THE SOCIOLOGY OF EARLY BUDDHISM

Early Buddhism flourished because it was able to take up the challenge represented by buoyant economic conditions and the need for cultural uniformity in the newly emergent states in northeastern India from the fifth century BCE onwards. This book begins with the apparent inconsistency of Buddhism, a renunciant movement, surviving within a strong urban environment, and draws out the implications of this. In spite of the Buddhist ascetic imperative, the Buddha and other celebrated monks moved easily through various levels of society and fitted into the urban landscape they inhabited. *The Sociology of Early Buddhism* tells how and why the early monks were able to exploit the social and political conditions of mid-first millennium northeastern India in such a way as to ensure the growth of Buddhism into a major world religion. Its readership lies both within Buddhist studies and more widely among historians, sociologists and anthropologists of religion.

GREG BAILEY has been teaching Sanskrit, Indian religions and Indian Literature at La Trobe University for the past twenty-four years. He has a PhD in Indian Studies from Melbourne University (1980). In the semester 1998 he was a visiting research fellow at the Seminar for Indian Studies and Comparative Religion at the University of Tübingen. He is a member of the International Consultative Committee of the International Association of Sanskrit Studies and a member of the Board of the Dubvronik International Conference on the Sanskrit Epics and Purāṇas.

IAN MABBETT, Reader in History at Monash University, Melbourne, was Professor of Indian and Buddhist Studies, Aichi Bunkyo University, Nagoya, 2000–2, and has made frequent research trips to India and South-East Asia (including visiting forest monasteries in Thailand). He is author of *A Short History of India* (1983); co-author (with David Chandler) of *The Khmers* (1995); and contributor to Jon Ortner (photographer), *Angkor: Celestial Temples of the Khmer Empire* (2002) and to reference books such as *The Cambridge History of Southeast Asia* (1992) and *Encyclopedia of Asian History* (1988).

THE SOCIOLOGY OF EARLY BUDDHISM

GREG BAILEY AND IAN MABBETT

CAMBRIDGE
UNIVERSITY PRESS

PUBLISHED BY THE PRESS SYNDICATE OF THE UNIVERSITY OF CAMBRIDGE
The Pitt Building, Trumpington Street, Cambridge, United Kingdom

CAMBRIDGE UNIVERSITY PRESS
The Edinburgh Building, Cambridge, CB2 2RU, UK
40 West 20th Street, New York, NY 10011–4211, USA
477 Williamstown Road, Port Melbourne, VIC 3207, Australia
Ruiz de Alarcón 13, 28014 Madrid, Spain
Dock House, The Waterfront, Cape Town 8001, South Africa

http://www.cambridge.org

First published 2003

Printed in the United Kingdom at the University Press, Cambridge

Typeface Adobe Garamond 11/12.5 pt. *System* LaTeX 2ε [TB]

A catalogue record for this book is available from the British Library

Library of Congress Cataloguing in Publication data
Bailey, G. M. (Greg M.)
The Sociology of early Buddhism / Greg Bailey, Ian Mabbett.
p. cm.
Includes bibliographical references and index.
ISBN 0-521-83116-4
1. Buddhism – Social aspects – South Asia. 2. Mediation – Religious aspects – Buddhism.
3. Monastic and religious life (Buddhism) – South Asia. I. Mabbett, Ian W. II. Title.
BQ4570.S6B35 2004
306.6′943 – dc21 2003048994

ISBN 0 521 83116 4 hardback

THE SOCIOLOGY OF EARLY BUDDHISM

GREG BAILEY AND IAN MABBETT

CAMBRIDGE
UNIVERSITY PRESS

PUBLISHED BY THE PRESS SYNDICATE OF THE UNIVERSITY OF CAMBRIDGE
The Pitt Building, Trumpington Street, Cambridge, United Kingdom

CAMBRIDGE UNIVERSITY PRESS
The Edinburgh Building, Cambridge, CB2 2RU, UK
40 West 20th Street, New York, NY 10011–4211, USA
477 Williamstown Road, Port Melbourne, VIC 3207, Australia
Ruiz de Alarcón 13, 28014 Madrid, Spain
Dock House, The Waterfront, Cape Town 8001, South Africa

http://www.cambridge.org

First published 2003

Printed in the United Kingdom at the University Press, Cambridge

Typeface Adobe Garamond 11/12.5 pt. *System* LaTeX 2ε [TB]

A catalogue record for this book is available from the British Library

Library of Congress Cataloguing in Publication data
Bailey, G. M. (Greg M.)
The Sociology of early Buddhism / Greg Bailey, Ian Mabbett.
p. cm.
Includes bibliographical references and index.
ISBN 0-521-83116-4
1. Buddhism – Social aspects – South Asia. 2. Mediation – Religious aspects – Buddhism.
3. Monastic and religious life (Buddhism) – South Asia. I. Mabbett, Ian W. II. Title.
BQ4570.S6B35 2004
306.6′943 – dc21 2003048994

ISBN 0 521 83116 4 hardback

Contents

Acknowledgements

The authors wish first to acknowledge the important contribution of Peter Masefield, whose assistance during the earlier stages of the research helped enormously with the assessment and ordering of a great mass of Pāli language material.

Responsibility for all that is said in the book rests wholly with the authors, but thanks are due to those who have made comments and offered advice at points during the various stages of the work. Detailed comments on some chapters were made by J. W. de Jong, whose recent death has been a great loss to all who work in the field. Also much appreciated have been the comments of Richard Gombrich, Don Miller, Steven Collins, Geoffrey Samuel, Jim Fitzgerald and Alf Hiltebeitel.

The book has benefited particularly from the very constructive criticisms of the anonymous reviewers of the manuscript. Kevin Taylor, Katharina Brett, Gillian Dadd and Joanne Hill of Cambridge University Press have helped improve the book in a myriad of ways.

We also acknowledge the financial assistance of the Australian Research Council, who provided three years of funding to facilitate the initial research for this book. We would also like to thank La Trobe and Monash Universities for the financial support offered to the two authors during the writing of this book.

Finally, the authors wish to acknowledge the patience and endurance of Jaccy and Kerri whose inspiration is always present.

Abbreviations

A	*Aṅguttara Nikāya*
AŚ	*Arthaśāstra*
BṛhU	*Bṛhadāraṇyaka Upaniṣad*
ChU	*Chāṇḍogya Upaniṣad*
D	*Dīgha Nikāya*
Dhp	*Dhammapada*
Dhs	*Dharmasūtra*
HR	*History of Religions*
IIJ	*Indo-Iranian Journal*
J	*Jātaka*
JAOS	*Journal of the American Oriental Society*
JESHO	*Journal of the Economic and Social History of the Orient*
JIABS	*Journal of the International Association of Buddhist Studies*
M	*Majjhima Nikāya*
Mbh	*Mahābhārata*
MP	*Milinda Pañha*
PTS	Pali Text Society
S	*Saṃyutta Nikāya*
Sn	*Sutta Nipāta*
Ud	*Udāna*
Vin	*Vinaya*
WZKSA	*Wiener Zeitschrift für die Kunde Südasiens*
ZDMG	*Zeitschrift der Deutschen Morgenländischen Gesellschaft*

Introduction

[If a monk] has utterly destroyed every vestige of worldly contamination, if he is not tied to any source of sustenance, if his territory is freedom, then the passing of such a one is hard to trace, like that of birds in the sky.

The idea of total detachment pervading this verse illustrates concisely the fundamental ambience associated with the early Buddhist quest: detachment, freedom from ties, renunciation of the world, celibacy. As both religious attitude and lifestyle practice, adoption of an attitude of total detachment has done much to define the image of the monk throughout the ages since the beginnings of Buddhism. In the world today, and in several recent centuries for which good evidence is available, there is no doubt that the Order of Buddhist monks has had plenty of interaction with society; in many countries it has necessarily been integrated within the pattern of social, cultural and even political systems. A fundamental dichotomy appears then as the monks who received the earliest Buddhist message were expected to live it as homeless mendicants, severing all ties with society in order to devote themselves fully to the search for enlightenment. The problem faced in this book is to explain how, right from the beginning, Buddhism has from a doctrinal viewpoint required of its Order of monks the practical application of an ethic of renunciation and detachment and yet this very same order has remained a vibrant *part* of society, culture or politics wherever Buddhism has flourished.

The present study confronts this problem by focusing on the relationships between Buddhism, understood as its teachings and the activities of the Buddhist Order, and its social context in northern India in about the fifth to third centuries BCE, assuming that these were the centuries during which the Pāli Canon took shape, though its formation could have continued for another two hundred years. Attention is given especially to the social dynamic of the growth of Buddhism, a dynamic understood within the terms of the opposition suggested in the first paragraph. Inevitably this dynamic must be tested by the material drawn from textual sources which centre above all on interaction between monks, nuns and the broader society, and the archaeological evidence which somewhat contextualizes this. If used with appropriate sensitivity, the available sources can furnish clues to the actual relationships, in all their permutations, between Buddhists and society when it first began to grow. Even the passing of a bird in the sky leaves some sort of trace, and in principle it should be possible to fashion the instruments to detect it.

Much has already been written over the past two centuries about the interaction of the Buddhist Order with society, as one side of the problem, and the implications of Buddhist teachings for social behaviour, as the other side of the problem. On the basis of this line of scholarship certain adumbrated positions have come to be taken as orthodoxy and have subsequently had a more than determinate influence on what scholars expect to find, or hope to defend, when looking at the broad field of early Buddhism and its larger social and economic context. Two of these positions are interrogated in this book and one of the book's aims is to convince those interested in Buddhism of the need to revise progressively the axioms governing our mode of reading the primary sources.

The first of these positions rests on what is virtually a starting point for the present book, the implication, if not proposition, that Buddhism began substantially as one possible response to the changes occurring in northern India in the two centuries from the sixth century BCE onwards. The classic view is given by Bareau:

> The most recent body of archaeological and philological works concerning the middle basin of the Ganges seems indeed to show that this region, in the course of the fifth century, underwent some very important and progressive changes: the beginning of urbanization; distinct economic development, notably in commerce and in the class of merchants (*vaṇij* and *śreṣṭhin*) with their caravans of ox carts; accentuation of political unification. Already in process beforehand and finishing in the following century with the Nanda dynasty, then that of the Mauryas, the latter seems to attain a decisive phase in the period of the Blessed One with the progressive affirmation of Magadha's power. These three kinds of changes – urbanization, economic development and political unification – are also quite probably interlinked.[1]

[1] A. Bareau,'Le Buddha et les rois', *Bulletin De L'École Française D'Extrême-Orient*, 80/1 (1993), p. 17. But cf. also G. von Simson, 'Die zeitgeschichtliche Hintergrund der Entstehung des Buddhismus und seine Bedeutung für die Datierungsfrage,' in H. Bechert (ed.), *The Dating of the Historical Buddha* (Vandenhoek & Ruprecht, Göttingen, 1991), part I, pp. 90–9; P. Olivelle, *The Āśrama System* (Oxford University Press, New York, 1993), pp. 55–62. More nuanced is Richard Gombrich, *Theravāda Buddhism. A Social History from Ancient Benares to Modern Colombo* (Routledge & Kegan Paul, London, 1988), ch. 2.

In our view the archaeological evidence, substantially filled out by textual evidence from the *Sutta Piṭaka*, is quite clear. Buddhism arose in a period when all these changes identified by Bareau, and assumed by most other scholars, had already occurred. The importance of this qualification – and given the observed differences between periods of great change and relative stability, it is much more significant than it seems – is that our understanding of early Buddhism must be of a religious movement developing within a period of relative prosperity and socio-economic consolidation, and not reacting against a period when change was occurring at breakneck speed. Responses to the latter often take radical forms, whereas survival during a period of slow change should be understood more as accommodation to a particular cultural setting. Buddhist literature reveals very little sign of a consciousness (repressed or otherwise) of a period of dramatic change having been traversed.

The second proposition is ultimately dependent upon the first, since if the situation implied in the first had not occurred, it would be impossible even to countenance the second. There is a view that Buddhism arose because it responded positively to a feeling of profound social malaise that gripped certain sections of the population of North India in the sixth and following centuries BCE. The ascetic tradition represented by Buddhism, the Upaniṣadic sages and the early Jains placed great emphasis on the transitoriness of human existence in any dimension that could be named. It is tempting, if not natural, for scholars to try and read the tone of socio-economic conditions in ancient Indian thought, especially where this is so concentrated chronologically and within a small body of texts, into the empirical conditions of the day. The tone of universal dissatisfaction expressed in the concept of *dukkha* has often been read back into a kind of social *Angst* operating somewhere in the psyche of the residents of the Ganges valley and inducing them to take up the renouncer's path; Buddhism represented such a vocation.

To recognize both these problems is to realize the difficulties of reasoning convincingly from two very central doctrines – *anicca* and *dukkha* – of Buddhism to socio-economic conditions that may have had a formative role in the Buddha's formulation of both doctrines. We see how insecurely founded is the glib notion that the early canonical texts both embody a teaching that must have appealed to the alienated, the disenfranchised, the dispossessed – whatever percentage of the total population these groups comprised – and also reflect a period of social dislocation occurring when they were composed. Not only are the arguments circular, the archaeological and textual evidence goes against them. The teaching of *dukkha* need not go with social distress – however this might be defined; the canonical texts might reflect any combination of the alienated, etc., and any or none of the times they reflect may have been characterized by either slow or rapid change. For the most part the changes wrought by urbanization and state formation had already occurred in their most far-reaching manifestations by the time the Buddhist texts took the form in which we know them.

Our desire to question these two assumptions means, of course, that we are required to offer alternative solutions to the main problems taken up in this book concerning the interaction between the Buddhist Order and wider society. Such an enterprise is likely to confront similar problems to those of our scholarly predecessors; the shortage of adequate appropriate evidence is conspicuous among them. It is not just the paucity of evidence that creates difficulties, however. Problems attend the way in which we may use the evidence. Even the concepts and presuppositions we bring with us to embark upon the study, as parts of the framework of thought, are fraught with ambiguity. Not the least of such concepts is that of Buddhism itself. It denotes no ready-made atomic reality: it has always meant many different things to different people. This is especially so for the concept of 'early Buddhism', which has itself provoked debate about what it can mean, even in principle. If this is not enough, it is compounded by the temporal disjunction between our literary sources. The Buddha lived in about the fifth century BCE; the texts upon which we must overwhelmingly depend to study the first few centuries of emergent Buddhism were not written down until late in the first century BCE. By then society had doubtless changed a great deal, and what was written down is all too likely to bear the imprint of a later period, an imprint difficult to remove from the earlier material.

We hope we have succeeded in advancing a coherent and plausible account of Buddhism in its social context by cutting away the clutter of unwarranted assumptions that are often made. We have tried to establish in broad outline what is really probable, and pointed to the often indirect evidence yielded by a close reading of the sources, both literary and archaeological.

This book is divided into two parts, which are interrelated in their treatment of particular aspects of Buddhism and its broader social context. Of these the first sets out our own view of the economic and social context within which the Buddha lived and the subsequent Buddhist Order developed, at least for the first two centuries of its existence. We finish roughly at the beginning of the reign of Aśoka, after which source material becomes more abundant and presents a picture of a more extensive Buddhism than what is likely for the pre-Aśokan period. It is necessary to set out the economic and social context in some detail because the second section of the book focuses on a specific role of the monk that makes full sense only within a particular view of society and economy. Our principal contention throughout the book is that Buddhism expanded and flourished, ultimately to a greater extent than its śramaṇic rivals, because the monk (and perhaps the nun, though there is little evidence for this) was able to function as an instrument of mediation between the forces – political and economic – benefiting from the changes that had taken place prior to, and perhaps during, the life of the Buddha, on the one hand, and those other groups for whom such changes were difficult to digest, on the other hand.

In this book there is scarcely any treatment of North India as it appears in middle and late Vedic literature. Details of the socio-economic conditions of this period are largely absent from the literature, but they would be relevant to this study only to the extent that it would be possible to locate a repressed memory of them (or nostalgia for them) in the consciousness of the early Buddhists. It is not possible to locate such a consciousness. Nevertheless, change there was. Erdosy summarizes it with great brevity:

> The emergence of what may be termed simple chiefdoms, datable to c. BC 1000, was the culmination of this process [of the reappearance of stable political structures following the collapse of Harappan urbanism]. They were characterized in material culture by an agricultural economy making limited use of iron, by low population density and by a two-tier settlement hierarchy whose central place coordinated the procurement, processing and distribution of vital raw materials . . .
>
> . . . By contrast, the next three centuries [after 550 BCE] witnessed dramatic growth in population size and agglomeration, the colonization of fertile but forested tracts away from the principal watercourses (facilitated by the introduction of iron into agricultural production) and the re-emergence of long-distance trade, of a monetary economy and – sometime before BC 250 – of writing . . .[2]

The first section of the book fills in with considerable detail the changes noted in the final paragraph of Erdosy's summary. Here we are concerned especially to define the principal elements of the environment of Buddhism in its early centuries and not so much to trace the process of transformation which had already occurred by the time of the Buddha.

This leads into the second section of the book where we analyse the role of the monk as mediator. Both sections are thematically interrelated. If in the first section one of the sub-texts is the emergence of the Buddhist movement

[2] G. Erdosy, 'City states of North India and Pakistan at the time of the Buddha', in F. R. Allchin (ed.), *The Archaeology of Early Historic South Asia* (Cambridge University Press, Cambridge, 1995), p. 99; cf. p. 107.

conceived as a response to already changed socio-economic conditions, the second section focuses on how members of the Buddhist Order helped other social groups deal with the on-going changes occurring as a result of the large-scale transformation outlined by Erdosy. As a form of interaction, mediation can take many different forms and operates with a range of goals. But it makes sense only within an environment where communication between certain groups has broken down, where there is a need to incorporate culturally diverse elements beneath a single umbrella and where unavoidable change must be explained.

The growth of Buddhism up until the time of Aśoka must be understood as the partially opportunistic response to large-scale urbanism, the presence of expanding state-based organizations and the rapid diversification of the economy. How should this be understood? Half the battle is to take a clear look at the way scholarship has so far treated the rise of Buddhism, and in this we observe a paradox.

In the first place, many writings on Buddhism focus on the needs of disadvantaged classes in society and support the view, without rigorous examination of the premises of the argument, that Buddhism appealed because of its message of *dukkha*, a concept defining a totalistic view of the ultimate incapacity of human existence to produce any possibility of permanent happiness. Social dislocation and alienation, it is argued, had caused distress; people heeded the message that life is *dukkha*. Working from this assumption Buddhism offered an alternative set of values, which must have been tightly defined to enable them to appear to be conspicuously different from other values with which they may have conflicted. This interpretation, however, leaves too many questions unanswered. Buddhism grew in an age of economic expansion, and although no doubt there were pockets of distress and poverty, there is nothing to suggest that the times and places which saw Buddhism thrive were more afflicted by socio-economic malaise than other times and places.

In the second place, many writings focus on the needs of the dominant classes – economic, political and religious – in society and sustain the view that Buddhism in some way reflected the values of the new rising kingdoms and provided their elites with an appropriate ideology. Some of the arguments here are appealing, except that they all presuppose Buddhism to have been something which, in its origin, it was not. In its origin it was a message for those who wished to forsake society, abandoning everything. It was not a rationale for the ambitions of holders of power and magnates. The gap between the austere ascetic impulse and the needs of expanding urban kingdoms is great indeed.

The two schools of thought contradict each other about the rise of Buddhism in its social context, and once the contradictions are clearly seen, it is easier to focus on the assumptions underlying such contradictions and ultimately to recognize how the Buddhist Order interacted with its social context and what the reciprocal relation of influence and borrowing might have been between Buddhist teachings and this environment. The texts certainly offer no reason for disputing that the earliest form of the Buddhist message was indeed the ascetic mendicant one, however rapidly differing responses to it effectively created new versions of it when it had attracted recruits and lay support. One obvious question arises from this. How could the original ascetic impulse play a positive part in the first place, attracting recruits and the support of a laity who could never practise the stringent eremitic lifestyle of the first monks? Our answer to this forms another sub-text of this book. The dynamics of society at the time are not best understood by analysing the needs of horizontal social classes, the precursors of what might have become castes, even though this approach has usually seemed overwhelmingly appealing. On the contrary, it is our contention that it is better to consider the tensions between groups in different geographical locations in relation to an urban/non-urban configuration of the landscape. When dominant core groups such as urban-based kingdoms were expanding rapidly, they encroached upon outlying communities which did not share any significant elements of culture with them. In this situation, there were clashes of cultures which manifested themselves in varying degrees of severity, and there was also a crisis of identity because of the clashes of culture and the mode of enforcement used by the dominant culture. The people being encroached upon needed to reconceptualize their culture, but they lacked an appropriate vocabulary to do so. It was here, precisely, that the wandering holy man, deliberately shunning society, could play an important role as middleman between the two incommensurable cultures, interpreting each to the other and trusted by both sides.

Initially this process took place as a result of the activities of the expanding states of Kośala and Magadha when their rulers and bureaucracies sought to institutionalize state rule and were required to deal with a patchwork of existing cultures and social forms. But expansion, though it may continue for some time, is a dynamic condition. Eventually outlying communities become more or less integrated within the ruling values of metropolitan societies: brahmins took on the mediating role, and there was less need for the figure of the wandering holy man. Where there were Buddhist monks, they settled in monasteries and became familiar components in the local scene with priest-like functions. This was probably an inevitable process, reaching some kind of mature development about 250 years after the founding of Buddhism. The texts of the *Vinaya*, concerned with monastic discipline, are often treated indiscriminately along with the books of the *Sutta Piṭaka* (narratives embodying the Buddha's preaching) as evidence of early Buddhism. However, it seems better to treat the *Vinaya*, and this concords with archaeological findings relating to the earliest *stūpas* and monasteries, as generally representing a later stage of development, when the monks were not typically wandering virtuosi seeking enlightenment but domesticated within society. Even so, the *Vinaya* does preserve for us some traces of the ways in which these monastic monks could play the mediating role within a narrowly defined locality.

But if the role of the monk as mediator is to be identified as one of the reasons why Buddhism survived amongst countless other śramaṇic groups, what are we to make of the postulated original role of the wandering ascetic, seeking to avoid social entanglements but increasingly drawn in because he was needed as middleman between expanding state and isolated village? That is, the capacity of the monk to act as mediator rests as much on his perceived detachment as it does on his capacity to operate at different levels of society and between various value systems. Can the transformation between social detachment in isolation from society to social detachment in society be detected from the sources as a historical change in the early centuries of Buddhism? The *Dhammapada*, one of the early books of condensed teachings, is taken as a case-study; an examination of it suggests ways in which it can reflect the different orientations of monks towards their ascetic calling, towards the local folk culture, and towards the political sphere. In addition, we also present our analysis of the *Sutta Nipāta*, one of the oldest texts of the canon, which lays great stress on the monk as renunciant ascetic being totally detached from all of his surroundings. In the many short texts collected here, the classic conditions for the monk as mediator are laid down.

BUDDHISM AS PROCESS: THREE VERSIONS OF BUDDHISM

If the role of monk as mediator dominates the second part of this book, the first part is mainly taken up with setting the context in which this role makes sense. Thus in some sense this book is about context. Especially it is about the social and economic context defining the fledgling Buddhist movement during the first three or four centuries of its existence. A focus on the context and the social aspects of Buddhism confirms our view that the best way to understand early Buddhism is to see it as a dynamic process dependent upon, and perhaps shaping, the societies in which it develops. Of course, it is necessary to reduce this process to specifics, which we have tried to do by dividing the book into two parts, one dealing with extra-Buddhist social roles, the other with the interaction between monks and society. This produces an impression of Buddhism as being many different things.

To illustrate what we intend by this, let us look at three Buddhisms. It comes all too naturally to think of Buddhism, just one noun, as just one thing, with a consistent character of its own. In reality, of course, any widespread movement must be many things to many people; an ideally complete history of Buddhism would identify a large number of often inconsistent Buddhisms representing the many images it has had for different sorts of people. The present study does two things – it insists upon the validity of multiple different versions of Buddhism in history, and for the purpose of understanding the Dharma's rise it focuses on the ascetic, other-worldly and asocial version as the most likely content of the original message. This can be contrasted with the various social versions according to which it played an active part in the community. Here, to exhibit the main different images of Buddhism both in history and among scholars, we can subdivide the 'social' version into two, roughly corresponding to the 'Great Tradition' and the 'Little Tradition' – political involvement and folk culture. Thus we can describe three Buddhisms.

The first represents (the original 'asocial') Buddhism as an ascetic quest embodied in a form of practice. It is exemplified above all in the *Sutta Nipāta*. It can be called 'ascetic' because of its rejection of the world, but of course the Buddha, unlike some of his contemporaries, rejected deliberate self-mortification, or extreme asceticism; his is a middle way, espousing calm detachment. In this view monks wander constantly, rejecting all social ties. Their object is to obtain a transcendent vision of the way things really are, abandoning all attachments in every sphere. In the absence of attachment and ignorance, one will cease generating *karma*, and thereby become enlightened and escape the unending frustration and distress inseparable from worldly existence. The aspirant is seen as being self-centred and dogged, as paradoxical as this might seem in the light of Buddhist doctrine.

The second version emphasizes the public (and frequently political) involvement of the *dhamma* and the *saṅgha*. In this view Buddhism becomes a system of teachings accessible to all. It offers a rich array of ethical precepts for the committed laity. Monks may seek salvation directly; laymen may set themselves the more modest goal of accumulating merit, which might help them gain enlightenment in a future life. Merit may be gained by supplying the needs of monks among other things. This is easier to achieve if there are settled permanent communities of monks with which the laity can live in symbiosis. Monks can provide education, give counsel to the laity, and even represent the local community to government. Buddhist teaching on this view is a practical system, one which can influence, if not regulate, the dealings individuals have with each other and rulers with their subjects.

The third approach relates Buddhism to the wide context of folk religion and deliberately leaves out the soteriological concepts and the ethical teachings codified in books. Such high-flown ideas, it is argued, are irrelevant to ordinary Buddhists. Real Buddhism must be sought in concrete manifestations in particular times and places, such as rituals to propitiate spirits, the building of *stūpas*, healing and divination, and miscellaneous dealings between monks and laity. Such evidences belong to the lifetime of the Buddha only by implication, working from the many passages evincing lay reverence to the person of the Buddha. It is therefore impossible directly to reconstruct original Buddhism (if it ever were a unitary thing) by direct evidence, but the analogy of later historical sources and modern anthropological studies points persuasively to the presence of a religion of immanent spiritual powers tapped by ascetic power or appropriate ritual, a religion also reflected in Hindu literature. Monks acquired powers that could be integrated within folk ritual and belief. It was believed they could acquire super-normal powers, and they taught devotion to the Buddha, whose presence or whose relics generated a field of communicable spiritual strength capable of guarding against harmful spirits. Buddhism was on this reading a source of talismans, amulets and apotropaic magic, and the monks were an elite of experts considered capable of concentrating and manipulating spiritual forces for the benefit of others.[3]

THE INCOMMENSURABILITY OF DIFFERENT VERSIONS

Each of these interpretations offers a coherent account of a postulated historical reality labelled 'Buddhism'. Each overlaps the others in many details, but each has its own patterned thematic structure and rationale which make it different from the others. All such interpretations treat Buddhism as an

[3] Cf. the three levels described by Melford Spiro in *Buddhism and Society: a Great Tradition and its Burmese Vicissitudes* (Harper and Row, New York, 1970), pp. 11–13: nibbāṇic, kammic and apotropaic. The present descriptions though are of ways of interpreting Buddhism as a whole, not of elements within a local system. Cf. G. Samuel, *Civilized Shamans* (Smithsonian Institute Press, Washington and London, 1993), ch. 2.

integrated, organic whole, working according to a particular logic, not as a name for a collection of disparate phenomena. Thus each of the three interpretations, describing an organic unity, is self-sufficient and has its own logic, not needing in principle to be supplemented by another mode of explanation.

But it is the words 'in principle' which are crucial here, and this for two reasons. First, there is the problem of how closely the empirical reality of a religious tradition ever fits to its scholarly description and the interpretation of the data producing this description. This, of course, may apply equally to the three interpretations. Secondly, there is an incommensurability in these approaches, and one of the most intriguing puzzles in the quest for an understanding of Buddhism in its early history resides in this incommensurability. Are they equally effective in helping us understand the rise and fortunes of the *dhamma* in ancient India? The key to understanding may be supplied by just one of the approaches, in which case the aspects of Buddhism addressed by the others must be set aside as marginal, 'theoretical' (and hence too distant from the empirical to be relevant) or corrupted manifestations; alternatively it may be supplied by a combination. In this case the empirical historical relationships must be discovered between aspects of religion seemingly belonging in different worlds of thought.

Given that one can think oneself into only one world at a time, though simultaneously be aware of others, it comes naturally to focus upon the explanatory power of one's single favoured interpretation to the neglect of the others, which are seen as incompatible with the essential hermeneutical thrust of the preferred image. The advocate of the ascetic, esoteric image of Buddhism is likely to regard the public and folk images as errors based upon subsequent misunderstandings of what he/she would identify as the essential message, which can often be found throughout history in ascetic revivals. Again, the protagonist of public Buddhism as a practical philosophy apt to guide individual life and social organization is likely to resist any suggestion that the *dhamma* was an esoteric message essentially only for the elect, and will be impatient with any account of Buddhism in historical practice that dwells upon the adaptation to rituals, magic or spirit cults. Similarly the advocate of Buddhism as an adaptation to folk culture will dismiss the contents of scriptures, however important they seem to modern scholars, as irrelevant to real life.

Nevertheless, there are good reasons for refusing to adopt just one of these approaches to the exclusion of the others. In this book we have utilized all of them. One good reason for this is that none of the aspects of Buddhism treated can be relegated to a marginal zone (a judgement such as 'theory' or 'superstition') deemed irrelevant to the main currents of the history of Indian Buddhism. The esoteric tradition with its austere dedication to enlightenment was written into the records of the faith, and it has at all times inspired the careers of holy men, hermits or peripatetics. Again, Buddhism as public morality holds the high ground, and its civic role has been written into history in every century. As for Buddhism as an element in folk culture, we very much need to know how the history of 'folk Buddhism' was affected by the patchwork of rituals and cults, governed by belief in immanent forces, that textured the world in which the Buddha lived and in which his teachings were transmitted.

I

The problem: asceticism and urban life

An instructive story tells of a Thai woman who had long lived in England. She became increasingly subject to a vague depression which eventually became quite disabling, until she realized what was wrong when she was introduced to a *vihāra* and was able to make religious offerings to the monks; it brought instant release from her burden of worries. 'That is what is wrong with living in this country,' she said. 'There are simply no opportunities to give.' Much could be learned from contemplation of this parable, but one simple fact matters here: the role of the Buddhist Order makes sense in a particular social environment with a particular culture, in terms of which people see each other and behave towards each other.

How, then, did Buddhism grow in the India of about 500 BCE? This India was not like modern England; it was not like modern Thailand either. So what sort of environment was it that shaped the emergence of the *dhamma* and the behaviour of the monks? What strikes the historian most is that cities were growing, many of them capitals of rising kingdoms. Agriculture and trade networks were developing. This environment must have been relevant to the appeal of Buddhism, and of the other new non-brāhmaṇical teachings.

Did the *dhamma* make sense to people because in some way it fitted the needs of these rising urban states? Or did it provide instead a spiritual salve, an opiate, for those who suffered from the effects of urbanization? These are two opposing sorts of interpretation; scholars argue strongly on both sides. The problem to be taken up here is just this fact; it is a curious fact, because scholars argue on both sides often without seeming to notice the contradiction.

THE EMPEROR'S CLOTHES

Let us take first the explanation that Buddhism fitted the needs of rising urban states. It goes somewhat as follows. The Buddha was a wandering holy man who insisted the only way to find salvation lies in the total renunciation of life in society and all its values. He sought disciples who should wear rags and eat left-overs, rejecting all responsibility to their families, seeking spiritual enlightenment, and rejecting all worldly involvement. His teaching earned royal patronage and social prestige. Why? Because it met the needs of a newly urbanized society; it appealed to the urbane, cosmopolitan values of ambitious traders surrounded by new luxuries and immersed in practical affairs; it found disciples whose outlook was shaped by an expanding economy, by the wider horizons of growing states seeking regional conquest.

It is difficult to resist a popular cliché: what is wrong with this picture? Buddhism, on the view of much relevant scholarship, is the ideology of a mature process of urbanism, and this is odd because the Buddha's message, as just described, appears to be as far removed as one can very well imagine from the needs and temper of urban life.[1] There is a further oddity, because little notice has been taken of the obvious inconsistency between the explanation and the thing explained; most accept that there was indeed a profound affinity between Buddhism (however other-worldly) and the spirit of urbanization (however mundane). It is as if people were to be swept by admiration for the naked emperor's clothes.

Certainly there are ways of accounting for these two oddities. One, which must be noticed at once but will here be put on one side for a while, is that the account of the Buddha's original message given above is false, or at least misrepresented by the omission of its public, ethical and social dimensions. This is a possible objection, for of course the social dimensions cannot be left out. They are indeed, in large measure, the subject-matter of this volume. A number of historians of Buddhism, especially those who belong to what has sometimes been dubbed the 'Franco-Belgian school', have rejected the ascetic, soteriological description of the Buddha's teaching in favour of something much more likely to appeal to ordinary people. A life-denying other-worldly figure could not have attracted crowds of supporters, they think. As Lamotte declared, 'We would search in vain for the transcendent quality which could attract crowds to the support of a personality so lacking in lustre and dynamism.'[2]

It will be argued here later on that this supposition misses the point; the dynamism of a holy man's appeal could be compelling, and the more

[1] One of the few who have commented upon this inconsistency is J. W. de Jong. 'It is however much more difficult to understand why members from the urban elite should abandon everything in order to strive for salvation.' J. W. de Jong, review of R. Gombrich, *Theravāda Buddhism*, *IIJ*, 32 (1989), p. 241.

[2] E. Lamotte, 'La légende du Buddha,' *Revue de l'Histoire des Religions*, 134 (1946), p. 40.

austere he was, the better. Here, though, three points must be considered. The first is that the scriptures themselves are not univocal; they contain evidence capable of supporting discrepant interpretations of the Buddhist teaching. On the one hand, it can be seen as the sort of private, inward-looking soteriological quest described above, and on the other it can be seen as a code of public morality. The two ingredients do not obviously mix. In a sense, this conflict need not matter; life does not imitate logic, and indeed, the quest for an internally consistent original Buddhism often encourages a mistaken view of Buddhism's social dynamics. However, the original message as intended by the Buddha himself is not the same thing as the subsequent dynamics of his teaching in society, and there was presumably substantial coherence to what he said and meant.

The second point is that, if there was an internally coherent original Buddhism embodied in the Buddha's own words and behaviour, the ascetic other-worldly version of it is as likely to be true as any. Therefore, the representation of the Buddha's teaching as a soteriological and transcendental message totally alien to any social form except ascetic isolationism is a reasonable initial hypothesis.

Thirdly, we must look beyond the Buddha himself in pursuit of the reasons for the attraction of a variety of classes of people to Buddhism as both philosophy and practice. Exploration of the texts dealing with monks other than the Buddha shows us that they adapted to several different role models, such as that of parish preacher (where the village functions like a small parish), charismatic teacher, and forest-dwelling ascetic – consistently with a complex society, even if all of them took some coloration from the values of the ascetic quest.

For the time being, though, we shall recognize two ways of describing the nature of the Buddha's message, acknowledging that the evidence may never allow us to prove just one to be correct. The first (the 'asocial' image) is to treat Buddhism as an austere, other-worldly quest for salvation, rejecting life in society. The second (the 'social' image) is to treat Buddhism as a system of religious life embracing society as a whole, with ethical and social teachings. This latter way is widely favoured by scholars. The first way is nevertheless favoured here provisionally; more will be said below to justify this.

TRADE, CITIES, CENTRALIZED STATES AND REMEMBERED TRIBALISM

The arguments relating the rise of Buddhism to urbanization and state formation can be classified under four headings according as they bear upon the relevance of Buddhism

(1) to the values of merchants,
(2) to the nature of city life,
(3) to political organization in the urban-based centralized state, and
(4) to the shift from pastoral to agrarian culture which economically underpinned the rise of cities.

A brief survey of these arguments follows directly, the intention of which is neither to endorse nor to reject the arguments described, merely to identify them. Some indeed offer valuable contributions to our understanding of the social appeal of Buddhism. The problem lies elsewhere. For in respect of each of the four aspects considered, we find that, confusingly, while some people have argued that Buddhism appealed because it legitimated or endorsed the values of the new urban state, others have argued that Buddhism appealed because it rejected them, offering an alternative ideology or style of life attractive to the dispossessed or the alienated.

Under each of the four headings we can find arguments claiming that Buddhism reflected the new values (which will be called here the positive style of argument), and other arguments claiming that Buddhism rejected them (the negative). The positive opinion can fairly be described as the majority opinion within the scholarship on the period of urbanization. It is so often met with in this context that it virtually amounts to a tenet of received wisdom that *Buddhism flourished essentially on account of its appeal in the urbanized society of the rising urban state.* The other view, the negative, does not so often appear in research on early Buddhist history, and is in that sense a minority opinion; but it is implicit in much of what has been written about ancient India and about Buddhism. It is often treated without examination, as self-evident, that Buddhism rejected the values of the urban state; it is implied wherever Buddhism's rise is attributed to its teaching about *dukkha*.

LEGITIMATION OF COMMERCIAL VALUES

Take first the values of merchants. Weber himself pointed to the appeal to the merchants and craftsmen of new schools founded by wandering mendicants.[3] Some scholars make explicit the parallel with Calvinism and capitalism, suggesting that, like Protestantism, Buddhism and the other heterodox

[3] M. Weber, *Die Wirtschaftsethik der Weltreligionen. Hinduismus und Buddhismus*, ed. H. Schmidt-Glintzer (J.C.B. Mohr, Tübingen, 1998 (Tübingen, 1921)), pp. 34–8. In this respect he gave particular attention to Jainism. However, the main thrust of his argument about India is that the brāhmaṇical order and the institutions of caste prevented the development of fully urban society uniting the interests of princes and merchants.

movements valued achieved, not ascribed, status, and offered self-respect to merchants, whereas orthodoxy (Roman Catholic or brāhmaṇical) discriminated against them.[4] Several commentators attach weight to the universalistic values of Buddhist morality, which meant that merchants, whatever their birth, would not suffer discrimination from co-religionists; Buddhism appealed to the *nouveaux riches* and found an affinity with the bourgeois ethic of thrift and diligence.[5] M. Carrithers recognizes an 'elective affinity' between Buddhism and city merchants,[6] and S. Collins suggests a consonance between the Buddhist idea of universal order and 'commercial rationalism'.[7]

Buddhism and the other new teachings suited the commercial classes in the cities and Buddhism, like Jainism, provided for the merchants the 'required ethic'.[8] Merchants, some have said, were out of sympathy with brāhmaṇical teachings, which offered them neither status nor sanction for their livelihood.[9] R. S. Sharma argues that, whereas brāhmaṇical sources despise commerce, Buddhism looked favourably upon trade, numbered great merchants among its early supporters, happily tolerated money lending (unlike brāhmaṇical authorities[10]), implicitly sanctioned usury and praised freedom from debt without condemning indebtedness on principle.[11]

The money economy, an important part of commercial culture, was on some views complementary to Buddhist values;[12] in a society where status

4 A. L. Basham, 'The background to the rise of Buddhism', in A. K. Narain (ed.), *Studies in History* (B.R. Publishing, Delhi, 1980).

5 Gombrich, *Theravāda Buddhism*, p. 78. Cf. von Simson, 'Die zeitgeschichtliche Hintergrund', pp. 92–4; U. Chakravarti, *The Social Dimensions of Early Buddhism* (Oxford University Press, Delhi, 1987), p. 179.

6 M. Carrithers, *The Buddha* (Oxford University Press, Oxford, 1983), p. 84, to which Carrithers adds that the message of the Buddha was universal and appealed to other classes besides merchants.

7 S. Collins, *Selfless Persons: Imagery and Thought in Theravāda Buddhism* (Cambridge University Press, Cambridge, 1982), p. 108. Collins refers to Weber's association of new religious ideas with urban life, but does not endorse his linking of the psychology of fatalism with mercantile culture.

8 Basham, 'Background', p. 73; R. Thapar, *Ancient Indian Social History: Some Interpretations* (Orient Longman, New Delhi, 1978), p. 73.

9 K. T. Sarao, *Urban Centres and Urbanisation as Reflected in the Pāli Vinaya and Sutta Piṭakas* (Vidyanidhi, Delhi, 1990), pp. 175ff.; cf. Thapar, *Ancient Indian Social History*, pp. 44, 61 n. 5.

10 The Vedic texts are not explored here, but the point is worth noticing. Āpastamba described usury as polluting. For instance, *Āpastamba Dhs* 1,18,22 prescribes that food offered by a usurer is not to be eaten by a brahman student and *Baudhāyana Dhs* 1,10,23 condemns buying cheap and selling dear. This brāhmaṇical stricture needs to be seen in the context of the traditionally sanctioned forms of payments for brahmans, namely, cattle, gold and women.

11 R. S. Sharma, *Material Culture and Social Formations in Ancient India* (Macmillan India, Delhi, 1983), pp. 123–6.

12 G. C. Pande, *Studies in the Origins of Buddhism* (Motilal Banarsidass, Delhi, 1974 (Department of Ancient History, Culture and Archeology, University of Allahabad, 1957)), p. 314, n. 27.

came to be based more on wealth, less on birth, a man was as good as the colour of his money.[13] The *karma* doctrine justified present wealth (reward for past merit), and assured future benefit for present merit.[14]

PROTEST AGAINST COMMERCIAL VALUES

In a word, the claim is that Buddhism displayed an affinity to the values of merchants. But it is possible to argue otherwise. In some ways, it might be said that Buddhism is antipathetic to the rise of commercial values, and this very claim has often enough been made in favour of the urbanization hypothesis, sometimes by the same people who argue that Buddhism appealed to the merchant classes. A. K. Narain's interpretation of the Buddhist appeal links commerce with the city environment as a cause of unequal prosperity which exacerbated problems of supply and demand, leading to unhappiness and disenchantment; Buddhism was in part a reaction against the 'mechanisms of affluence'.[15] The Buddhist community of monks forbade its members the use of money and the accumulation of possessions; their customs represented a rejection of new social elements such as love of money, private property and luxury. The monks' lifestyle was austere; they were not to accept money or engage in buying or selling; their code reflects 'to some extent a reaction against these new elements'.[16] The renouncers represented a universal code of behaviour apt for the laity in cities where 'now there were merchants who, through command of the impersonal instruments of money and trade, could wreak a new damage on others'.[17]

This form of the argument is perhaps easier to understand than its reverse. If original Buddhism was (on the initial hypothesis adopted provisionally here) a movement that rejected all social values and sought transcendent illumination outside society, we can imagine how its appeal might be related to commercial culture as a reaction against it, not as a legitimization of it. People disgusted by what they saw as an excess of selfish greed, passion and delusion might turn to their opposite.

LEGITIMATION OF CITY LIFE

There is a similar oscillation in the forms taken by the argument for Buddhism as a response to the nature of city life. For some authorities,

[13] Gombrich, *Theravāda Buddhism*, p. 81.
[14] von Simson, 'Die zeitgeschichtliche Hintergrund', pp. 92–4.
[15] Narain, ed., *Studies in History*, p. xvi.
[16] Such as textiles and leather goods. Sharma, *Material Culture*, p. 128.
[17] Carrithers, *Buddha*, p. 86.

the new teaching supplied an ideological sanction for urban culture.[18] Weber wrote: 'Like Jainism, but even more clearly, Buddhism presents itself as a product of the time of urban development, of urban kingship and the city nobles.'[19] The fluid structure of urban society demanded a cosmopolitan culture in which people could question the values of the old particularistic traditions.[20] Gokhale argues that Buddhism as a teaching for society reflected the 'demands of the New Man'. He wrote: 'The new age that was dawning demanded new forms of political organization and a revaluation of norms of social behaviour and formulation of new social goals. The history of early Buddhism reflects the elements of crisis as also the attempts made to crystallize and express the new social outlook.'[21]

The old brāhmaṇical culture was, at least in the early period of urbanization, antipathetic to city life. The priestly codes of law and ritual found no place for state officials, or for traders; brāhmaṇical authority advised against visiting cities, and forbade the recitation of the Vedas in their polluting environment.[22] Buddhism, unlike the ritualistic priestly codes, could countenance a way of life that included eating houses (whereas *Āpastamba* prohibited the consumption of shop food) and prostitution (a famous benefactrix of the *saṅgha* was a courtesan).[23]

PROTEST AGAINST CITY LIFE

So Buddhism was an ideology to serve the new age of urbanism. But, alternatively or perhaps even simultaneously, it was a reaction against this new environment, from which many sought spiritual refreshment in the wilderness. This point of view is succinctly argued by A. K. Narain:

18 Duad Ali sees a subtle isomorphism between the Buddhist *Vinaya* discipline and the principles of urban sophistication: 'Technologies of the self: courtly artifice and monastic discipline in early India', *JESHO*, 41 (1998), pp. 159–84.

19 Max Weber, *The Religion of India: the sociology of Hinduism and Buddhism*, trans. and ed. Hans H. Gerth and Don Martindale (Free Press, Glencoe, Ill., 1958/1962), p. 204.

20 Carrithers, *Buddha*, pp. 10f.

21 B. G. Gokhale, 'The Buddhist social ideals', *Indian Historical Quarterly*, 32 (1957), pp. 141f.

22 P. Olivelle, *Saṃnyāsa Upaniṣads: Hindu Scriptures on Asceticism and Renunciation* (Oxford University Press, New York, 1992), pp. 38ff. *Āpastamba Dhs* 1, 32, 19–21 warns a brahman teacher against frequenting crowds and entering towns (cf. Gombrich, *Theravāda Buddhism*, p. 55). See also *Baudhāyana Dhs* 2, 6, 33, ' "A man who keeps himself well under control will attain final bliss even if he lives in a city with his body covered with the city dust and his eyes and face coated with it" – now that is something impossible.' (Trans. Patrick Olivelle, in *Dharmasutras: the law codes of Āpastamba, Gautama, Baudhāyana, and Vasiṣṭha. Annotated text and translation* (Motilal Banarsidass, New Delhi, 2000), p. 265.

23 Sharma, *Material Culture*, p. 126. See *Āpastamba Dhs* 1, 17, 14, 'He should not eat food obtained from the market.'

> This urbanism led to material prosperity . . . suffering on account of tensions of life and insecurity of the person, and also to a concern for the preservation of the fauna and flora, which were being destroyed by the rise of cities and self-indulgent, savage rituals and games. All these factors were indeed sufficient to drive some out of the cities to wander forth in search of an end to suffering . . .[24]

One feature of city life that could have bred disenchantment with materialism was the suffering brought by disease, for in the warm wet lower Ganges area plague is likely to have been rife; as McNeill has suggested, the rise of the bigger cities could well have contributed to the spread of disease.[25] Such facts have been adduced by some scholars in support of the view that Buddhism appealed to those who suffered as a result of urbanization.[26] Using Drekmeier's concept of 'tribal trauma', F. Reynolds has argued that the social changes attending urbanization eventually alienated people and engendered 'lostness and despair';[27] people were acutely conscious of the extremes of wealth and poverty, and economic developments often involved oppression and brought social distress in their wake. Gombrich suggested a link between urbanism and spiritual malaise as a condition for the appeal of Buddhism.[28] Pande refers to the 'pessimistic Weltanschauung' developing at the end of the Vedic period as population moved into new regions difficult to pioneer: 'These circumstances must have created a feeling of distress and despair in the minds of many.'[29]

LEGITIMATION OF THE CENTRALIZED STATE

With the rise of cities went the rise of a new sort of state, more centralized in its organization and impersonal in its political culture, with a growing corps of bureaucrats. The canonical scriptures often refer to early Buddhist teachers as being consulted by the rulers of some of these kingdoms, and one could well link the Buddhist *dharma* with the new political order, whether as a rationalization of it or as a reaction against it.

On the one hand, Buddhism appealed as an ideology for the new commonwealth, which needed a set of uniform standards that would apply

[24] Narain (ed), *Studies in History*, p. xxvi.

[25] W. McNeill, *Plagues and Peoples* (Anchor, New York, 1976), pp. 81ff., 95.

[26] See Gombrich, *Theravāda Buddhism*, pp. 58ff., and Olivelle, *Saṃnyāsa Upaniṣads*, pp. 34f. McNeill's argument (see previous note) – linking epidemiology with political, social and cultural structures – indicates a direction in which future research could profitably move. See also de Jong, review of Gombrich, *Theravāda Buddhism*, pp. 239–42.

[27] F. Reynolds, 'The two wheels of *dharma*: a study of early Buddhism,' in G. Obeyesekere, F. Reynolds and B. L. Smith, *The Two Wheels of dharma: Essays on the Theravāda Tradition in India and Ceylon* (The American Academy of Religion, Chambersburg, Pa., 1972), pp. 6–30.

[28] Gombrich, *Theravāda Buddhism*, p. 57.

[29] Pande, *Studies*, pp. 264, 328.

equally to all the cultural groups beneath the ruler's sceptre instead of being rooted in the traditions of any one. Buddhism filled this need; it cut across lineage and caste ties. Further, according to R. Thapar, its doctrines of *karma* and *saṃsāra*, reconciling men to a life of suffering, were a sedative to quell dissidence and encourage the acceptance of authority.[30] It was much more apt as a public code than the brāhmaṇical prescriptions; it offered scientific values instead of moralizing restraints.[31] Buddhism's opposition to many of the brāhmaṇical claims made it a natural ally of the *rājanya*,[32] who sought to enlist the heads of mendicant orders as agents of central control, managing recruitment into their sects to serve state interest and giving moral support against the brahmins.[33] Buddhism favoured the values of the new political order, describing the *kṣatriya* as the 'protector of the fields' and denying ordination to deserters and criminals in acknowledgment of obligations to the ruler.[34]

PROTEST AGAINST THE CENTRALIZED STATE

On the other hand, Buddhism can be seen as a voice of protest against the new political order of the centralizing monarchies of the Ganges basin.[35] Buddhism, it might be argued, could appeal to those alienated by the new state, such as the *kṣatriyas*.[36] Buddhism and the other heterodoxies, especially Jainism, embodied with their teaching of *ahiṃsā* (non-injury) an alternative public morality to a state gospel that increasingly recognized official violence and coercion.[37] Again, it has been claimed that Buddhism represented a rejection of the demands made by the new state apparatus, which the economy was scarcely able to support.[38] Injustice accompanied official violence; cities became 'centres of corruption and bribery',[39] compelling citizens to look for spiritual solace. Kings waged wars in pursuit of

[30] R. Thapar, *From Lineage to State* (Oxford University Press, Delhi, 1984), p. 150.

[31] von Simson, 'Die zeitgeschichtliche Hintergrund', p. 96.

[32] Collins, *Selfless Persons*, p. 38.

[33] A. K. Warder, 'On the relationships between Buddhism and other contemporary systems', *Bulletin of the School of Oriental and African Studies*, 18 (1956), p. 48.

[34] Sharma, *Material Culture*, p. 126.

[35] J. W. de Jong, 'The background of early Buddhism', *Journal of Indian and Buddhist Studies*, 12 (1964), p. 46, offers an account of early Buddhism and the state which combines positive and negative. Buddhism's rationality suited the new rulers, whereas the old aristocracies they marginalized were alienated, ready to turn to Buddhism.

[36] Chakravarti, *Social Dimensions*, pp. 147–8.

[37] Thapar, *Ancient Indian Social History*, p. 55.

[38] McNeill, *Plagues*, pp. 94ff. points to a sense in which Buddhism (and in this view Hinduism also), with its rejection of political involvement, could be imagined to have appealed to those who turned their backs on a nascent state whose exactions were too heavy to bear.

[39] Sarao, *Urban Centres*, pp. 175ff.

their imperial dreams, bringing untold suffering to their subjects,[40] who were thus ripe for a religion predicated upon the prime fact of suffering as a condition of life. A fatalistic system like that of the Ājīvikas was 'eminently suited' to transforming society in a strong, dominant state; 'In this environment Buddhism, and to a lesser extent Jainism, reflected the desire to . . . evade or soften autocratic government.'[41] In such respects as these (some have argued), Buddhism gained support in reaction against the political order of the centralizing regional kingdoms, not as a legitimizing ideology for it.

LEGITIMATION OF POST-TRIBAL CULTURE

A fourth way in which Buddhism can be related to urbanization concerns its relations with the values of agrarian society. Agricultural surpluses supported, and were perhaps politically created by, the needs of the Ganges valley cities. Agrarian values evolve as part of the same process that generates urban societies. Buddhism might be thought of, in this case, either as a celebration of sedentary agrarian values superseding the nomadic tribal ways, or as thriving on nostalgia for them in reaction against agrarian values.

Several scholars have taken up the theme of animal sacrifice, which might well be regarded as an emblem of the tribal Vedic culture with its elaborate ritual. The idea was perhaps first given currency by D. D. Kosambi.[42] Others have taken it up. R. S. Sharma, for example, refers to the Vedic texts requiring senseless slaughter for sacrifice and argues that Pāli scriptures express values appropriate to the new agricultural environment.[43] One can see this value as utilitarian – in the crowded lands of the doab, cattle were a scarce resource to be husbanded, not wasted in conspicuous sacrificial consumption. Alternatively, one can see the opposition to Vedic animal sacrifices as the expression of a moral value – non-injury or *ahiṃsā*.[44] In this

[40] Pande, *Studies*, pp. 327ff. Contrast T. W. Rhys Davids, who (being overly romantic) thought that material conditions for ordinary people in the Indian cities were not oppressive; 'of want, as known in our great cities, there is no evidence'. T. W. Rhys Davids, *Buddhist India* (T. Fisher Unwin, London, 1903), p. 101.

[41] Warder, 'Relationships', p. 44.

[42] D. D. Kosambi, 'Early stages of the caste system in northern India', *Journal of the Bombay Branch of the Royal Asiatic Society*, 22 (1946), p. 45, who argued that the old Vedic order was predicated on a religious idea involving slaughter for sacrifice; the new order similarly based its rejection of slaughter upon religious grounds but had economic justification in rejecting practices that were uneconomic in the change to agriculture.

[43] Sharma, *Material Culture*, pp. 109, 118ff., 121. Cf. Thapar, *Ancient Indian Social History*, p. 54.

[44] T. W. Rhys Davids, *Dialogues of the Buddha* (PTS, London, reprint 1973), vol. 1, pp. 160–6, comments that the ironic disparagement of elaborate animal sacrifices found here reflects a big victory for *ahiṅsā* in India.

case the Buddhist adoption of it can be regarded as a feature of urban culture, for it was city folk who could afford to abstain from harming animals; farmers followed a way of life in which strict *ahiṃsā* was impossible.[45] Either way, Buddhism stood for the new civilization of the northeast and the rising kingdoms, while brahmanism remained linked with the civilization of the northwest and the Vedas. Von Simson has argued that the Vedic religion, with its ideas of sacred place and time, its divinization of the forces of nature, its calendar myths, its seasonal rituals and above all its exalting of the concept of sustenance, is wedded to the agricultural or pastoral way of life, in contrast to the quest for salvation represented by the heterodox teachings such as Buddhism.[46] From this point of view, Buddhism needs to be aligned with urban civilization, as opposed to both agricultural and pastoral values.

PROTEST AGAINST POST-TRIBAL CULTURE

Equally, however, Buddhism might be seen as a reaction against the whole movement of civilization from its pastoral origins in the hills, where men were surrounded by nature and governed by its rhythms, to the artificiality of the man-made landscape and the urban anonymity of the relatively densely populated agricultural plains.[47] D. P. Chattopadhyaya has pointed to the fact that the *Aggañña Suttanta* represents the move from gathering to hoarding grain as a part of the degeneration of society; Buddhism looked back to the values of the 'tribal collective'. The 'early rules envisage a kind of primitive communism based on low standards of pre-field agriculture and of pre-trade, tribal life'.[48]

One strand of argument aligns Buddhism with the old tribal society by identifying the non-monarchical *gaṇa* communities of the northern foothills and the northwest as representative of the old culture. Some have considered that Buddhism represented the world view of the older aristocratic *gaṇa* communities in opposition to centralized power, preferring the 'utopian egalitarianism of pristine society'.[49] Again, Buddhism and Jainism have been seen as a 'moral counter-attack' by the

45 Thapar, *Ancient Indian Social History*, p. 54.

46 von Simson, 'Die zeitgeschichtliche Hintergrund', p. 93.

47 Sharma, *Material Culture*, p. 128.

48 D. P. Chattopadhyaya, *Lokāyata. A study in ancient Indian materialism* (People's Publishing House, Delhi, 1959/1973), p. 481.

49 Thapar, *Ancient Indian Social History*, p. 88. The author also suggests, however, that perhaps the *gaṇa* communities with their less authoritarian ideology acted as safety valves for the 'containment of political dissidence'.

indigenous culture of the tribal oligarchies against encroaching Indo-Aryan stratification.[50]

CRITIQUE OF THE ARGUMENTS CONCERNING URBANIZATION

In respect of each of the four identified aspects of urbanization, scholars have argued variously that Buddhism can be seen to have appealed because it was in tune with the changes associated with urbanization, being apt to legitimate or encode them, and that on the other hand Buddhism can be seen to have appealed because it was apt as a voice for those who suffered from the changes and sought an alternative world view. Some of the arguments embody valuable insights. Some others are too glib and as they stand leave too many questions unanswered to carry conviction. There is something precarious about the whole framework of the discussion. (It is not exactly a debate, for the protagonists normally do not acknowledge, or seek to resolve, the contradictions that divide them.) Too often, highly speculative assumptions are treated as self-evident.

The arguments just summarized do not amount to a convincing case, on either side. Let us first look at the claim that Buddhism favoured the values of merchants. We cannot deny the connection between the new religions and the mercantile classes, yet we can ask why these classes demanded an intellectual contextualization and justification for their style of life. Commerce, like agriculture, was certainly not new. Both are recorded frequently, if lacking in detail, in the *Brāhmaṇas*.[51] If they had already existed, why did they demand intellectual justification in a new form and reorientation of culture in respect of a new set of values?

One can indeed appeal to the presumed congruity between the commercial spirit and the peripatetic Buddhist tradition. But is this enough? To draw out more fully the analogy as forming the basis of a strong material and intellectual interaction between Buddhism and mercantile activity, it is necessary to show why traders, shopkeepers, small businessmen and wealthy farmers experienced a need for intellectual validation, and how this need was met by Buddhism. Moreover, if such a need can be isolated, we must still ask whether the 'mercantilist sphere', to use a very general term,

[50] G. Erdosy, 'Early historic cities of northern India', *South Asian Studies*, 3 (1987), p. 15. Chattopadhyaya (*Lokāyata*, pp. 483 and 491) also regards the organization of the Buddhist Order as modelled on the (assumed) collective communities of old tribal culture.

[51] See W. Rau, *Staat und Gesellschaft Im Alten Indien nach den Brāhmaṇatexten Dargestellt* (Harrassowitz, Wiesbaden, 1957), p. 52. Cf. R. Thapar, 'The First Millennium B.C. in northern India', in R. Thapar, ed., *Recent Perspectives of Early Indian History* (Popular Prakashan, Bombay, 1995), pp. 92–3.

was attracted to the Buddhist message, to its practitioners, or to both. Regrettably, the situation portrayed by the literature is sketchy: mercantilism is a distinctive part of an expanding economy, self-confidently aware of its own role and capable of engaging in a kind of sumptuary display. If Buddhism did have a function in its rise and continuing expansion in a growing economy, this function must have been to promote its distinctiveness and to value positively the material achievements of the mercantile class. In one sense the merchants were a sort of counterweight to the brahmins. These were the two most visible groups to emerge with late Vedic culture. Neither held coercive power; both were fashioning highly distinctive values and subcultures, the one with a material *raison d'être* and the other with a religious. It was natural for the Buddhists to support the mercantile groups as these (1) provided them with material resources, and (2) were not obliged to regard them as competitors, as the brahmins clearly did. In so far as there was a mercantilist ideology, it was natural for the Buddhists to seek an affinity in it. But of course, the claim that Buddhism favoured merchant values would be more convincing if we had some specific knowledge of the content of these values. Everything rests at present on inference,[52] except perhaps what we can glean from texts like the *Sigālovādasutta*.[53] More obviously congruent with the original message of Buddhism is the opposite view, arguing instead that Buddhism was a counter or alternative to the materialist society of the new cities where money ruled. This view, though, fails to clarify in what precise manner the renouncer would have represented a universal code of behaviour for the laity in cities.[54] By a certain stage of economic development (probably later than the rise of Buddhism), the laity were required to deal with money, and certainly did not have the luxury of doing without it or begging for their food. For them this kind of activity was not an option, whereas for the monks it was obligatory. If the universal code of monks was translated into a form taken up by the laity, it could only have been a limited section of this code – whatever could guide the dealings of the laity with other people.

[52] Even in the otherwise useful article by B. G. Gokhale, 'The merchant in ancient India', *Journal of the American Oriental Society*, 97 (1977), pp. 125–30, we find little about mercantile values either in an ideological or in a behavioural sense.

[53] The *Sigālovādasutta* (*D* III 180–3) certainly appears to endorse 'bourgeois' values, and has been abundantly cited in the modern literature as evidence of the Buddha's social concerns. The very fact that it is so often cited is evidence of its special character. It is not representative of the concerns of the early Nikāyas as a whole.

[54] Sarkisyanz can argue in the opposite direction; the universalistic ethics of Buddhism were economically *less* practical than the Hindu mercantile caste ethos, or the Realpolitik of Hindu kings, for they were abstract and pious, not geared to action in the real world. See E. Sarkisyanz, *Buddhist Backgrounds of the Burmese Revolution* (Nijhoff, The Hague, 1965), pp. 80ff., 143.

They still had to conduct their lives within the secular economic order. We would rather argue that the renouncers represented the higher ideals associated with transcendent values, and we are yet to see how these values translate into those of the laity except as rather abstract high-flown moral principles.

So what about the claim that Buddhism favoured the culture of the new urban society? We could well question whether people at the time recognized themselves as entering a 'new age'. Were they not, more likely, encountering ad hoc a range of piecemeal changes, some of which they tried to insulate themselves against, while attempting to adapt to others? It is the recognition of the 'new' and the consciousness of this that require more elaboration here. Buddhism was more attuned to the context of city life than brahmanism, more tolerant of institutions such as brothels and communal eating-places, and in this sense it was broader in its acceptance of people of divergent classes and customs than was brahmanism in a practical sense. Yet there was not just one brāhmaṇical religion, there were several under one broad rubric, which changed dramatically and became much more adaptable under the influence of devotional values and practices. These were emerging at the same time as Buddhism was initially expanding. Moreover, it was very likely that brahmins followed a variety of occupations whilst still calling themselves brahmins, and retained the privileges that went with that title.

What then of the claim that Buddhism at least had universal values, apt for the cosmopolitan city environment, unlike the particularistic brāhmaṇical code? Indological scholarship seems to assume brahmins had no universalistic theories, though the much later *varṇāśrama* theory and the *trivarga* do indeed aim at a totalistic world view of universal scope. This lack of recognition arises perhaps because many find it difficult to recognize compatibility between a universalistic outlook and a particularistic view of social class, yet the two need not be mutually exclusive.

If Indologists persist in accusing brahmins of lacking universalistic theories, it may be because brahmins are believed to have been preoccupied with ritual theory, as embodied in the huge ritual texts – the *Brāhmaṇas*. These texts, like much of late Vedic and early post-Vedic literature and certain of the *śrauta* rituals, promote the image of the brahmin as obsessed with ritual performance, as indeed do certain famous passages in the Buddhist *Sutta Nipāta* and the *Jātakas*. Yet what nomadic economy could have supported a large group of non-producing ritual and legal specialists who claimed to be both within and outside of society? True, society did eventually support economically the (much cheaper) ascetic groups, but this was well after the social pre-eminence of the brahmins had been firmly established. As we will see in chapter 5, the brahmins were much more adaptable and worldly than is commonly thought, and this was one reason for the Buddha's own antipathy towards them.

But what about the claim that Buddhism appealed to those who suffered from urbanization? Some have argued that the alienating environment of the city engendered feelings even of despair. The argument turns on a view of change in history. The ascetic tradition represented by Buddhism, the Upaniṣadic sages and the early Jains placed great emphasis on the transitoriness of human existence in any dimension that could be named. It is tempting, if not natural, for scholars to try and locate some kind of direct connection between the socio-economic conditions and the emergence of a theory of change, both sophisticated and universal, in ancient Indian thought. The tone of universal dissatisfaction implied in the concept of *dukkha* has sometimes been read back into a kind of social *Angst* somewhere in the psyche of the residents of the Ganges valley. The reasoning is scarcely convincing. The notion of *dukkha* is normally formulated in broad generic terms that do not allow us to identify, as specific causes of dissatisfaction, particular changes in the non-religious and non-speculative areas of life. As for the doctrine of impermanence, we still do not know from where or how the Buddha himself developed his universalistic theory. If there is any real connection between doctrine and social environment, we cannot know it without a much more detailed understanding of the background than is at present possible. We would need to know whether the rate of change, however it might be defined, was especially pronounced during the Buddha's time, and whether the elites with whom the Buddha interacted retained nostalgic memories of a more stable, peaceful era.

To recognize this problem is to see the difficulties of reasoning convincingly from even a very central doctrine of Buddhism to socio-economic conditions that may have contributed to the Buddha's formulation of this doctrine. We see how insecurely founded is the glib notion that the early canonical texts both embody a teaching that must have appealed to the alienated, the disenfranchised, the dispossessed, and also reflect a period of social dislocation occurring when they were composed. Both propositions are problematic. The teaching of *dukkha* need not go with social distress; the canonical texts might reflect any combination of times, and any or none of these times may have been characterized by either slow or rapid change. For the most part the changes wrought by urbanization and state formation had already become well established by the time the Buddhist texts took the form in which we know them; at any rate, parts of them offer a picture of urban society that had been maturing for some time.[55]

It is not clear that urbanization in itself must have created such a feeling of despair in the minds of so many. These people were not so unadaptable as to be incapable of responding to changes which came upon them, particularly since (we have no grounds to doubt) these changes were gradual. Few who argue in this way spell out, in detail, the mechanism by which traumatic alienation is supposed to have engendered a spiritual turn and the emergence of the ascetic groups. Yet we surely need to have it fully explained, since all of the ascetic groups place so much emphasis on *dukkha* as a universal condition, without any emphasis upon the particular conditions of city life. (As we saw, it is brāhmaṇical texts which spurn city life.) A really convincing answer has not been given to the question why city dwellers in particular should have turned to a doctrine of total detachment from society. We conclude that, on the available evidence, early Buddhism, as embodied in its monks and laity, is a social and religious movement *adapting itself to an expanding society where the economy is experiencing steady growth and a degree of prosperity.*

By and large, what goes for the urban environment goes for the new rising state, which normally was based in a growing city. Some claim that Buddhism favoured the rising kingdoms, and that monks often gave rulers advice. But it is really only the Buddha and perhaps Ānanda, and Devadatta from a different perspective, who are portrayed in this role. One could hardly mount a strong argument upon the canonical evidence.

Perhaps there is a better argument that Buddhism supported the state because its doctrines of *saṃsāra* and *karma* provided a rationale for acceptance of authority, a sort of fatalism that would legitimate an authoritarian regime. This remains problematic given that ancient India does not present a picture of acceptance and submission, nor do any of the literary sources, Hindu or Buddhist, provide good evidence for such a conclusion. The doctrine of *karma* (and *puruṣakara* in the *Mahābhārata*) could equally support the contrary view: that the only way to confront universal *dukkha* was to work hard at producing good *karma* (including political reform) for the future (and hence future happiness).

So what about the opposite argument that Buddhism appealed to those alienated by the rising monarchical regimes, notably the *kṣatriyas*? Once

55 A similar view has been put by M. Witzel, 'Tracing the Vedic dialects', in C. Caillat (ed.), *Dialectes dans les littératures indo-aryennes* (Institut de Civilisation Indienne, Collège de France, Paris, 1991), p. 245. Cf. W. Rau, *Zur vedischen Altertumskunde* (Akademie der Wissenschaft und der Literatur, Mainz, 1983), p. 21, n. 12.

again this argument assumes that the only possibility for the 'alienated aristocracy' was to seek a new ideology. Why should this be so? Were no other possibilities available in a society and economy expanding with scarcely any restraint on available resources?[56]

But it was not only the *kṣatriya* elite within the dominant culture, it was the mass of ordinary people now subjected to the expansion of autocratic power that can be seen as the natural audience for the Buddhist message. With monarchy came the ladder of degree, and we can imagine Buddhism as a voice of protest against it. However, to the extent that the Buddhists formed part of any form of social organization, they maintained a separate community, operating with achieved status, alongside the increasingly stratified secular world. While the Buddha criticized ascribed status, he did not actively seek reforms or fight stratification. As an actor in society Buddhism was complex and multi-faceted, resisting any simple characterization.

The austere and parsimonious lifestyle of the monks may be thought to imply a criticism of the hierarchical state; but equally it could reflect a repudiation of the self-indulgence fostered by an expanding economy. This leads us to the fourth and last category of interpretation: Buddhism as either a protagonist or a critic of the older nomadic or agrarian society, in contrast to the new urban one. Those who see Buddhism as standing for the new society emphasize its contrast with the sacrificial and ritual character of the old Vedic religion that went with tribal society. The contrast is real enough, but we must beware of simplistic categorization, pigeonholing ritual with tribalism and the inner religious quest with urbanism. *A priori*, such an alignment is counter-intuitive, and later history scarcely bears it out; highly urbanized royal capitals became centres of brāhmaṇical ritual.

On the other hand, it would be unwise to assume glibly that Buddhism stood for the old ways of a simpler, kindlier society, where a tribal collective protected people from the abuses of 'individualism'. We can scarcely identify the early *saṅgha* with a primitive subsistence economy. Surely those who steered the Buddhist Order through its formative period knew well how much they depended upon an expanding economy. Accordingly, they adapted skilfully to the new socio-economic conditions, without compromising their fundamental religious position.

[56] It could further be asked how we know the ruler bypassed the *kṣatriya* as his agents. Perhaps they were potential competitors with an aspiring sole ruler, an interpretation supported on the analogy of the kind of alliances portrayed in the *Mahābhārata*. Again, the armies of officials described in the *Arthaśāstra* may reflect the practice of recruiting 'new men', but this text is not evidence for the late Vedic period. We must recognize how speculative is any argument about the social dynamics of the rise of kingship.

BUDDHISM AS A REMEDY IN AN AGE OF SUFFERING

These considerations collectively show the inconclusiveness of the discussion in the terms so far deployed. But, given the nature of the Buddhist message as one of ascetic renunciation for the sake of spiritual salvation outside society, it might seem appropriate to seek an explanation of the rise of Buddhism by abandoning all the positive arguments (to the effect that Buddhism was in tune with the new society) and maintaining only the negative ones (to the effect that it attracted the alienated).

The negative ones constitute an important undercurrent in modern perceptions of Buddhist teaching, often glibly labelled 'pessimism', if not even more misleadingly 'fatalism'. This is one strand of a broader argument focusing on the negative effects of dislocation and displacement, providing a ready audience for teachings like Buddhism, which reinforced and fed on this negativism. It is not uncharitable to assert that it stands or falls on the success with which we can demonstrate that pre-Buddhistic India was free of such tensions, as this view implies.

On the available evidence it is difficult to argue one way or the other. Kosambi has been the most eloquent and convincing exponent of this view, associating the success of Buddhism with the rise of individualism and with the collapse of community, by which he meant the collapse of the Vedic tribe. For example, in the political sphere this manifests itself in the rise of a more individualistic sort of society in kingdoms not founded on any older traditional loyalties, and the process of emergent individuality has economic consequences that can only aggravate the personal anxieties provoked by the reconfiguration of political power.[57]

Kosambi's arguments link the collapse of the old tribal solidarity to the rise of religious movements feeding on the frustrations of displaced and dispossessed groups. They are persuasive arguments, but it is difficult to find evidence from the literature sufficiently transparent fully to confirm them. Moreover, the counter-argument also needs to be overturned if Kosambi's is to be accepted: all the available evidence portrays a fluid economy, one which is impressively diversified, and offering increasing opportunities to the enterprising. Whatever mental anxieties were created by the emergent attitudes of possessive individualism, and we do not know how widespread such attitudes were, these grew in generally favourable economic conditions.

[57] D. D. Kosambi, *An Introduction to the Study of Ancient Indian History* (Popular Book Depot, Bombay, 1956), pp. 156, 159. Cf. p. 167, 'truth, justice, non-stealing, not encroaching upon the possessions of others show that a totally new conception of private, individual property had arisen'.

Kosambi's argument would be all the more convincing if it could be shown that there were large numbers of displaced individuals and displaced groups, people who had suffered rapid decline in their living conditions. Whilst the Pāli texts do offer us some images of an idealized and frozen past (as exemplified in the ideal image of the brahmin of old), they offer us no images of groups who harbour a strongly nostalgic vision of a time when everything was better than it is now.[58] This does not mean such groups did not exist. Rather it simply confirms the canon to be primarily a religious document set within the particular historical context of its day; within this context the belief in secular decay figures purely as a general doctrinal formula. Buddhists accepted the myth of a decline into decay from a golden age, something akin to the Hindu *yuga* theory, but before we can draw conclusions from this we need to know why they told the story of decline in the first place. Such stories, which may be told in any age (not just ages of urban expansion), can be accommodated within the anthropology of religion as messages emphasizing the contrast between the sacred (however defined) and the profane.

However, one must not fall into the trap of defining ancient Indian culture in purely religious terms. The temptation to exaggerate the religious character of everything arises because our primary textual sources are almost exclusively religious. But there can be no natural presumption that disaffected urbanites unhappy with their conditions would be thereby disposed to join a religious movement requiring them to forsake their families and become wandering mendicants.

Further, it does not make sense to claim that people turned to a doctrine of withdrawal from a world full of suffering as a response to the fact that they were actually suffering more than in previous ages. This interpretation, attributing Buddhism's success to its pessimism, is in a way anachronistic. It supposes that people in the Buddha's time saw history from our own (modern) perspective, and made the sorts of comparisons which we might make, thereby recognizing that conditions were worse than in previous centuries and feeling unhappy as a result. We do not find texts drawing the conclusions we would expect – that historical decline is a cause of *dukkha*, that life in urban kingdoms is unhappy, and that therefore people should

[58] Except perhaps for the *Aggañña Sutta*, which presents a myth or parable of social and moral decline. See M. Carrithers, review of S. J. Tambiah, *World Conqueror, World Renouncer*, *Journal of the Anthropological Society of Oxford*, 8 (1977), pp. 95–105. Carrithers sees the *sutta*'s use of the theory of successive stages of decline as a satire upon brāhmaṇical lore. Cf. S. Collins, 'The Discourse on What is Primary (Aggañña-Sutta). An annotated translation', *Journal of Indian Philosophy*, 21 (1993), pp. 301–95.

turn away from the world. The hypothesis simply does not fit comfortably with the evidence of what people believed.

In fact, people can suffer from all manner of afflictions caused by war, oppression, inequality and malnutrition without necessarily comparing their lot with a past situation inferred from historical evidence or turning to creeds based upon the diagnosis that a modern historian might make.

Is it anyway proper to treat Buddhism as pessimistic? This may be justified to the extent that we can identify a pessimistic world view with the notion of *dukkha*, a concept which acquired an axiomatic status in Buddhist teaching. *Dukkha* is an untranslatable word connoting unsatisfactoriness, disillusionment, anxiety, physical pain and insecurity in every possible modulation and dimension. So the point of the doctrine may be found in a doctrinal, not a social, context: the doctrines of impermanence and non-self entail that human experience, based on the belief in a continuing self, should in all circumstances be shot through with frustration or unsatisfactoriness. On this view the concept arose from a philosophical tenet; it does not represent pessimism inspired by social disruption and alienation.

SIMULTANEOUS LEGITIMATION AND PROTEST

Some explanations of Buddhism's appeal favour the positive side (Buddhism legitimated and supported the new society), and some the negative (Buddhism attracted those alienated by the new society); there are also some who have argued on both sides.[59] The temptation to present arguments portraying Buddhism both as a sigh of the oppressed and as a legitimizing device to prop up the authority of tyrants has also affected anthropologists such as Marvin Harris. On one side:

> The great universalistic religions can also best be understood as products of the misery the Old World imperial systems created in their futile attempt to relieve reproductive pressures by intensification, exploitation and warfare . . . Buddhism preached the overthrow of the hereditary priesthoods, declared poverty a virtue, outlawed the slaughter of vital plow animals, and converted the de facto vegetarianism of the semi-starved peasants into a spiritual blessing.[60]

[59] Most notable in this respect is R. S. Sharma, *Material Culture*, pp. 123–6, who argues that Buddhism was in tune with urbanization because it permitted usury, eating houses, and prostitution, and rejected the old brāhmaṇical ways such as animal sacrifices which could not be afforded in the new economic conditions. On the other hand it was a reaction against urbanization in its rejection of 'gross social inequalities' and values based on money, luxuries, or private property; it condemned the urban way of life with its inequality and suffering and the disintegration of the social order. See pp. 128–31.

[60] M. Harris, *Cultural Materialism: the struggle for a science of culture* (Random House, New York, 1979), p. 109.

On the other hand, it appears, Buddhism was a weapon of elite domination:

> The demystification of the world religions begins with this simple fact: Confucianism, Taoism, Buddhism, Hinduism, Christianity and Islam prospered because the ruling elites who invented or co-opted them benefited materially from them.[61]

Generally, as here, the apparent inconsistency goes unacknowledged. Sometimes, though, scholars have pointed out explicitly that Buddhism seemed on their accounts to have played opposite parts; Uma Chakravarti refers to a 'dialectical relationship' between Buddhism and new socio-economic forces.[62] Such a 'dialectical relationship', however, is not an explanation. How, in detail, could a single protagonist both oppose and unite with socio-economic changes? What, in fact, was this Buddhism?

There is nothing wrong with eclecticism if the author is presenting a coherent synthesis that orders and explains the various ways in which Buddhism could tap into different, even conflicting, aspirations. Such eclecticism is not self-evidently absurd; but it needs to be justified by a consistent account of the 'Buddhism' seen as a protagonist in cultural history. The problem we confront is that a coherent synthesis is generally lacking.

Other interpretations which seek to deal relatively comprehensively with the positive and negative aspects find similar difficulty in dealing with the gap between them.[63] A basic problem is that it is not at all easy to see how a thoroughly ascetic movement is likely to have gained real popularity or social relevance in the first place.

THE FALLACY OF TREATING EFFECTS AS CAUSES

The actual mechanism of Buddhism's likely appeal during its early years has not in fact been analysed with any finesse. We confront an issue in the logic of explanation. Whenever any movement *M* follows more or less closely

[61] Ibid., p. 110.

[62] Chakravarti, *Social Dimensions*, p. 64, 'It has been suggested that Buddhism had a dialectical relationship with the new system of production and the new society emerging . . . demonstrating simultaneously both an opposition to and unity with it.'

[63] There is no space here to discuss Weber's impressive attempt at a synthesis, but see G. Bailey, 'Max Weber's *Hinduismus und Buddhismus*: a new interpretation', and I. Mabbett, 'Weber, Protestantism and Buddhism', papers contributed to *Max Weber, Religion and Social Action*, conference in Canberra, September 1999. Gokhale, 'The Buddhist social Ideals', argues that Buddhism first appealed negatively, then changed its nature and appealed positively. It is not easy to see how an organization which so blatantly switched its policies could have subsequently succeeded so well after radically changing its character. Too much remains difficult to digest.

upon the operation of any process P, it is possible to identify those features of *M* which might be described as in harmony with P and declare that they 'explain' how *M* arose as a natural effect of P; it is also possible to identify those features which might be described as discordant or incompatible and declare that they 'explain' how *M* arose as a reaction against P. Sometimes, as with Buddhism, one can do both at once. Yet in no case is a real explanation thereby achieved. Any randomly chosen process and any randomly chosen movement may, if they are complex enough, render up to an appropriate investigation some features of harmony and some features of discordance. To identify the features is not *ipso facto* to discover any causal links. The claim that Buddhism was a legitimator of urbanization or a reaction against it is not an explanation.

When we look closely at the urbanization hypothesis, therefore, we can see how easily it might fall into the *post hoc ergo propter hoc* fallacy. During a certain period, the Gangetic plain witnessed the rise of cities. During a later but overlapping period, the *dhamma* became an important element in urban culture. The first is therefore used to explain the second.

There is a simple process by which this manner of explanation is made to seem plausible, and the outline of causal connections is blurred:

1 Buddhism in its original conception, and brahmanism in its earlier form before the rise of cities and kingdoms, had distinctive characteristics which were not congruent with the processes of urbanization and state formation.
2 Both Buddhism and brahmanism, in different ways, came to terms with the rise of cities and kingdoms, adapting to changing society and themselves changing in the process. At the latter end of any process of adaptation, an institution becomes more or less integrated into, and comes to serve the purposes of, the social structure in which it is lodged.
3 Thus, in different ways, Buddhism and brahmanism acquired characteristics that were wholly congruent with the culture of the city-based regional kingdom, with distinct roles to play in this culture.

In the case of Buddhism, these characteristics were grafted upon the traditions that eventually found written form, and thus come to be available as explanatory principles – they are assumed to have been characteristics of original Buddhism, making it easy to see how the teaching must by its nature have appealed to the citizens of the urbanizing societies, filling an ideological gap. The result of Buddhism's popularity is treated as its cause. Meanwhile, the traces of a much earlier and quite different sort of teaching (surviving awkwardly alongside the results of adaptation) were available to explain how people reacting against urbanization took to something quite different. These considerations are important if we are to see how delusive is 'urbanization' as a ready-made 'explanation'. What looks like a cause of Buddhism's appeal might well be its effect.

Where the question of historical causes and effects is in view, it is impossible to ignore Max Weber, often called the father of modern sociology. To be sure, his research on Indian religion is now, in detail, superseded; but his ideas remain influential, and his insights still have something to offer. There is no space here to deal with them properly, but we need to notice where he stands on the explanation of the rise of Indian Buddhism.

We noticed above his alignment of Buddhism with 'urban development, of urban kingship and the city nobles'.[64] This seems to place him with the proponents of the 'positive' argument, the view that Buddhism became popular because of its aptness to express the urban ethos, but in fact the central intent of *The Religion of India*, the work most often cited in English to identify Weber's views on the matter, is to advance an interpretation of Indian religion, Hinduism as well as Buddhism and others, as essentially other-worldly, world-fleeing.

To be sure, as Ilana Silber has observed, Weber's focus is on withdrawal from the world in a general sense, without detailed attention to 'the more radically individual and/or withdrawn eremitic forms of virtuosity'[65] (which indeed will be given importance in the present study). There is no doubt, however, that for him the Indian religions take their place in the grand scheme of the history of religions in the category of world-denial. The grand scheme in question is not one that can be fully understood by taking in isolation any one of the well-known essays translated separately into English. It is one which evolved throughout his oeuvre, and it finishes by proposing that, in general, human culture is governed by all manner of factors, material and social as well as religious, but that at certain crucial points societies take decisive turns towards one or another of a limited number of cosmological belief systems, and once such a turn has been taken, certain possible futures are closed off. India, for Weber, took a turn towards the ideology of world-denial, and this foreclosed the possibility

[64] Weber, *The Religion of India*, p. 204.

[65] I. Friedrich-Silber, *Virtuosity, Charisma, and Social Order: a comparative sociological study of monasticism in Theravada Buddhism and medieval Catholicism* (Cambridge University Press, Cambridge, 1995), p. 33.

of subsequent progress towards rational, this-worldly and (in Weber's own special sense) 'ascetic' culture.[66]

This is a sort of modified determinism of ideas, however qualified. It will not be adopted here, but it is important to follow Weber in recognizing the complexity of the causal factors that are in play, and to assess the social role of a religion carefully in relation to its material and social context. The following chapters are addressed to this context.

66 See particularly F. H. Tenbruch, 'The problem of thematic unity in the works of Max Weber', *British Journal of Sociology*, 31/3 (1980), pp. 315–51.

Context

2

The social elite

In order to define properly the mediatory role of the monk it is necessary to review the evidence concerning the structure of society in the period with which this book is concerned. It is not our intention to present in exhaustive detail all information in the texts pertaining to social classes, occupational positions, kinship terminology and *varṇa* affiliation, though some of this will be mentioned. These have been well treated in other publications and any extended treatment here would simply duplicate them.[1] Rather, the emphasis in this chapter will be focused on three areas: (1) a summary of the principal characteristics of the various elite groups as they receive more emphasis in the texts than any other groups; (2) a description of the concurrent operation of various forms of classification which operate within similar groups that otherwise might be different; and (3) the difficulties in determining whether a demonstrably pluralist society needs a universal ideology to provide it with the possibility of political and social homogeneity. Put in another way, the question we have set ourselves in this chapter is to ask whether the many groups and social units mentioned in the Pāli Canon (and tribal names found in late Vedic literature) reflected a society, highly diverse in a number of ways, such that we need to speak of semi-autonomous groups and even of distinct small-scale societies existing side by side. Or do we have to argue a case that the texts present us with a veneer of diversity, underneath which there is really a tendency towards socialization and uniformity along the lines of the brāhmaṇical *varṇa* model?

Society is never monolithic. Textual and archaeological evidence suggests ancient Buddhist and Hindu literature was informed by both small and large-scale societies. These must have included tribal-based rural societies, city-based societies, rural communities probably centred on villages

[1] See N. K. Wagle, *Society at the Time of the Buddha* (Popular Prakashan, Bombay, 1966); Chakravarti, *Social Dimensions*.

and, because of the importance of the various ascetic movements, many highly visible individuals wandering from urban centre to countryside and back again. Within this essentially spatial and social configuration of people, different possibilities of personal identity and social interaction were being developed. These ranged from forms of possessive individualism to group-based forms of identity where the group severely restricted the limits available to wholly individualized behaviour. More likely, in an empirical sense, such views existed side by side and offered possibilities of identity rather than clearly delineated pathways of social behaviour.

There are two approaches we can adopt in exploring through Buddhist sources what is in reality pre-caste society. We can study the society itself, apart from Buddhism, simply using the Buddhist sources as a window upon it; or we can try to understand it by looking at the relations between Buddhist monks and nuns and the rest of society. In adopting the first, it is important to recognize that the society described in Buddhist texts should not be thought of as something unique to Buddhism. We are not looking at two different societies when using Hindu and Buddhist sources, but one society, certainly not monolithic in any sense. There was substantial cultural and social diversity in ancient India just as there is now. Widespread mining of the Buddhist texts has tended to reinforce an assumption that in using those sources we are dealing with some entity called a Buddhist society. Such a thing may exist in the case of certain Theravāda Buddhist countries in present-day South East Asia and including Sri Lanka, but it could never have been the case in ancient India.

This view needs more nuancing. It is not so much that we find these ideas being explicitly developed in the secondary sources. Rather, there is an implication that a Buddhist society could possibly be realized. The *Sigālovādasutta* presents the outlines of a social ethic, as does the *Vinaya* everywhere, but this is not the presentation of a society. It is the presentation of a set of standards for action, strongly coloured by a Buddhist ethical view, designed to produce a particular result conducive to medium- and long-term success and contentment in every aspect of life.

The second approach, on the other hand, demands that we do not ignore the interrelation between monk, nun, *saṅgha* and society. In the *Vinaya*, the *Majjhima* and *Dīgha Nikāyas*, the conditions for these interrelations are laid down prescriptively and explored in some detail in narrative form to illustrate how they might apply in given historical situations. Much of what we find in the Pāli Canon dealing with subjects of a social nature is included expressly to illustrate these interrelations, and it is from this specific perspective that the social material in the Canon must be read.

These, then, are the two ways of approaching the study of pre-caste society: examining the Buddhist texts (among other sources) as a window upon it, and examining it through the interaction between Buddhists and others. A failure fully to appreciate these alternatives may lead to the fallacious conclusion that whatever picture of society scholars see in the literature was strongly coloured by Buddhism in all of its doctrinal and behavioural permutations. In the present chapter our focus is primarily on the first of these alternatives, even if, and this is a crucial condition, we can only glimpse social conditions using the second alternative as the vehicle. To put this in other words: we envision ancient Indian society as it is depicted in Buddhist texts mostly by extrapolating from social conditions encountered in contacts of monks and nuns with laypeople, many of whom would not have been lay Buddhists. We deal with the second alternative more fully in the second section of this book.

It should, finally, be noted that the material in this and the next chapter has been placed into conceptual abstractions that likely meant very little in this form to the agents of the actions the texts describe. That is, in order to create some control over our data we have been required to use categories, taken largely from the social sciences, that abstract material in such a way as to present a more simplistic picture than would really have existed. It is our hope that the use of such categories as 'economy' or 'urbanization' will be found to have illuminated the sources rather than to have obscured them.

CATEGORIZATION OF SOCIAL GROUPS IN BUDDHIST LITERATURE: SOCIAL DIVERSITY

Any wide reading of the earliest texts relating to the period covered in this book demonstrates that the articulation of society did not lend itself to any simple scheme of division into stable classes or what later became castes; it consisted rather of a patchwork of miscellaneous groups, each united by a sense of kin, either authentic or constructed, or by whatever other factors, especially occupational, tribal or political, gave it functional unity. The overwhelming impression given by literary sources is that, however powerful a king might be, his power rested upon his success in manipulating the relationships between innumerable local groupings, defined in various ways, which in the normal course of things conducted their affairs more or less autonomously. Members of each such group were likely to cluster together for mutual support in a dangerous world. What we observe is that there was a variety of such groups – lineage groups, extended families or clans, merchant or craft organizations, *gaṇa* communities, unassimilated tribes on the borders, and so forth. A convenient general term for these groups is *vargas*, separate groups; in law such communities were recognized by the time of the *Kātyāyanasmṛti* as contracting parties to agreements made between local communities for specific purposes.[2] The task for the social historian is to determine whether there is any substance behind these names and to what extent social cohesion was maintained only within the group or between the individual groups when they came into contact with emerging large-scale societies.

The existence of many such groups, and many of them are just names, beyond which we know nothing, may give the impression that we are dealing with a highly complex society with many different status levels and political, religious and economic networks. However, it is our view that whilst there may have been individuals in the society where the Buddha lived who perceived society in a broader manner than whatever existed in a set of individual villages and towns – after all the *varṇa* theory is a theory of society – it is better to distinguish between small-scale and large-scale societies. In this sense much of what the Buddhist texts tell us applies at the level of small-scale societies, though it is clear that, at least on the level of the expanding monarchies, large-scale societies were developing. Roughly speaking, then, a total account of the society reflected in this literature makes sense only when we consider it operating as a set of mini-societies, where the rough distinction is between complex urban societies and small-scale rural and forest groups, where the socio-economic structure is necessarily simpler than the former though interpersonal relationships could be equally complex.

Canonical and later sources alike furnish evidence of a large number of groups which made up the kind of small-scale social structure that would characterize a village. They were not, as Rhys Davids pointed out long ago, like castes as later known, and they included numbers of named occupational or tribal communities on the fringes of brāhmaṇical society, such as the *Caṇḍālas*, Nesādas, Veṇas, *Rathakāras*, and Pukkusas. A text dealing with these groups is repeated almost verbatim several times in the Canon:

> There are degraded families: a caṇḍāla family, a family of hunters, of bamboo workers, of chariot-makers and of refuse-removers. A person is born in such a family which is poor, one in which food, drink and possessions are few, in which the lifestyle is difficult, in which animal fodder and covering are gained with difficulty. And he is of poor complexion, ugly, dwarf-like, frequently sick, or else

[2] *Kātyāyanasmṛti* 225, 349, 682.

he is blind, or deformed, or lame, or a cripple; nor does he possess food, drink, clothing, vehicle, garlands, scents and ointment, nor a bed, a dwelling and a lamp plus things to light it with.[3]

There is a triune implication in dealing with these groups. They are simultaneously occupational, low status and marginalized, the latter two probably because they are tribal. Note that the standards of classification here are possession or otherwise of material wealth, method of occupation – the implication being that all these names, except for *rathākara*, indicate unskilled occupations – and location, all of them being forest dwellers. Beyond this they are all of bad appearance and sickly – judgements expressive of prejudice. They are poor but not beggars. One reason for this almost wholly negative evaluation is that they are reborn into their position through bad *karma* (*S* II 85–6). Yet we must assume these figures were not picked out of a vacuum, that they were regarded within the culture, undifferentiated between Hindus and Buddhists, as being of low occupational status, relatively speaking, and of marginal value.

Two passages containing this list also present its opposite, a man who is born in a high family:

In such a case a particular person is reborn in a high family, a wealthy warrior family, or a wealthy priestly family or a wealthy householder family, which is opulent, has much grain, much wealth, abundant gold and silver, abundant possessions and means, abundant wealth and good fortune. In addition, he is handsome, good looking, pleasant, has an exquisite lotus-like complexion, possesses food, drink, clothes, a vehicle, garlands, scents and ointments, a bed, clothes and a lamp plus things to light it with.[4]

In every way this is the opposite of what is described as being characteristic of the incumbent of the low occupation. Wealth is once again a categorical feature and this is combined with *vaṇṇa* and what is essentially an agrarian elite (*gahapati*) category, thus reflecting a triune classification. Note this group is in no sense marginalized, being rather the accepted elite of the society described in the Pāli Canon.

If there is a difference between these two groups, it is that the low occupational types are marginalized and probably tribal groups, unlike the elite categories which were forming one of the central elements in the emerging

[3] *M* III 169–70; *S* I 93–4; A I 107, II 85–6; *Vin* IV 6. (See also *PTS Dictionary*, s.v. *caṇḍāla*, on the 'low castes', *nīcā kulā*. Note that *Vin* IV 6 has *jāti* (possibly suggestive of lineage instead of family) instead of *kula*, *hīna* instead of *nīca*, and *ukkaṭṭha* instead of *ucca*. From the *Brāhmaṇas* see the very comprehensive list of names given in Egon Brucker, *Die Spätvedische Kulturepoche nach den Quellen der Śrauta-, Gṛhya und Dharmasūtras. Der Siedlungsraum* (Steiner, Wiesbaden, 1980), pp. 85–7.

[4] *S* II 94–5.

large-scale societies. The difficulty of distinguishing between a tribal group (with its own inherited way of life, language, kinship system and religious tradition) and what later becomes a caste (with its endogamous structure, prescribed occupation and distinctive rituals) can be very hard to draw. As A. Béteille says, 'Tribes have existed at the margins of Hindu civilization from time immemorial, and these margins have always been vague, uncertain and fluctuating.'[5] Aśoka refers in an inscription to the forest dwellers, the rough untamed people who belong to the wilds on the borderlands and follow a different way of life;[6] they must be dealt with circumspectly, for their loyalty is always uncertain. The *Arthaśāstra* refers at many points to the same forest tribes, *aṭavika*, as potential antagonists who must be controlled by cunning.[7] We also cite in this connection *Śaṅkhalikhitadharmasūtra* 7:

> The *ārya* land is excellent and lies to the east of the sunset and to the west of the sunrise, and runs as far as the high mountains reach and as far as the sacred rivers flow . . . To the east of Sindhu-Sauvīra, south of Himālaya, west of Kāmpilī and north of Pāriyātra the brahman splendour is impeccable. The traditions of all the rules of life of castes and families of other lands are different from this.[8]

Here the classification turns on ritual purity and impurity, where the standard of the former is the brahmin, and denotes Āryāvarta as that area between the Gaṅgā and Yamunā rivers valley in contrast to everything outside of it.

These mini-societies had a variety of forms. There were craft villages, where trades were passed on from father to son. Villages of *caṇḍālas*, a despised group, are also mentioned.[9] It is unclear whether this specific term relates to a group permanently polluted by occupation or derives its status from other factors. *Jātakas* speak of a village of 500 robbers, and elsewhere we learn that forest guards belonging to guild-type organizations would escort travellers in the forest areas.[10] Such communities ran their own affairs. Heads (*settha*) of clans (*kula*) were responsible for peace and stability; one *sutta* attributes the cosmic decline of the age to crimes and lack

[5] A. Béteille, 'On the concept of tribe', *International Social Science Journal*, 32 (1980), pp. 825–8, at p. 827.

[6] Rock Edict 13, *M*; see *Corpus Inscriptionum Indicarum, Vol. 1 Inscriptions of Asoka*, new edn ed. E. Hultzsch (Indological Book House, Delhi and Varanasi, 1969), pp. 67 and 69 n. 3: Devānāṃpriya even pacifies the *aṭavi*; see also C. Caillat, 'Aśoka et les gens de la brousse (XIII M-N)', *Bulletin des Etudes Indiennes*, 9 (1991), pp. 9–13, at p. 9. Also H. Kulke, *Jagannātha-Kult und Gajapati-Königtum* (Steiner, Wiesbaden, 1979), pp. 6–7.

[7] See for example *AŚ* 9.2, advising a king on conditions in which to recruit *aṭavikas* into his own army.

[8] Text cited in Brücker, *Spätvedische Kulturepoche*, p. 95.

[9] *J* IV 390.

[10] *J* IV 430; R. Fick, *Die Soziale Gliederung in Nordostlichen Indien zu Buddhas Zeit* (Kiel, 1897), pp. 176f.

of respect for parents and *kulasettha*.[11] Communities called *kula*, literally 'family', appear to be equivalent to *jāti* ('birth'), the later common term for the local caste group.[12] In at least certain cases, communities such as guilds, a kind of economic grouping, had their own regular courts for the trying of offences; in the *Majjhima Nikāya* for example we find reference to different types of court including guild courts along with the royal family court and others.[13] We cannot know, however, whether these refer to different kinds of villages or to different forms of assembly and judicial bodies within a single village or town, suggesting a large-scale society.

The economic imperative as a basis of classification is very important in Buddhist literature, and not just because it was easy to recognize, but also because it accurately reflected the situation in the area the early Buddhists inhabited. Examples such as these cited below are reflective of this mode of generalization.

> If a kṣatriya were to prosper in wealth or corn or gold or silver, he could have another kṣatriya to get up earlier than he would, to go to bed later, doing what pleases him and speaking affably, or he could have a brahmin . . . vaiśya . . . śūdra . . . [to do the same. Similarly a brahmin, vaiśya and śūdra could have any of the four classes to serve him.][14] Brahmins hold that a brahmin, kṣatriya, vaiśya or śūdra may serve a brahmin; that a kṣatriya, vaiśya or śūdra may serve a kṣatriya; that a vaiśya or śūdra may serve a vaiśya; and that only a śūdra may serve a śūdra.[15]

> If a kṣatriya . . . brahmin . . . vaiśya . . . śūdra were to engage in house-breaking, or carry off plunder, or rob an isolated house, or wait in ambush, or commit adultery, the king would kill him or ruin him or banish him or deal with him as he liked, for the designation of kṣatriya . . . brahmin . . . vaiśya . . . śūdra would be irrelevant for him and he would be reckoned simply as a robber.[16]

There are several contexts in which this mode of categorization would have made sense to the authors of the text. At the most basic it is simply a difference between rich and poor and directly implies that other forms of categorization will be overtaken by wealth, a standard which overturns other forms of classification. Such passages also contain traces of an acceptance that economic considerations could theoretically determine social relationships. These passages do not vitiate the relevance of the *varṇa* system because a brahmin remains such even if he works for any of the three lower *varṇas*. The problem then becomes not that there exists a hierarchy, but of the possibility of moving between levels, especially where they are defined in classificatory systems different from the *varṇas*.

[11] *D* III 70. [12] Wagle, *Society*, p. 122. Cf. n. 3 above. [13] *M* I 288; cf. *M* III 48.
[14] Summary of *M* II 84. [15] Summary of *M* II 177–8. [16] Summary of *M* II 87–8.

Uma Chakravarti, in some measure following Romila Thapar, argues that Buddhist society was ideally conceptualized in terms of 'khattiya, brāhmaṇa, and gahapati representing categories in the social world, and the samaṇa or recluse representing the asocial world'.[17] In fact, the texts tell us the *samaṇa* was very active in the social world even if the ideology shaping that role evaluated the social in a quite different way from the other categories mentioned here, turning above all on the image of the *samaṇa* as an isolated figure. Leaving aside the *samaṇa*, the other three who are said to represent categories in the social world cross two classificatory systems. *Brāhmaṇa* and *khattiya* are the highest two rungs of the *varṇa* system, no doubt a brāhmaṇical invention, but probably recognized by all groups in the society, irrespective of their adherence to Hindu beliefs and practices. It is possible, occupationally speaking, that the *gahapati* should be taken to represent the *vaiśya* class, though the Pāli texts frequently mention compounds joining *brāhmaṇa* and *khattiya* with *gahapati* as the final member. It is more likely that these three names represent the elite in the social world depicted in the Buddhist texts, and that individuals could easily operate within several different classifications found within the same locality, though probably these classifications would have had to be derived from different areas of culture. That is, a man could not be both *brāhmaṇa* and *vaiśya*, though he could be *brāhmaṇa*, a wealthy landholder and perhaps a member of a guild as well. This is the least we would expect in the highly pluralistic society which marked the urban areas of the Buddha's time and the succeeding centuries, though less so the rural villages and their surrounding lands and scarcely at all the tribal groups. What this means is that it is likely the urban areas show the highest degree of diversity in social classification and frames of social classification, though they need not have cohered less as social groups than more isolated and localized communities.

ELITE GROUPS AND THE BASIS OF ELITE STATUS

An investigation of the status of elites in and around the rise of Buddhism falls firmly within the second of our assumptions about Buddhism and society – where we opt for a concentration on the relationships between Buddhists (monks) and the rest of society – suggested at the beginning of this chapter. Whom are we entitled to identify as elites in the societies of the time this book covers? In both Hindu and Buddhist sources *brāhmaṇas* and *kṣatriyas* emerge as social, cultural and political elites. If we rely mainly

[17] Chakravarti, *Social Dimensions*, p. 67.

on Buddhist sources it is necessary to add the *gahapati*, the *seṭṭhi* and the *rājan*, all of whom are mentioned in the passage from the *Kūṭadantasutta* cited below (p. 48). It would be immensely helpful if we knew what percentage of the total population was constituted by these groups and details of the various levels of difference within the elite itself. Scholarship has traditionally suggested that of these elites, the *gahapatis* and *seṭṭhis* were newly emergent, *brāhmaṇas* were raising an already high status, and *kṣatriyas* and *rājans* were struggling to determine their status in emerging societies where a single ruler reigned and the others became mere soldiers and, perhaps, absentee landlords.

It is necessary to say something about the meaning of the word 'elite' in the context of early Buddhist literature. Most of the secondary literature dealing with ancient Indian society uses notions of an 'elite' or 'elite status' implicitly, without defining in any precise sense what is meant by either term. Gokhale, in a much cited article, defines the Buddhist elite using two criteria:

> In the first instance the person's intellectual, spiritual attainments and/or organizational skills would be the most obvious qualifications for his inclusion among the elite. Such is the case with Sāriputta and Moggallāna, Ānanda . . . The other is the attribution of an elite status to the person either by the Buddha himself or some of his eminent disciples or the redactors of the Pāli Canon who thought it fit to include information on them or their utterances in parts of the Pāli Canon.[18]

This is scarcely adequate as an evaluation of elite status as it includes only the *saṅgha*. This in itself makes it too narrow to encompass elite groups in the wider society. A more recent book by Murray Milner[19] argues that elite status is primarily constructed in terms of economic, political and religious categories, each of which either works to confer some kind of intellectual legitimacy on the elites amongst the larger body of non-elites or provides channels whereby the means of production can be controlled and distributed. Both are necessarily interrelated. Whilst this may not seem a spectacular insight, it does provide a frame for discussion of particular kinds of social groupings where otherwise this might not have been available.

The social categories pertaining to the religious, political and economic spheres, even if they overlap constantly, strike us continually when reading the early Buddhist texts. Reflections on the interactions between representatives of the groups defined within these categories and monks form a

[18] B. G. Gokhale, 'The early Buddhist elite', *Journal of Indian History*, 42 (1965), p. 392.

[19] Murray Milner, *Status and Sacredness. A General Theory of Status Relations and an Analysis of Indian Culture* (Oxford University Press, New York, 1994), pp. 65–79.

large part of the content of this book. Statistical analysis of the *vaṇṇa* ranking status of all the named individuals, populating the *Sutta* and *Vinaya Piṭakas*, carried out by Sarao, Chakravarti, Ray and Gokhale respectively, suggests that the Buddha interacts mostly with members of three particular groups: brahmins, prominent politicians (i.e., kings) and the wealthy. We cannot be certain how much he interacted with other groups, even though the lower ranking groups would have formed the majority of the society. Here too, once more, the texts are limiting in their focus on the Buddha himself, who originally came from a noble background. Would the picture be different if we had more information about the interaction of other monks with lay Buddhists and the rest of the non-Buddhist population?

If we were to rely on the perspective taken in the indigenous literature we would find a focus on brāhmaṇical categories, especially *varṇa* and *jāti*, both of which take up religious as well as occupational characteristics, or concentrate on the emerging figure of the *gahapati* as a means of tying elite status into processes of economic change. Certain texts, such as the following from the *Kūṭadantasutta*, conflate the two main sources of elite status, *varṇa* classification and economic wealth. The passage in question concerns a king who wishes to perform a sacrifice. His purohita tells him to invite the following groups, all of whom are qualified as living either in the town or the country: *kṣatriyas* who are vassals of the king; ministers who sit in his assembly; wealthy brahmins and wealthy householders.[20] Whilst there is nothing particularly exceptional about this passage, it does, we believe, define the socio-economic constituents of a kingdom whose influence the king may have found necessary for his support. In this case he harnesses support by reaffirming his kingship through performance of a *śrauta* sacrifice, the presence of certain groups to witness the display being necessary as a demonstration of his qualification to be king.

Where the text becomes interesting and germane to the present argument is in its rehearsal of some of the qualifications of the participants. Of the king eight qualities are listed: his lineage was well born on both sides, he was physically imposing and handsome, he was fabulously wealthy in property, precious metals and grain, he had a powerful army and was a mighty warrior, he was generous and a supporter of beggars and mendicants, he was learned, he could analyse sayings, and, finally, he was intelligent and could predict the future. The text goes on to tell us about the four qualities of the brahmin, which set him apart from others. He too is well born on

[20] *D* I 136 and often. See below, ch. 11.

both sides back to seven generations, he knew the entire field of Vedic knowledge, he was virtuous and skilled in performing the sacrifice.[21]

This text is more informative about the king than it is about the brahmins or any of the other elite classes. It compiles a list of qualities affirming elite status within the frame of the characteristics assigned to the first three *varṇas*, following the manner in which these are formally listed in the *dharmaśāstras*, and by measure of wealth. Thus the king, as a metaphor for the kingdom in its entirety, brings within his person all the cultural, economic, military and religious factors necessary for the kingdom to survive and prosper. This is scarcely an original vision but it has the virtue of presenting elite status as a combination of wealth, lineage, physical power and knowledge. The king is perhaps unique in possessing all of these in his own person. Not so for the other classes. For it is clear from this description and others elsewhere that the brahmin held, relatively speaking, elite status because of his possession of religious knowledge and the capacity to transmit it. He may also have held monetary wealth and/or land, but his status was independent of this.

That we have so much information on groups who could justifiably claim elite status is a problem in itself. It gives us a highly skewed view of the society of the time. It is almost certain that those who composed the text were literate – if writing was being practised at the time when Buddhism began –, thus placing themselves amongst the educated elite. Their treatment of the lower socio-economic groups is, therefore, minimal and makes it extremely difficult for scholars to penetrate the veil created in the texts.

Gahapatis were heads of some of the smaller units in the kaleidoscope of semi-autonomous social units. Fick considered that in some respects the class of *gahapatis* could be compared to caste groups, with a real sense of status as members of a high class, but without the community customs or judicial powers which he regarded as essential to the definition of a caste.[22] Sometimes they are enumerated as a class alongside (and thus not overlapping with) brahmins and *kṣatriyas*, but at other times there is an overlap and the term *gahapati* is a label for the social eminence of pillars of the community including brahmins.[23] Brahmans are included in the class, in the case of brahmin villages.[24] Thapar has related the *gahapatis* to the rise of the new kingdoms based on agrarian societies in the northeast after the

[21] *D* I 139. [22] Fick, *Soziale Gliederung*, p. 165.
[23] R. Tsuchida, 'Two categories of brahmins in the early Buddhist period', *The Memoirs of the Toyo Bunko*, 49 (1991), pp. 57–60.
[24] Wagle, *Society*, pp. 18f.; cf. pp. 151–6.

Vedic period, describing them as representing a distinct stage in economic evolution – a stage in which economic management was fragmented.[25]

The *brāhmaṇa-gahapati* has an ambiguous status in early Buddhist texts. On the one hand, he seems ideologically and actually to be the opposite of everything for which the *bhikkhu* stands. As such he is presented almost as an ideal type even if we can glimpse many cracks beneath the surface in looking at this type. He was not a homogeneous figure on the measure of occupation and wealth, even if representations of him are collected into a single symbol which can be used to contrast him with the *bhikkhu*, and this may well have been the function of this symbol in the context of the early texts. On the other hand, he was a source of material support for the *saṅgha* and its principal source of recruitment. Both *monk* and *brāhmaṇa-gahapati* were mirrors each of what the other one was not.

If the *gahapati* was anything in early Buddhist literature it was an overlapping social (householder = the male head of the family) and economic (landowner) category and was flexible enough to be attached to some of the *varṇa* titles. He worked on the land himself, supported a family group including servants, gave gifts to religious organizations and worked to extend the use of arable land. A passage like this taken from the *Majjhima Nikāya* illustrates the *gahapati*'s overwhelming connection with material wealth:

> And it is like a householder or his son, rich, of great wealth, of great possessions, with a mass of abundant gold ornaments, a mass of abundant corn, a mass of abundant fields, with a mass of abundant raiment, with a mass of abundant wives, with a mass of abundant men slaves, with a mass of abundant women slaves.[26]

But his wealth is not just in money and land. It is also resides in his capacity to mobilize human resources as an employer and to demonstrate status by possession of multiple wives.

We prefer to identify the various groups who include *gahapati* in their name as being representative of a horizontal form of social classification in contrast to the vertical form of distinction based primarily on lineage or *varṇa* and focused on by Thapar in two recent studies.[27] Disputes over lineage and succession dominate the two Sanskrit epics, but appear to be of little importance in early Buddhist literature except where a criticism is made of the succession of seven generations used by *brāhmaṇas* to legitimize their claim to a higher status than other groups in society. What we note is a picture of a society focused on householders who showed a preference for agriculture and rural life rather than residence in those areas

[25] Thapar, *From Lineage to State*, pp. 41f. [26] *M* I 452.

[27] Thapar, 'The First Millennium' and *From Lineage to State*.

unambiguously urban in character. The *gahapati* is the foundational economic position in the transformed agrarian economy centred on all of the rural areas now supplying the cities and other developing conurbations. This position makes sense only in relation to the urban areas even if it is economically centred in the agrarian areas. Whatever his spatial location, he could not have remained untouched by the process of urbanism.

Finally, we note an important point made by Milner about the nature of the dispute that often characterizes the interrelations of economic elites:

> In the realm of material production, a cleavage often arises between economic elites who control alternative means of production. Typically, this involves a conflict between ascendant means of production and more traditional ones. In agrarian societies, those who control and manage land are threatened by those who specialize in more movable forms of resources, for example merchants, traders and bankers.[28]

This could easily be a description of the economic base of what were becoming large-scale societies in northeastern India during the time the Buddha flourished. What is certain is that both groups of economic elites were present, yet it cannot be confirmed whether the one (the agrarian elite) was regarded as being traditional, the other not. Of course, the basic thesis of much recent scholarship is that the early growth of Buddhism benefited substantially from the development of a mercantilist attitude in society and from the appearance of a group of people who could be generally called traders and financiers, even if this is not the exact translation of the term *seṭṭhis*. Even if these people made money through dealing in goods or financial services, they may still have owned parcels of agricultural land. It is more accurate to say that the *gahapati* were the village and country elite, whereas the *seṭṭhi* formed the urban elite, with the king, high members of the army, and any bureaucracy.

SOCIAL COHESION, VALUES AND ELITES

The texts do contain clues about what the up-and-coming aspirants to wealth were doing, those who seemed so eager to sustain the Buddha with the things of life the *saṅgha* itself could not produce by dint of its essential calling to inactivity. It is these groups of people who were the economic and political elite and who were enjoying the fruits of the rapidly expanding economy and its emergence into some kind of complex intra-regional entity. Some of the Buddha's activity was concerned with attracting a portion

[28] Milner, *Status and Sacredness*, p. 66.

of the new wealth being created by the new elites and with positioning himself and his followers in the cultural mainstream without, for all that, compromising the originality of his own theoretical position. This would explain why the Buddha was supportive of a work effort focused upon self-help and why he was so inimical towards status based on birth, for him a sure cause of indolence, corruption and arrogance. And this, as has been frequently observed by scholars, was consistent with the kind of ideology the new economic elites in society would have needed in order to have retained whatever privilege they had acquired through their wealth.

There is certainly evidence of the Buddha taking up with real gusto the task of providing appropriate ethics for the new 'secular' elite classes. That he was successful in it – judging from the continuous stream of lay followers he attracted – is a testimony both to his own marketing skills and *to the deep need in the people to have their desire for upward mobility legitimated.* A brilliant instance of his teaching technique and the content of his thoughts in this area is given in a passage from the *Mahāvagga*,[29] which we cite at length. On one of his journeys the Buddha had reached Pāṭaligāma with 1,250 monks. Some laypeople came and offered the use of a rest house and provided lamps and washing facilities. In the morning (it is not clear if the Buddha had spent the night there) the Buddha went to the rest house which was filled up with monks and laypeople. Then he made a speech to all of them:

'There are these five disadvantages, householders, for a person of poor morality who fails in morality. What five? Now, householders, a person of poor morality who fails in morality suffers great diminution of wealth owing to laziness; this is the first disadvantage for a person of poor morality who fails in morality.

Then again, householders, an evil reputation of a person of poor morality who fails in morality is spread abroad; this is the second disadvantage for a person of poor morality who fails in morality.

Then again, householders, when a person of poor morality who fails in morality approaches any company, whether it be a company of nobles, a company of brahmins, a company of householders or a company of recluses, he approaches it diffidently, being ashamed: this is the third disadvantage for a person of poor morality who fails in morality.

Then again, householders, a person of poor morality who fails in morality dies entirely confused; this is the fourth disadvantage for a person of poor morality who fails in morality.

Then again, householders, at the breaking up of the body after dying, a person of poor morality who fails in morality arises in the hell of loss, the realm of misery,

[29] *Vin* I 226ff.

the hell of ruin, hell;[30] this is the fifth disadvantage for a person of poor morality who fails in morality. These, householders, are the five disadvantages for a person of poor morality who fails in morality.

There are these five advantages, householders, for a moral person who cultivates morality. What five? Now, householders, a moral person who cultivates morality acquires a great mass of wealth due to his conscientiousness; this is the first advantage for a moral person who cultivates morality.

Then again, householders, for a moral person who cultivates morality an excellent reputation is spread abroad; this is the second advantage for a moral person who cultivates morality.

Then again, householders, when a moral person who cultivates morality approaches any company, whether a company of nobles, a company of brahmins, a company of householders or a company of recluses, he approaches it confidently, not being ashamed; this is the third advantage for a moral person who cultivates morality.

Then again, householders, a moral person who cultivates morality passes away entirely unconfused; this is the fourth advantage for a moral person who cultivates morality.

Then again, householders, at the breaking up of the body after dying a moral person who cultivates morality arises in the happy heaven, in heaven; this is the fifth advantage for a moral person who cultivates morality. These, householders, are the five advantages for a moral person who cultivates morality.'

When the Lord had gladdened, rejoiced, roused, delighted the laypeople of Pāṭaligāma far into the night with talk on *dhamma*, he dismissed them saying: 'The night has now almost passed, householders; now do whatever is timely.'

The set of five precepts announced by the Buddha in this lecture recur elsewhere[31] in the canon, though only the version found in the *Mahāparinibbāṇasutta* includes the narrative context given here. All the others contain only the barest summary of the five disasters arising from immoral behaviour and the five advantages (*ānisaṃso*) accruing to the moral man. They offer no context for the oral delivery given by the Buddha.

This passage is highly significant for the kinds of qualities it groups together as constituting both positive and negative images of a man in the society of the time. Of course, the man envisaged here is not a monk but a layman and by implication a *gahapati* or a *seṭṭhi* who has accumulated wealth or sees this as one of his principal goals in life. Whatever his exact status, it is assumed he falls into that class of person we recognize, following the texts, as constituting the new elite. What the Buddha proposes the layman should cultivate is material wealth, good reputation, confidence, self-knowledge

[30] *apāyaṃ duggatiṃ vinipātaṃ nirayam*. Each of these words refers to a particular hell, but they could also denote loss of money as well, and as such should have a metaphorical sense.

[31] See A III 252f.; *D* III 85–6, 236 and *Ud.* 86.

and a good rebirth of the kind a layman would have expected. Translating this into concepts familiar in the West today, we would argue that the Buddha is promoting a modest 'get rich' scheme, a scheme proposing self-confidence, self-assertiveness and self-knowledge (in the sense of goal-setting) and negotiating skills that will facilitate advancement in all spheres – except that of the monk, deliberately excluded here – in which the layman may find himself. So complete is this self-help programme that it even makes allowance for the acquisition of good merit leading to a desirable rebirth after death, a prospect never considered by hawkers of self-development schemes in the contemporary West. The parallel can only be stretched a certain distance, beyond which its validity fails. What the Buddha taught in the discourse cited above was only a small part of his overall teaching, though it does sum up admirably his conception of the normative role for the layperson in society, the rest of the teaching being of such sophistication as to exclude all but the most well-educated monk and the occasional layperson (as evidence from contemporary Buddhist countries indicates). One further example comes from a list in the *Aṅguttara Nikāya*[32] where five reasons for a person to become rich are enumerated. Wealth (1) makes himself and others happy, (2) makes his friends and companions happy, (3) allows him to ward off danger from water and fire, from *rājas*, robbers, enemies and heirs, (4) allows him to make the five oblations to deceased ancestors and so on, and (5) allows him to perform offerings that will take him to heaven.

Where there is a continuity with the teachings pertinent primarily to the monk is in the emphasis on conduct – *sīlā* – and its acquisition (*sīlasampada*) (*D* II 236) or loss (*sīlavipatti*) (*D* II 235). Whilst this is one of the three limbs of the eight-limbed path, it also falls within the general ambit of conduct in the sense that the *Vinaya* provides a set of rules observance of which will be conducive to the cultivation of the more imposing aspects of Buddhist life.

These teachings are definitely not those conceiving exclusively of a society of renouncers. On the contrary they could be interpreted as strengthening the foundations of civil society in a collective sense even while they focus primarily on the development of the individual within that society. Therefore we are compelled to ask what the Buddha was intending to achieve in offering teachings like this, which are, if it be asked, widespread through the Canon, if not in a systematic form, but rather as part of an overall

[32] III 45. This passage could be profitably compared with arguments for the acquisition of wealth put forward in *Mbh* 3, 36 and 12, 8.

ethical ambience which is offered. What we can be certain of is that it is not the kind of teaching any brāhmaṇical ascetic would have offered. It is much too close to the urban perspective dominating Pāli literature and it is far too individualistic in its tone, the latter in the sense of defining the individual's status primarily against a social and not a spiritual standard. Any discrimination is restricted to where it reflects relative status apparently held by those within the respective classes.

If what is being taught is individualistic it is also communalistic. The Buddha is not only teaching a form of behaviour which will benefit the individual in both this world and the next, he is also prescribing the means whereby the individual will be treated positively by other people within the groups in which he moves. It is this sense of offering a standardized ethics[33] applicable to anybody of any class or occupation that makes this passage an important one for presenting a concern for social cohesion. That it is directed towards an elite, and in the language typically associated with mercantilist values, does not lessen the social breadth of its message.

[33] J. D. Ryan, 'The Civakacintamani in Historical Perspective' (unpublished thesis, University of California, Berkeley, 1985), pp. 14–15.

3

Economic conditions

An acceptance that Buddhism originally began as an elite movement requires us to extend our discussion into a study of the economic conditions associated with elite status, the relationship between these conditions and the development and survival of Buddhism. Weberian analysis has long shown the complex interplay between material development and ideological support or denial from religious groups. Buddhist doctrine appeared to provide active encouragement to the most striking of the newly emergent groups exploiting changed political and productive conditions, namely the merchants and farmers. The former group, while certainly not homogeneous, was not only developing into a major producer and disseminator of new kinds of goods, but was also very active in promoting its own status and its concerns as being central to those of society. The perception that Buddhism provided an ideological support to this group leads us to confront a number of questions rising in part from the previous chapter:

(1) Why would an ascetic group disdainful of material wealth, and the motivations leading to its accumulation, give ideological support to such a group?
(2) Why would this group in return provide material support to the fledgling Buddhist group?
(3) What kind of economy was it that allowed this group to emerge and apparently become so successful?

To answer these requires us first to investigate the economic conditions of the time. It is difficult to envisage an 'economy' existing in the Buddha's time. The economy is at best an abstract term used to categorize and describe particular aspects of human interaction. But economic activity is clearly described in Buddhist literature. We must, however, be constantly vigilant to avoid applying the terminology of contemporary economics to events and conditions that are distorted by the use of such technical terms. We assume, following Pearson, that 'the economy at all levels of material existence is a *social* process of interaction between man and his environment in the course of which goods and services change form, are moved about and change hands. The shape of this process, i.e., its institutional form and the motives which make it run are determined not by any single factor either in nature or man, but are the resultants of several interdependent levels of human existence, ecological, technological, social and cultural.'[1] Taking this as a lead we treat social and economic conditions together, even at the risk of confusing two overlapping conceptual categories.

THE NATURE OF THE ECONOMY

Following archaeological and literary evidence, we have noted in earlier chapters that the Buddhist texts depict economic conditions based on agriculture, pastoralism, small-scale manufacture of material goods of a large variety of types and the incipient development of an industry making money out of money itself. Production was for both subsistence and trade. Money was an important means of exchange.[2] Money lending was no doubt common, judging from the presence of wealthy bankers, and forms of taxation were probably beginning. Inequalities based on differences in possession of capital and land, and access to resources, were beginning to emerge in a perceptible way. All of this is easy to read as a collection of perhaps discrete data. What we lack is a sense of what a large-scale interconnected economy might have been like and the hard statistical data which would enable us to put flesh on the economy's interconnections.

In contrast to the equivocal evidence about the nature of the economy depicted in Vedic texts, and presumably prior to the emergence of early Buddhism, evidence from the Buddhist sources suggests a prosperous economy in a state of expansion. Nor is this a swift conclusion produced by an impressionistic reading of the texts which are only concerned incidentally with what today would be called economics. Our knowledge about the nature and strength of the economy in the Buddha's time and the following centuries is substantially based on inference. Yet the inference of an

[1] H. W. Pearson, 'The economy has no surplus: critique of a theory of development', in K. Polanyi, C. M. Arensberg and H. W. Pearson (eds), *Trade and Market in the Early Empires* (Free Press, New York, 1957), p. 326 (his italics).

[2] J. Cribb, identifying the errors that inspired some scholars to date Indian coins to earlier times, concludes that the earliest Indian coins, the various punch-marked silver issues, originated in the Gandhāra area from imitations of Greek coins early in the fourth century BC, and that developments from these soon took place in the Ganges valley during the same century. See J. Cribb, 'Dating India's earliest coins', in J. Schotsmans and M. Taddei (eds.), *South Asian Archaeology 1983* (Istituto Universitario Orientale, Naples, 1985), vol. 1, pp. 535–54.

expanding economy is confirmed by more solid evidence derived from the study of food remains and settlement patterns.

In Vedic literature, the economic conditions hinted at define a much narrower base of production and consumption. It is accurate to speak of a tribal economy, where there was some trade with other tribal groups and with people leading a sedentary lifestyle, but where the social extent of the economy was substantially defined by the members of the tribe, and its physical extent by the area where the tribe wandered. Whilst measures of wealth exist in nomadic tribes in the varied holdings of flocks particular individuals might have, every person was ultimately protected by the safety net offered by the social group defining the tribe. If at various times such an economy were evaluated as 'weak' (and this could only be done on the basis of the archaeological record), it could only be on the measure of its incapacity to feed its own people in a totalistic sense or by a measure of food insecurity (where the availability of food is highly variable), a situation we would usually retrospectively attribute to drought, some other natural calamity or war. What we can glean from Vedic literature provides a simpler picture than this, however. Using the *Brāhmaṇas*, Rau gives a pessimistic view of the quality of life they depict:

> [I]n spite of the fertility of the Indian soil and the favourable climatic conditions, it could have been by no means easy to nourish themselves and their herds. Again and again the texts assert that the real enemy of men is hunger. It is identical with death and darkness, while heaven is explained as the place where hunger and thirst are unknown.[3]

In reading the Pāli texts we are immediately struck by the difference in landscape in which economic conditions are projected. Noteworthy is the presence of large cities which became large precisely because they are located at the junction of trading routes or because they are administrative centres and allow for increasing division of labour, diversification of production techniques and the use of capital. A further aspect of this landscape is the juxtaposition of city and (rural) hinterland, reflected strongly in the inter-regional trading featured so heavily in the texts. Whilst the idea of micro-economies focused on the village or group of contiguous villages has relevance in this situation, it has to be seen in relation to the dramatic increase in trading. Additionally, the idea of levying taxes across a large region, especially when it is populated by distinctive groups, suggests the presence of an economy definitely increasing in size, complexity and centralized control. Development of industries and class differentiation based on property

[3] Rau, *Staat und Gesellschaft*, p. 31.

ownership could allow a situation where relative prosperity coexisted with relative poverty, including denominated debt. The economy could still be vibrant and showing increased productivity even though some groups in society were economically depressed.

The Buddhist texts provide us with much evidence about rural and urban trade and production. Here we present some of this evidence in order to allow us to step back and draw some inferences about the economy as a whole. The style of description in the text is idealized. Here, for instance, is a *Jātaka* description of a city pullulating with business activity: 'a city furnished with solid foundations and with many gateways and walls . . . behold the drinking shops and taverns, the slaughter-houses and cooks' shops, and the harlots and wantons . . . the garland-weavers, the washermen, the astrologers, the cloth merchants, the gold workers, the jewellers . . .'[4] Other evidence suggests the likelihood that every city had its quarters for the carrying on of specific crafts, such as the street of ivory carvers in Kāśī;[5] beyond the walls were dedicated craft villages serving the city's needs, such as communities of carpenters, potters, and smiths making axes, hatchets, ploughshares, spikes and so forth.[6] Communities of actors worked under the direction of stage managers to produce upon the stage a deceitful illusion of reality.[7] The first three examples are all taken from the *Jātakas*,which are late in comparison to the other sources we are using, and should be taken as indicating changes that had occurred by the end of the period of Buddhism's early development.

Craftsmen were divided into communities; the hereditary character of their occupation was taken for granted, and there are references to trade organizations approximating to guilds.[8] A passage in a *Jātaka* refers to a hereditary grain merchant.[9] Buddhist canonical sources refer to communities of carpenters, vulture trainers, cowherds, liquor distillers,[10] dyers, garland makers, cattle butchers, pig slaughterers, fowlers, horse trainers, jailers, bath attendants, potters and ivory workers, goldsmiths, ditchers, fletchers, joiners, archers, conch-blowers, trappers, bamboo plaiters, cartwrights and scavengers.[11] The last four in this list are identified as low-class occupations, as are those of leather workers, reed workers, potters, tailors and barbers.[12] Service occupations culled by Wagle include those

[4] *J* VI 276. [5] Fick, *Soziale Gliederung*, p. 180. [6] Ibid., p. 181.
[7] *S* IV 306–8. [8] Fick, *Soziale Gliederung*, pp. 177–9.
[9] *J* III 198 where a grain merchant's son is said to go into the same business.
[10] *M* I 119, 130, 220, 228.
[11] See, for example, from the first two books of *M*; *M* I 343, 385, 387, 396, 412, 446; *M* II 15, 18, 23, 65, 105, 152 and 205. In these passages numerous crafts and trades are mentioned, frequently chosen as suitable topics for familiar metaphors.
[12] See Wagle, *Society*, pp. 135ff.

of the washerman-dyer, painter, tailor-weaver, cook, messenger, servant-companion and attendant.[13]

These references all derive from literary sources across a span of several centuries, beginning in perhaps 400 BCE, but extending with the *Jātakas* to the early centuries of the Christian era. That there should be so many classifiable occupations in a developing urban society should not surprise us and the archaeological evidence also confirms this. However, we have no way of knowing anything like relative numbers of the people in such professions. It is possible that there were only two vulture trainers in each large city, for example, and fletchers presumably would have waxed and waned in numbers as demand for their services changed depending on external military situations. In addition, we cannot be certain about the spread of these occupations across the urban/rural divide, though we would expect the greater number of new occupational classes to be associated with urbanization and the sources confirm this.

It is possible that brahmins often entered such occupational classes. Brahmins are referred to as supporting themselves by various occupations other than acting as priest, including 'calculation' or accountancy (*gaṇanā*),[14] though it was not thought right that a brahmin should follow secular occupations. The *Sutta Nipāta* declares that if one lives by mechanical arts one is an artisan, not a brahmin.[15] The reality is that many brahmins were farmers, the economy not being sufficiently rich to support an entire class of people who simply lived off the paid performance of ritual activity. High-status professions – perhaps based on remuneration as well as social class – would have included accounting, money-changing, surgery, medicine and writing.[16]

Inscriptional evidence joins literature in reflecting the richness of the urban economy. At Mathurā there were perfumers, bankers, metalworkers, and the treasurer of an association; the same city is mentioned also by Patañjali in about the second century BCE as a source of kettledrums, garments and coins, hence of intra-regional trade.[17] To this we can add archaeological evidence, but it remains more opaque than the literary or inscriptional evidence as we cannot often attribute direct occupational categories to particular data. Erdosy sums up some of the archaeological evidence: large-scale production of iron is indicated at a number of sites where iron slag abounds, especially Ujjain; Rairh has hundreds of silver punch-marked coins, and there are coppersmiths' furnaces there, with moulds. At

[13] Ibid., p. 136. [14] *M* II 1. [15] *Sn* 613. [16] Wagle, *Society*, pp. 140ff.

[17] F. R. Allchin, *The Archaeology of Early Historic South Asia* (Cambridge University Press, Cambridge, 1995), p. 295.

Rājghat there were bone arrow factories; beads were made at Ujjain and jewellers' moulds have been found at Campā. Crafts are generally very well represented in the larger settlements.[18]

The Buddhist texts are clear in attesting a dynamic economy with a high degree of occupational and product diversification. Cities were homes for a highly differentiated and fully urbanized commercial society in the period for which the texts can be considered to vouch. But we cannot draw any firm conclusions about whether we are dealing with a whole set of micro-economies that trade with each other, especially those operating in the larger urban areas. The view that there existed some kind of developing macro-economy rests on the impression of possibilities as much as anything else, possibilities unavailable in micro-economies because of their absence of economies of scale and a body of consumers demanding a wide differentiation of products. Included amongst such possibilities would be: the existence of long-distance trade as evidenced by caravans and demarcated trading routes; the protection of such routes by large-scale political authorities; the widespread production of luxury goods and the existence of a surplus.

TRADE

A sure sign of the development of an effectively functioning macro-economy is the presence of a very large intra- and inter-regional trading sector. Buddhist literature is full of references to trading caravans, guilds of merchants, market towns and roads along which trading caravans moved.[19] So frequent are the references that it is clear intra-regional and inter-city trade was already regarded as a typical activity requiring no comment, therefore a standard component of the economic life of the time. For our purpose the importance of these references is that they not only provide information about one aspect of an emerging macro-economy, they also tie the dispersal of the Buddhist Order and Buddhism directly into the expansion of trade, such that early Buddhism may well have been associated with the trading vocation.

Long-distance land trade took groups of merchants in caravans through wilderness[20] and forest to seek out markets in all the towns of northern (and increasingly southern) India. Intra-regional trade, which probably meant

[18] Erdosy, 'City states', p. 112.

[19] Much of the relevant information for a period two centuries later is catalogued in G. M. Bongard-Levin, *Mauryan India* (Sterling, New Delhi, 1985), pp. 133–6.

[20] See *J* I 107, 99.

between the large urban centres, flourished, though to speak of international trade would require the recognition of international boundaries. Trade routes linked the pioneering new world of the middle Ganges, with its rising cities, to the rest of northern India and beyond to the zones of Achaemenid and later Hellenic culture, as well as to the south. It is specially to be noted that the arteries of commerce passed through the home territories of Buddhist tradition, linking the centralized monarchies along the Ganges with the more sparsely settled upland territories inhabited by tribal confederacies or oligarchies (*gaṇas*) such as the Buddha's own natal community and, further afield, with the sources of cultural influence in Afghanistan and Iran that became so conspicuous in the fourth and third centuries.

Whilst the literary sources do not give us detailed descriptions of trading caravans as they must have operated over a long and continuous period of time, they do allude frequently enough to such caravans. For instance, in one text we are told that whilst en route to Rājagaha the Buddha came into contact with 'Belaṭṭha Kaccāna who was going along the main road from Rājagaha to Andhakavindha with five hundred wagons all filled with jars of sugar'.[21] Another *Jātaka* tale speaks of two caravan leaders, plus 500 wagons, journeying from east to west for trade, returning to Sāvatthi with large profits.[22] The *Vinaya* refers to regular caravan settlements[23] and a Jain story tells of a caravan of merchants in the desert.[24] Despite this we are not in a position to be able to determine the relative percentages of production for local consumption and production for trade beyond the immediate locality of the area in which the goods were produced. Nonetheless we can be certain production was for profit and where there was the idea of profit, the idea of a disposable surplus developed. Perhaps this was related to the high level of risk associated with long-distance trade and the consciousness of wilderness as a category defining risk.[25]

It is possible trade was mentioned ubiquitously in Buddhist literature not just because it was conspicuous in the society reflected in the texts, but because the actual development and expansion of Buddhism was so closely connected with it. Buddhist monks often travelled with caravans of merchants and there is an example of the Buddha allowing a monk to pass the rainy season in the company of a caravan.[26] It is likely the extension of Buddhist culture into the Deccan was closely associated with

[21] *Vin* I 244ff. [22] *J* II 181, 335. Cf. *J* I 377f., 107; *Vin* I 152; III. 46; *D* II 342.
[23] *Vin* III 46. [24] Basham, *Ājīvikas*, p. 59, citing the *Bhagavatī Sūtra*.
[25] See *J* I 99 distinguishing five different types of wilderness. Cf. Fick, *Soziale Gliederung*, pp. 175ff.
[26] *Vin* I 152.

trade. An itinerary in the *Sn* traces the route of Bāvarī's disciples along a route from Amarāvatī to Kapilavastu that takes in the Krishna, the western Deccan, Patiṭṭhāna, Ujjenī, Vedisā, Sanchi, Kosambī, and Sāvatthi, and pre-Sātavāhana remains suggest trade along this route.[27]

THE TONE OF THE ECONOMY: LUXURY GOODS AND STRATIFICATION OF ACCESS TO RESOURCES

Much of the evidence so far adduced tells us unambiguously that Buddhism was linked with economic advance and commercial expansion. In addition, the evidence of both texts and archaeology is of a vibrant economy producing a substantial range of goods for a whole set of consumption preferences. It would be tempting to say this is primarily a picture of an urban-based economy supported by a large agricultural sector, operating at different levels of development, and with inter-regional trade providing luxury goods. To say there is enough evidence to evaluate the economy as strong or weak begs too many questions to be meaningful, but we do need also to look at any evidence suggestive of weakness in economic conditions during the time reflected in the early Buddhist texts. This would have relevance to questions of income distribution and access to resources as both of these are factors essential in the determination of economic stratification in a given society and the emergent class differentials based on income inequality. If the Pāli sources are indeed indicative of a vibrant, growing economy (which does not automatically translate into economic equity), we must be able to explain any evidence to the contrary. Mostly what we have been able to find are references to food shortages in particular areas and to mentions of despised groups such as Caṇḍālas who might also have been economically depressed. Usually the references to famines use stock expressions to describe a condition of food shortage. Food is said to be difficult to obtain either by gleaning or by gift, white bones are seen and people dig out little pieces of grain from holes in the ground using sticks. Places such as Verañjā, Sāvatthī and Vajjī are mentioned as experiencing such conditions.[28] Other cases just use one of the words (usually *dubbhikkham*)

[27] *Sn* 1011–13. Cf. H. P. Ray, *Monastery and Guild. Commerce under the Sātavāhanas* (Oxford University Press, Delhi, 1986), pp. 64 and 82ff.

[28] "At that time Verañjā was short of alms-food (*dubbhikkhā*), which was difficult to obtain (*dvīhītikā*), it was white with bones and people were living by digging out little pieces of grain from holes in the ground using sticks (*salākāvuttā*). Nor was it easy to nourish oneself by gleaning or by favour." *Vin* III 6, 64, 87. For the whole phrase Rhys Davids and Stede (eds), *Pali-English Dictionary* also gives *Vin* II 175; IV 23; *S* IV 323 amongst eighteen references in total. The translation of the compound *salākāvuttā* is based on the explanation given in *Divyāvadana*, p. 131 line 21. See also I.B. Horner, *The Book of the Discipline* (Luzac & Co. (PTS), London, 1938), vol. 1, p. 11, n. 4.

of the stock description.[29] In such circumstances a monk is recorded[30] as having stolen food, thereby committing a *parājika* offence, or people take food to the monastery rather than monks making begging rounds.[31]

It may be that these and other references are little more than allusions to an occasional famine. A more conservative view would stress the conclusion that the stereotypical style of many of the statements conveying the impression of food shortage betray a sub-text of restricting the kind of diets available to the monk or nun and therefore allude only to hypothetical conditions. No doubt there were crop failures – a disaster if sufficient seed stock and supplies from previous years had not been saved –, droughts and damage to agricultural production and production of consumer goods caused by war. The texts are largely silent on this and the negative evidence suggestive of failure to provide for the basics of life is weak. It is not, however, entirely absent and such cases as the following do occasionally occur:

> Once when Sāvatthī was short of alms-food (*dubbhikkhe*), a certain monk deliberately stole a handful of rice belonging to a shop-keeper. [Though he was remorseful this was considered a *parājika* offence.[32]]

> At that time when alms-food was scarce [the families of a village] offered only a small amount of a food to the monks who refused it after some consideration.[33] [The text goes on to cite several other times when food was scarce and monks resorted to eating, all of which the Buddha prohibited.]

These passages suggest the monks did share the privations encountered during famines, even if they still did have access to food given as a result of begging. They are more informative for what they tell us about the privileged status of monks *vis-à-vis* the rest of the population than serving as signs for some endemic long-term weakness of the economy.

The other sign of possible weaknesses in economic conditions – in an environment where resources were not being exhaustively exploited – is to be found in the occasional descriptions of groups regarded as being depressed in one form or another. As broadly descriptive as they are, such passages definitely point to groups which were already being stigmatized as economically weak, but more generally they should be taken as further evidence for the increasing differentiation of society along the lines of wealth and access to wealth. This differentiation need not have been directly correlated with other forms of social differentiation such as the *varṇa* scheme. A few

[29] *Vin* I 211–14. Cf. *Vin* I 219ff., where monks are offered elephant-flesh, horse-flesh, dog-flesh and snake-flesh, at a time when food is scarce, yet the Buddha prohibits them all.

[30] *Vin* III 6. [31] *Vin* I 211. [32] *Vin* III 64. [33] *Vin* I 214.

passages have been cited above in the context of distinguishing between high and low occupations and marginalized groups.[34] A further passage describes a king Serī who used to have alms given, at each of the four gates to his city, to brahmins and recluses, those suffering great hardship, tramps, charlatans and beggars. When members of his harem (*itthāgāraṃ*), and others, then ask to be allowed to do the same, he lets them and then finds himself giving nothing, so he decrees that of the revenue coming in from the outlying provinces, half should be brought into the palace and half given to those who ask for it.[35]

If the evidence for economic and social distress in early Buddhist literature is sparse and opaque of interpretation, the same cannot be said for indications of the presence of luxury goods and the conspicuous display of material wealth. The following examples may seem hyperbolic, but are too common to be omitted. Luxury goods are often mentioned in the possession of monks and, primarily, to illustrate the great variety within a single category, we cite several examples from the fifth book of the *Mahāvagga*:

(1) 'At that time the group of six monks used various kinds of ointment boxes, made of gold or silver.' After criticism from laymen, the Buddha allowed only ointment boxes made from bone, ivory, horn, reed, bamboo, wood, resin, crystal, copper and the centre of a conch shell.[36]

(2) 'At that time the group of six monks used, for their high beds and large beds, the following: a sofa, a couch, a long woollen cloth, a cloth of many colours, a white woollen cloth, a woollen cloth embroidered with flowers, a mattress, a woollen cloth decorated with animals, a woollen cloth with hair on the upper side, a woollen cloth with a fringe, a silken cloth studded with jewels, a silken cloth, a dancer's carpet, an elephant rug, a horse rug, a chariot rug, a rug of black antelope skins, the precious hide of the kadali-deer, a sheet with an awning above, a couch with a red cushion at either end.'[37]

(3) 'At that time the group of six monks wore sandals with straps around the heels . . . moccasins . . . laced boots . . . sandals stuffed with cotton . . . sandals coloured like partridges' wings . . . sandals pointed with rams' horns . . . sandals with a ram's horn tied on . . . sandals with a goat's horn tied on . . . sandals having scorpions' tails . . . sandals bordered with peacocks' tail feathers . . . coloured sandals.'[38]

Whether all of these products were available for sale, or whether the authors of the text sought to be exhaustive in their prohibitions, will always remain open to speculation. Nor should we be surprised to find most of them were forbidden to monks because they would have violated the image of poverty

[34] *S* I 93ff. See above, pp. 42–6. [35] *S* I 58. [36] *Vin* I 203. [37] *Vin* I 192. [38] *Vin* I 186.

and modesty the monk was required to cultivate.[39] What is of importance for the present discussion is that such diversity within specific categories of goods was available in an economy probably not long expanded from a subsistence base, and that they fall into the range of what today would be called luxury goods.

The presence of luxuries is also reflected in other measures besides the diversity of products. Many wealthy courtesans, charging high prices, are mentioned in the texts.[40] Entertainment of other kinds is sometimes recorded as attracting large payments[41] and wealthy merchants and brahmins are recorded as offering sumptuous gifts.[42] Wealthy men are also recorded as having guards, which would be expected for trading caravans because they were travelling through wilderness areas, but not perhaps in urban areas. All of this clearly shows that wealth was concentrated in certain hands, but that this did not exclude the bulk of the population having access to at least a subsistence level of resources.

THE IDEA OF A SURPLUS

The emergence of changed economic conditions, methods of production and patterns of consumption went hand in hand with the rise of Buddhism. Whilst this does not establish a necessary causal connection, it is a basic truth that an ascetic movement like Buddhism could not have survived in the absence of a broadly based disposable surplus of production beyond subsistence needs. That such a surplus existed is inferable from the presence of luxury goods, social stratification based in part on access to resources and, finally, on the increasing expansion of bureaucratic structures whose financial support[43] was necessarily derived from taxes and other imposts. We cannot even guess at what the size of the surplus might have been because this would not only require a valuation of the total production of North-Eastern India in the Buddha's time, it would also require a breaking up of the value of this production into distinctive categories – capital, taxes, luxury goods, expenditure for sumptuary display – not available to us. Nonetheless, surplus there was and the new religious groups certainly

[39] Cf. also T. Brekke, 'The early *saṅgha* and the laity', *JIABS*, 20/2 (1997), pp. 28–9.

[40] *J* III 435, 261; *D* II 96, where the Licchavi princes offer Ambapālī a hundred thousand [*kahāpaṇa*] if she will give up her meal with the Buddha.

[41] *J* II 431, 294. [42] *J* II 428, 291; *D* II 182.

[43] On the latter see H. P. Ray, 'Trade and Contacts', in R. Thapar (ed.), *Recent Perspectives of Early Indian History* (Popular Prakashan, Bombay, 1995), p. 143. Cf. also von Simson, 'Die zeitgeschichtliche Hintergrund', pp. 91–2.

benefited from this, a benefit predicated on the belief in society that it was proper to support these new groups financially.

McNeill argues that, on the basis of epidemiological factors, any surplus produced in the Ganges valley during the period covered in this book would have been small. He suggests, 'From a distance India looked wealthy, since its imports were gems and spices, but in spite of that reputation it seems likely that the subcontinent as a whole was always comparatively poor inasmuch as a rather slender margin existed in most times and places between what an average peasant family could produce and what it needed for survival.'[44] He uses this argument as one reason why asceticism developed so strongly in ancient India. Ascetic practices involved dietary and bodily restraints, a practice well suited for a society producing only a small food surplus.[45] However, the idea of an absolute surplus of production over a subsistence level of living may well be irrelevant to the very idea of surplus, even of a minimal surplus as implied by McNeill. Pearson has argued that the level of surplus is not biological, but social:

> A given quantity of goods or services would be surplus only if the society in some manner set these quantities aside and declared them to be available for a specific purpose. Into this category might then fall such things as food set aside for ceremonial feasts or in anticipation of future dearth, war chests, budgetary surpluses, or savings for whatever purpose. The essential point is that relative surpluses are initiated by the society in question. It is true that such surpluses may be made to appear along with a wind-fall increase of material means, or a more permanent rise in productive capacity: but they may also be created with no change whatever in the quantity of subsistence means by re-allocating goods or services from one use to another.[46]

Accepting this broader view of surplus compels us to ask not what the minimal level of economic subsistence might be, but what cultural forces within society – such as prestige or access to the sacred – resulted in economic goods being acquired for purposes other than the material subsistence of those who produced them.

To understand how this surplus might have been used a dichotomy should be drawn, no doubt historically based, between Buddhism conceived primarily as a group of eremitic monks and as a religion focused on monastic institutions and parish priests. There must be implications for the utilization of economic resources arising from the activity of the monk who wanders around from house to house begging for food. We assume that on a very small scale such a monk would place minimum pressure

[44] McNeill, *Plagues and Peoples*, p. 92. [45] Ibid., p. 93. [46] Pearson, 'Economy', p. 323.

on his begging environment except in times of famine. The agricultural surplus required to feed such figures would not have been excessive and any given village could probably support a few monks with relative ease for a long period. If though, a century after the death of the Buddha, there are many (say twenty) monks and a small monastery on the outskirts of the village, then the situation becomes quite different. The presence of the Buddhist institution could become a veritable drain on the economic prosperity of the village, though any one monastery could have survived off several neighbouring villages. Ultimately we cannot give precision to the question of how the presence of monks and monastic organizations materially and ideologically affected the economic impulses of individuals or socio-economic groups in ancient northeastern India. What is needed here is a systematic effort in locating and statistically analysing the number of villages grouped in close proximity to a given monastery. Nor, and maybe this is of greater significance if only because of the potential size, do we know how the presence of a monastery might have increased demand in the local economy of the area in which it was located. Two factors should be relevant: (1) the simple function of the *saṅgha* as a purchaser of goods and services from the local area, hence a stimulator of demand for certain goods, and (2) the role of the *saṅgha* in creating an ideational motivation for increasing production or in modifying the methods of distribution.

An early proponent of this focus on the monastery as stimulant to economic activity was D. D. Kosambi, who noted the presence of Mother-Goddess cult sites along prehistoric tracks. H. P. Ray succinctly summarizes his findings: 'Many of these became prosperous and prominent Buddhist centres developed at these spots in the Early Historical period. These were well-endowed with land and money donations both by the ruling Sātavāhanas and by members of the trading community. Analogies with Buddhist monastic establishments in China led Kosambi to postulate a symbiotic relationship between the monastic centres and the local populace.'[47] Since the time when his work was first published an increase in the rate of archaeological excavation, and new evidence for the details of distinctive regional cultures this has produced, have allowed us to offer more precision to the exact nature of this relationship.[48] H. P. Ray has called

[47] Ray, 'Trade and Contacts', p. 148.

[48] An example would be the site of Dharaṇikota, associated with the Amarāvatī *stūpa*, which is likely to be very early; claims have been made for the fourth century BC, and there is certainly evidence suggesting occupation at the time of Aśoka, with Buddhist activity also attributed to the third century: R. Knox, *Amaravati: Buddhist Sculpture from the Great Stūpa* (British Museum, London, 1992), pp. 10–13.

attention to the possible role of pilgrimage in the symbiosis of commerce and Buddhism as both travelled the trade routes.

Apart from the obvious point that the monasteries are centres of consumption[49] little more is said about their economic implications. The results of recent archaeological research, however, entails that the relationship of dependence between monasteries and centres of economic activity must be re-theorized in a more comprehensive manner than has hitherto been done. Consider the view of Heitzman:

[A]round 500 BC, a pattern of settlements occupied on a permanent basis, spread from North India throughout South Asia. By the third century BC, major institutional forms of imperial power and long-distance trade were centred in nodes of permanent settlement connected by trade routes. Buddhist monastic sites grew up at these nodes and along the routes, serving as symbolic structures mediating social hierarchy within a new urban complex. The triad of political power and commerce centred in stable occupational sites, associated with Buddhism as a major religious component, lasted into the Christian era.[50]

This suggests that monastic centres survived as much because they fulfilled certain secular functions (i.e., demonstrating social hierarchies by means of prestatory gifts) as because of performing particular pastoral and educative functions. But this secular function was not necessarily associated with trade, or if it was, we have not yet understood what its precise relationship with trade might have been. Heitzman is instructive, once more:

Although Buddhist monastic sites were consistently associated with non-monastic locations and with the two institutional components – empire and trade – which organized the network of permanent settlement, there is little archaeological evidence to suggest that the Buddhist sites themselves had any purely political or economic role. In the vast majority of cases, monasteries are situated at a distance from the non-monastic structural concentrations . . . The location of the Buddhist monastic sites at a distance from the scenes of political and economic activity made their direct participation in such activity inefficient. There is, furthermore, no artificial or structural evidence pointing to military, storage, or industrial functions within monasteries . . .[51]

49 Jonathon Walters' arguments about the holding of Buddhist festivals in Aśokan India might also relate to this subject, as they would be centres of heightened economic activity, even if only at intermittent times during the year. See J. Walters, 'A voice from the silence. The Buddhist Mother's Story', *HR*, 33/34 (1994), p. 368.

50 J. Heitzman, 'Early Buddhism, trade and empire', in K. A. R. Kennedy and Gregory L. Possehl (eds), *Studies in the Archeology and Paleoanthropology of South Asia* (Oxford and IBH Publishing Co., New Delhi, 1984), p. 121.

51 Ibid., p. 131.

Morrison presents a picture which makes the prevailing view seem even more contradictory. She notes: 'Monastic sites situated at this boundary [of Ghat passes] would have been in a position to take advantage of the produce of both environmental zones. Further, the earliest monastic sites were located in the areas of most secure agricultural production, pointing to their need for surplus produce and their close relationship with cultivated produce.'[52] This point is not as obvious as one might think. Clearly, a large non-productive institution will necessarily be in close proximity with food-producing areas in order to survive, though this does not guarantee a particular kind of stimulus to the expansion of trade in that area. Furthermore, in Morrison's words, affirming Heitzman's point cited earlier, 'Monastic sites are notable for their lack of evidence for large-scale storage, craft production, or any other indication of participation in exchange networks other than as recipients of gifts.'[53] It is quite significant that none of this can be confirmed for the very early period of Buddhism as the available texts simply lack detailed descriptions of monasteries. Nor can much be gleaned from them about the interaction between the monastery and the regions and social groupings in immediate proximity with it. The overwhelming impression is that the *Vinaya* and the *Nikāyas* are providing a description of a Buddhism where the interaction is between individual monks and the laity, except where it is a question of portraying the heretical activities of the group of six monks, whose standard of behaviour is always condemned. Of course, the *saṅgha* was present in a group then and in small sub-groups relating to particular areas and the *pātimokkha* rules obviously imply the presence of a large organization requiring a degree of administrative control. So too do the donations received by the Buddha from the wealthy, most of which were used to purchase land or construct buildings for the emerging order. Yet we have great difficulty in extrapolating from the texts themselves to the post-Aśokan situation (depicted in the archaeological record) where Buddhism had become substantially a monastic order.

ECONOMIC SUPPORT FOR THE BUDDHIST ORDER

The principal religious motive for providing support was for the personal acquisition of good merit and because generosity was part of the expected role of a lay Buddhist. Like any holy figure, a monk was a field of merit from

[52] K. Morrison, 'Trade, urbanism and agricultural expansion: Buddhist monastic institutions and the state in early historic western Deccan', *World Archeology*, 27 (1995), p. 216.

[53] Ibid., p. 217.

which positive returns could be gained by giving. In addition, as we argue in a later chapter, providing material support to the *saṅgha* made available the possibility for demonstration of sumptuary acts, the purpose of which may have had more to do with social status than acquisition of merit. Support for the *saṅgha*, at the level at which it must have been practised – especially when Buddhism began to expand rapidly after the reign of Aśoka – must have been too large for the produce of a subsistence economy. No doubt, in some small villages it must have been the case that individual monks were supported by families who could at times have scarcely raised enough to feed themselves. We are not in a position to know if the bulk of support during the growth of Buddhism in its earliest centuries came from this source or whether it derived from the highly conspicuous support from the most successful of the social elites.

Buddhist donors as they are reflected in the texts, or later in inscriptions, can be divided into two categories corresponding to small and large, on the one hand, and institutional or individual, on the other hand. The majority of the examples concern monks being supported by individual families in specific villages:

'Once, as a certain monk was going to the village, he said to another monk: 'Your reverence, let me speak on your behalf[54] to the family which supports you (*upaṭṭhākakulaṃ*).' He went there, had an outer cloak brought and used it for himself (*attanā paribhuñji*). After finding out about this the other monk reprimanded him with the words, 'You are not a true recluse' (. . . *asamaṇo 'si tvan ti*).[55]

'At one time in Campā, a nun who was the pupil of the nun Thullanandā went to the family who supported Thullanandā, and said: "The lady wants to drink rice-gruel containing the three pungent spices." She had it cooked, took it away with her and ate it by herself (*attanā paribhuñji*). After finding out about this, she reprimanded her with the words, "You are not a true female recluse" (*asamaṇī 'si tvan ti*).'[56]

'Once in Vesālī, the householder who was the supporter (*upaṭṭhākassa gahapatino*) of the venerable Ajjuka had two children, a son and a nephew . . . '[57]

Another passage alludes to an entire village of monks and yet another to a commercial guild supplying robes to the six heretical monks.[58] The latter, in particular, is quite revealing in showing how dependence can become too strongly displayed, almost to the point where it becomes emotional blackmail. Here the moral is that the whole giving relationship has become

[54] 'let me speak on your behalf', *vutto vajjemīti*. On this phrase see Horner, *The Book of the Discipline*, vol. I. p. 102, n. 1.

[55] *Vin* III 61. [56] *Vin* III 66, 67. [57] *Vin* III 66. [58] *Vin* I 149 and III 265, respectively.

too individualized and that giving should be regarded as to the Order as a whole. The group of six monks has asked a guild for robes:

> [The guild speaking:] 'Honoured monks, we will not give them. Every year we designate alms-food and robes for the Order.'
>
> [The monks reply:] 'Good people, the Order has many donors and many devotees (*bhattā*). We live here because we depend on and look to you, but if you won't give to us, then who will give to us? Good people, give this robe material to us.'
>
> Being pressured by the group of six monks, the guild then gave the group of six monks the robe material and served the Order with a meal which was prepared appropriately.
>
> The other monks, knowing that robe material and a meal had been prepared for the Order, but not knowing it had been given to the group of six monks, said this:
>
> 'Good people, give the robe material to the Order.'
>
> 'Honoured monks, there isn't any: the masters, the group of six monks, appropriated for themselves the robe material that was prepared.'
>
> [Then the modest monks asked how the six monks could take material for themselves that was meant for the Order as a whole. The Buddha declared this to be a *nissaggiya* offence.][59]

These examples, especially the first, imply that monks cultivated relationships of support with individual families. This in turn implies two more things, first, that the family was a lay Buddhist family, and secondly, that the monk was either a local in the area who had known the family before he became a monk or a newcomer to the area who had developed a relationship with a family he knew to be Buddhist in sympathy. How long these relations would have taken to develop is not possible to determine from the texts, though there are many examples of laypeople giving spontaneously to individual monks and groups of monks as well as others who deal with only one set of monks. All three also imply there were some misgivings about the donor–monk relationship, the expression 'enjoyed/used it himself' suggesting a critique of any idea of individual ownership of donated goods, that the gift is to the Order not to the individual monk.

But begging rounds did become almost formalized and there are cases in the *Vinaya* of prior preparations being made for a visit of the Buddha, preparations very similar to the kind of fund-raising occurring whenever the present Dalai Lama visits a particular country. An illustration is found in the first book of the *Vinaya* where the Buddha is depicted setting out for Ātumā with his retinue of 1,250 monks. There dwelt a barber who renounced when he was quite old, and still had two lay sons living in the village.

[59] *Vin* III 265.

He had two boys who had sweet voices, were intelligent, skilled, and good at the barber's trade because of their own teacher.

The barber heard that the monks were coming and decided to organize food to feed the Buddha and the monks. He said to his sons: 'It is said, sons, that the Lord is coming to Ātumā with a large Order of monks, totalling twelve hundred and fifty monks. Boys, go and take a barber's kit, wander from house to house for *nāḷi* measures of offerings, and collect salt, oil, husked rice and solid food, and when the Lord comes we will make him a drink of rice milk.'

'Yes, father,' said these boys, agreeing with him who had renounced when old. They took a barber's kit, wandered from house to house for offerings equal to a *nāḷi* measure, and collected salt, oil, husked rice and solid food to a measure of a *nāḷi*. When they saw these intelligent boys with their sweet voices, even the people who did not want to make offerings made them and gave much. So these boys collected much salt, oil, husked rice and solid food.[60]

No doubt a small group of monks could have easily been accommodated, in this case by the barber, in either an urban or a rural area as long as there was not a major famine in process. It is likely too that a larger group could have been fed for a short time if it was known by the donors they were on a preaching tour as the Buddha is portrayed as doing in the *Mahāvagga*. In this latter sense they would almost be like an army[61] or a troupe of wandering players.

Similar examples are given in the two following passages, one seemingly offering one-off support, the other establishing a long-term offer of support.

(1) [A]t that time a certain layman offered garlic to the Order of nuns, saying: 'If these ladies need garlic, I will supply it.' And he instructed the keeper of the field: 'If the nuns come, give two or three bundles to each nun.'

At that time there was a festival in Sāvatthī and the garlic was gone as soon as it was brought in. The nuns went up to the layman and said, 'Sir, we need garlic.' He said, 'There is none, ladies; the garlic is gone as soon as it is brought in; go to the field.' The nun Thullanandā went to the field, but did not exercise moderation and had too much garlic taken away.

[Then she was criticized by the keeper of the field and a folk tale is recited showing that, due to past *kamma*, she really is greedy.][62]

(2) 'A householder who had nice food gave a continual supply of food of four kinds to the Order. With his wife and children, he stayed in the kitchen and served food. One offered boiled rice, another curry, another oil and another offered

[60] *Vin* I 249–50.

[61] The following passage even suggests the possibility of camp followers. 'Then the Lord, having stayed in Benares for as long as he wanted, set out on tour for Andhakavinda with a large group of monks, totalling twelve hundred and fifty. At that time the people of the area (*jānapadā manussā*) loaded much salt, oil, husked rice and solid food into wagons and followed close after the group of monks (*buddhapamukhassa bhikkhusaṃghassa piṭṭhito-piṭṭhito anubaddhā honti*) . . .' *Vin* I 220; 243–4.

[62] *Vin* IV 258–9.

tit-bits.' [Conflict arises when he does not wish to give food which had been apportioned by Dabba, the Mallian, to the followers of the monks Mettiya and Bhummajaka, whom the householder considers to be depraved. He serves them poor food and the monks blame Dabba.][63]

The gift-giving relationship was one that could be abused on both sides and was sometimes transparent enough to bring out divisions between monks within a particular area and, as in the case with Thullanandā, to raise the possibility of monks/nuns offending their donors.

The usual reward for generosity was merit transferred implicitly to the donor family, but there must have been cases where a more tangible reward was required and the monk obliged. In the *Vinaya* there are situations[64] where monks are approached to find abortive preparations or fertility drugs for women. These monks are said to be dependent on the women's family for alms and are subsequently condemned by the Buddha for agreeing to find the abortive drugs. Another kind of dependence is reflected in a story told several times in the *Vinaya*. A monk en route to Sāvatthi arrives at Kiṭāgiri. He goes looking for alms-food, adopting a comportment of great modesty. People see and ridicule him, saying that their own (monkish?) masters Assaji and Punabbasu are much more polite and that they should receive the alms instead of this monk. He received nothing until a layman invited him to his own house, where he invited him to eat. Then he criticizes the monks who are followers of Assaji and Punabbasu, because 'Those who formerly were channels for gifts (*dānapatha*) to the Order are now cut off, they neglect the well-behaved monks, and the depraved monks stay on.' He informs the Buddha who tells Sāriputta and Moggallāna to banish those monks from the Order.[65]

The point in all these and other examples[66] is that they impose obligations on the monks who are involved in the formalized exchange of alms. Of course, this is to be expected, especially when a close relationship would build up over time between a monk and his supportive family. This would be the minimal condition for allowing the flow of alms to continue on a permanent basis, unless the prestige of dealing with a monk – a prestige enhanced by his reputation as a recipient of psychic power – was sufficient to guarantee continuity of alms, irrespective of whether there was personal knowledge of the monk on the part of the lay family.

Each of these examples restricts a single monk to a single family, or a single village, and whether or not this was coincidental cannot be determined from

63 *Vin* III 160–1; cf. I 292. 64 *Vin* III 83–4. 65 *Vin* III 181.

66 See *Vin* I 83, where the family supporting Sāriputta sent a youth to him requesting that the youth be allowed to renounce.

the textual sources. We are, however, entitled to speculate whether it was a deliberate policy of the Buddhists who were sensitive to the quantity of resources available to a family. The burden of feeding another person on a daily basis would have depended on the total and expected income stream of the family and the overall conditions pertaining to agriculture in a society still substantially based on agrarian activity.

CONCLUSION

Because we do lack precise details of monastic developments in the early centuries of Buddhism, it is not possible to make an informed guess about the split between individual monks/nuns and groups of monks/nuns as percentages of the entire Order. After perhaps the end of the second century BCE we witness the widespread construction of monastic centres across many areas of South Asia, and it is likely that institutional support would have been required for their construction and maintenance. In the early centuries, though, we speculate that much of the support would have come from individual families of widely diverging degrees of wealth. A preparedness to offer such support already bespeaks an acceptance of Buddhism by a certain percentage of the population and either an on-going surplus of production over subsistence needs or a willingness to engage in self-sacrifice on the part of the laity, if not both of these.

It is important to speculate in this way because if we can demonstrate that individual family support for monks was substantially a product of an on-going productive surplus, that did not impinge on the security of food for the family, this has direct implications for the strength of what must have been an expanding economy in the Buddha's time. The evidence constituted by the large-scale and institutional donations of the wealthy is not as good as that provided by the arrangements with ordinary individuals and families, because such a surplus, as implied by their sumptuary activity, could have been produced as a consequence of a wealthy and armed elite oppressing the rest of the population who necessarily lived at a bare subsistence level. Evidence from the early centuries before and after the beginning of the Christian era is suggestive of small-scale contributions being of major importance for the material basis of Buddhism. V. Dehejia points to the sustained patronage received from the non-regal laity for the construction of *stūpas* and cave temples:

> With a few exceptions, the artistic monuments produced in these kingdoms were not dependent on royal patronage. Stable political conditions apparently led to considerable economic prosperity, and surplus money seems to have accumulated

in the hands of a wide section of the community. The patronage of the religious art was not the prerogative of the merchant and the banker. Apparently, the wealth necessary to indulge in such a luxury belonged also to persons of humbler professions like the ironmonger and stone mason, the gardener and the fisherman.[67]

She provides ample evidence from epigraphy that many of the donors, leaving aside the large percentage of donor monks and nuns, were from people whose occupations would disqualify them from being brahmins or elite merchants. A similar conclusion can be drawn from a reading of the early literature, yet it must remain impressionistic as we possess no hard figures.

This whole question of a surplus shades off into the question of how monks could gain access to this surplus both at an institutional and at an individual level. It may not be too much of an exaggeration to see the Buddha (or is it really Ānanda?) as the first of the institutional fund-raisers. In this sphere of activity the method of raising resources could not have been based on any form of market exchange, though this need not mean competitive attitudes were not present. It is more accurate to use a prestatory model[68] in the sense that Buddhism may have provided an opportunity for those persons at various class and status levels within the urban environment to express and confirm their positions through ostentatious display in a way previously undertaken through the *śrauta* sacrifice, the performance of which was probably always beyond the reach of any but the most wealthy. The relative magnificence of donations was a method for establishing the divisions in a hierarchical elite. Only the wealthy could afford to have a monument built; only the wealthiest could afford the richest and most ornate designs. Changes in the composition of the classes which held economic power could be mirrored by variations in the style of their donations. The very fact that all parties participated 'meant that Buddhist institutions could perform a unifying role at the same time that they symbolized social and economic divisions',[69] and enables us to make some sense out of the huge donations to the *saṅgha* made by Anāthapiṇḍaka et al. which may have been no more or less legitimate than the offering of a bowl of rice to a wandering monk.

[67] V. Dehejia, 'The collective and popular basis of early Buddhist patronage: sacred monuments, 100BC–AD250', in B. Stoler Miller (ed.), *The Powers of Art. Patronage in Indian Culture* (Oxford University Press, Delhi, 1992), p. 44.

[68] See ch. 11 below. [69] Heitzman, 'Early Buddhism', p. 133.

4

Urbanization, urbanism and the development of large-scale political structures

Society and economy in the Buddhist texts are still dominated by a physical (and conceptual) landscape where the contrast between village and forest is pronounced in a geographical sense and not just in an ideological sense as it is in the Brāḥmaṇa texts.[1] But it is much more than a question of village. The universal quality of landscape given by early Buddhist texts is that of urbanism, of cities sufficient in size to have harboured large populations who did not derive their income from agriculture. Such cities were surrounded by small villages and lots of open space, both wooded and cultivated. Buddhist monks did not have to make a decision between accepting urbanization as a process, the presence of large political states as a reality, or not accepting them. Both were realities when Buddhism developed. We presume *they did not have an attitude to it as a process of landscape change* and as a conceptual frame for particular forms of behaviour, because through their habitual touring the monks must have witnessed a wide variety of landscapes and forms of habitation. Not that all monks or nuns came from large towns or cities, but there was not a repressed memory of a sharp break between an urban and a non-urban landscape, even if there remained in both Buddhist and brāhmaṇical thought a sharp conceptual (and physical) distinction between village and forest. This distinction is considered important as it brings out the real significance of a group of wanderers locating themselves – forest/village, urban/rural countryside, village/trade route – simultaneously in several different areas, each having its own symbolic resonance. Further, it is an integral part of certain theories relating to the origins of Buddhism within its spatial context.

The question of urbanism, rather than urbanization, must be treated in any history of the socio-economic conditions associated with the rise of Buddhism, not just because it may have been contemporary with, or have

[1] See C. Malamoud, 'Village et forêt dans l'idéologie de l'Inde brāhmaṇique', *Archives Européennes de Sociologie*, 17 (1976), pp. 3–20.

just preceded, Buddhism's rise. In focusing on urbanism we are dealing with values rather than process, although we must inevitably also reflect on the process of social change accompanying the growth of the city in size and population. Both may be direct consequences of the change in political structures, though to assert distinct causality is difficult given the simultaneous arising of both phenomena. The differential features of the spatial landscape are well presented in the literature as places where Buddhist monks wandered and with which they had familiarity. But it is likely that from the time of the Buddha's life onwards the variability of social groupings associated with the variability of landscape was coming under the unifying and homogenizing tendencies associated with the pressures imposed by the newly arising states. He moved easily amongst political elites, of which group he himself had been a member. It is possible, and this is our view, that the Buddha offered the kind of teaching about the human condition that transcended any kind of spatial distinction between city and non-city, monarchical state and tribal confederacy, and that the universalism which was a concomitant of this helped legitimize the rising state by providing an ideology capable of transcending ethnic, tribal, social and linguistic differences. Such a universalistic teaching became a means of encoding in several interrelated layers the values of a socially and culturally heterogeneous state. From the centre an ideology of kingship and social coherence, centring on an absolute monarch, could be disseminated, an ideology which allowed the outlying tribes and states to retain a semblance of their cultural uniqueness. If this theory is correct then it has as a corollary that the particularistic values of the brahmins were inappropriate for the same task. Accordingly the tremendous feats of cultural codification we find in the *Dharmasūtras*, and especially in the *Mahābhārata*, must be seen as a recognition by the brahmins of the particularity of their values and an attempt to broaden them out.

Intra-regional trade, finance, agriculture, division of labour, a diversified production base, a currency system, the idea of surplus and the ideological conditions required to give intellectual cohesion to all of these factors, are a sub-text of the entire Canon and appear incidentally everywhere. None of these could be present without urbanization.

THE URBAN SITUATION AT THE TIME OF THE BUDDHA AND LATER CENTURIES

An excellent broad summary of the state and character of urbanization between 550 and 400 BCE is offered by George Erdosy, working primarily from archaeological sources for the region containing Kauśambī:

Period II [in Kauśambī and dating from BC 550–400] shows an exceptionally high increase of size, and therefore rate of population growth, at .68 percent per annum, much of which is absorbed through agglomeration – the total occupied area changes from 35.8 to 100 hectares, but the number of sites grows only by five, to 21. Clearly we are witnessing rapid political and economic centralization: the concentration of population in sites clearly graded in size, the regular spacing of central places along all major arteries of communication, and the overwhelming dominance of the largest settlement all point to this . . .

. . . On the lowest rung of the ladder were villages, predominantly nucleated and inhabited by those practising agriculture and herding. Above them were minor centres which revealed traces of the manufacture of ceramics and lithic blades, as well as of iron-smelting, and to which marketing, policing and tax-collecting functions may also be attributed on the basis of the literary evidence. Next in the scale were towns providing a full complement of manufacturing activities, including the production of luxury items: unfinished beads of semi-precious stones and shells, as well as copper slag, were among the surface finds at such sites as Kara. Although several of these towns were fortified, they were dwarfed in size by the capital city of Kausambi which, in addition to possessing all the functions of smaller settlements, acted as the centre of political power.[2]

This spatial arrangement corresponds well with what Makkhan Lal has presented in his important work on proto-historic settlement patterns in the Kanpur region.[3]

The Pāli Canon does not so much chronicle the development of this situation as reflect its fully developed condition, but one can recognize a similar picture to that suggested by the archaeological evidence. The Buddhist literary sources speak as often of villages (*gāma*) as they do of large towns which are normally referred to by the name of the town, rather than by a generic term. From the texts we must assume the landscape was one where a few large cities existed, surrounded by many smaller villages, either providing services to the large city and/or subsisting from agricultural production, in between all of which must have been wasteland and jungle. Over the centuries this would have been progressively removed, though in the Buddha's time much seems to have remained. Chattopadhyaya is substantially correct when, writing of the impressions about the city derived from ancient Indian literature, he notes:

Literature thus gives two initial impressions about the city. As an apex centre, it is not at a distance from other settlements; in other words the essence of the city is in its centrality in the togetherness of settlements. Also, there is a graded hierarchy,

[2] Erdosy, 'City states', p. 107.

[3] See for example his *Settlement History and Rise of Civilization in Ganga-Yamuna Doab, from 1500 B.C. to 300 A.D.* (B.R. Publishing, Delhi, 1984) and other works cited below.

between village, town and royal city, and not just a sharp distinction between the village and the city.[4]

Thus the physical distinction between town (city) and village should not be drawn too sharply, the conceptual opposition between urban area and forest/mountain remaining much stronger.

The Buddhist texts recognize a hierarchy of communities consisting of villages, towns, cities and countries.[5] Terms used include *gāma* (village), *nigama* (country town), *janapada* (large community, country), *nagara* (town) and *puṭabhedana*[6] (a market town). In the *Jātakas*, which represent a much later environment, there are references to *dvāragāma* (satellite villages) and *pacchantagāma* (frontier villages).[7] The texts do show some inclination to classify the urban conurbations in several different ways: size, economic function, political status (border towns as opposed to capitals) and perhaps methods of internal governance (*negama*). Although the texts do not allow us any precision in determining the respective sizes of these kinds of urban arrangements, except that is for the difference between the cities and the small villages, it is clear that there was an acceptance of the landscape as it was. Whilst from the perspective of Vedic literature and archaeological data this was a new kind of built environment, the Pāli texts show no signs of its newness, but only of familiarity.

Buddhist canonical literature sets many or most of its stories in or near cities and villages, and in sum we are not given much more information about them than the names themselves. Any details are given in an entirely unsystematic manner. B. G. Gokhale has counted 1,009 references to various settlements, of which 842 are to just six cities – Sāvatthī, Rājgir, Kapilavatthu, Vesālī, Kauśambī and Campā.[8] What became Benares must have also been a large city with many satellites – fitting the archaeological pattern –, if we go by the following reference from a *Jātaka*:

4 B. D. Chattopadhyaya, 'The city in early India: perspectives from texts', *Studies in History*, 13/2 NS (1997), p. 183.

5 *D* III. 37: *gāma, nigama, nagara, janapada*. A fuller discussion of these, complete with textual references, is given in Sarao, *Urban Centres*, pp. 36–47.

6 Kölver suggests it is a regional centre, a market town where an official breaks seals on goods for sale in controlled markets. See B. Kölver, 'Kautalyas Stadt als Handelzentrum: der Terminus *puṭabhedana*', *ZDMG*, 135 (1985), pp. 299–311.

7 A. Ray, *Villages, Towns and Secular Buildings in Ancient India* (Firma K. L. Mukhopadhyaya, Calcutta, 1964), pp. 26f.

8 B. G. Gokhale, 'Early Buddhism and the urban revolution', *JIABS*, 5/2 (1982), pp. 7–22, esp. p. 10. The figures for numbers of references are: 593 Sāvatthī, 140 Rājgir, 56 Kapilavatthu, 38 Vesālī, 15 Kosambī; 6 Campā. Distribution of places: 35 cities/towns, 8 market places, 45 villages, 3 countryside. Savatthi is so much represented because the Buddha is said to have spent 25 vassas there.

Not far from Benares was a village in which 500 carpenters lived. They would go up the river in a vessel and enter the forest, where they would shape beams and planks for house building and put together the framework of one-storey or two-storey houses, numbering all the pieces from the mainpost onwards; these then they brought down to the river bank and put them all aboard; then rowing down stream again, they would build houses to order.[9]

The number 500 is a formula meaning 'a lot', and is not evidence of anything, but, when we consider textual evidence for the spatial concentration of particular occupations, there must have been a large conurbation to sustain the services of a craft village like this. Moreover, this conurbation must have been increasing in size for a large number of carpenters to have remained gainfully employed.

However, these various fragments of evidence are scattered over many centuries. Apart from the naming of the six cities, none of the more economically advanced stages of urban life are mentioned in the earliest sources. Descriptions in the *Jātakas* are of no relevance to the pre-Mauryan period of Buddhism's growth. The same goes for Buddhist sculpture associated with early monuments which certainly presents an image of bustling city life with splendid buildings and throngs of well-dressed idlers. None of this is evidence of sophisticated urbanization as early as the fifth or fourth centuries BCE. Nonetheless archaeological evidence is highly suggestive that the six cities mentioned above, and some others, were fortified for military reasons and that they may also have doubled as administrative centres. The earliest dating of ramparts around cities that is now generally accepted is some time in the sixth century BCE; probably the earliest is Old Rājgir (New Rājgir dates from the second century).[10] By 550 BCE, there were ramparts at various city sites, all identified as capitals of kingdoms: Atranjikhera, Rājgir, Campā, Ujjain and Rājghat. By 400 Śrāvastī was added, and by 300 also Besnagar, Mathurā, Tripuri, Vesālī and Pāṭaliputra. Ghosh recognizes two periods of construction of city fortifications, the first beginning about 600 BCE and the later in the second century BCE, after the Mauryas.[11] These were both periods of severe political instability.

The few canonical descriptions of cities are conspicuous for their brevity. Here are some of the more substantial:

[9] *J* II 18, 14.

[10] Erdosy, 'Early historic cities', pp. 4–6; Erdosy points out that there is however no evidence to corroborate the association of Old Rājgir with the King Bimbisāra mentioned in Pāli texts; the date of this king cannot be regarded as a fixed point, given the doubt about when the Buddha lived.

[11] A. Ghosh, *The City* in *Early Historical India* (Institute of Advanced Study, Simla, 1973), pp. 11, 66.

Lord, this town of Kapilavatthu is rich, prosperous, populous, crowded with men, with congested thoroughfares. Now, Lord, when I entered Kapilavatthu at eventide after waiting upon the Blessed One, I met a wandering elephant, a wandering horse, a wandering chariot, a wandering cart and a wandering man.[12]

[Ānanda speaking to the Buddha,] 'Let not the Blessed One die in this little town of mud huts, which is in the midst of the jungle, a minor town. For, Lord, there are other great cities, such as Campā, Rājagaha, Sāvatthi, Sāketa, Kosambi, and Benares. Let the Blessed One die in one of them. In them there are many wealthy warriors, brahmins and householders who are well disposed towards the Tathāgata. They will honour the Tathāgata's body.'

[The Buddha says no and praises Kusinārā where he intends to die:] ' . . . This Kusinārā, Ānanda, was the royal city of King Mahāsudassana, under the name of Kusāvatī, and on the east and on the west it was twelve leagues in length, and on the north and on the south it was seven leagues in breadth.

That royal city Kusāvatī, Ānanda, was successful, prosperous, and full of people, crowded with men, and had good food. Just, Ānanda, as the royal city of the gods, Ālakamandā by name, is successful, prosperous, and full of people, crowded with the gods, and has good food, so, Ānanda, was the royal city Kusāvatī successful, prosperous, full of people, crowded with men and had good food.

Both by day and by night, Ānanda, the royal city Kusāvatī resounded with ten cries; that is to say, the noise of elephants, and the noise of horses, and the noise of chariots; the sounds of the drum, of the tabor, and of the lute; the sound of singing, and the sounds of the cymbal and of the gong; and tenthly, with the cry, "Eat, drink and chew" '.[13]

A later description given in the *Milindapañho*[14] allows us to notice the rich texture of a much more fully developed city. Most of the description is taken up with the occupational types in the city, but the brief description of the architecture is of a large city containing defensive features, regal buildings, ponds, wells and bazaars. What is most conspicuous in the description are the various occupational categories. The groups of people listed are classified according to at least five separate categories: (1) the brāhmaṇical *varṇas*, (2) a diverse set of military roles, (3) occupations, trades and crafts one would expect to find in a large city, though not in a village, (4) people of different nationalities, and (5) people from different Indian cities and regions. Of these categories the third is, not unexpectedly, the largest. It comprises various classes of occupation necessary for providing the basics of life and adds to this others whose role is to produce luxury goods. The breadth of different categories and the range of occupations in category three could scarcely have been supported in a nucleated village economy.

[12] Summary of *S* V 369. We have followed the translation and amendments to the text of Bhikkhu Bodhi, *The Connected Discourses of the Buddha: A New Translation of the Samyutta Nikāya* (Wisdom Publications, Boston, 2000), vol. II, pp. 1848, 1956 nn. 336–7.

[13] *D* II 146–7.

[14] *The Milindapañho*, ed. V. Trenckner (Luzac, London, 1962), pp. 330ff.

In addition, the range of military positions listed here would apply only to a standing army, not to an ad hoc militia cobbled together to fight off cattle rustlers.

What is absent from this list are farmers, pastoralists, financiers of the type made famous in Buddhist literature by the example of Anāthapiṇḍika, and large merchants. The absence of the first two is hardly surprising, but the other two are mentioned frequently as residents of large towns such as Sāvatthi, Rājagaha or Benares.

TWO STAGES OF URBANIZATION

When we inspect the quality of the evidence category by category with an eye on its chronology, it is necessary to realize that even by the period 600–400 BCE, we do not yet confront convincing evidences of mature urbanization with the sorts of sophisticated technical developments we might expect, especially from sources like the *Vinaya* and some other parts of the canon. Several scholars have drawn attention to the absence of many of the features normally associated with urban civilization until relatively late. A. K. Sinha has pointed out that most of the features of full-fledged urbanization do not turn out (despite some earlier claims) to belong to the period before the fifth century BCE.[15] R. S. Sharma identifies as a major stage of cultural progress the Mauryan period, when there were advances in the numbers of coins, iron tools and burned brick buildings, and the appearance of tiles and ring-wells.[16] Erdosy speaks of a third-century boost in urbanization, with baked bricks, elaborate sanitation, town planning, monumental religious architecture, and writing.[17] Niharranjan Ray, reminding us that Pāli literature is not useful as evidence for urbanization even for some centuries after the Buddha, argues that urbanization proper needs to be dated to the Mauryan period, built upon Nanda dynasty fourth-century foundations, as well as the probable impact of Hellenic culture mediated by Alexander's campaign.[18]

[15] A. K. Sinha, 'The Historical Urbanization – a Suggestive Date', *Purātattva*, 11 (1979–80), pp. 151–5.

[16] Sharma, *Material Culture*, pp. 105f. However, he also gives great weight to a major stage of urbanization in the sixth century BCE.

[17] G. Erdosy, 'Early historic cities', p. 14. Erdosy identifies a phase of maturation in 500–300 BCE marked by technological flourishing – baked bricks, wells, drains, paved roads and religious monuments. See also G. Erdosy, 'Origins of cities in the Ganges valley', *JESHO*, 28 (1985), p. 96.

[18] N. Ray, 'Technology and social change', *Purātattva*, 8 (1975–6), pp. 132–8. He discusses the archaeological sites at Rājgir, Benares, Śrāvastī and Vesālī to show that there is no evidence that in early times these places were actual cities, as opposed to settlements with big but primitive fortifications. Even Kauśambī exhibits no more advanced culture pre-dating the Mauryas, and a stone circular construction at Ujjain cannot alone make this site a city even if it is pre-Mauryan.

These positions converge upon the claim that advanced urbanization needs to be recognized in a variety of sophisticated cultural developments that did not in fact become important features of Ganges settlements until the rise of the Mauryan dynasty towards the end of the fourth century, or a little earlier. Such a claim implicitly identifies urbanization with aspects of material culture in some combination, not necessarily all regarded as necessary conditions – large settlement size, coinage, writing, large-scale application of iron manufacture to the economy, and so forth. Whatever may have been the combination of stimuli responsible for the rise of state and city in ancient India, it is clear that we should recognize two distinct stages.

In the first appear new larger communities representing much denser clusterings of people than before, living in central settlements where manpower is organized on a really large scale. For this to happen there must first be a major shift in the pattern of social relationships; settlements grow to a new and unprecedented size with a new hierarchical structure and a substantial degree of political centralization, instead of constantly splitting, with groups migrating elsewhere. This requires the rise of centralized political power: instead of being *primus inter pares*, a chieftain is able to subordinate surrounding groups to his own authority, employing his own livery to execute and enforce central decisions and engaging in various prestatory and regal activities intended to demonstrate his own pre-eminence. These conditions appear to have been fulfilled by the rise of important centres by about the sixth century, each marked by a relatively very dense concentration of population in one place, bounded by a massive rampart, and linked by a network of commercial or administrative connections to a complex pattern of smaller settlements in the hinterland. These developments can be seen to have occurred substantially in advance of the second stage, one marked by the appearance of sophisticated material culture, with money, writing, major advances in architecture, and the use of iron tools in agriculture from the fourth century.

The succession of stages is masked by the fact that not all the technical advances of the second stage had to wait until then to be invented. Some (notably, iron manufacture) had been invented long before, some (such as written language) perhaps somewhat before, but they found their widespread application only then. Mature urbanization, with a growing economy and technical advance, involved not so much new inventions as the burgeoning of technologies whose time had come. Northern Black Polished Ware pottery began rather earlier, but came in its later stages, only from the fourth or later centuries, to be associated with major brick fortifications, drainage, coins, seals, and a big expansion of settlement size.[19] The use of burned bricks in house construction is negligible before the third century BCE.

To whatever extent the process here recognized is typical, the clear sequence of stages comporting it, first political and then technical, is rich in implications for the process of state formation, to be considered in the second section of this chapter – it suggests that political change can come *before* social and economic change. It is therefore interesting to notice that in South East Asia, where sophisticated forms of economic and political organization eventually developed with the adoption of Sanskrit culture in the royal capitals, there was a similar earlier stage in which large settlements appeared ringed by ramparts. They appeared, for example, in northeastern Thailand,[20] and in eastern Cambodia many smaller earthworks with moats suggest the same thing.[21] It appears that, in the prelude to the rise of Indian-style kingdoms in the region, there were chiefdoms with relatively advanced stages of political centralization and control of manpower, which had developed independently.[22]

EARLY BUDDHISM IN ITS URBAN ENVIRONMENT

So far as any sort of chronological associations can be made, it is our view that the rise of Buddhism accompanied the beginnings of the second stage. What is clear, though, is that the canonical texts took shape as a whole somewhat later, when the full-fledged urban environment of the second stage was thoroughly familiar and taken for granted.

Most Buddhist countries have been basically agrarian, and an unreflective reading of the obvious facts of geography and Buddhist history might suggest that monks in early times would have been most at home in an agricultural environment. To be sure, there are references to agriculture which

[19] A. King, 'Some archaeological problems regarding Gangetic culture', in K. A. R. Kennedy and Gregory L. Possehl (eds), *Studies in the Archeology and Paleoanthropology of South Asia* (Oxford and IBH Publishing Co., New Delhi, 1984), pp. 114ff. At Atrañjikhera the evidence is that the occupied area in the Painted Grey Ware phase was only about 1300 square metres, while in the subsequent Northern Black Polished phase it multiplied to about 850 × 550; it turned from a village into a town (Ghosh, *City*, p. 60). Burnt brick is securely attested in northern India only from late N.B.P. levels (ibid, pp. 68f.).

[20] E. Moore, *Moated Sites in Early North East Thailand* (British Archaeological Reports, Oxford, 1988).

[21] See R. Mourer, 'Préhistoire du Cambodge', *Archéologia*, 23 (1988), p. 52.

[22] Referring to such communities attested by early Chinese evidence for Indochina and Java, and archaeological sources for the middle Irrawaddy and the delta of the Mekong, P. Wheatley observed that 'it is in these pre- and protohistoric paramountcies that much of the dynamism of the so-called Hinduization process should be sought': P. Wheatley, 'Presidential address: India beyond the Ganges – desultory reflections on the origins of civilization in Southeast Asia', *Journal of Asian Studies*, 42/1 (1982), pp. 13–28.

are of interest to the social or economic historian. An exclusive emphasis upon the rural background, however, would mask a capital fact about the life and organizational culture of the early *saṅgha*. The monk was expected to move back and forth between the empty spaces, however remote, and the towns, however bustling and densely populated. The monks' stamping ground was not just the forest and not just the city; it was both, as references to Rājagaha tell us. Rājagaha was a large city dominated by a bureaucracy, a king and a military garrison, but it was also surrounded by wooded hills which would allow monks to escape if they wished.

The *vihāra* could be regarded as a compromise between the two. Textual evidence, confirmed in some measure by archaeological research, reveals that the great majority were built on the outskirts of villages, enabling the monk to practise a certain isolation within the monastery whilst viewing the life he has renounced when in the village or town. A monastery allows the monk to be both within and without, to coin a phrase. It also enables lay Buddhists to see the monks in their own environment, if, that is, we can draw this conclusion from *Vin* I 192 where people are described as touring around the dwelling places of monks and being critical of what they see.

If one reads the *Nikāyas* and the *Vinaya* extensively, one is struck by the few references dealing *in extenso* with city life. It is standard practice for the Buddha's delivery of individual suttas to be announced as having occurred at particular locations, often Sāvatthi or Rājagaha. But the locations only form the spatial backdrop for the sermon and the references to the town or city end there. Allusion has already been made to statistical counts of the number of locations mentioned in the entire Canon and the frequency of the Buddha's visits to them.[23] This in itself is useful for giving us a rough indication of where the Buddha preferred to spend his time, but it does not reveal an attitude towards an abstract concept like urbanism or the process that is urbanization.

The time the early Buddhist monks spent in particular places can be summarized in respect of five spatial locations:

(1) Temporary residence in large conurbations raising money, collecting alms and preaching the *dhamma*.
(2) Travelling 'on tour' from one large city to another, often along trade routes.
(3) Temporary residence in villages whilst on tour.
(4) Life in monasteries on the outskirts of villages and large towns.
(5) Wandering in uninhabited areas such as mountains and jungles.

[23] See Gokhale, 'Early Buddhism', p. 10. See above, p. 80.

We are not able to assess the respective time monks might have spent in these locations; in earlier times, it appears the monks and nuns spent the three months of the rainy season in monastic shelters, and in later times, with the process of 'domestication', settled monasticism became increasingly normal. The Buddha himself clearly spent much of his forty-five years after his attainment of nirvāṇa undertaking tours between the large cities, yet it is clear he also spent much time in Rājagaha and Sāvatthī, no doubt because he needed to be there to keep his finger on the pulse of political affairs and to raise material support for the *saṅgha*. We should not, however, assume the Buddha was the model for all other members of the *saṅgha*. At all times there must have been those who wandered about bringing publicity to the newly emergent religion, others who remained in one monastery and built up a network of influence in particular villages and still others, probably a minority, who isolated themselves in order to lead a solitary life.

Even if a given monk/nun were to spend time in villages or large conurbations, they still, nonetheless, located themselves primarily in a 'religious' environment by virtue of living on the outskirts of a village. We can be certain of this by the huge number of times a given sutta tells us that a certain monk went into/returned from a particular village before/after an alms round. Taking village/town and cultivated/uncultivated outskirts into account means that any geographical location must be considered the appropriate spatial location for the monk, an echo of which is given in a *Vinaya* passage where Rājagaha is said to be overcrowded with monks:

> At that time the Lord spent the rains, the winter and the summer only in Rājagaha. People grumbled, took offence and became irritated, saying: 'The district is overcrowded with recluses, sons of the Sakyans, because of whom the area around can hardly be seen.' Monks heard these people who . . . spread it about. Then the monks told the Lord about this problem.

In response, we are told, the Buddha took a small number of monks to Dakkhiṇāgiri. He did not answer the critique but did lay down conditions whereby monks could live independently, presumably away from their own teachers.[24]

Apart from the spatial locations of the Buddha and the early monks, there is also evidence pertaining to this subject which can be derived from the large number of non-Buddhists who inhabit the early texts. One estimate can be derived from figures collected by K. T. Sarao.[25] Of the total of members of the four *varṇas* mentioned in the *Sutta* and *Vinaya Piṭakas* the

[24] *Vin* I 79–81. [25] Sarao, *Origin and Nature*, p. 69.

following figures pertaining to origin from urban, rural or unknown areas can be collated.

Class	**Urban**	**Rural**	**Unknown**
brāhmaṇa	231	43	124
khattiya	671	8	21
vessa	101	7	6
lower classes	86	17	44

The sample is small, but these figures seem overwhelming in support of the conclusion that an urban environment was more central in the Buddhist texts than any other.

That this is so may be the reason why one of the most conspicuous features of the picture of social life given by Buddhist sources is the prominence of crafts and other miscellaneous occupations other than just herding or farming. We see a remarkably diversified economy, in which the monks find themselves constantly in contact with people following a huge variety of occupations. Further, it is notable that stories told for didactic purposes time and time again use homely similes that presuppose their hearers' familiarity with all manner of craft operations; the suggestion is that the *dharma* found itself specially at home among craftsmen. This surely is a point of some importance: crafts are referred to not by dead metaphors that might be presumed to have been part of everybody's active vocabulary (which is arguably the case with the agricultural metaphors), but with images carefully chosen to make the teaching clear. For example, in the *Majjhima Nikāya*, moral straightening out and edification are compared to the action of a wagon maker who shapes a felloe, shaping away its crookedness, 'its twist and notch, so that the felloe . . . might be clear and placed on the pith'.[26]

URBANISM AND ISOLATION

In the discussion of the strong urban ambience depicted in early Buddhist literature what is significant is precisely that the transmitters of the *dhamma* should have represented the Buddha as a wanderer, constantly visiting the most important centres of power and wealth in spite of his concern with the peace best found in seclusion.

From the perspective of Buddhist teaching and monkish practice the framework for the Buddha's requirements given an urban environment is summarized by King Bimbisāra of Magadha, reflecting on a meeting with the Buddha:

[26] *M* I 31.

Now, where could the Lord stay that would be neither too far from a village nor too close, suitable for coming and going, accessible for people whenever they want, not crowded by day, having little noise at night, little sound, without a whiff of people, where a man can sleep alone, suitable for seclusion?[27]

Hence monastic life and the location of monasteries on borders. Textual and archaeological evidence are in agreement that most monasteries were located on the border of the village or town and this is constantly reinforced by the references to monks entering into urban areas in order to go begging. The Buddha and his retinue are commonly depicted going from house to house and spending some part of the day, at least, in concourse with laypeople. The traffic goes both ways, with lay supporters coming into the monastery with supplies (as in modern times); in the *Vinaya* we find laypeople bringing oil, husked rice and solid food to the monastery, even in times of scarcity.[28]

This, then, is what we learn, chiefly from the literary evidence, of life in the urban and commercial environment. Of course, the literary references reviewed (especially the *Jātakas*) come from sources unlikely to provide historical evidence of advanced urbanization in the earliest period of Buddhism, but the significance of such material here is simply that so much comes from Buddhist sources. What is remarkable is that the numerous casual allusions to the experience and knowledge to be expected in the city dweller are met in just the same contexts as allusions to the need for seclusion, the delights of the wilderness, and the incomparable states to be attained by the ascetic lost in private meditation. There is no clear separation of contexts representing different chronological layers. The *Nikāyas*, like other texts, were compiled by people familiar with the isolation of the forest and the hurly-burly of the market place. Like the holy men of other ages, they were wanderers who frequented the most cosmopolitan cities and the remotest hamlets. They lived in two worlds, which they were thus well placed to interpret to each other. That is the important lesson to be learned for the purposes of our enquiry.

STATE FORMATION

If urbanism within the context of early Buddhism has to be studied both as a process of environmental change and as a transformation in cultural and mental attitudes, so too does the development of political structures from the sixth to the fourth centuries BCE. They are implemented in a twofold

[27] *Vin* I 39. [28] *Vin* I 211.

way: in the extension of geographical boundaries and in the assimilation of prior social and political structures under the loose control of hereditary kings. If urbanism is one unstated context for the development and growth of the incipient Buddhist *saṅgha*, so too is the presence of large political formations in much of the area where Buddhism first took hold. Such formations consisted primarily of the states of Kośala and Magadha, and the political history during the Buddha's life is dominated by two processes: the conflict between the two expanding states and the continuing tendency of Magadha to threaten and eventually impose its will on the smaller settlements. Accepting that these tendencies, and the policies implementing them in a pragmatic sense, were givens during the life of the Buddha, and that the expansion of Magadha continued on after this, did they have a formative influence on the developing religion and what role could the activity of Buddhists have played in the role of governance associated with these states?

Both questions are relevant to the study of early Buddhism: on the one hand, according to the texts the Buddha was often in contact with Bimbisāra, King of Magadha, and with Pasenadi, King of Kosala, and on the other hand, if there was substantial dislocation in northeastern India during and after the Buddha's time it was caused by the on-going efforts of the Magadhan state to incorporate the many quasi-independent small groups that had existed in the area prior to the development of the large state-like formations. We are arguing that Buddhism offered a particular brand of transcendent teaching, performing some kind of ideological function enabling a corresponding political/social ideology to be used that transcended ethnic, tribal, social and linguistic differences. Allied to this, Buddhist teachings with their emphasis on individual effort and ethics offer a universalist teaching available for legitimizing what would otherwise have to be achieved ultimately by coercion or the socially divisive teachings of the brahmins.

CULTURE AND STATE FORMATION

Much of the scholarship on the connection between religion and social organization in ancient India is based upon the belief that social organization was shaped by ideas formulated by brahmins or other elite groups to serve their own material interests as a class. This assumption is methodologically inadequate. Here, we shall seek to improve upon an explanation of social and political change that appeals only to the calculus of purely material interest. We need to speculate in order to achieve some sort of working hypothesis which will provide a better framework for the discussion of religious change in the period of state formation. During the time of elementary state formation (600–400 BCE) communities were increasingly supported by agriculture and growing in population, and began to encroach upon each other. Conflict became endemic, as indeed it was to remain, on and off, throughout most of India's subsequent history. Some communities, favoured by superior weaponry or access to other valued resources, made themselves centres of patronage and protection for others. Attracting clients of various status and interests, they became centres of ritual and social activity, creating markets for goods from far away and providing minimal security, where none before had existed, for the growth of long-distance trade, which may have occurred even before the use of money. Leaders found themselves able to accumulate roles and responsibilities. The functions of garrison, market and ritual centre converged in centres of administration. Kingship evolved out of chieftainship.

This constitutes a bare hypothesis for the beginning of large-scale political formations which were characterized by an administrative/military capital city, an incipient bureaucracy, an impulse to territorial expansion and consolidation of prior political/social entities, protective measures to foster inter- and intra-regional trade and patronage of the most conspicuously successful religious groups. Such political groupings are ultimately backed up by whatever coercive powers the king can deploy, but some kind of ideology of kingship, as manifested over a large geographical area, was emerging and received expression in both Buddhist sources and later in both Sanskrit epics as well as the *Arthaśāstra*. But the idealistic and normative views they offer cannot in any sense be used as mirrors of what actually happened.

It is necessary to take account of the whole problem of group identification if we are to justify our opinion that one of the principal problems confronting the emerging large-scale kingdoms was that of dealing with groups all operating with different sets of factors causing identity formation. Such factors elicit some of the deeper springs of human nature, self-perception and social values. People feel loyalty to some groups, perhaps two, though scarcely to more, and can be induced to make sacrifices in a common cause with little or no coercion. Sometimes political circumstances change, creating new loyalties, and often to their own surprise people find themselves confronting former comrades as enemies.

One danger of proceeding along this path is in assuming Indian society in the Buddha's time was articulated in horizontal classes like those of modern industrial society, each class pursuing its own recognized group interests. We have argued against this view in the previous chapter, but some published writings, for example, tend to treat ancient Indian politics as if 'the brahmins' and 'the *kṣatriyas*' were cohesive communities, competing or co-operating according to their perceived advantage; but we cannot know to what extent, or on what occasions, such generalizations capture the realities of motivation and behaviour. Much of the time, no doubt, particular brahmins and *kṣatriyas* were driven by local or kin interests that were largely unaffected by any considerations of *varṇa*. Suppose that we knew as little about the later Muslim states (and their intense political intrigues) as we in fact know about the Buddha's time; with such sketchy knowledge we might seek to generalize about the political behaviour of 'the Hindus' and 'the Muslims', but we would be unable to catch any of the subtlety of the cross-cutting and constantly shifting categories that made up the networks of alliance and affinity, and governed the dynamics of political action in the Muslim period.[29]

Let us propose the hypothesis that religion becomes dominant in certain crisis situations where people's group identities are dramatically challenged – in war, or when a political order is dissolved, or a social order is seriously threatened, especially where these had had very settled and conspicuous boundaries. In such circumstances people turn to their inherited religious ideas in order to know who they are, and their loyalties are redefined accordingly.[30] The extension of political and cultural influence outwards from rising states like Magadha and Kośala must certainly have presented many people with just such a dramatic challenge. But who precisely were these 'people'? The historical record does not allow us to examine them in detail, for almost by definition they were non-literate communities on the fringes, capable of entering the light of history only to the extent that they found redefinition as parts of the larger expanding

[29] The complexity of cross-cutting and nesting categories defining strong group loyalties and political action is well brought out by Mary Searle-Chatterjee's study of 'Caste, religion and other identities', in M. Searle-Chatterjee and U. Sharma (eds.), *Contextualising Caste: Post-Dumontian Approaches* (Blackwell, Oxford, 1994), pp. 147–66. See p. 164, 'Sect, tribe, caste, class, language and regional origin may each provide a basis for solidarity, and even mobilisation.'

[30] The study of group identity in modern India just cited points to the importance of religion: 'When the religious label enters the situation, the numbers of deaths in the riots appear far greater, as if religion *is* a crucial differentiating identity,' ibid., p. 164. However, we cannot extrapolate from this period to early historical India. Cf. H. Kulke, 'THE RĀJASŪYA. A paradigm of early state formation', in A. W. Van Den Hoek, D. H. A. Kolff and M. S. Oort (eds.), *Ritual, State and History in South Asia. Essays in Honour of J. C. Heesterman* (E.J. Brill, Leiden, 1992), p. 196 who points out that early state formation probably occurred in India at a time when the performance of the *śrauta* rituals was at its height. His view is that such rituals 'not only reflected, but sometimes even influenced socio-political developments through their impact on "public" opinion'.

states, and the role of monks and brahmins in dealing with these people during the process of change is not charted.

What is at stake here is the problem of 'ethnicity', a concept that is awkwardly named because, in the course of discussion, the term has lost touch with its origin. Groups often feel very strongly that they are united as a community or a people, but actual biological ancestry (even though it may be theoretically prominent among the concepts celebrated by the group), or even religion or language, may not provide any over-riding criterion for this unity.

What is perhaps lacking in the theoretical literature on ethnicity is a refined analysis of the role of cosmology, the beliefs people have about the order governing the universe, and the particular place which their own community has within this order. This subject will be touched on in a later chapter. What needs to be noticed here is the importance of the radical dissonance between cosmological ideas and life experiences that confronts people in periods of rapid change. When an urban culture expands and encroaches upon hinterland communities that have nothing much in common with it, and threatens their cultural integrity, the dissonance is maximal. What is then required is a new cosmology that can make sense of an otherwise intellectually incoherent universe. Such a system needs specialists; and these may in certain circumstances be ascetics, wanderers who in specific symbolic ways claim to have divested themselves of the entire *habitus* of their inherited cultures. If their status is generally accepted, these people can play a part in helping an outlying community to redefine itself in confrontation with an alien dominant culture which threatens people's ideas of who they are without initially offering any recognizable alternative. Thus they can play a part in the articulation of social relationships in the real world that is directly represented by the transcendental and soteriological values celebrated by their scriptures. This is the argument developed here.

STATE FORMATION IN NORTH-EAST INDIA: A WORKING HYPOTHESIS

Here we introduce a hypothetical description of the process of state formation in the Ganges valley and its environs. Into this process, religious developments fit naturally as interactive components with functions to perform in specific social situations: first the sort of ritual-dominated forms which the Vedic *Brāhmaṇa* texts typify, and at a later stage the ascetic forms represented by Buddhism and the *śramaṇa* schools. A warning should be given in advance that this description offers a picture which is much purer than what must have actually occurred. Given the deep concern of all the available literary sources with religion, any hypotheses about the change in political structures (of any size) can only ever be inference.

The description is generic and can apply to a wide range of possible situations. It is the dynamics of interaction that are abstracted to embody the hypothesis. Essentially, the proposal denies that a central political authority can arise only as a result of victory in violent conflict with those communities or institutions (villages, tribes, clans, guilds or *janapadas*) which, being subordinated, subsequently constitute the body of citizens. It denies, equally, that authority must be built upon a contract, however informal, between citizen communities and the central authority, offering obedience and services in return for protection.[31]

What happens is that, where a particular community is privileged above its fellow communities in the same broad cultural group by special access to desired goods, and if it maintains its edge over them in its own culture for long enough, these other communities may in the natural course of change accept ritually subordinate terms of association with it in order to obtain a share in the exploitation of the goods, rather than competing violently. This ritual subordination gradually turns into political subordination and the ritual eminence of the privileged community's leaders gradually turns into the exercise of political power with the natural growth of economic activity promoted by exploitation of the goods.

We can call the economic resources the *field of exploitation*; it can be any sort of resource-rich area, strategic position (on a pass or river mouth, for example), or subordinated alien population (such as farmers belonging to a different culture, subordinated by pastoralists with warrior skill and the use of the horse). The privileged community we can call the *bridgehead community*. This may obtain its privilege by luck, when it moves into a zone which turns out to offer economic advantages, or by adaptation in a marginal zone, taking advantage of the possibilities of its environment to add new resources to its repertoire (adding farming to pastoralism, or trade to both).

The bridgehead community has varying relationships of alliance and enmity with other communities which share the same culture; they have common myths, perhaps a common language, but are frequently in conflict. If the privileged group establishes a marked superiority in the control of manpower given it by its control of economic goods, these others may find

[31] Cf. Kulke, 'RĀJASŪYA', p. 192, focusing on the newly emerging *grāmin* having to both coerce and attract the 'subjugated' residents of his village.

it advantageous to link themselves politically to the bridgehead community rather than fight it, sharing in the benefits of taxing, looting, trading or otherwise benefiting from the zone of exploitation.

The process can operate in any number of situations. What matters in every case is that a particular community should experience a special advantage enabling it to establish pre-eminence among its fellows. The pre-eminence should be sufficient to deter the fellow communities from attempting direct competition and to induce them to accept a measure of subordination, and the duration of the situation should be sufficient to enable the bridgehead community to become the nucleus of a new political unit. As it grows, the smaller communities lose their ability to compete with it on equal terms. So long as there are visible benefits from sharing in the benefits of economic exploitation and, presumably, of the mere maintenance of the traditional status quo, they may co-operate with the rising centre, accepting their junior status.

But co-operation does not come naturally. People can adjust to a new political environment only by drawing upon existing cultural resources, which effectively perform a mediating function. This places heavy demands upon the various ritual institutions by which the larger group as a whole recognizes and celebrates its own unity and distinctness. Certain individuals symbolize the shared culture of the society by their birth, prowess or ritual office (or any combination of these), and they are able to command some degree of loyalty, if only on ceremonial occasions or in brokering military alliances. Their role in ritual relationships is therefore called upon to dampen resentments and stifle competition in the cause of the general good (*sarvabhūtahita*?). With co-operation, it is felt, the fruits of exploitation may be adequate to please everybody.

Leaders can engage in activities calculated to magnify their fame, particularly the sponsoring of lavish ceremonial gatherings and the organization of labour for symbolic monumental construction. P. J. Wilson has stressed that, in organizing labour for such community activities, a chief is adding value to the labour by organizing it so as to gain a community benefit (such as the refertilization of the Earth by the performance of *śrauta* sacrifices) that could not otherwise be obtained; the construction of tombs in particular connects chiefly power with the presence of ancestors whose spiritual power thus comes to be available for the community.[32] 'Architecture,

[32] P. J. Wilson, *The Domestication of the Human Species* (Yale University Press, New Haven and London, 1989), pp. 90f., 133. For how this is applicable to the domesticated and socially evolved forms of Buddhism see G. Schopen, 'Burial *ad sanctos* and the physical presence of the Buddha in early Indian Buddhism: a study in the archeology of religions', *Religion*, 17 (1987), pp. 193–225 and P. Mus, *India Seen from the East* (Centre for South East Asian Studies, Clayton, Victoria, 1975).

especially funerary architecture, is ritual materialized and perfected.' Tombs are 'as near as mortals can get to incarnating absolute real power. Their building and existence testify to and legitimize the right of some people to be empowered by others so that they may assume all power, divine power.'[33]

Hand in hand with the construction of these monuments must have gone the centralized organization of labour mobilized for such construction projects. The bureaucracy required for the planning of the constructions and the organization of the labour force must have been considerable. This, as well as the actual structure itself, was clearly a symbol of the king's power, a symbol effective to anybody who lived in the general area of the respective cities.

All forms of display may be exploited to magnify the ritual centre, with increasingly grand ceremonies designed to manifest the spiritual energy thought to imbue it. Feasts require the levying of more produce from affiliated communities; co-operation in the management or subjugation of other cultural groups requires more complex processes of discussion and policy execution. In such ways the activities of a chief would bring about a centralization of manpower that was originally ritual but had the potential for political reorganization.

Such activities are important in giving a *raison d'être* to the office of ruler, whose superiority is given firm foundations in the material world by the support of armed bands capable of levying tribute from lesser client communities in return for protection, especially if they are well armed with the best weapons. New types of activity at the ceremonial centre attract groups of hired craftsmen and retainers, and increasing market activity with a substantially wider range of consumption goods. Thus, step by step, a qualitatively new and centralized form of political authority associated with a larger settlement comes into being. Such an authority promotes the production of trade goods by extracting and redistributing a surplus; trade and political authority evolve together, each feeding the other. In this way a state can grow by stealth, gradually creeping up on its constituent groups, even while they cherish their autonomy.

The emphasis placed here upon ritual centres is, however, intended to depict only the preliminary stages of state formation, not its mature development. The ritual repertoire which can be drawn upon for changing self-perceptions of the communities involved during the transition to a state belongs to the culture of the old society which lacked effective political centralization. By the time a state's rulers are in a position to organize

[33] Wilson, *Domestication*, p. 130.

an apparatus of government capable of calling forth surpluses, generating urban architecture, and stimulating crafts and sciences, the state begins to demonstrate a much more secular character. Indeed, in the current state of archaeological knowledge ritual principles are not conspicuous in the layout of early urban sites, and massive funerary monuments do not dominate them.[34] The best examples of town planning dominated by ritual came from much later, even medieval, times. The role of ritual in state formation may nevertheless be plausibly hypothesized for an *earlier* stage, in which chiefs still dwelled in village settlements, and the processes of political integration had yet to advance. In India it makes more sense to recognize the heyday of the large public ritual as a phase at the very beginning of the elevation of chiefs to rulers, a view that Hindu texts confirm. After about 500 BCE only the large kingship rituals continued to be performed with anything like a regular frequency. But in this early phase, religion reflects a state of society that is ripe for the growth of a higher-order political authority, but in which, if other conditions are lacking, it may not proceed to maturity. This phase of elaborate ritual and of enhanced claims for ksatriya eminence thus lies just before the rise of the state. The evidence of the late Vedic sources fits this scheme rather well, and although the Vedic literature is not a focus in this study, we shall shortly turn back briefly to notice its significance.

To the extent that the reality of the state's emergence is perceived by the exploiting culture in ritual terms, its legitimacy is cultural in the sense that it functions as a tool for communicating symbolically both to those at the centre of the culture and those on its fringes. This means there is no natural boundary, other than the boundary of the whole culture, defining the scope of a potential state. In India, emergent kings were automatically in competition with each other, for the *raison d'être* of each kingdom lay in the sense of cultural unity that linked the exploiting communities together. In practice the area of a state's rise was determined by the geography of competition. In the Ganges-Yamuna drainage area, the first steps towards state formation (unlike the later developments in Magadha and Kosala of the mid first millennium BCE) took place in upriver sites where a number of settlements enjoyed access to scattered iron deposits. However, if iron for weapons had anything to do with the story, no one part of the whole region was uniquely privileged.

[34] Certain men, especially holy men who had stepped outside the Vedic orthodoxy of the sacred fire and therefore could not be ritually cremated, were honoured by burial mounds, and this custom is clearly at work in the evolution of the mythology of the Buddha's funeral and the construction of *stūpas*.

Finally, it should be noted that the adequately successful integration of a number of communities into a proto-state is a process requiring a reorientation of world view. People draw upon the myths and rituals of common culture to represent to themselves the now more complex ordering of a changing world. But what when there is no common culture, or no culture perceived by those affected to be shared between them? Even if there are no alien communities in range at the beginning of the process, it is virtually inevitable that the activities of a growing state will encroach upon outlying communities unable to draw upon shared cultural motifs to allow the psychological transition to belonging in a larger society. From the point of view of the expanding state, these communities present a challenge to the state's own view of itself and the world. They may be seen as intrusive and potentially dangerous. No ritual manipulation of shared traditions is available to create an integrating framework. If alien cultures are to be absorbed within an expanding state, some quite different type of ideological scheme must come into play. As will appear in the second part of this book, this is where Buddhism had a particular role, while brahmanism served the needs of integration *within* the exploiting culture.

In the centuries surrounding the life of the Buddha the most convincing material evidence for this kind of process is found in the huge, possibly defensive, ramparts built around the earliest cities of northern India. The necessary construction activity could in some cases require the organized full-time labour of many thousands of men for months or years; it is on its own adequate evidence of the central direction of manpower and hence of the appearance of at least some degree of political centralization. The subject is therefore significant for the study of state formation in the Ganges valley.

The cities that grew in the north were generally characterized by perimeter constructions consisting of a wide moat and a rampart made from the moat excavation. Among the earliest ones, the largest was at Ujjain, which was sixty to seventy-five metres wide at its base, fourteen metres high, and more than five kilometres long.[35] It has been estimated that this rampart contains two million cubic metres of earth and probably required three and a half million man-days of work (or ten thousand men working for a year). This represents centralization of manpower on a huge scale, especially when we consider that the population of the city would not have been much more than 30,000.[36] The Kauśambī rampart I would have required the labour

[35] Erdosy, 'City states', p. 109 and 'Early historic cities', p. 7.

[36] Erdosy, 'Early historic cities', p. 7; cf. R. A. E. Coningham, 'Dark Age or continuum', in F. R. Allchin (ed.), *The Archaeology of Early Historic South Asia* (Cambridge University Press, Cambridge, 1995), pp. 67–71.

of 10,262 men for 150 days for its construction; Sisupalgarh's outer rampart needed 14,000 men for 150 days, Ujjain 34,666 men for 150 days.[37]

In the earlier centuries, ramparts had sloping sides (arguably not good against frontal attack); brick revetments reinforced them, and eventually brick walls made them more effective against assault. It may be a mistake to identify the earliest phase of rampart-building as defence construction.[38] Among the earlier fortified cities (about the sixth to fourth centuries), only Rājgir has a stone wall; others were of earth, only later topped by brick walls. It has been debated whether these ramparts made sense as military defences,[39] when they failed to offer vertical faces difficult to scale; some have argued that, on the other hand, they made little sense as flood protection since they often occur at sites on the inside of river bends, where flood danger is not great, but (especially in conjunction with the large moats created by their construction) made good perimeter defence lines.

Apart from the archaeological evidence pertaining to the development of particular cities implying a high degree of (probably) state organization, changes in ritual performances and the extent of warfare can be used as clues for helping us understand the development of the state in ancient India. The way of framing the social and political history of the first millennium BCE in India finds place for the elaboration of ritual religion in the period when political authority first began to be centralized, and for a religion based more strongly on ascetic practices and ideology in the period when states first expanded into hinterlands populated by sparse scattered communities lacking shared cultural traditions.

Here it is appropriate to look back at the ritualism of the phase when the state was in embryo. Initially the political authority was centred in Vedic chieftains, the ideological basis of their rule and their ritualization of the world by the medium of the *śrauta* sacrifice being the responsibility of brahmins. Some members of this group became ritual specialists and defined themselves as *ārya* in relation to other groups who existed outside of the ritual sphere or did not recognize the authority of the brahmins. The large-scale rituals, requiring up to eighteen priests for their performance, were usually paid for by wealthy warriors. They were lavish, spectacular affairs, easily capable of lending themselves to the practice of sumptuary

37 Coningham, 'Dark Age or continuum', pp. 67–71.

38 F. R. Allchin, 'City and state formation in early historic South Asia, I' *South Asian Studies*, 5 (1989), pp. 3f.; King, 'Some archaeological problems', p. 114.

39 Erdosy has discussed the problem of identifying the functions of the massive ramparts found round early city states, concluding that it is difficult to identify them confidently; he gives some weight to the possibility that they were symbolic structures, marking sacred space. See 'Early historic cities', p. 8.

display. Certainly the two main kingship rituals – the *rājasūya* and the *aśvamedha* – performed the instrumentalist function of legitimizing the king both within and without the territory he claimed to rule, but were also an opportunity to display his wealth. It was probably much easier to perform the latter in those cases where the territory to be covered was not too large, as the larger the territory the greater the cost of sending warriors to follow a horse wherever it went and the greater the likelihood of conflict with outlying groups. As for the other *śrauta* rituals we have only prescriptions for their performance, not descriptions of their actual conduct; hence we cannot assess their immediate effects on those who might have witnessed them.

Rituals celebrate the cultural motifs that different (potentially rival) groups have in common. Implicitly, they appeal to cultural unity as a way of avoiding excessive conflict, drawing boundaries and expressing claims in symbolic form. They represent aspirations when the reality is more elusive. The absence of any over-arching political authority capable of resolving conflict encourages the proliferation of ritual. The first stages in the rise of such an authority will make ritual all the more important as tensions increase; but as soon as central political authority is successfully established, this will diminish the social importance of rituals in the territory where it is effective.

Few though they are, there are in the *Brāhmaṇas* and the *Upaniṣads* various indications of the rising importance of chieftains who attracted the services of ritualists. Some stories in the *Upaniṣads* represent *kṣatriyas*, rulers, as patrons on a lavish scale, and deliberately exalt their wisdom, setting them even above the learned brahmins. For example, in *Bṛhadāraṇyaka Upaniṣad* 2.1.1, the learned brahmin Gārgya offered to teach Ajātaśatru, Lord of Kāśī (who offered a thousand cows in return), about the nature of Brahma. However, Gārgya's characterization of Brahma is entirely unsatisfactory, and Ajātaśatru turns out to know better.

> 'Let me come to you as your pupil,' said Gārgya. 'Let me come to you as a pupil.' Ajātaśatru replied, 'Isn't it a reversal of the norm for a Brahmin to become the pupil of a Kṣatriya, thinking, "He will tell me the formulation of truth (*brahman*)?" But I'll see to it that you perceive it clearly.'[40]

The same *Upaniṣad* sets the *kṣatra* estate above that of the brahmin: Brahma existed before all things, but, being alone, 'he further created a superior

[40] *BrhU.* 2.1.14–15. Trans. in P. Olivelle, *The Early Upanishads: annotated text and translation* (Oxford University Press, New York, 1998), p. 65.

form, the kṣatrahood'.[41] Such statements are not untypical. At many points the older *Upaniṣads* represent *kṣatriyas* not only as magnificent patrons with enormous wealth to bestow but also as repositories of wisdom.[42] The intent seems to have been to depict the brahmin and the *kṣatriya* in a symbiotic relationship, a view further developed, but also questioned, in the two epics. Buddhism also, in its turn, recognized a formula for the *varṇas* which elevated *kṣatriyas* above brahmins. That brahmins themselves should do this clearly reflects the rise of *rājans* as important sources of patronage and attests the birth of the state from the womb of ritual within a dominant exploiting culture.

> Janaka, Lord of Videha, once set out to perform a sacrifice at which he intended to give lavish gifts to the officiating priests. Brahmins from the Kuru and Pañcāla regions had flocked there for the occasion, and Janaka of Videha wanted to find out which of those Brahmins was the most learned in the Vedas. So he coralled a thousand cows; to the horns of each cow were tied ten pieces of gold.[43]

The ritual exaltation of the figure of the chieftain stems not just from the ambition of particular chieftains but from the needs of the people in the communities which were scarcely yet integrated. It reaffirms the relationship of hierarchy and function operative between them, as well as symbolically communicating their cosmology. The ritual exaltation will not, by itself, make a state come into being; but if the conditions such as those outlined above are present, this may happen.

Initially, the only valid reasons that can be recognized for accepting the increased authority of a leader are ritual ones. Yet as the case of the Ganges valley clearly shows, there is no natural equilibrium guaranteed under this system. If what begins as a ceremonial centre survives long enough in an economically strategic zone, it may become a big city and a royal capital. But in this case the new political authority will elicit new patterns of economic exploitation (creating incentives for technical advance and extracting an agricultural surplus, for example). Expansion from a hub of prosperity may make the old social boundaries, and the rituals which expressed them, obsolete. No sooner is the job of the brahmins at the ritual centre complete than they are marginalized, for the expanding state quickly acquires component elements that cannot be moulded by the brahmins' ritual technology.

41 *BrhU* 1.4.11. 42 *ChU* 1.8–9; 5.3.7; 5.11.4f.; *Kauśitakī Upanisad* 4.19.
43 *BrhU.* 3.1.1. Trans. Olivelle, *The Early Upanishads*, pp. 75, 77.

The population subject to the bearers of the dominant exploiting culture may soon come to comport a majority of aliens,[44] and from the ruler's point of view these are at least as important as the structure of the state. If expansion provides economic space for all groups, and indeed encourages it by means of securing communication and trade routes, society becomes more fluid, boundaries are relaxed and large-scale ritual becomes less important. In the India of the second half of the first millennium BCE the large *śrauta* sacrifices became less frequently performed, while from that same period to the present day cheap household rituals have continued as a framework whereby brahmins could bring about adaptation to new cultural conditions via a form of ritual homogenization.

In concluding this section we note two articles in which H. Kulke laid the groundwork for a theory of formation of political units in the late Vedic period.[45] On the basis of a selection of late Vedic texts detailing the *kāmyeṣṭi* rituals and the *rājasūya* ritual, he demonstrated an increasing process of social stratification between the *kṣatriyas* who became possessers of villages (*grāmins*) and the *viś* – incorporating relatives, slaves and depressed labouring groups – who fell under the subjugation of these new kinds of landlords. The brahmins emerged as the group who would legitimize this new social structure through the performance of rituals and, presumably, by the telling of mythic narratives which would rehearse this new social structure. Thus the *kṣatriyas* and brahmins become an elite in a newly stratifying society and stand against the *viś*. He sees proto-states developing in the following way:

> After having established himself as the uncontested chief of a village (*grāmpati* [sic], *grāmin*) and its *viś* population, he subdued several villages and their hinterland with its *jana* population thus becoming a *svarāja*, viz. a "self-ruler" or autocrat, of a *rāṣṭra* chiefdom. In the final stage of early state formation the chieftains (*rājā*) tried to subdue other rājās in order to become an overlord of these rājās (*rājñām adhirāja*). These different stages of early state formation can be, at least partly, recognized in the Vedic royal consecration rituals.[46]

Kulke's arguments are convincing and certainly provide signposts for further research, but in the final analysis do not detail the transition from a

[44] As was perhaps recognized by Bareau, 'Le Bouddha et les rois', p. 19: 'The Magadhans were undoubtedly aryanised at a more recent date and, therefore, more superficially than the Kośalans and the Kaśis. The autochtonous elements of the population were undoubtedly proportionally more numerous amongst them than they were amongst these other two peoples.'

[45] Kulke, 'RĀJASŪYA'; H. Kulke, 'Grāmakāma – "das verlangen nach einem Dorf". Überlegungen zum Beginn frühstaatlicher Entwicklung im vedischen Indien,' *Saeculum*, 42 (1991), pp. 111–28.

[46] Kulke, 'RĀJASŪYA', p. 190.

kṣatriya ruling over several villages and the emergence and growth of large states like Kośala and Magadha. In the present book these states are assumed. Indeed, the sources scarcely allow any detailed chronicling of the rise of these states; such a chronicling will not be attempted here.

WARFARE AND INSTABILITY IN THE EARLY INDIAN STATE

States began to grow at a number of places in the middle reaches of the Ganges, and although they were initially far enough apart to allow the process of state formation to advance to a certain extent, it was not until most of them had been subsequently subordinated by the most powerful (by the third century BCE, if not the fourth) that expansiveness and pluralism came to characterize court culture, a culture constantly alluded to in both the Canon and the two Sanskrit epics. But even these conditions were consistent with large-scale warfare, armies being sent campaigning far afield. Warfare was endemic, then as in later history. And whilst Buddhist sources cannot be treated as secure evidence for conditions at the time of the Buddha, they appear to reflect a period of multi-state competition before the Mauryan ascendancy.[47] They attest that war or preparations for war were a normal part of life.[48] After the Mauryas, we have testimony from the *Jātakas* to chronic instability, punctuated by war uprisings and pillaging in border areas.[49]

The scale of war, given the centralized control of manpower and organization, probably promoted enormous disruption to normal life, though this can only be inferred from the literary sources. We cannot, however, ignore the much-quoted inscription where Aśoka laments the enormous slaughter entailed by his conquest of Kalinga, after which he claims to have abjured conquest by arms.[50] Aśoka's figures are of course conventional hyperbole, but the scale and complexity of warfare in its impact on society are reflected by the growing elaboration of military weaponry, strategy, tactics, logistics and commissariat. Armies contain elephant riders, cavalry, charioteers, archers, standard bearers, billeting officers, supply corps and others including perhaps specially detailed disposers of corpses and camp

[47] Cf. Bareau, 'Le Buddha et les rois', p. 19: 'The memory of the struggles between the Kośalans and the Kāśis therefore remained alive, but in the time of the Buddha the second had, at all appearances, been definitively defeated and conquered by the first.'

[48] *M* III 7f.; *D* II 86. [49] Eg. *J* II 217; I 409, 437; II 74. See also Fick, *Soziale Gliederung*, pp. 69ff.

[50] Rock Edict XIII; and see J. Bloch, *Les Inscriptions d'Aśoka, traduites et commentées* (Société d'édition 'Les belles Lettres', Paris, 1950), p. 150. According to this inscription 150,000 people were displaced, over 100,000 were killed on the battlefield, and many more died as a result of war.

followers.[51] The importance of warfare as a normal department of kingly activity is made conspicuous in the *AŚ*, where it occupies a substantial part of the content of the work.[52]

What calls for attention here is the striking fact, demanding some sort of explanation, that warfare was embedded in Indian culture as a natural condition of life. To be a king was to be a *kṣatriya*. *Kṣatriyas*, like other *varṇas*, were theoretically a hereditary class, but reality was accommodated by certain śāstric texts which acknowledged that, 'When one who is a non-*kṣatriya* does the work of a *kṣatriya*, he should do all this [that is prescribed for a king], in view of the principle that by taking on the function of a particular person or thing one receives the *dharma* of the other.'[53] The Nandas were technically supposed to have been śūdras, and the Śunga dynasty which firmly supplanted the Mauryas was founded by a brahmin. In later times, dynasties founded by people recognized as śūdras cropped up more often than the theory of the *varṇa*s would lead one to think.[54] As is clear enough, the recognition of dynasties of non-*kṣatriya* origin as having *kṣatriya* status typically reflects the acceptance of realities of power created by the rise of rebels or bandit leaders, over any inherited social conditions.

To discover the ultimate reasons why India should have experienced such a high degree of disruption and militarization would require a major study of a type which cannot be undertaken here. It is likely that part of the explanation lies in India's openness to invasion through the passes of the northwest. Here, over the centuries, wave after wave of aggressive aliens pressed in. Their incursions set up ripple effects which destabilized power balances and provoked conflict over much of India. Endemic warfare was built into the institutions of Indian society from a very early period and is alluded to often in both Hindu and Buddhist sources as well as being discussed in a theoretical sense in the *AŚ*. The *AŚ* may look like an exercise in outrageous cynicism, but it takes its place in its own context as a practical manual of politics. Renaissance Italy was torn apart politically in much the same way: no enduring internal empire could develop to the point of paramount power, presiding over a stable arena of states, because Italy was made the plaything of great-power ambitions. It is no coincidence

51 See Wagle, *Society*, pp. 143ff.

52 The *AŚ* contains fourteen substantial books, of which numbers 7, 9, 10, 12, 13 and 14, plus part of 8, are devoted to warfare.

53 Aparārka on *Yājñavalkyasmṛti* 1.366. Similarly, Medhātithi, commenting much later on *Manusmṛti*, 4.84, declared that whoever performs the function of king should be called a king. Cited by R. Bajpai, *Society in the 7th Century* (Chand, Delhi, 1992), p. 19, n. 190.

54 Numerous examples are given in Bajpai, *Society*.

that Machiavelli, the Italian Kautilya, arose to map out a similar science of statecraft.

It is easy to see how this chronic instability may have affected the way Indian politics evolved, inhibiting the development of stable cultural units within which political centres could preside over other emerging centres of power. People recognize themselves as part of an encompassing community if over time that community maintains a stable unity underwritten by institutions of language, belief and economic interaction. The growth of such a community consciousness requires a recognized dominant set of traditions embodied in an elite which can be emulated by the rest of the population. In the long run intermarriage and changes of custom, with the adoption of common language, origin myths, legends, rituals and belief systems, will promote homogenization around the culture of this elite. The consolidation of the dominance of an elite in its earlier stages requires to be supported by enduring political power, because the development of a large-scale political unit requires a stable political centre.

But political centres were not stable. Even where the name of a dynasty was perpetuated for many generations, in-fighting at court and simmering conflict around the frontiers thwarted the evolution of a large-scale empire within any very large territorial unit. Clients of great men were liable to dispossession when their masters foundered, and dominant elite strata were constantly liable to lose political eminence. It is likely, therefore, that the power centres around which large homogeneous communities might have grown did not last long enough.

In these circumstances, it is perhaps not surprising if the class of brahmins came to play, in some respects, the role which a politically dominant elite could not, and in Indian history this role became institutionalized to such an extent that it acquired its own momentum. Society was permanently atomized, each local *varga* functioning as a miniature 'state' and looking for protection to whatever lord in the vicinity might be able to afford temporary protection. Meanwhile, the crystallization of cultural identity, lacking any enduring focus of political power, came to be centred upon the ritual and cultural elite – the brahmins, who had always been the mediators of high culture.[55] Political and ritual hierarchies came to be awkwardly conflated; people adapted cultural identities for themselves in

[55] R. Kahane, 'Priesthood and social change: the case of the brahmins', *Religion*, 11 (1981), pp. 353–66, argues that the religious values of the brahmins gave them their social role: 'In a highly diversified society, such as that of India, in which groups are institutionally separated from one another, a special mechanism is required to unify them. Since it is likely that the "this-worldly" values will be different for each group, it is the "other-worldly" transcendent values which can unite the entire collective.'

the world by using a map supplied by brāhmaṇical lore or tribal lore, not by a centralizing political force. Notions of ritual hierarchy, based on the axis of purity and pollution, were forcibly superimposed upon notions of place in the local power structure. Brāhmaṇical religion, with its infusion of devotional practices, aligned with the world view of insecure and highly self-conscious groups, in a situation which favoured the entrenchment of religious traditions appealing to personal gods and focused on ritual.

L. Dumont has described the abstract structure of this social order for us in his classic study;[56] what has been lacking is an explanation of the concrete historical circumstances through which such an order first acquired its *raison d'être*, so unlike that of other agrarian social orders, and its massive authority which has given it a longevity greater than any raj. Of course the suggestions just advanced here necessarily raise more questions than they answer, but they may help point us in the right direction.

These observations have a direct relevance to the subject of the Buddha's social role. In its early social forms, Buddhist teachers were offering an ascetic message during a period of expansion characterized by interaction between encroaching state power and local communities who could not recognize themselves as in any sense 'Aryan' and were unable to assimilate themselves easily to the encroaching culture. This sort of interaction was a transient phenomenon of the relationship between expanding states and the fringes of Ārya civilization. The brāhmaṇical social order, on the other hand, was fed by an opposite situation: paradoxically, it derived its considerable stability and longevity from the constantly fractured unity of a political order bred of endemic warfare. The brahmins were the ritual specialists who were needed to provide a cosmology for the self-perceptions of ill-integrated groups who recognized themselves as culturally Aryan in some sense but were unable to find definition within a secure and durable political community. Thus the caste system, in its classical form, was bred of instability, of the enduring tension between aspiring large-scale political structures and small face-to-face communities.[57] In the long run, fracturing and political realignment were more characteristic of Indian history than the expansion of unitary states, and the schizoid politico-ritual social order of the brahmins was destined to prevail.

56 L. Dumont, *Homo Hierarchicus* (Paladin, London, 1966).

57 A tension of this kind is identified as a factor of the caste system by Declan Quigley: 'The common structure underlying caste systems is rather to be found in constraints given by kinship on the one hand and kingship on the other, both of which are set against a particular material backdrop which allows a territorially limited kind of centralization to develop.' 'Is a theory of caste still possible?', in M. Searle-Chatterjee and U. Sharma (eds), *Contextualising Caste: post-Dumontian approaches* (Blackwell, Oxford and *Sociological Review*, Cambridge, Mass., 1994), p. 42.

The kind of teachings offered by the Buddha to kings is clearly independent of any class considerations in the way it is presented to us in the texts. This must be regarded as its principal claim to neutrality. A teaching on diligence (*appamāda*) taken from the *Samyatta Nikāya* is illustrative. The Buddha is depicted in discourse with King Pasenadi of Kosala and reproduces a teaching the Buddha made to Ānanda, where the former says,

> In truth the whole of this life of celibacy consists of friendship with auspicious people, association with auspicious people and intimacy with auspicious people. Of that monk who is a friend of auspicious people, who is an associate of auspicious people and who is an intimate of auspicious people, there will be the cultivation of the noble eight-limbed path, there will be an enlarged exposition of the noble eight-limbed path.[58]

But this is inappropriate for a king and so the Buddha recommends the cultivation of the three forms of association with the auspicious person and recommends this be applied in respect of *appamāda*. He says, 'You must live on one single basis: diligence in respect of all good things'.[59] This will, the Buddha says, bring praise from the court ladies, his warrior dependants, his army, and those who live in towns and the countryside, all of whom will say, 'This diligent king lives basing himself on diligence' (*S* I 89), with the final result that he himself, the house of his women, his treasury and storehouses will be guarded and protected. The generality of this teaching gives it universal value and enables it to be translated into various levels to accommodate people of various levels of economic development and access to political power.

[58] *S* I 87–8. [59] *S* I 89 *eko dhammo upanissaya vihātabbo apamādo kusalesu dhammesu.*

5

Brahmins and other competitors

In some senses, no doubt, Buddhism is a coherent and self-contained object of study; but for historical purposes it is essential to place it within a context supplied by brahmanism. The two are not totally independent entities; they belong together, in a complex and ambivalent relationship, as aspects of Sanskrit civilization. It is misleading to create the impression of a monolithic civilization centred on the use of the Sanskrit language, though it remains respectable to argue for the centrality of values expressed most prominently in Sanskrit literature as providing a kind of filter through which cultural motifs passed to constitute the repertoire of the Great Tradition. Possibly this notion of core culture as a compilation is unduly influenced by the analogy of the case of the *Mahābhārata*, which grew by accumulation; but if so we must still ask what role the urban state played in the nurturing both of Sanskritic values and of intellectual movements that reacted against them.

It is within this framework that we can legitimately see in the teaching of *śramaṇas* like the Buddha a systematic critique of the brāhmaṇical programme. The brahmin goal of penetration to sacred truth by spiritual cultivation was heartily commended, but the perceived exclusivism and moral bankruptcy of worldly brahmins, clinging to ritual formulae to justify themselves, was rejected; and this rejection was a means of appealing to all those in society who had their own reasons for resisting the claims of brahmins to have a monopoly on access to sacred power or the means of religious legitimation of secular power.

It is a truism, familiar in the anthropology of Buddhist societies in modern times, that ordinary villagers do not understand the inwardness of the nirvāṇa and the *anātmān* doctrines and do not bother themselves with them, however important they may be in some philosophical sense. Southwold, studying village Buddhism in Sri Lanka, observed that only the middle classes had any real attitude towards nirvāṇa, namely, an attitude of repugnance; as far as villagers are concerned, nirvāṇa is very remote and irrelevant. 'We might perhaps say that village Buddhists are protected from not wanting Nirvana by being taught that they are in no danger of getting it.'[1] Spiro, studying Burma, writes: 'Although almost every villager whom I interviewed had learned about anatta, less than two percent knew the meaning of this term.'[2]

It therefore becomes a puzzle how such doctrines can have had sufficient popular appeal to gain the support they did. The puzzle disappears when we visualize a zone – the north-east of India, with its frontier society and ambitious city-based rulers – in which a form of ideological underpinning specifically bound to the unique claims of Vedic myth was likely to seem counter-productive in any kingdom where multiple races, languages and traditions, mutually alien until yesterday, had to be welded into one. As Collins observes about the 'non-self' concept, the negative Buddhist teaching 'preserves the identity and integrity of Buddhism as an Indian system separate from brahminism'.[3] Thus a metaphysical point serves to introduce our discussion of the relationship between Buddhism and the brāhmaṇical orthodoxy; the Buddha was not a student of the Vedic scriptures, but he knew enough about brāhmaṇical teachings to construct a system that in many ways was the opposite of them.

The common view of the status of the brahmin in its Buddhist depiction in the Pāli Canon has been predicated on the oppositional relationship between the Buddha and the brahmins. This reflects a view that both were competitors for souls, and that the principal form of attack on the Buddha's part was to question strongly the social pretensions of the brahmins and the metaphysical claims they adduced in support of their status.[4] If the relationship really was an oppositional one we need to explore, with much more sensitivity than has hitherto been applied, the actual dynamics of this opposition, whether it was regarded as being oppositional by both sides and, as a corollary of this, why both groups revealed a need to market themselves in an aggressive manner, if, indeed, this is the correct way to characterize this aspect of their activity. By marketing we understand the deliberate application of a panoply of techniques to parade, in an intentionally persuasive manner, the ideology each group claimed to embody and its corresponding lifestyle. If this really was marketing, and implied a backdrop of competition such as we in the contemporary West associate directly

[1] M. Southwold, *Buddhism in Life: the anthropological study of religion and the Sinhalese practice of Buddhism* (Manchester University Press, Manchester, 1983), p. 203.
[2] M. Spiro, 'Buddhism and economic action in Burma', *American Anthropologist*, 68 (1966), p. 1163.
[3] Collins, *Selfless Persons*, p. 183.
[4] For an axiomatic statement of this opposition see Chakravarti, *Social Dimensions*, p. 42.

with the whole culture surrounding marketing, was it really a question of gaining and applying a form of power, capable of influencing deep values and of shaping cultures, that was in play here? Was it seen as something that could slip from the hands of its possessors into those of another group adjudged as manifesting 'religious status' of a kind conducive to mobilizing economic or other resources? Why did either group want status if it was not for economic or political reasons? Can we conceive of other reasons in the ancient Indian historical milieu which would explain a desire for power?

Scholarly opinion on this subject is further predicated upon the high-status position of the brahmins in relation to the Buddha and other monks who were marked as existing in (a) another space outside of the social structure circumscribed by the brahmins, or (b) in the *khattiya* class and therefore located within the former social structure. The first of these is usually held to embrace the position of the *samaṇa*, often regarded as the appropriate opposition in a conceptual space occupied by those social categories most clearly defined by a particular mode of practising religion and making it the centre of all values. It includes a ragbag of non-brāhmaṇical ascetics. However, to restrict oneself only to this aspect of the question means that one narrow referent is being retrospectively allowed to define the activities of these classes, even when their socio-cultural functions were probably much wider. Defining them only, or even substantially, in religious terms will result in a neglect or concealment of other aspects of their positioning within society and culture.

All the questions associated with the oppositional relationship between the Buddha and the brahmins need to be reformulated in another way to take into account the massive success both groups achieved in their capacity to flourish on Indian soil. We should ask whether in their portrayal in the Pāli Canon both groups emerge as direct products of their culture or were simply passengers mirroring and confirming the dominant trends of their time in such a way as not to threaten these, but to accommodate themselves to ever changing conditions. It is, of course, exceedingly difficult to expect any kind of precise answer to these questions from the narratives the texts make available to us. Above all they do have as a basic frame a context of antagonism and repeat this ad infinitum, always muting the antagonism between the Buddha and a given brahmin by also locating it within a conversion frame. Moreover, the manifestations of the success of the respective religions are surely as different as the different positions their representatives have always held in Indian society. The brahmins have as much a social significance as they do a religious significance, and they cannot be defined exclusively in terms of either. Their ability to act as the cultural vanguard of the socio-economic and religious system which has long guaranteed them a place at the pinnacle of society, and which has ensured their survival as the embodiment of that particular image in Indian society which other groups sought to emulate or trenchantly criticize, is the most evident sign of their success. Witzel has shown on the evidence of late Vedic literature that the eastern kings recognized the status of the brahmins and imported them to their own kingdoms, perhaps as a sign of status. *'It is important to note that the eastern "kings", both of Kosala and of Videha, adopt western schools as their new Vedic śākhās,* and not the central North Indian (Taittirīya, Śāṭyāyani-Jaiminīya, Kauṣītaki).'[5]

An initial signpost for the study of the portrayal of the brahmins in early Buddhist literature is provided in an important article by R. Tsuchida. He takes much more seriously than hitherto the need to define the brahmin simply as a religious specialist. He writes:

> In a number of modern publications on early Buddhism the Buddha's antagonism toward or disrespect for the Brahmanical tradition is simply taken for granted, as if in the Buddha's mind that tradition amounted to little more than mere rubbish to be discarded by his followers. Such an assumption derives mostly from a partial and inadequate comprehension of the Brahminhood, in which one mere aspect of it is regarded as representative of the whole. For example, the practice of the animal sacrifice seems to have acquired such a preponderance in the minds of many scholars, when they speak about the Brahmanical tradition in relation to the Buddha's teaching, that they fail to pay enough attention to several other aspects of Brahmanical religion at the time of the rise of Buddhism . . . In reality, the practice of śrauta-sacrifices including animal rites, was by no means obligatory for every socially important brahmin.[6]

It is true that the killing of animals in the *śrauta* sacrifices is widely condemned in parts of the *Suttanipāta* and the *Jātakas*, leading D. D. Kosambi to speculate whether this was because of the Buddha's fear about the amount of livestock habitually wasted in this practice. It is equally true that the oblations offered in many rituals mentioned in Buddhist texts were vegetable offerings. But even these correctives are mere trifles. It is the presumption that the basis of the difference between the two had to be substantially a religious one that lies at the heart of our concern.

5 See Witzel, 'The development of the Vedic canon and its schools: the social and political milieu', in M. Witzel (ed.), *Inside the Texts. Beyond the Texts* (Harvard Oriental Series, Opera Minora 2, Cambridge, Mass., 1997), p. 312, Cf. p. 313: 'In line with Sanskritization as a means of raising the status of local chiefs, the extensive materials in the late Vedic eastern texts regarding the "coronation" (*abhiṣeka*) of kings (AB 8.5) must be considered.'

6 R. Tsuchida, 'Two categories of brahmins', pp. 51–2.

At the same time it is equally true that in many Buddhist texts the interaction of the Buddha with prominent brahmins forms the subject of a large quantity of *suttas*. This is especially marked in the second and third volumes of the *Majjhima Nikāya* and also in the first volume of the *Dīgha Nikāya*.[7] Not only do these texts contain considerable material about doctrine, the refutation of false views, descriptions of meditational states and guidance leading towards the achievement of mindfulness, they also contain much material that can be mined for sociological purposes. In this sociological material the dominant emerging theme is the jostling for status between brahmins and Buddhists on the one hand and between the Buddha and other groups on the other hand. This should not necessarily be taken as antagonism. But it is competition. We do not find significant tension expressed in the texts between the Buddhists and other classes classified, by whatever means, as lower than the brahmin. This is clearly noteworthy in placing some meat on the thesis that Buddhism was primarily a movement of elites, but equally it may be a consequence of the fact that only the historical memories of those who had control of literacy and textual transmission survived.

Frequently in the Buddhist canonical literature, the terms *brāhmaṇa* and *śramaṇa* occur as a compound, *brāhmaṇaśramaṇa*, making it clear that the two categories belonged naturally together.[8] We have seen elsewhere that Buddhist monks were often designated with the Pāli equivalent *samaṇa*. The pairing occurs in Aśokan inscriptions.[9] Commonly in the Pāli texts the use of the compound suggests that the two categories together form a homogeneous class for the purpose of some generalizations, so that the sense could be something like 'experts in sacred knowledge'. There is some evidence that the life of the *śramaṇa* was originally sometimes thought to be appropriate only for brahmins, and the compound *śramaṇabrāhmaṇa* could on occasion mean 'a *brāhmaṇa* who is a *śramaṇa*'; but equally the frequent criticism of brahmins and the constant opposition announced between the lives and values of brahmins and the teaching of the Buddha make it clear that the relationship was also thought of as an opposition. That this

7 Once again this raises the problem of how narrow it is to study Buddhism simply on the basis of the figure of the Buddha alone. It is a truism to say that he lies at the centre of most Buddhist narratives, but this means we may simply end up with a study of how certain elite figures competed with each other to achieve superiority in certain areas of life.

8 See V. Fausbøll, *Sutta Nipāta* (Sacred Books of the East, Oxford, 1881), vol. x, p. xii, which contains a list of places where the two are mentioned together. See also *Sn.* p. 15 prose; p. 19 vs. 110; p. 22 vs. 129–30; p. 32 prose; p. 33 vs. 191–2; p. 48 prose, p. 76 vs. 443; p. 91 prose, etc.; *DhP* (P.T.S. edn) p. 21 lists together *brāhmaṇo, samaṇo* and *bhikkhu*.

9 At many places in the Rock Edicts (e.g. Girnar R. E. XIII line 3) Aśoka preaches respect for *brāhmaṇas* and *śramaṇas*. See also Collins, *Selfless Persons*, p. 270, n. 7.

was not just a Buddhist prejudice is apparent from Patañjali's treatment of the compound *brāhmaṇaśramaṇa* as an example of an oppositional *dvandva* compound.[10]

THE QUESTION OF THE BRAHMIN'S ELITE STATUS

To understand the source of the brahmins' prestige and power even in the Buddha's time, we can go no further than Milner's highly incisive perception that:

> Their [the brahmins'] genius, though, was to avoid making the control of land and labour, or the control of force – the two are intimately related in agrarian societies – the primary basis of their power. These resources are the most alienable and easily appropriated by outside conquerors or upstart discontents, and in India's long and complex history frequently were; in contrast, a highly elaborate lifestyle, emphasizing ritual purity, among other things, was nearly impossible for outsiders to copy or appropriate.
>
> The Brahmins had another genius: they rejected the notion that ritual purity required renunciation and lifelong otherworldliness.[11]

This position is both highly problematic and suggestive at the same time. If we take into consideration the evidence derived from the Pāli sources it is clear many brahmins were attached in a very real sense to material possessions in their capacity as property owners. In his study of eleven brahmins who figure prominently in certain Pāli texts Tsuchida shows convincingly that such figures were well known as landowners and farmers. Of course, this was not the whole story, nor was it the only source of their prestige in society:

> . . . the group of wealthy Brahmin-householders (lists 1–2) and that of eminent scholars of the three Vedas (list 3), although not quite identical, overlap to a considerable extent. This fact indicates the existence of a special class of Vedic masters living as Brahmin-landlords, who exerted great influence over the society both as cultural authorities and as agents of economic power. It is precisely this class of affluent Vedic masters to which most of the important Brahmin-figures in the canonical narratives seem to belong.[12]

10 *Mahābhāṣya*, II 4 9 (ed. F. Kielhorn, 1880, vol. 1, p. 476 line 9). The *dvandva* compound *śramaṇabrāhmaṇa* appears as an example of *virodha*.

11 Milner, *Status and Sacredness*, pp. 68–9.

12 Tsuchida, 'Two categories of brahmins', p. 65. Much earlier Fick, *Soziale Gliederung*, ch.viii had documented the presence of brahmin farmers in the *Jātakas*. Though later than the Canon the evidence presented by Fick corresponds in some measure to the existence of similar data in the *Dharmasūtras*. See E. Ritschl, 'Brahmanische Bauern. Zur Theorie und Praxis der brahmanischen Ständeordnung im alten Indien', *Altorientalische Forschungen*, 7 (1980), pp. 177–87.

If this makes Milner's position somewhat problematic, other evidence in the Canon supports the general thrust of his view. Most of the brahmins who are given anything like a biographical treatment are portrayed as figures attracting social prestige not through their property holdings, but because they are skilled in Vedic knowledge. Perhaps even more important, they are capable of rehearsing constantly, and in a convincing manner, those arguments used everywhere to place the brahmin at the centre of society and culture. Nowhere do the brahmins make anything out of the materiality of their wealth, although they do receive criticism from the Buddhists on this account. What they are depicted parading is their learning. Of course, given the strength of renunciation and its associated values as a standard against which all other forms of behaviour could be tested, there is a degree of perceptible ambivalence about this. Brahmins were having it both ways in the image projected of them: as property owners and as learned religious specialists. As we will see, and has been noted many times, this was their Achilles heel exploited by the Buddha and others of his contemporaries.

The brahmin is the most prestigious non-Buddhist figure in the Pāli Canon and this elite status is both religious and economic. The term *mahāsālā*, used to designate a person possessing wealth in land, money, food and good appearance, is employed specifically to qualify the brahmin as well as the *khattiya* and the *gahapati*.[13] There is evidence that brahmins were often enlisted as royal functionaries early on in the development of states; there were semi-autonomous brahmin settlements with wealth and power, and brahmins increasingly figured as officials engaged in administrative work. No doubt the canons of the high brāhmaṇical tradition stood for a more ancient set of ideals, according to which city life was polluting, and texts such as the *Baudhāyana Dharmasūtra* disapproved of brahmins being contaminated by urban occupations or serving the king;[14] but the very fact that royal service was condemned is the best evidence that it was happening.

Brahmanical texts may have disparaged urban culture, but it was also a period when, as Buddhist sources richly attest, according to current perceptions many people identifying themselves as brahmins were supporting themselves not by religious practice but by employment in all manner of secular occupations. This practice never disqualified them from being brahmins, however, as long as, in subsequent centuries, they observed the correct procedures of ritual purity and impurity. The *Sn* portrays brahmins

[13] Cf. Tsuchida, 'Two categories of brahmins', pp. 60–1. See also *S* I 74, *D* I 136–7.

[14] See Thapar, *From Lineage to State*, p. 88.

living by various crafts. The *Jātakas* (which of course may speak for perceptions belonging to a later time than is targeted here) frequently enough represent brahmins engaged in all sorts of employment, sometimes quite lowly. Sometimes they bring to their trade the sort of skill that men of sacred power might have been expected to possess; for example, brahmin snake charmers (*ahiguṇṭhika*) tame snakes with herbs and incantations.[15] This may also be seen in a more abstract sense in the power brahmins can develop when they accumulate large amounts of *tapas*. Examples are legion in the epics and *Purāṇas* and complete the multi-faceted image of the brahmin developing in Buddhist times as a figure who was a man of learning as well as a caster of spells and a reader of horoscopes, as the *Brahmajālasutta* tells us in such great detail.[16] Some brahmins engage in trade and in many cases become rich, while others follow despised callings like hunting. Such secular brahmins, though they might (as nowadays) be technically qualified by their brahmin birth to officiate at rituals, had frequently lost touch with the sacred techniques and knowledge pertaining to their lineage; the *Somadatta Jātaka* refers to a brahmin farmer unable to remember or repeat a verse of scripture properly.[17] But none of this vitiates the image they have continued to have to the present day of being learned, wedded to an ideal lifestyle of renunciation, and role models for all other *jātis* to follow.

What we do not know about the brahmins is how much their economic status also flowed over into, or derived from, a more general cultural status such that they became role models for other groups within the society in areas of life other than the specifically religious. Such a question is difficult to answer because the brahmins appear to have operated in a range of networks, interdependencies and status positions. Was it this capacity to act opportunistically and in several different areas at once that caused the Buddha to have such an animus against certain brahmins? Increasingly there appears to have been a tension between the old idea of brahmins as specialists in sacred lore, associated pre-eminently with the ritual of sacrifice, and the newer reality of brahmins as primarily secular figures. As time wore on, they often had little but a retreating ancestry of sacred function to give them any claim to special status. In these circumstances the rise of the ascetics posed a serious challenge to the standing of brahmins in the community. The brahmin response was to incorporate asceticism within the brahmin ideology, ritualizing it in the process.

15 Fick, *Soziale Gliederung*, p. 237 cites *J* IV 457.

16 Fick, *Soziale Gliederung*, 159–61. 17 Ibid., 249ff.

It is likely the Buddha may have actually encountered the brahmins as an expanding group in the geographical areas with which he was most familiar. The innovation of granting whole villages to brahmins under the form of *brahmadeyya* may have been especially widespread in the Magadha and Kosala regions.[18] As Thapar says, of the northeastern kingdoms: 'The association of land with brahmins becomes more common at this time, and it is probable that in the process of establishing kingdoms those who performed the legitimizing rituals for the new kings may well have been given grants of land.'[19] In the *Nikāyas* occur references to land grants made by kings to brahmins.[20] The term *brahmadeyyo*, used in Pāli to denote such grants, does not necessarily indicate an outright gift of land, but may mean (as the later epigraphic sources clearly enough show for land grants in general) that various rights including at least a part of royal revenue went to the beneficiaries with the land granted. The element *brahma-* does not have to mean that the gift is for brahmins, and it is not obvious that these grants carried full civil and judicial powers with them. It is not clear what was the nature of the relationship of brahmins to the land in the so-called brahmin villages; the expression could have meant that brahmins owned or controlled the land, or simply that they were numerous or powerful.[21] This apparent economic wealth, substantially underplayed by their claims to function intrinsically as religious specialists, and their capacity to extend in an authoritative manner over an ever expanding geographical area, along with their proclivity to exhibit an ostentatious lifestyle, would have marked them out as targets either for attraction or repulsion. Hence the Buddha's focus on brahmins to the apparent neglect of other classes in society.

There is a fundamental problem here, but it is one that requires us to read back to early Buddhism on the basis of data derived from later sources. This problem becomes apparent when we study the social stratification of donors as reflected in inscriptions between the second century BCE and the fourth century ACE. As Thapar tells us, continuing conclusions drawn from other scholars:

> Examples of this category of patronage become evident during the period from the second century BC to the fourth century AD in the patronage extended to the building of *stūpas* such as those at Sanchi, Bharhut and Amaravati and the rock cut caves of the Western Deccan, all of which had at source donations to

[18] Wagle, *Society*, pp. 18–19. [19] Thapar, *From Lineage to State*, p. 88.

[20] *D* I 87, where land is granted by King Pasenadi to a brahman, land which is 'in the king's gift (*rājabhoggaṃ*). . . . a gift of the king (*rājadāyaṃ*), worthy to be given to a brahmin (*brahmadeyyaṃ*). Cf. *D* I 111; 127 and 224, where similar terms are used of other prosperous estates enjoyed by brahmins.

[21] Gokhale, 'Early Buddhism', p. 17.

the Buddhist *saṅgha*. The donations came substantially from artisans, guilds of craftsmen, traders, monks and nuns, small-scale landowners and to a lesser extent from royalty and families in high political and administrative office.[22]

Apart from *stūpa* construction which was sponsored financially by kings and royalty, the financing of other smaller monumental structures was largely in the hands of all the non-elite classes. This seems universally to be so judging from the inscriptions. Yet these classes are not mentioned much, except in passing, in the Pāli texts. Of course, to be fully convincing the argument would have to draw on the basis of comparative counts of the occurrence of the respective groups in literature and inscriptions. Then and only then could a more sensible comparison be drawn.[23] It is likely to be the case that we are really dealing with two different historical periods, one where Buddhism – still in its incipient stage – has to impress its principal competitors in claims to a universal vision, the other – a later stage – when it was firmly anchored in Indian soil and had extended its base of material support across the entirety of society, measured in occupations and religious proclivities.

THE IMAGE OF THE BRAHMIN IN EARLY BUDDHIST LITERATURE

The renunciant ideal associated with *saṃnyāsa* began in the brahmin tradition perhaps about the fifth century BCE.[24] Buddhist canonical sources refer to ascetic brahmins who have fully embraced the principles of rigorous austerity; the Jaṭila ascetics wear animal skins and have matted hair. They do not beg for alms but live on gleanings; brahmin ascetics also maintain Vedic traditions, teach pupils, and perform sacrifices. As Tsuchida has argued, we should distinguish between true wandering ascetics and the brahmins

[22] R. Thapar, 'Patronage and Community', in B. Stoler Miller (ed.), *The Powers of Art. Patronage in Indian Culture* (Oxford University Press, Delhi, 1992), p. 22. A fuller treatment is given in the same book by V. Dehejia, 'Collective and Popular Basis', pp. 35–45.

[23] Using data based on 2,426 men and women mentioned in both sets of texts, Sarao (*Origin and Nature*, p. 69) has shown that of the 1,371 people who can be identified by *varṇa*, 51.50% (706) are *khattiyas*, 29.18% (400) are *brāhmaṇas*, 11.30% (155) are low caste and 8.02% (110) are *vessa*. In addition, a much cited study by Gokhale ('The Early Buddhist Elite') replicates the general tenor of these figures, but only on the basis of a much more restricted source, the *Thera-* and *Therīgāthās*. Do these statistics help us read as social texts the manifestly ambivalent messages the rich narratives in *M* convey to us? There is no one-to-one correlation between frequency of meeting with members of a particular class and the attitude the Buddha manifests towards them. This would be simplistic in the extreme, even in literary constructions, and, furthermore, we should never assume that the caste grouping was monolithic in any sense other than the adoption of the caste reference as a source of identity itself.

[24] See Olivelle, *Saṃnyāsa Upaniṣads*, p. 52.

who, by contrast, lived in *āśramas*, performed sacrifices, took fees and kept wives.[25] Some brahmin renouncers, perhaps, cut themselves off completely from society in the way that the thoroughgoing *śramaṇa* ideal demands; but to the extent that renunciation became institutionalized, it was doubtless quickly ritualized and modified. Olivelle says: 'The image of a renouncer totally divorced from and unconcerned about ordinary people and about his relatives is purely a theological (and perhaps scholarly) figment.'[26] In later centuries, life in a woodland hermitage became a subject for detailed prescription in the *smṛtis* and *śāstras*, with rules about diet, clothing and so forth, and the absence of outward ritual performance proper to brāhmaṇical rule was reinterpreted as an internalization of ritual within the self, with the body being seen as the sacrificial altar.[27] Yet the life of the renouncer is supposed to be the very antithesis of established ritual, a rejection of worldly concerns and of constraints imposed from outside the self. This process of domestication shows how different images of religious life, even when they can well be represented as mutually contradictory, may slide one into another; just as folk, public and ascetic Buddhisms were superimposed upon one another and often believed in by contemporaries as a single truth, so in brāhmaṇical tradition the ritual and renunciant traditions could be perceived as aspects of a single system.

The Canon was ready to twin brahmins with *śramaṇas* as holy men deserving of respect. In portions of the Canon which may be the oldest, the verse *gāthās*, the term 'brahmin' occurs in application to the sage or the ascetic with perfected virtues, but the later prose portions rarely use the term without qualification in this way. This implies that in early times the brahmins still had prestige. The *Sn*, for example, describes *śramaṇas* and brahmins alike as worthy mendicants (though of course not all brahmins were mendicants); the same text refers, however, to palatial complexes bestowed by kings upon brahmins in the time of brahmin decadence, indicating that Buddhists perceived a distinction between brahmin ideals and practice.

By the time of the Buddha, then, the status of the concept of a brahmin had evolved in complex ways. An old tradition, conventionally believed to be maintained in its greatest purity in the northern areas, associated the life of the brahmin with the cultivation of sacred wisdom, while in practice the families claiming brahmin status had increasingly become secularized,

[25] Tsuchida, 'Two categories of brahmins', pp. 80ff.; 83ff. [26] Olivelle, *Saṃnyāsa Upaniṣads*, p. 73.

[27] See especially M. Biardeau and C. Malamoud, *La Sacrifice dans L'Inde Ancienne* (Presses Universitaires de France, Paris, 1976), pp. 75ff.

partly as a result of success in attracting the patronage of the wealthy and powerful. The support given by such people inevitably had the same sort of effects in 'domesticating' the brahmins as it has in the history of Buddhism, and similar social mechanisms must be recognized.

Many scholars have alluded to the Buddha's development of a concept of the brahmin that would stand outside of received images of Buddhist monks and brahmins. Masefield has developed the point that there is a contrast between the behaviour of the brahmins of the Buddha's own day and this idealized construction mentioned in the previous paragraph. He evaluates the significance of this normative image – as a point of comparison – for the historical development of the early *saṅgha*:

From the foregoing it will be clear that by the period covered by the Nikāyas a group of individuals, from the Buddhist point of view of dubious ancestry, had arrogated to themselves a position of religious power and wealth on the basis that they alone embodied the sacred power of Brahman. The Buddhists, feeling that their unariyan behaviour disqualified them from this, openly criticized what they took to be a band of indigenous opportunists, but in this they were motivated by no egalitarian ethic on behalf of the despised class. Indeed it was rather the other way round for the evidence of the Nikāyas suggests that it was the altogether more conservative cause of the kṣatriyas that the Buddhists favoured. The kṣatriyas were so intent on preserving the purity of Āryan blood that they took to incest whereas the brahmins would go with any varṇa or indeed a woman of the despised clans[28] (A 3.228), accepting, unlike the kṣatriyans, any offspring.[29]

It is a possible view, even if an extreme one, that the normative image of the brahmin has nothing to it other than its rhetorical power. It is hardly an image of what brahmins could ever have been like in practice, though it might have been successful as a means of eliciting a deep set of values summarizing the ethos of the *varṇa* in its broadest, yet abstract, cultural sense at the time the Buddha lived. That is, it stood centrally enough within the brahmins' perception of themselves to be easily recognizable to them as a set of images bearing close relations with what some of their kind still were and hoped to be. In this sense it could be seen as one pure and very clearly defined image meaningful to all brahmins as a sign uniting the few disparate qualities associated with the class. It also served the important function of defining some kind of imputed essence against the two other principal classes and any other occupational groups that had previously gained visibility in the society.

[28] A III 228.

[29] P. Masefield, *Divine Revelation in Pali Buddhism* (Allen & Unwin, London, 1986), p. 160.

Its rhetorical power resides in its capacity to function as an unachievable standard against which any contemporaneous group can be measured, a standard held to be legitimate because of the strong grounding it has in a historically defined cultural tradition. It must have been valuable also because of the difficulty of finding anyone able to meet that requirement, a fact instrumental in strengthening its exclusivism given that some brahmins might have been recognized as having at least one foot in it. On the basis of texts cited by Masefield it is the *arahant* who is projected in the Buddhist texts as having the potential for fulfilling the requirements of the true brahmin. As an assessment of its cultural function within the Buddhist arsenal of rhetorical arms, we perhaps should take this as another instance of the well-cited Buddhist process of appropriating to itself certain rituals and ideals central to brāhmaṇical culture.

Indeed, the idea of brāhmaṇical corruption and impurity is emphasized. Most especially, brahmins are found wanting in the comparison with *kṣatriyas*. For some, this comparison has seemed to fortify the supposition that, in the structure of very ancient Indian society, it was already possible to identify priests and lords as distinct classes in competition with each other. Since the two classes are defined by different sorts of criteria and have different functions, the notion of competition seems inappropriate. At all events, it is clear that Buddhist teachers made the comparison of the two classes directly, to the advantage of the lords.[30]

Brahmins are criticized for their corrupt behaviour. 'These brahmin folk are greedy for money'; a set of noblemen is represented as assuming that a brahmin minister can be won over by money and women.[31] Brahmins are so greedy for the rewards of assisting at a sacrifice that at the mere smell of it they run up to it like dung-eating animals.[32] A similar attitude is conveyed in the *Jātakas*, where brahmins are portrayed as avaricious.[33] They are not only greedy; they are superstitious. Many brahmins, often unlettered and poor no doubt, made their living by divination and allied techniques, and in Buddhist sources they are ridiculed.

COMPETITION

The Buddhist teachers, then, were highly sensitive to the comparison between themselves and the brahmins. This comparison needs to be seen in

[30] See *D* I 92ff., 97ff., *M* II 84, 87ff. For the critique of contemporary brahmins for being materialistic and marrying anybody see A III 220.

[31] *D* II 244ff. [32] *M* III 167.

[33] For this and the following see Fick, *Soziale Gliederung*, p. 229.

its ideological context. Individual brahmins are very often mentioned by name in the canon, but this does not necessarily mean that the Buddha very frequently met and converted people of brahmin stock. It means that those who later collected and codified the remembered stories of the teaching were particularly interested in setting out the points at which they saw their master as having offered values and teachings the brahmins lacked or did not clearly understand. Modern scholars have given a great deal of attention to the concrete detail of these references to brahmins,[34] often with valuable results, but we cannot of course expect to wring quantitative historical data about the biographies of individuals or the composition of the *saṅgha* from such sources. The way in which the *Nikāyas* duplicate incidents in different settings inevitably makes them seem to have happened more often than it is likely they actually did. Tsuchida, emphasizing the dangers of treating the *suttas* as historical records, gives the example of the brahmin Jānussoṇi, who was mentioned in six different sutta contexts as having been converted.[35] We cannot assume that the number of references to conversion of brahmins has a close relationship with the actual number of conversions of brahmins.

Clearly, there was a great deal more to the Buddhist attitude towards the brāhmaṇical orthodoxy than that it could constitute a field for conversions. A heterodox or minority tradition needs to relate itself to the orthodox or mainstream practice;[36] almost necessarily, Buddhism mapped itself upon a structure supplied by the brahmins, defining itself by reference to what it was not; a series of systematic oppositions identified its relationship to the pre-existing orthodoxy. Even though the canon does not contain detailed analysis of brāhmaṇical texts, the *dhamma* displays in all sorts of ways a disposition to contrast itself systematically with what they preached.

Several writers have commented on the systematic superimposition of Buddhist concepts upon the brāhmaṇical ones which they invert or supersede.[37] Gombrich, for example, has argued that the teachings of the

[34] See especially Chakravarti, *Social Dimensions*, pp. 125–8; appendix C, pp. 198–206.

[35] Tsuchida, 'Two categories of brahmins', p. 77. For Tsuchida, it appears likely that comparatively few brahmins actually entered the order as a result of conversion by the Buddha; those who did would have been from the special class of brahmin ascetics rather than from among the many ordinary brahmins following secular careers; see p. 66 and n. 47. But these ascetic brahmins could have constituted a large proportion of the *saṅgha*.

[36] A graphic example of this is the way in which, in Tibet, the Bon religious practice involves the performance of circumambulation of a shrine anti-clockwise, to contrast itself to the Buddhist *pradakṣiṇā*.

[37] See I. W. Mabbett, 'Buddhism and freedom', in D. Kelly and A. J. S. Reid (eds.), *Asian Freedoms* (Cambridge University Press, Cambridge, 1998), pp. 19–36.

canon are much more closely modelled on the Vedas than is generally realized.[38] For example, against the brāhmaṇical myth of the origin of the four ritual orders of society, the *varṇas*, Buddhism proclaims a different version in which the brahmins lose their divinely ordained privilege; and Tambiah comments that 'the real thrust of the Buddhist story is that it is self-consciously an inversion of the Vedic theory of the origin of the varna'.[39] Tsuchida refers to the Buddhist habit of redefining brāhmaṇical terms in a new sense, subordinating the original sense to the Buddhist conceptions without actually rejecting the brāhmaṇical meaning, as in cases such as *vijjācaraṇa*, *yañña*, and of course *brāhmaṇa*.[40]

Again, Gombrich points to the way in which the Buddhist doctrine of *karma* consistently inverts the brāhmaṇical notion of action, turning it, paradoxically, into the morality of the actor's state of mind, which is not a physical 'action' at all; similarly the Buddhist emphasis upon psychological action entails a recognition that mechanical acts of austerity are without value compared to true insight leading to enlightenment, and Rhys Davids compares this valuation with the new emphasis in the *Upaniṣads* upon gnosis as against sacrifice or asceticism.[41] Of course, it is true that the Pāli Canon does not discuss the philosophy of the *Upaniṣads* as such, and it is not obvious that Buddhist texts can be said to reflect any knowledge of the content of the brāhmaṇical texts. It has been argued though that the *Alagaddupama Sutta* demonstrates the Buddha's familiarity with the *Bṛhadāraṇyaka Upaniṣad*, because the former systematically attacks or redefines the latter's theses point by point.[42]

The Buddhist treatment of the threefold sacred fire of brāhmaṇical ritual is another instance; Buddhism identified fire with the saṃsāric entanglements of life in the society that the *bhikkhu* left behind, representing these as the three fires of *rāga*, *dveṣa* and *moha*. Likewise the three Vedas of the priests are paralleled by the three higher knowledges of Buddhism, *tevijja*, and the brāhmaṇical sacrifices are matched by the *bhikkhu*'s metaphorical ones. Boris Oguibenine has detected a parallel threefold structure in the

[38] R. F. Gombrich, 'How the Mahāyāna began', *Journal of Pali and Buddhist Studies*, 1 (1988), pp. 29–46; reprinted in T. Skorupski (ed.), *The Buddhist Forum: Seminar Papers 1987–88, Volume 1* (School of Oriental and African Studies, London, 1990), pp. 5–20. This article suggests that probably the Pāli *sutta* represents *sūkta* 'well spoken', and that *suttānta* deliberately parallels *vedānta*.

[39] S. J. Tambiah, *World Conqueror and World Renouncer: a study of Buddhism and polity in Thailand against a historical background* (Cambridge University Press, Cambridge, 1976), p. 22.

[40] Tsuchida, 'Two categories of brahmins', p. 75.

[41] T. W. Rhys Davids (trans.), *Dialogues of the Buddha* (PTS, London, reprint 1973), vol. 1, p. 211.

[42] K. R. Norman, 'A note on Attā in the Alagaddupama Sutta', in *Studies in Indian Philosophy. A Memorial Volume in Honour of Pt Sukhlalji Sanghvi* (Ahmedabad, 1981), pp. 19–29.

brāhmaṇical sacrifice and in the Buddhist transfer of merit, wherever this latter notion may be said to apply.[43]

This almost obsessive mapping of Buddhist teachings upon the structure of brāhmaṇical tradition clearly demonstrates that the Buddhists saw themselves as competitors with the brahmins, in spite of the obvious differences in their concerns. When all was said and done, the Buddha identified himself as a protagonist of brāhmaṇical ideals, revived and purified. His teaching could be seen as wholly consistent with brāhmaṇical ideals understood in a special sense – the sense which in fact corresponded, not to the values and institutions of brahmins in ordinary social life, with their rituals and their memorized texts, or even to the priesthood of the ancient Vedic pastoral society, but to the ascetic brahmin programme, a programme which itself originated within the priestly fold probably in large part as a response to the influence of the heterodox *śramaṇas* and could be accommodated within brāhmaṇical orthodoxy only at the cost of much tension and ideological indigestion. This ascetic brahmin was conceived of as the truly self-sufficient being independent of others, as the arch-renouncer, 'with no provisions even for the next day', and his ascetic way of life was the highest sacrifice. But it is the worldly lifestyle of the allegedly corrupt eastern brahmins that is most obtrusive in the Buddhist literature, and the *dhamma* is set up as an alternative to their ritualism, to their monopolism, and their ignorance. Yet, however much difference there may have been between the brāhmaṇical ideals and brāhmaṇical behaviour as thus described, the disciples of the Buddha recognized some form of threat or rivalry in the activities of their priestly opponents. This must reflect competition in their actual social relationship, however incommensurable their programmes may appear. The nature of this competition must hold the key to an understanding of the needs to which the Buddhists were able to respond in an urban society with the accompanying process of urbanization.

To appreciate fully the rich image of the brahmin and the attitude of ambivalence – emphasizing the rejection and attraction the Buddha felt towards the brahmins and their social success – it is necessary to refer directly to a series of passages from the *Majjhima Nikāya*. These are of more significance for our purpose than passages in other texts, except perhaps for the *Vinaya*, in so far as they portray in a very full sense the social interaction between the Buddha and individual brahmins. That it is individual brahmins whom the Buddha is depicted as confronting, not groups of them,

[43] B. Oguibenine, 'From a Vedic ritual to the Buddhist practice of initiation into the doctrine', in P. Denwood and A. Piatigorsky (eds), *Buddhist Studies Ancient and Modern* (Curzon Press, London, 1983), pp. 118–20.

may make for better dramatics. This supposition holds validity even in the light of the view sometimes expressed in the texts that if one leader of a group defeated another one in debate, the followers of the defeated became followers of the victor. The first text to be cited is significant primarily in showing the kind of protocol the brahmins use in addressing the Buddha. It recurs elsewhere, hence is clearly a stock passage conveying one sense of the ritualized relations between a designated class of religious figures and a particular holy man. In the *Apaṇṇakasutta* the Buddha is described going to a brahmin village of the Kosalans named Sālā. The brahmin householders hear of his reputation, one communicated to them in highly devotional terms. Here is a description of the ritualized initial meeting between the brahmins and the Buddha:

> Then the brahmin householders of Sālā went up to the Lord. Some who had gone up greeted the Lord and sat down at a respectful distance. Some exchanged greetings with the Lord, conversed pleasantly and politely, and sat down at a respectful distance. Some saluted the Lord with joined palms and sat down at a respectful distance. Some declared their names and clans in the Lord's presence and sat down at a respectful distance. Some became silent and sat down at a respectful distance. The Lord said this to the brahmin householders of Sālā when they were sitting down at a respectful distance.[44]

After this greeting the Buddha proceeds to give a teaching on *dhamma* in the traditional manner, though not a progressive talk.

There are various markers of relations designated here between the Buddha and the brahmin *gahapatis*, wealthy householders. Spatial difference is immediately established between all the brahmins and the Buddha. They sit down at a respectful distance, not to one side as the monks do when in close proximity with the Buddha at a time when he is giving a teaching, but in a way still giving emphasis to distance, though there are variations on this in other passages. Not all brahmins do sit down at a respectful distance, as we will see soon, but spatial isolation amidst a group of people is a standard device for reinforcing the Buddha's charisma and maintaining a distinction that was as much for dramatic purposes as for reasons of emphasis of religious difference. Four different modes of greeting are enumerated here:

(1) 'Some who had gone up greeted the Lord'
(2) 'Some exchanged greetings with the Lord, conversed pleasantly and politely'
(3) 'Some saluted the Lord with joined palms'
(4) 'Some declared their names and clans in the Lord's presence . . . became silent'

[44] *M* I 401, 290–1; *M* II 55.

Each of these implies a different level of confidence in greeting a figure whose reputation precedes him, who has the general bearing of a holy figure – although the impression given in the texts is that he is a towering figure, even if this impression is implied rather than made explicit – with all the behavioural implications that brings with it, but who, nevertheless, is a highly social being. Other modes of address have been studied in detail by Wagle, but we need to be aware how important it was for the marketing of the Buddha's message that he be portrayed always at the centre of the appropriate spatial or social location.

A more expansive exploration of the relation between a prominent brahmin and the Buddha is conveyed in the *Selasutta*.[45] The narrative brings out all the themes we find elsewhere in the *Majjhima Nikāya*:

The Buddha arrived at the town of Āpaṇa. Keṇiya the matted hair ascetic heard about this and, knowing of the Buddha's reputation, he heard the words, 'The sight of arahants of such an appearance is certainly very good' (*kho pana tathārūpānaṃ arahataṃ dassanaṃ hoti'ti*).

Keṇiya went up to the Buddha and invited him to a meal on the following day. The Buddha said to him, 'But, Keṇiya, the Order of monks is huge, twelve hundred and fifty monks, and you are strongly disposed (*abhippasanno*) towards the brahmins.' Initially he declined, but after Keṇiya's perseverance, the Buddha finally agreed to come for a meal.

Keṇiya organised all his relations to help him with the job and they constructed a pavilion for him.

Then a celebrated brahmin named Sela arrived, saw the preparations and asked, 'Is the honourable Keṇiya now holding the ritual journey to the bride's house or the ritual departure from the bride's house? Or has a huge sacrifice been organised or has King Seniya Bimbisāra of Magadha been invited tomorrow together with his troops?'

Then he told Sela the Buddha was coming. Sela began theorising about the Buddha's titles and asked to meet him. He sat down in front of him with his three hundred disciples and speculated in his mind about the Buddha's thirty-two special bodily marks. Knowing his thoughts, the Buddha revealed the two hidden marks as a means of demonstrating empirically his possession of them.

[Then occurs a series of verses summarising in a formulaic manner the career path of a Buddha. After this the Buddha declared himself as a self-awakened one in the context of the Cakkavattin theory and his role as a turner of the wheel of dhamma.

Sela and his followers then all declared they would go forth and become renouncers.

[45] *M* II 146ff. Not printed in the PTS edn, but included in the digital version of the International Buddhist Research and Information Center. Other versions are found in the *Sn*, p. 103 and *Vin* I 245ff. *D* I 87–110 is similar in intent.

The Buddha arrived for the meal and Keṇiya himself served the Buddha as a sign of respect. The Buddha then recited certain verses expressive of dhamma and Sela became perfected.]

The celebration of brahmins here and elsewhere in the canon serves just to strengthen the rhetorical power of the conversion frame enclosing the narrative. The power of the Buddha is defined both by the transformative capacity of his teaching and by his physical uniqueness expressed through the possession of his thirty-two marks.[46] This becomes an important component of his charisma, a judgement confirmed in the text itself when Keṇiya expresses the opinion about the positive value to be had simply from seeing the Buddha, an attitude found not infrequently in the meal narratives. The problem of charisma arises because of the centrality of the act of *darśana* in Indian culture. Is the charisma independent of the set of qualities defining this subject as an object of vision, or is every figure who is the object of vision in possession of charisma?

This kind of treatment of the Buddha is crucial in telling us about the pressures working on the composers of the text to depict him in this heightened manner and, conversely, about the brahmins in defining themselves as that social group having the highest level of sanctity in a society where sanctity was assuming increasing importance as one of the central elements in defining social rank. But why would people entitled to confidence in their own social and cultural position, as Sela is, so easily abandon that aspect of their life – *varṇa* affiliation – which defines them so clearly at the pinnacle of society?[47] It is obvious why the Buddha should be depicted in this position. In a highly competitive situation, the highest stakes will be brought into play and the underdog destined to be revealed as superior and filled with a quiet confidence in his own capacity to transform individuals and society. But this does not explain why the brahmins would be converted with what appears to be such relative ease – unless, that is, the historical situation in which the narratives were composed was not just one of considerable social and economic fluidity, but also one where there was a serious decline in confidence about personal and social identity.

46 A further contributing factor, building up the reputation of the Buddha as a man of power, would be the kind of miracles performed by the Buddha and other monks. See Phyllis Granoff, 'The ambiguity of miracles. Buddhist understandings of supernatural power', *East and West*, 46 (1996), pp. 79–96.

47 A passage at *D* III 81 is instructive here. In it are criticized brahmins who have become monks. They are charged with abandoning a superior *vaṇṇa* for an inferior one, namely that 'of shaveling recluses, who are menials, offspring of their kinsman's feet'.

A related narrative is the *Brahmāyusutta*.[48] Again the problem turns on the question of the existence of the thirty-two marks.

[Brahmāyu, a prominent brahmin, sent his young brahmin student Uttara to discover whether the Buddha really had the thirty-two marks. He discovered that he did but only after the Buddha, using his psychic power, consciously revealed the 'penis sheath' and 'the tongue'.

When Brahmāyu heard that the Buddha was nearby, he announced his wish to see him in Makhadeva's Mango Grove. But he had a misgiving,] 'It definitely doesn't seem right to me that I should go up to see the recluse Gotama without being announced first.'[49] So he sent a brahmin youth to inform the Buddha that he would be coming. The youth was instructed to inform Buddha that Brahmāyu was a brahmin of extremely high standard, educated in all branches of knowledge. He says, 'Of all the brahmins and householders who live in Mithilā, sir, Brahmāyu the brahmin is declared to be the foremost in wealth, Brahmāyu the brahmin is declared to be the foremost in mantras (142); Brahmāyu the brahmin is declared to be foremost in longevity as well as in renown. He wants to see the good Gotama.' (141–2)

[The Buddha agreed and,]

'Then Brahmāyu the brahmin went up to the Lord. His assembly saw the brahmin Brahmāyu coming in the distance. When they saw him near each made room for him because he was well known and renowned. Then Brahmāyu the brahmin said to the assembly: "No sirs, each of you sit on your own seat. I will sit here near the recluse Gotta."' (142)

[Then he sat down at a respectful distance from the Buddha and asked to see all the thirty-two marks. Using his psychic power the Buddha showed him these, after which Brahmāyu asked how one becomes a brahmin, how one is perfected. In response the Buddha offered a speech about how one could attain enlightenment.] Impressed by this, when this had been said, 'Brahmāyu the brahmin got up from his own seat, arranged his upper robe over one shoulder, placed his head at the Lord's feet, kissed them all around with his mouth and stroked them on all sides with his hands, and declared his name "I, good Gotama, am Brahmāyu, the brahmin." Then the assembly was filled with wonder and astonishment, and said: "It is quite amazing, it is quite astonishing that the psychic power and the majesty of the recluse are so great that Brahmāyu the brahmin, well known and renowned, pays such deep respect."'

[Then the Buddha told Brahmāyu to sit down on his own seat and then spoke to him about a range of topics, after which Brahmāyu asked to be accepted as a lay-disciple.

[48] *M* II 134–46. Because of its length we have summarized it here.

[49] *M* I 141. *Na kho m 'etaṃ patirūpaṃ yo'haṃ pubbe appaṭisaṃvidito samaṇaṃ gotamaṃ dassanāya upasaṅkameyyan ti.* The translation does not exactly capture the strength of the self-expression of Brahmāyu's self-worth created linguistically by the occurrence of the first person pronoun *me* with the repetitions of the third and first person pronouns *yo 'ham.*

As if in recognition of this acceptance, he invited the Buddha and the Order to a meal on the following day and fed them himself by his own hand.]

This narrative points to some of the likely tensions framing the encounter between the Buddha and early monks and the brahmins. It takes no acumen to see that the Buddha himself rests on some kind of austere pedestal, that he does not at any time reveal a need to see the brahmin. At all times he is doing the brahmin a manifest favour in providing him with an audience. Never is he impressed by the qualities the brahmin is reputed to possess, qualities making him renowned and widely known, implying that his own status is such that he need not concern himself with the attracting power of such qualities at all.

It is this fame the Buddha is most concerned about. Of course, this is never stated so baldly in the texts themselves since it is in such broad contradiction to the Buddhist axiom that a Buddha and his followers must be those who have made an incontrovertible decision to abandon any desire, even desire for social status. Yet, for all that, it is the unstated sub-text beneath so many of the narratives detailing the encounter between the Buddha and brahmins. The presentation of the brahmin in this formulaic manner builds up the climax of the encounter where the conversion is not necessarily the most important element. It is the act of undermining the social and cultural qualities of the brahmin – qualities implicitly repudiated when Brahmāyu becomes a lay Buddhist – that assumes primacy in the narrative. For it is these social and cultural qualities the Buddha seeks to undermine. Not that he did not take culture or society seriously. In order to renounce them he had to understand them. Rather, at the heart of his message and his own example is the conviction that a person must develop himself and constantly test his progress within the strictures of a clear-cut moral path and doctrinal framework laid down by the Buddha himself. This framework is valid irrespective of the social and cultural forces operating on it.

All that the texts offer about the Buddha is his status as a perfected being and the possessor of those particular qualities enabling him to offer *darśana* and to be approached as one who is worthy of being gazed upon. But in the ancient (and contemporary) cultural context this is of enormous importance. In a sense the texts are presenting us with a confrontation between two different sets of values. As has been commented upon frequently, the brahmins were reinforcing their identity in society by successfully keeping their feet in both the secular and religious camps, where the latter had been reinterpreted to encompass alike the all-inclusive ritualist tradition and the renunciatory lifestyle which in various of its forms offers a substantial rejection of the ritual cosmology. The Buddha by his own example offers a radical renunciation as the standard for all behaviour, and this is used by the Buddhist apologists both to undermine the brāhmaṇical position and also to present a unique path that offers the possibility of standing out firmly and distinctively against this very position.

THE BUDDHA'S CHARISMA AND SOCIAL MARKETING

Though there may be a competitive tinge in the great majority of encounters the Buddha has with brahmins, the Buddha is always depicted as standing aside in some way from the brahmins – or anyone else for that matter whom he encounters. This has the effect of distinguishing him from them as a special, if not unique, figure whose distinctive nature was inseparable from his teaching and experience. The kind of aloofness, social distancing and lack of emotion present in so many of these portrayals is both a representation of an enlightened being and a marketing device to underline the Buddha's own superiority in respect of those against whom he is implicitly in confrontation. Therefore if we are analysing the portrayal of the brahmins in Buddhist literature primarily from the perspective of their capacity to promote themselves as a distinguished high-status group, it is important to see what strategies the texts use to mark up the Buddha as a unique and high-status figure. The texts take pains to present the Buddha as a charismatic figure. Reginald Ray has made an excellent analysis of the bases of this charisma and there is no need to repeat his conclusions here.[50] In a previous chapter we analysed a passage, one of many, where the Buddha offers very broad guidance to the laity directed towards the achievement of success in a whole range of areas – mostly non-religious.[51] On such occasions, which presumably must have occurred with great frequency during his preaching career, the Buddha taught a wide range of people of differing intellects and interests, many of whom would have hardly had a particular interest in the kind of religious message he usually sought to offer. Many other examples of a more specific kind are concentrated in the second book of the *Majjhima Nikāya*. In these texts the kind of activity in which the Buddha is portrayed derives its legitimacy from the content of the message, but also assumes the drawing power of his status as a figure whose appeal derives from his fame and his charisma. Both of these – content of

[50] R. Ray, *Buddhist Saints in India* (Oxford University Press, New York, 1994), pp. 44–61.
[51] See ch. 2, and cf. *Vin* I 226ff.

message and charisma of the messenger – must be interrelated because even if the Buddha was highly charismatic (according to the standards of ancient India), this charisma would not have sanctioned him to say anything at all. There had to be recognition of the cultural needs of a variety of devotees as well as of his own capacity to deliver a talk on any range of subjects relevant to the time and milieu.

The mythology and darśanic material so common in the Pāli texts do not necessarily magnify the Buddha's charisma. Both, however, add to its mystique and ground the Buddha in several deep religious streams – especially a devotional one – that must have existed in India prior to his time. Both provide a background serving to consolidate an image that might have otherwise easily come to lose its potency. The extraordinary nature of the figure flows into the message he offers and gives it a measure of authority. To this charisma needs to be contrasted the practicality of the message he delivers. It is all of this that those who would deal with him must confront, and the texts never tire of offering us this uniquely constructed figure around whom everyone else must make their own way.

But the Buddha's charisma and whatever is associated with it make sense only in comparison with the other kinds of charismatic figures inhabiting Buddhist texts. And there are masses of them, judging from the numbers of followers they have, though such charisma is not often attributed to the brahmins, a characteristic which must arouse our interest. Their authority lies in their role as spokesmen of a tradition they are required neither to defend nor to substantiate. They can speak for this tradition because it has been successfully established as the standard against which most other cultural forms will be measured, and the dominant groups in the society accept this as such. Against this the Buddha, presenting a new message (even if it is claimed to be old), has constantly to present his message in the face of an ideology already fundamentally grounded in both theory and practice. If his charismatic reception preceded him, this would undoubtedly have helped him confront a tradition that had always proved impossible to overturn. All he could do was allow himself to be accommodated at its side.

In the second book of the *Majjhima Nikāya*, as well as in parts of the *Dīgha* and the *Samyutta Nikāyas*, the portrayal of the Buddha continually alternates between a figure possessed of supernatural powers (though these are never used extravagantly and only as a means of self-revelation to others) and a 'rational' human being who has worked towards and attained a state of enlightenment using only human capacities. Both positions avail themselves of particular modes of representation and, presumably, were meant to be conveyed to different constituencies. We cannot say simply that the figure of the Buddha with the thirty-two marks, who at various times deals in a superior manner with the gods at an everyday level and who has attracted a profuse mythology, was simply created for the benefit of lay Buddhists and potential converts. Surely the figure must have appealed to individuals coming from right across the spectrum of levels of articulation, intellectual development and capacity.

To whom was the image of the rationalistic 'self-help' Buddha attractive? To some putative *arahant* or late commentator, or is it substantially a twentieth-century construction? Certainly, the many passages in the *M*, where the Buddha takes such pains to deliver stern, if highly systematic, discourses on the *jhānas* and the formless states, on the hindrances, the five graspings etc., strongly convey a highly didactic Buddhism propagated by a pedagogical Buddha. These are teachings extending far beyond the understanding or interest of all but the most highly sophisticated devotee. And, as if to highlight the high stakes in play, these teachings are framed by narratives of conversion, thus communicating the drama of an intellectual victory.[52] If both images were viable (and given the frequency of their occurrence, we must assume they were) as communicative devices, what did they sustain beyond the specific messages they were intending to communicate and to what extent were they intended for groups of differing socio-economic origins? We cannot underrate the importance of the social origin, economic status and the *varṇa* affiliation of these groups, for if they were analysed in tabular form they would depict a highly complex society of potentially conflicting status. Even if the groups are usually only described in broad stereotypical terms, the texts provide enough evidence for us to be confident that the Buddhist message was being addressed to the whole of society in the broadest possible measure. However, even when we know this, the textual evidence, with a few exceptions, does not enable us to focus on what the Buddha conveyed specifically to those groups who were of a lower class[53] than the various elite groups we have outlined in an earlier chapter.

[52] It is noteworthy that in such instances the Buddha never speaks highly of his own teaching. He only presents it in a highly modulated manner and the praise is placed in the mouth of the recipient of the message. The kind of stock response usually offered is given at *S* I 161, for example.

[53] Unless we take the Buddha's encounter with *yakkhas* and other 'folk deities' as falling within the ambit of non-brāhmaṇical religion and therefore of not requiring such a sophisticated response as necessitated for the former. See Greg Bailey, 'Problems of the interpretation of the data pertaining to religious interaction in ancient India: the conversion stories in the *Sutta Nipāta*', *Indo-British Review*, 19 (1991), pp. 16–17.

If the ritual meal is one means whereby the interaction between the Buddha and potential (initially antagonistic) converts is mediated in a non-competitive manner, and reciprocity applies as the means of exchange, other narratives provide us with instances where the competition is much more pronounced. In raising the theme of competition they also reflect intensely, if unintentionally, on the Buddha's charisma. Two instances will suffice. The first comes from the Caṅkīsutta.[54]

The Buddha is wandering in a particular region inhabited by Caṅkī, an eminent brahmin, who indicates to his fellow brahmins that he wants to go and see the Buddha (*Sādhu kho pana tathārūpānaṃ arahataṃ dassanaṃ hotī'ti*). Other brahmins tell him that the Buddha should come and see Caṅkī, as he is a brahmin of high renown in his own right.

He is:

(1) of pure birth on both sides back through seven generations;
(2) prosperous, very wealthy and rich (*aho mahaddhano mahābhogo*);
(3) learned in all the accepted areas of scholarship including knowledge of the marks of a great man;
(4) very handsome, of sublime complexion and unblemished appearance;
(5) very moral;
(6) possessed of excellent communicative skills and an auspicious voice;
(7) an accomplished teacher;
(8) revered by King Pasenadi of Kosala;
(9) revered by the brahmin Pokkharasti;
(10) dwelling as overlord in Opasāda, given to him as a gift by King Pasenadi.

In response to this Caṅkī provides a set of reasons as to why the Buddha should be visited. Of these the following are listed:

(1) The Buddha is of pure birth on both sides back through seven generations.
(2) The Buddha renounced, giving away much gold.
(3) The Buddha renounced when he was still young.
(4) The Buddha renounced even though his parents were very upset.
(5) The Buddha is very handsome, of sublime complexion and unblemished appearance.
(6) He is very moral.
(7) He has excellent communicative skills and an auspicious voice.
(8) He is the teacher of many teachers.
(9) He has destroyed attachment to sense pleasures.
(10) He teaches about *kamma* and has no evil intentions (*appapurekkhro*) towards brahmins.
(11) He has renounced from a distinguished family of khattiyas.
(12) He has renounced from a family both prosperous and very rich (*aḍḍhakulā . . . mahaddhanā mahābhogā*).
(13) People come from distant countries to question him.

[54] *S* II 164–77.

(14) Thousands of deities have gone to him for refuge on account of (or 'with') living beings.
(15) He is a fully perfected one, a Buddha etc.
(16) He has the thirty-two marks of a great man.
(17) King Bimbisāra goes to him for the same reason.
(18) The brahmin Pokkharasati goes to him for the same reason.
(19) He is a guest and guests must be honoured by brahmins.

In addition, all sorts of prominent figures, including kings and brahmins (whom he names), have previously gone to see him.

The two lists of qualities overlap considerably. They are important for providing clues as to why cultural elites in the Buddha's time accorded him a status that would attract to him those members of society who were so confident in the worth of their own traditional status and the acceptance of this status by the majority of the members in that society, especially by those who were of lower status. Moreover, this importance is enhanced by the clear competitive context in which this list is constructed. Perhaps competition is a misleading word to use. Rather, the monks supportive of Caṅkī are strongly concerned about status disjunction, and presumably in offering a list of qualities possessed by Caṅkī, they are making two implications: that these are the qualities of traditional brahmins, and that non-brahmins, even those who are renowned religious teachers, do not possess them. That Caṅkī comes so quickly and firmly to the Buddha's defence may be a device of the Buddhist editors of the text to put down the other brahmins by repudiating them with one of their own.

In the distinction between the qualities attributed to the Buddha and those attributed to Caṅkī, three categories can be isolated:

(a) Those common to the Buddha and to Caṅkī. These are attributed to the Buddha in order to place him on a par with a renowned brahmin of the householder type, who is learned in all the traditional skills as well as the traditional marks of the great man, an attribute which once more narratively subordinates the brahmin to the Buddha in this particular context.

(b) Those the brahmin alone possesses. These relate specifically to the brahmin's possession of wealth, an essential attribute if he is to fit the depiction of the householder brahmin in the Canon, and his knowledge of the sources of traditional brāhmaṇical learning. These the Buddha would not normally have, both because he is a critic of them and because what they teach is scarcely consistent with the eight-limbed path encapsulating his own teaching.

(c) Those exclusive to the Buddha himself. The first relates to the brahmin's possession of wealth. The Buddha does not now have wealth, but he has had it in the past and gave it all up. Thus, he was a successful householder, as symbolized by his possession of this wealth, but by rejecting it has simultaneously fulfilled his credentials as a renouncer.

There are nine common features to both lists. Several elements (1, 4, 6) derive directly from the Buddha's charisma, another (1) from his pure birth, a feature the brahmins continually claim in support of their own status, two others (2 and 3) because he fits a particular mould, that of the religious specialist, and finally, because of his renown (7).

The charismatic qualities conferring a special status upon the Buddha, certain brahmins and other holy men can never be underrated in their utility as marketing the attraction of these figures to the majority of the population believing themselves not to possess such star quality. Inevitably a strong competitive element must emerge as well as a need to develop criteria to distinguish these stars from each other. But it would not be enough just to read into these apparent competitive encounters a further indication that Buddhism developed in an environment of elites. If we reverse the line of approach two other questions become evident. First, why would the mercantile groups plus other financial and cultural elites have been so eager to make themselves seen to be so closely associated with the Buddha, both physically and financially? Secondly, what interest would it serve for narratives of this kind to be included in the Canon?

In response to the first question, let us initially note that these elites were of two kinds, roughly divisible into brahmins and others. The two groups are treated differently in the narratives dealing with the ritualized meal and in other contexts where someone is depicted deriving favour from the Buddha or becoming a candidate for conversion. The brahmins do not appear to engage in competition with each other, though their activity is always undertaken against a backdrop of a very broad competitive attitude operating between the Buddha and brahmins, both offering different religious positions. Often the conflict with the Buddha becomes almost heated as in the verbal conflicts occurring in the 'brahmin suttas' of the third book of the *Dīgha Nikāya*. The brahmins defend their traditional position and the Buddha rebuts it, though never is he depicted in any stance other than one of repose. Continually the brahmins are depicted as reactionaries, the Buddha as progressive and logical. But knowing this does not answer the question as to the apparent attraction of some brahmins to the Buddha's message and to the figure of the Buddha himself. Was it that the traditional hegemony of the brahmins' message was breaking down, that as a result of a changing society the brahmins were really questioning their past intellectual heritage? Evidence derived from the immense speculation about ancient Indian society in the *Mahābhārata* might be taken as a support of this argument, for there a society is depicted that is quite unsure of its cultural foundations. Alternatively, this text could equally be taken as reaffirming brāhmaṇical hegemony by showing that the brahmins really were capable of questioning their own intellectual presuppositions and of adjusting them to altered socio-economic and political conditions.

Without any evidence to the contrary, it seems better to postulate a range of factors explaining this attraction towards the Buddha. In the first instance, brahmins were definitely being required to recognize that their environment had changed, though this did not mean it had become more negative in an economic sense. Their own power had not been threatened because it was not primarily dependent upon ownership of material assets. Yet they must have been coming into contact with different ethnic groups, inhabiting land they had to colonize, and they had to defend their own world view against others of equal sophistication and breadth to their own. Given the charisma of the Buddha and his capacity to win arguments, it is not surprising that he should win some of the brahmins over to his side. This being the case, the texts dealing with the conversion of brahmins do not really tell us if the conversion of individual brahmins was a consequence of individual crises, alienation from the system or genuine attraction to the Buddha's message.

A second factor must have been the figure of the Buddha himself. Here was a person who had appeared to master the vagaries of time, one to whom even death itself held no fear. Fear of death and the development of a ritual means to overcome death are paramount in pre-Buddhist brāhmaṇical thought. Thirdly, but related to the second, the *Upaniṣads* themselves do offer an alternative to death in their emphasis on liberating knowledge and a break from the circularity of *karma*. Yet the associated lifestyle practice, with the exception of meditation and *tapas*, is absent from there, whereas in the appropriate teachings of the Buddha, subsequently codified in the *Vinaya*, this kind of practice is given in great detail and with very little room left for doubt.

As to why the composers of the Buddhist texts would have been so keen to include so many narratives dealing with the brahmins, one can only suggest the following reasons. It is quite possible they may have been presenting a particular historical situation, albeit interpreted through their own beliefs and reframed accordingly, where the brahmins were the principal cultural elites in a society where production and warfare were valued less highly than the ability to disseminate religious and cultural knowledge. Any victory over the brahmins would have been a victory for the supporters of the Buddha, though it could not have been shown to be such for the Buddha, whose textual persona was such that he was beyond this kind of ambition. To develop this argument fully we need to know much more about the actual networks of influences brahmins had in the villages and towns where the Buddha spent much of his time, but the texts simply do not allow us access to this knowledge. Secondly, it enabled the Buddhists to be appearing to stand with the elites of society. Despite their professed disinterest in *varṇa* as a source of prestige, the capacity to be accepted substantially by that group, known from time immemorial to set the cultural agenda for the entire society, must have been a major bonus for the fledgling Buddhist community. This does not fit awkwardly with their desire to stand alone. For them, the cultural Other were certainly the brahmins, but they envied them at the same time as viewing them as antagonists, in one area of life at least. This is not to suggest that the Buddhists wished to usurp the position of the brahmins, just that they would have liked to have the same status as an alternative in a society awash with sects offering their own pathway to liberation.

CONCLUSION

Of all the groups who populate the social and cultural world depicted in the Pāli Canon it is with the brahmins and members of his own order that the Buddha has most interaction. That it is this group reinforces the point that Buddhism began as an elite movement before expanding to encompass most levels of society in its embrace. Nor is it simply a question of economic elites, though this factor cannot be left out of any discussion of the problem, as there is much substantive textual and (later) inscriptional evidence that brahmins were materially wealthy. Rather, we must recognize in this interaction a concern to place the Buddha on an equal or superior footing to any group placed at the pinnacle of society in the specific sense that it was both the origin and custodian of the dominant (if not hegemonic) values in that society. In this its role had been fêted for centuries, although we are still at a loss to know exactly how this was manifested in practice. Nor do the Pāli texts elaborate on the details of the management of this custodianship. What is significant is that they assume it. And in spite of the Buddha's equanimity and aloofness in the face of the brahmins there can be no doubt his reaction to them was not just a simple one of tolerance and acceptance. His creation of an image of an ideal brahmin was an attempt to undermine the perceived superiority of the brahmin in his time on the grounds of corruption and immorality. Neither the Pāli Canon nor the

Hindu texts are sufficient to enable us to test the validity of these implied criticisms.

What the Buddha does tell us – both through his implied criticism of the brahmin and the conditions established for him which enabled him to be portrayed as a unique religious figure in relation to his peers – is that the brahmins had so successfully made themselves into the embodiment of tradition that they were treated as the natural and legitimate heirs of cultural transmission. No other conclusion can be drawn from the texts' portrayal of the Buddha in a posture constantly superior to the brahmins in wisdom and from the lack of emotion attributed to him in the face of brāhmaṇical anger.

6

Folk religion and cosmology: meeting of two thought worlds

The image of Buddhism which has been inherited from past cultural perceptions is dominated by the austere and authoritative figure of the monk; and this image of practice is supplemented by a virtuoso tradition of spiritual cultivation. This tradition is embodied in a rigorous set of intellectual propositions about the mind, the world and action, alongside rigorous meditational techniques to plumb the deepest truths.

Of course, there is much in it that belies the real character of Buddhism in history, and it is increasingly contested. It is true that the act of becoming a monk can be seen as a cutting off of all the intellectual, social and economic ties that would bind a person, and that *vipassanā* meditation in particular may be seen as a method of reversing acculturalization. But a Leitmotif of our discussion so far has been that the Buddhist monks and laity inhabited a range of thought worlds and cultural milieux. Acceptance of the Buddha's intellectual message, however qualified, did not automatically mean rejection of the totality of the thought world into which one was born, and which was embodied in one's *habitus*. Even if some monks managed successfully to become single-minded in their religious pursuits, they were still required to deal, often daily, with others who had not and did not wish to.

The Pāli texts are absolutely filled with references to other meaning systems competing within the same cultural arena. Already we have touched in passing on those of the Jains and the Ājīvikas, and on brahmanism in some detail. They are the most well profiled in the texts, probably because they very early on caught the imagination of the elites in society. But lurking in the background, lying behind all of these and enjoying a complex and fragmented relation with them, were the various religious beliefs scholars often refer to misleadingly as 'folk religion'. We might choose to regard the references in the texts to gods, *bhūtas*, *yakṣas*, *nāgas*, tree deities and sacred festivals of all kinds as a concession to popular belief, to the world of the ordinary folk who were struck dumb by the complexities of Buddhist metaphysics. This interpretation has often enough been advanced. But it both underrates the capacity of laypeople to cope with complex theological ideas and overestimates the extent to which a monk could deny his inherited past. Most of all it fails to allow us to place Buddhism within its total context, that of daily life, which must be its most important context of all, even if the least studied. Our purpose in this chapter is to bring together some of the fragmentary strands of beliefs and practices associated with non-metaphysical and (in the narrow sense) non-brāhmaṇical belief, hoping to suggest some of the features of a more sensitive understanding of the thought world in which the Buddha's contemporaries lived.

RELIGION AND BELIEF, COGNITIVE AND AFFECTIVE

It is necessary first to look critically at the modern habit of identifying religion with belief. This must be done in order to distance ourselves from some of the inappropriate categories built into the cultural vocabulary of modern western thought.

There are, of course, different meanings of belief. Belief *in* can be seen as an aspect of practical religion, or alternatively as an aspect of intensely private commitment; belief *that* can be contrasted with both of these, as an abstract intellectual claim. In modern western society, religion has quite widely (though no doubt inappropriately) come to be seen as reducible to adherence to a set of propositions. The reciting of the Creed, after all, encourages the outsider to think of Christianity as something that can be summed up in this way. When we turn to meaning systems in other cultures, it comes naturally to treat them as systems of thought about what is ultimately true. The role of philosophy in Buddhist history particularly encourages the enquirer to treat Buddhism as an intellectual pursuit. It should be clear enough from all that has gone before that this is very far from the case.

However, there is more to this than is likely to be obvious so far. Religions usually comport cosmological ideas, which are developed or adapted for their followers; and cosmology at least, belief about the way the world works, seems to be both an essential part of the meaning of a religion and something expressible in propositions capable of being accorded truth-value. But this too is misleading. Cosmology, belief about the way the world works, has, in modern society, come as close as any culture has attained to neutral intellectual functions. Scientific propositions are not supposed to reflect social ideas; they are supposed to reflect laws of nature. Of course, this is ideal rather than reality, and for some time now reflective scholarship has explored with finesse the ways in which 'scientific' beliefs are moulded by social forces. Every science periodically turns out to have been based upon paradigms now shown by evidence to be inappropriate, and new paradigms subtly responsive to current attitudes to the universe must be adopted. All this is familiar; but it remains fair to contrast the habits of thought in modern culture with those of most traditional cultures.

In the case of traditional cultures, it comes naturally to us to suppose that people 'believe' the cosmological propositions comported by their religion in just the same way as we 'believe' that there are elephants in Africa or that monsoon winds in India bring seasonal rain. Ancient Indians, or the people of traditional 'unmodernized' societies today, are similarly supposed to accept the existence of particular gods, or of principles of magical manipulation, in the same way and with the same confidence. It is therefore a little disturbing when people in traditional cultures evince the same sort of scepticism about the efficacy of magic rituals that a modern westerner might. When rain duly followed a rain ritual performed by !Kung Bushmen, anthropologists asked if the ritual had caused the rain, and were greeted with ridicule.[1] Another example would be the case of an old village woman commenting that it was a waste of time for the menfolk to make a ritual pilgrimage to the Ganges for water – the village well would have produced water just as good for their purposes.[2] Or again, an African tribesman hurrying home pauses a moment to tie together a bundle of grass beside his path, a symbol of delay supposed to ensure that dinner at his home is not started before he arrives; but we are told that he knows perfectly well that the act of tying these shoots has no actual direct effect on events at home.[3] So why does he do it?

An obvious way of dealing with such cases is to say that some people in the societies we study have been contaminated by the values of the modern world, by the visiting anthropologist if not by other agencies sooner; but it does not always work very well and should not be regarded as necessarily correct. The old woman in the Indian village is supposed to be more tradition-bound, surely, than the younger folk going on pilgrimage. The African man still ties his grass, though he ought to conclude from his attitude to the belief that it is a waste of time. There must be another motivation.

The explanation, surely, is just that people behave in ways that imply certain beliefs as a way of fitting together an image of the world they

[1] Cited by M. Douglas, *Purity and Danger: an analysis of concepts of pollution and taboo* (Routledge and Kegan Paul, London, 1966), p. 58.

[2] D. Miller, personal communication. [3] Douglas, *Purity and Danger*, pp. 63ff.

live in. Gombrich's distinction between cognitive and affective beliefs is to the point;[4] he discusses the offerings (*pūjā*) (usually flowers, incense or lights) made to Buddha images and relics by certain modern Ceylonese communities. Such offerings are commonly accompanied by prayers in Pāli. The ceremonies, in varying degrees, imply the treatment of the Buddha as a super-monk or as an emperor, and sometimes clearly as a living, potentially dangerous, presence. These attitudes represent affective belief; however, they are arguably in conflict with the cognitive beliefs that go with Theravāda professions – the Buddha is not supposed to be a living presence. Individuals engaged in *pūjā* often know the doctrine and seek to explain their actions in harmony with it.

The underlying logic of affective beliefs, which may be inconsistent with cognitive ones, may be difficult to recognize, but it is usually there. It need not reside substantially in the overt and orthodox teaching; it may be in some ways incompatible with such professed beliefs; but it coheres at a deeper level with a cosmological scheme which is embedded in culture and is learned by socialization.

A clue to the character of affective beliefs is furnished by the concept of an 'anthropic' cosmology. This term has been applied to meaning systems in which the course of events, the things that happen to people in their lives, can be explained by anthropocentric principles. That is, the causes of events are not random, not coldly impersonal, not blind to human desires or merits; they conform to a pattern that makes human sense, they serve moral purposes or answer human needs. Instinctively and affectively, people tend to subscribe to such systems. We find the instinct attested by the saying that there is no such thing as an atheist on a sinking ship, or in popular attitudes to Buddha images, in Theravāda or Mahāyāna contexts alike. Perhaps, the more impersonal the principles of a publicly accepted cosmology, the more people are likely to reach out for an anthropic version of it, either by reinterpreting official belief, or by digging up anthropic principles from somewhere else in their cultural heritage.

The meaning of 'affective' beliefs does not primarily reside in the specific formal propositions they imply (such as 'the Buddha is a living accessible being' or 'the tying of this grass will slow down dinner preparations at home' or 'if I touch wood the thing I fear will not happen'). Their meaning resides in the actions expressing them, and these actions have value in articulating, confirming and reinforcing a total (anthropic) world view that makes sense

4 R. Gombrich, *Precept and Practice. Traditional Buddhism in the Rural Highlands of Ceylon* (Oxford University Press, London, 1971), pp. 114–40.

of human experience and offers the possibility of predicting and controlling it. The effect of an action is not so much a specific, perhaps magical, result produced directly; it is rather to assert the validity of the entire cosmological scheme within which order can be imposed upon experience and related to human desire or merit. This assertion has value for the individual by making sense of the confusing and by mitigating fear or suffering. The cognitive content of a formal system of cosmological belief may be virtually diametrically opposed to some affective beliefs.

THE NEED FOR A COSMOLOGY OF ORDER AND MEANING

Human experience of reality has jagged edges that often bewilder, frighten or hurt (a fact which itself is in a sense the starting point of Buddhist teaching), but human culture everywhere dedicates itself to the elaboration of schemes of order that contain and make manageable the booming, buzzing confusion, explain and justify the hurt. A grid of order is laid over the perceived disorder, and a means created to interpret experience in rational ways.

Religious symbols provide assurance of the existence of ways to reduce suffering. For example, a Navaho curing rite is directed to sustaining an effect which 'rests ultimately on its ability to give the stricken person a vocabulary in which to grasp the nature of his distress and relate it to the wider world'.[5] The dramatic Barong-Rangda ritual in Bali is not in origin just an aesthetic performance; it produces religious states of mind and reveals to participants the inherent ordered structure of the world.[6] In various ways, religious belief orders and explains tragic or unpredictable events by giving them a meaning which is not necessarily a causal explanation but an assurance of meaning.[7]

Religious statements are not to be read on a surface level; they point to subtle connections between things and qualities that constitute a framework of order.[8] To an extent greater than we usually notice, the will to

[5] C. Geertz, 'Religion as a cultural system', in *The Interpretation of Cultures* (Basic Books, New York, 1973), p. 105.

[6] Ibid., pp. 114–17. [7] Ibid., pp. 123ff.

[8] 'A man who says he is a parakeet is, if he says it in normal conversation, saying that, as myth and ritual demonstrate, he is shot through with parakeetness and that this religious fact has some crucial social implications – we parakeets must stick together, not marry one another, not eat mundane parakeets, and so on . . . this placing of proximate acts in ultimate contexts . . . alters, often radically, the whole landscape presented to common sense, alters it in such a way that the moods and motivations induced by religious practice seem themselves supremely practical, the only sensible ones to adopt given the way things "really" are.' Ibid., p. 121.

fit experience within a known scheme of understanding and expectation can dominate what is given to the senses, censoring and selecting to create an ordered world. Of course there are limits; and whenever brute creation threatens the security people feel within their construction of order, they instinctively turn to ('anthropic') affirmations of the whole scheme.

Some societies, for political and social reasons, have a greater need than others to favour public rituals, but no society or culture can do entirely without rituals in some sense, for the act which affirms the validity of the whole scheme or declares its application to a particular experience is a ritual act. Rituals cannot obliterate unwanted realities, but can make them acceptable; in many societies for example it is made possible to cope with the pain of childbirth or the anguish of mourning by elaborate ritual observances which accompany them.[9]

ORDER AND ABSENCE OF ORDER

The imposition of a constructed world upon the facts of experience naturally produces tensions, and these are perceived in cosmological terms as expressions of the eternal antagonism between order and absence of order. Every cosmology expresses, in one way or another, the polarization of order and absence of order, form and formlessness.[10] Such polarizations may not be constantly in the forefront of daily consciousness, but ritual and myth, when they express cosmology, bring out in an abstract sense the structure of such polarities that is, perhaps, embedded deep within the psyche.

All or most cosmologies recognize the extreme importance of closing the gaps between the ordered structures of time and place which pattern the world; social groups that are subject to the forces favouring ritual will do this abundantly in ritual ways, while more secular cultures will prefer the symbolism of inner states. Rituals commonly identify as dangerous the various in-between places and states, such as the suspension between two

9 The vexed question of divine kingship needs to be seen in this context. To say that Indians, or anybody else, *believed* that their kings were gods does not mean that people treated their rulers in practice as superhuman beings, gullibly accepting absurd claims. History demonstrates otherwise. What the ritual assertion of divine kingship suggests is that people accepted a total cosmology within which kingship was a divine function. This was a theory which helped make sense of the experience of state power. In dealing with actual kings in the real world, though, people used the cognitive parts of their minds.

10 F. B. J. Kuiper abstracts from the earliest Vedic texts an evolving scheme of order and absence of order, with the gods presiding over the world of being, *sat*, as it superseded absence of order, *asat*. In his reconstruction it is a set of abstractions, but many texts and rituals show its transformation into empirical categories framing other ideas and practices. See his *Varuṇa and Vidūṣaka. On the Origin of the Sanskrit Drama* (North Holland, Amsterdam, 1979), ch. 1.

stages of life enacted in an initiation, or pregnancy, or the shedding of menstrual blood; Mary Douglas points to the sense of danger often provoked by these things.[11] There is danger in formlessness, uncategorizability, undefined gaps. Menstrual blood, for example, is regarded as what could have become life, but did not; it is between life and not-life. Festivals marking the end of one year and the beginning of another often involve the warding off of chaotic dark forces pressing into the gap. Eclipses are in-between states; in Indian tradition, a vigorous ritual commotion must be made to scare off demons.

Such ideas necessarily find expression in underlying affective cosmological belief, whether or not a culture is highly ritualized. We have to recognize how even the austere and impersonal culture of early Buddhism fitted into a social world where the polarity of form and formlessness governed cosmological perceptions. To be sure, it is all but impossible for us today to enter imaginatively into the thoughts of those who first sallied forth, *pra-vraj*, as mendicant wanderers passing through tracts of wilderness, for the world that surrounds us has so little left in it of raw nature; it is a construct, an artifact. What we must also remember is that the priests and monks who wrote down the literature on which we depend for our knowledge of ancient religion were also separated by a cultural abyss from the world of the early *śramaṇas*. An urban revolution, still under way in the Buddha's time, had long been completed, transforming the cultural landscape in which they lived. When the scriptures were first written down, huge tracts of land had been tamed and brought beneath the plough, and the scholarly classes had become accustomed to life in cloisters situated within a short stroll of massive city fortifications or busy markets.

The cosmology of their civilization, however, preserved a lively sense of the duality of forest and town, human settlement and wilderness, a duality which was built into society's perception of the operation of cosmic forces. Until comparatively recent times, the wilderness has always loomed around the edges of consciousness, often within walking distance in any direction; it was a permanent presence with its lurking dangers and opportunities, reminding people that the world of order and artifice was an unstable and hard-won creation beset by the unpredictable forces of nature.

The Ganges valley is bare and tamed now, following continuous deforestation over millennia, most especially in the last two centuries, but it has not always been so. In Vedic times there was dense luxuriant forest. The area of the Indus-Ganges divide, between the Gagghar and the Gandak,

[11] Douglas, *Purity and Danger*, pp. 94–113.

was a wooded area, made cultivable by fire. Hastināpura, the Kuru capital, was in the forest; the Pāṇḍavas were said to have cleared forest to build Indraprastha; the Pañcāla kingdom was described as being in the Kuru jungle.[12] According to Lal, pollen records from Hastināpura show a variety of botanical species to have flourished in ancient times which are now found only in the Nepalese *tarai*; the region was 'quite densely forested' before the Christian era, and the fauna attested, including numerous carnivores, was consistent only with a thick forest cover as late as the fifteenth and sixteenth centuries ACE.[13] There are references in the Pāli literature to four 'great forests' (*mahāraññā*) occupying parts of northeastern India.[14] We have the testimony of Hsüan-tsang that the area between Allahabad and Kausambi was still densely forested at the time of his visit in the seventh century ACE: 'From Prayāga the pilgrim went . . . through a forest infested by wild elephants and other fierce animals.'[15] As Deloche said, 'The forest appears, more than the mountains, the desert and the rivers, to have been the principal barrier to the movement of men.'[16]

Even the most urbane of urbanites at any time during our period, therefore, was permanently aware of the forces of untamed nature always lurking on the edges of civilized life. Society itself was envisaged as patterned by the classical duality of settled and wild lands, each with its own lifestyle. Some classes of people frequented the wild places, and were on that account seen as separate, governed by a different sort of ethic. As J. C. Heesterman has put it, 'While the family and caste were at home in the agricultural village, the wastes were the home of the warrior and his war band.'[17] *Kṣatriya* leaders jealous of their autonomy have always liked to make the forest tracts their stamping-ground; Rajput leaders within more recent centuries have even preserved belts of forest around their fortresses, and with different motives communities of forest monks seek to re-create the wilderness environment in patches of woodland that are artificially preserved around the *vihāra*.[18] In the *Śatapatha Brāhmaṇa*, we find that the forest which surrounds the

[12] M. Lal, 'Population distribution and its movement during the second-first millennium B.C. in the Indo-Gangetic divide and Upper Ganga plain', *Purātattva*, 18 (1987–8), p. 38.

[13] Ibid., p. 50. [14] S. Sharma, *Material Culture*, p. 102.

[15] T. Watters (trans. and ed.), *Yuan Chwang's Travels in India* (Munshiram Manoharlal, Delhi, 1961), p. 365.

[16] J. Deloche, *La Circulation en Inde, avant la Révolution des Transports* (École Française D'Extrême-Orient, Paris, 1980), vol. 1, p. 7.

[17] J. C. Heesterman, 'Was there an Indian reaction? Western expansion in Indian perspective', in H. Wesseling (ed.), *Expansion and Reaction: Essays on European Expansion and Reaction in Asia and Africa* (Leiden University Press, Leiden, 1978), p. 47.

[18] The forest movement in northeastern Thailand illustrates this. For example, Wat Pah Nanachat outside Ubon is in a patch of woodland surrounded by paddy fields.

site of a sacrifice is a haunt of dangerous powers natural and unnatural – ogres, man-tigers, thieves, murderers and robbers –, and some sacrifices are said to be able to annihilate the wilderness tracts separating villages.[19]

The polarity of settlement and wilderness is a valuable clue to the organizing principles of the ancient Indian thought world. It is at work in Vedic society, where the terms *grāma* and *araṇya* carry connotations that are as much psychological as environmental: the one signifies order, familiarity, predictability, and the other (traceable to Indo-European **al*, **ol*, and related to words meaning 'other' such as *alter*) represents otherness, separation, in-between space. The Vedic *araṇya* meant a distant land, and by the time of the *Atharva Veda* acquired its meaning of 'forest', 'desert', 'wilderness'. *Araṇya* means the opposite of human settlement – 'das Fremde, das Feindliche', whereas the term *vana* was, up to the time of the earlier *Upaniṣads*, quite different, referring to areas around settlements.[20] In the Vedic sacrifice, sacrificial animals from the wilderness, *araṇya*, are placed in spaces between the sacrificial posts; on the other hand the domesticated fire, *agni* (which burns up the forest), represents the village order with its familiar patterns and seasonal cyclic repetition.[21]

The wilderness stood for chance, unpredictability, the primal lack of order whose raw energy could be a source of awful power if subdued, but was dangerous in the extreme to whoever would tangle with its forces. The people who lived there were people apart, alienated, outsiders. According to the *Āpastamba Śrauta Sūtra*, the wilderness, *araṇya*, was a place of 'retirement, isolation or banishment'.

The meditations of brāhmaṇical hermits on the self, *ātman*, draw on the powers of the wilderness, and the later development of the concept of *vanaprastha*, the woodland-dwelling life of the recluse, Malamoud argues, is a utopian combination of the forces of wilderness and settlement, marrying family life and routine sacrifices with closeness to nature and an ethic of non-injury to living beings, *ahiṃsā*.[22] *Upaniṣads* associate the two cosmic principles with the two Vedic paths followed in the afterlife, leading respectively to the world of the forefathers and that of the gods: those who carry out their observances in the forest go to the world of the gods, and thence to the sun and the fire of lightning, while those who live in the

[19] *Śatapatha Brāhmaṇa* 13.2.4.2–4.

[20] J. F. Sprockhoff, 'Āraṇyaka und Vanaprastha in der vedische Literatur', *WZKSA*, 25 (1981), p. 84.

[21] Malamoud, 'Village et forêt', pp. 5, 9, 13 and passim. Some sacrificial spoons, associated with village animals, are used repeatedly; others, associated with wild animals, are thrown away after a single use (see p. 13).

[22] Ibid., pp. 11–20.

village and carry out sacrifices return to earth.[23] Jain texts commemorate the same polarity of village and wilderness.[24]

That the symbolism of kingship came to embrace the subjection of the forces of the wilderness therefore follows logically; kings both subdued them and maintained them as a source of power. Nancy Falk has argued for a cosmological link between royal power and wilderness: 'It appears that a king had to have some kind of transaction with the wilderness and the beings that inhabit it to acquire or hold his kingship.'[25] Among the forms taken by this relationship, it is worth noticing the importance of the shrine in the royal park, symbol of wilderness, where a throne consisting of a stone slab constitutes a ritual focus for the king's absorption of cosmic energies.[26] The special role of the king's pleasure park is commemorated in the *Jātakas*: he receives homage from wild creatures there, and his occupancy of its throne legitimizes his rule.[27] Royal patron deities were sometimes associated with the wilderness spirits: Jagannāth was originally a forest god, and the Buddha tooth relic has been traced back to a *yakṣa* cult.[28]

It is quite clear that the rootless lifestyle of the early Buddhist monks made them familiar with the ways of the wilderness; they were professionally required to confront its dangers, and no doubt they were widely perceived to absorb its powers. Certainly, many monks, including the Buddha himself, must have wandered through forests and wasteland, but the later career of the Buddha seems to have tended much more to an itinerary that led to and from urban centres, accompanied by an entourage. Nonetheless, the connection between the wandering monk and the ambiguous powers of the forest remains integral to the image and style of the holy man's career.

The *Jātakas* are a rich source of information about the types of people who made their living in the frontier areas – pioneer villagers, foresters, hunters, sometimes carpenters, and often enough refugees[29] or

[23] *BrhU* 6.2.15ff.; *ChU* 5.10.1–3.

[24] J. Bronkhorst, *The Two Traditions of Meditation in Ancient India* (Steiner, Stuttgart, 1986), p. 29, citing the *Āyāraṅga Sūtra*.

[25] N. Falk, 'Wilderness and kingship in ancient South Asia', *HR*, 13 (1974), p. 1.

[26] J. Auboyer, *Le trône et son symbolisme dans l'Inde ancienne* (Pressses Universitaires de France, Paris, 1949), esp. pp. 51–61. The royal throne is absorbed within the evolution of the iconography of the altar and linked with the spirits of sacred trees in consecrated spots. It is invested (pp. 61ff.) with mythical value and is considered to be the predestined seat of a great being.

[27] *J* IV 40, V 247ff., VI 39, where strangers destined for kingship are discovered lying on the stone slab in the royal park; II 227, where a king receives the homage of fish and tortoises in his park.

[28] Falk, 'Wilderness and kingship'.

[29] *J* II 356, IV 306ff., where the bodhisattva dwells in seclusion, in one case as a tree spirit in the forest. On *Jātaka* references to forest dwellers in general see Tracy Taylor, 'The Interaction of the Settled and Wild Lands, According to the Jātakas' (unpublished thesis, Monash University, 1983), pp. 27–9, and passim.

exiles.[30] Unassimilated tribal communities lived in the forest areas, as they have until modern times, and relations with them were constantly a complex and vexatious problem for kings;[31] the *AŚ* at a number of points gives advice about the treatment of such tribes, *āṭavika*.[32] Buddhist monks constantly passed through the wilderness in their wanderings, though naturally they could not take up residence, even briefly, far from the settlements upon which they depended for their food; but these settlements were often enough small outlying hamlets in the hinterland areas.[33] Buddhist monks might lodge with the nomadic groups of cattle herders, moving when the herdsmen moved.[34]

To judge from the *Jātakas*, Buddhists knew the wilderness well. It was regarded as a place of untamed spirits, especially *yakṣas*.[35] The concept underlying the figure of a *yakṣa* perhaps connoted primal lack of order, as represented also by the waters that frame the cosmos; upon the waters reclines the figure of the creator deity, sometimes called a *yakṣa*; from his body the gods arose.[36] The forest is a place of animals, spirits and birds.[37] It is especially a place of danger from spirits, exciting fear and numinous dread which must be quelled by meditation:

> So I . . . stayed in such frightening places as park-shrines, forest-shrines, tree-shrines. As I was staying there, brahmin, either an animal came along, or a peacock broke off a twig, or the wind rustled the fallen leaves. It occurred to me: 'Surely this is fear and dread coming . . . Why am I staying longing for nothing but fear?'[38]

Merchants passing through were doubtless impelled by the hope of profits, but they did not like it.[39] Some of the dangers no doubt were mundane ones, like those of Sherwood Forest while Robin Hood was at large, but others were supernatural, and no very sharp distinction was made between different types of danger. *Jātakas* tell us stories of the adventures that befell travellers in wild places: one merchant was tricked by a malicious spirit into

[30] Certainly it is a recurrent theme of Indian literature that victims of successful conquerors should be banished for long periods. See R. Thapar, 'The Rāmāyaṇa: theme and variation', in S. Mukherjee (ed.), *India: History and Thought* (Subarnarakha, Calcutta, 1982), pp. 221–53.

[31] *J* II 74 (a border rebellion); see also Taylor, *Settled and Wild Lands*, p. 43, for *Jātaka* references to frontier problems.

[32] *AŚ* 9.2, for example, advises a ruler on the circumstances in which it is appropriate to recruit wild tribes into his army.

[33] *Vin* III 46 defines 'village' (*gāma*) as a settlement of any size starting from one hut, or two, three or four huts; though part of the old commentary, this passage may be late.

[34] *Vin* I 152: monks could stay in a cow pen, *vaja*, and move on with it when it was moved.

[35] Taylor, *Settled and Wild Lands*, p. 14.

[36] A. K. Coomaraswamy, *Yakṣas* (Munshiram Manoharlal, Delhi, 1971), part II, p. 25.

[37] *J* V 416. Creatures dwelling in the region are listed, and immediately after animal species come 'horse-faced *yakkhas*, sprites, goblins and ogres'.

[38] *M* I 20ff.

[39] For example, *M* I 276.

throwing away his drinking-water; a group of merchants died of poisonous wild fruit; bands of robbers fell upon hapless travellers passing through; captives were taken, and ransom demands made; plundering war-bands emerging from the wilderness raided villages and caused the villagers to run away.[40] The famous Buddhist convert, Aṅgulimāla, had in his career of crime caused villages to become 'non-villages' in this way.[41] Whilst we have no way of generating crime statistics for ancient India, it is still the case that the fear of the forest was not based just on the ambiguity intended by supernatural powers, but equally on real physical danger, the cause of which could be easily ascertained.

Now, in all this, we can recognize the foundations of a cosmological structure that is essential to the world view of the people upon whose support the *śramaṇa* orders depended, a world view which inevitably moulded the evolution of religious attitudes and behaviour.

PERSONAL AND IMPERSONAL COSMIC FORCES

We need first to recognize the division of beliefs into those that postulate gods or spirits, beings possessed of will and consciousness, capable of recognizing prayers or insults and of influencing human life, and those that postulate impersonal processes, inanimate forces that operate according to their own laws regardless of human interests, potentially dangerous if uncontrolled but capable of being manipulated by the use of special knowledge. The latter are sometimes left altogether out of account in any enquiry into religion, or if noticed they may be considered to represent a debased or inferior sort of religion, called magic. Both approaches are mistaken.

In the world view that developed under the influence of these cosmological principles, then, there were two types of power affecting human life, the impersonal and the personal. Quite a long time ago now, Durkheim recognized this well enough. He sought to give causal and chronological priority to the impersonal conceptions of religion; without necessarily following him in this, we can recognize the perceptiveness with which he analysed the intermeshing of personal and impersonal forces in the cosmologies of traditional religious beliefs.[42]

[40] *J* II 295ff., where a *nāga* lord slays merchants in a forest; II 335ff., where a merchant caravan is attacked in the forest by a robber band. See also Taylor, *Settled and Wild Lands*, p. 24.

[41] *M* II 97, 100.

[42] E. Durkheim, *The Elementary Forms of the Religious Life*, trans. J. W. Swain (Free Press, New York, 1965), pp. 229ff., 'What we find at the origin and basis of religious thought are . . . indefinite powers, anonymous forces . . . whose impersonality is strictly comparable to that of the physical forces whose manifestations the sciences of nature study . . . so it is not surprising that even in the religions where

In the Indian cosmology, where form and order must be imposed upon a threatening disorder or lack of order, we find that the formlessness of the wilderness is characterized, and in large measure defined, by the disordered mingling of the personal and the impersonal; the form and order of human life in society is characterized by the proper separation and demarcation of the personal and the impersonal.

It may not be going too far to suggest that, at least in Buddhist thought, the same distinction needed to be made in the imposition of order upon the mind. It is precisely the intermeshing of purpose and sentience with mindless thinghood that gives an edge of numinous dread to the encounter with disordered nature. The spirits that haunt the forests, mountains and deserts have consciousness and can do us harm or good, but their personalities are apt to dissolve into faceless, remorseless energies. Conversely, the elements of blind nature that embody the cycles of day and season have within them germs of purpose and consciousness that need to be negotiated with; it is always possible that real communication can be established with them by the use of expert knowledge. It is just this ambivalence of personality and thinghood that makes the dark unpredictability of raw nature dangerous and frightening.

On the other hand, the realm of settled order is established by the clear demarcation of unambiguously inanimate things or forces and unambiguously conscious beings; the latter are able confidently to manipulate the former. Boundaries are drawn, ritually and juridically. There are familiar gods whose behaviour is more or less predictable, and therefore capable of being managed by appropriate ritual. Magic is technology, which can be learned by apprenticeship to a specialist. Life is capable, often if in practice not always, of being planned and made predictable.

The old problem of the nature of the Ṛgvedic religion illustrates the pattern. Though Max Müller's concept of henotheism may have been false to the real character of the old Vedic cult, he had a point. The Vedic gods were indeed seen as stable conscious individuals, each unique and separate, and thus far belonging to the domesticated religion of the ordered microcosm, but they were not completely and safely personalized. They were envisaged in part as clusters of transferable properties (creation, shining, killing demons, giving life etc.); in a sense they were not so much unique

there are avowed divinities, there are rites having an efficient virtue in themselves, independently of all divine intervention . . . Even should [the energy of this efficient virtue] happen to concentrate itself especially in a rite, this will become a creator of divinities from that very fact. That is why there is scarcely a divine personality who does not retain some impersonality . . . Zeus is in each of the raindrops which falls, just as Ceres is in each of the sheaves of the harvest.'

individuals as nodes in a web of impersonal forces. Their fierce and often dangerous powers meant that they were always imperfectly tamed and domesticated; they were still liable to retreat into the forces of raw nature. It is this, indeed, that imparts a glimmer of truth to the old simplistic conception of Vedic religion as worship of nature; but this perception identifies only one pole, from which the gods were receding under the influence of myth and ritual. It was the prescriptions of the *Brāhmaṇa* texts that effectively bottled the gods' personalities within the confines of a set of rules which could not be transgressed; the gods became uninteresting, and the activities of the priest all-important.

A further development was liable to take place with the increasing elaboration of an ideology of domestication and order. The effect of confinement by rules, of ritual power over the environment, was in the first place to separate the personal from the impersonal, so that sentient beings (including gods and spirits, and the inhabitants of the other realms to which a being might go for rebirth) were clearly distinguished from the inanimate elements and forces of nature; but in the long run the ritual worked against the true autonomy of sentient beings, who were liable to retreat to the status of passive components within a deterministic system. The Vedic gods suffered this fate early, to the extent that they were tamed and subordinated by the mechanisms of brāhmaṇical ritual.

Ultimately, the same process of depersonalization could engulf all beings as they came to be seen as instruments of a cosmic order. What used to be vital purposeful forces could turn into intellectual abstractions. (Māra, lord of the underworld, for example, could turn into a metaphor for transmigration; a *stūpa* could become a diagram to aid recollection and meditation; human personality could turn into an elaborate psychological chart tabulating interactions between various defined components in successive moments.) In modern industrial culture, materialist philosophies such as mind-brain identity theory have advanced the process practically as far as it can go, though philosophical puzzles remain.

This complex cycle of relationships is something implicit in the cosmology which Indians more or less instinctively accepted, not a map of intellectual history. Any particular doctrine may take its place in a number of different cosmological contexts, and be reinterpreted accordingly. Thus, although it is certainly useful to think of Buddhism and the *śramaṇa* movements as emerging, in some sense, from the unpredictable and unbounded environment of the wilderness, and of brāhmaṇical religion as belonging to the ritually circumscribed order of settlement, there are many complications. Something of the original danger and energy of primal forces may still be felt by ordinary devotees to inhere in any religious artifact or concept,[43] while for the scholarly monk that same thing may be little more than an intellectualization; and different religious traditions or styles of life can be related to the cosmic environment of personhood, thinghood or abstraction in different ways.

It is easy enough to recognize the values of brāhmaṇical tradition in the minutely regulated religious environment of settlement, where disorder is kept at bay, the cosmos can be mapped, and divine forces are predictable and familiar. But major qualifications have to be made. For one thing, brahmanism was not a simple monolithic structure; with the concept of the fourth stage of life, it incorporated within itself the originally alien values of the holy man in the wilderness. For another, the individuality of gods within the system did not remain static: no sooner did ritual threaten to erase their personality altogether, turning them into no more than inert vehicles, than devotional religion, *bhakti*, came to give them back all their former autonomy, but in a different way.

In the third place, it is easy enough to recognize the values of the wandering holy man in the religious environment of the wilderness. By braving dangers and exposing himself to the powerful half-animate forces that haunt the lonely places, he absorbs power.[44] By his intense self-control, in a sense by his impersonality, he prevents the supernatural hurricane around him from tearing his being apart, and learns to control the fierce energies of the cosmos; he internalizes them, using them to obtain supernatural skills and insights. He is a living symbol of precisely defined order and predictability amidst all that is the opposite of this. This at least is the manner in which the ordinary villager is liable to regard the mendicant who comes out of the forest, his gaunt emaciated frame attesting his confrontation with powerful psychic forces. As a result of his sojourn in the wilderness he is made alien, other; he is a dweller in the spaces between, detached from the interests and concerns of ordinary humanity. He is almost a spirit himself. It is essential to recognize this context – like the experience of initiation, in a sense – if

[43] See, for example, Douglas, *Purity and Danger*, pp. 94–113 and passim. The massive importance of the duality of form and formlessness in traditional societies is fundamental to the structure of ideas described here.

[44] This is very much like the brāhmaṇical concept of *tapas*, the mystic heat which the ascetic is able to absorb by austerities and meditation. It is important to distinguish between *tapas*, yoga, Buddhist meditation, and gnosis, which although they overlap a great deal in various ways are distinct techniques or concepts; but from the point of view of Indian cosmology, what matters is that the behaviour of the holy man, Buddhist or otherwise, presented the image of an ascetic building up *tapas*. See W. O. Kaelber, '*Tapas*, birth and spiritual rebirth in the Veda', *HR*, 15 (1976), pp. 343–86.

we are to make sense of the way in which *śramaṇa* movements such as Buddhism developed.

BUDDHISM, FOLK RELIGION AND MAGIC

Buddhism inherited these cosmological premises without seriously criticizing them, and Buddhist literature presents us with the same duality: wilderness spirits that are not clearly animate or inanimate, and the microcosm of the settled community, within which the animate and the inanimate are kept apart.

This way of regarding the background of belief about cosmic principles makes sense of some of the ambiguities we meet in Buddhist texts. For example, the Buddhist concept of the *nāga* oscillates teasingly between snake, human and superhuman; Rawlinson has argued that the oscillations represent not a multiplicity of discrepant traditions but different manifestations of a consistent cosmology in which both personal beings (including *devas*) and abstract principles are manifested in a hierarchy of forms linked by correspondences of essential nature. Thus the *nāga deva* becomes the principle of water and is equivalent to sap, semen, soma and fire, and is embodied in snakes and in certain people whose nature possesses the appropriate qualities (fiery, sharp, fierce and so forth).[45]

Buddhism came out of the wilderness, and was domesticated. It also domesticated the forces of the wilderness. These are symbolized, for example, by the figures of Aṅgulimāla and the *yakkhas*, tamed in various ways by the Buddha.[46] We cannot doubt that many generations of Buddhist monks and followers believed (or instinctively accepted, having in their bones a profound sense of the ubiquity of cosmic forces) that it brought with it an armoury of powers that might be animate or inanimate or an explosive mixture of both. Such powers were commemorated in Buddhist stories of gods and spirits, in the potency of ritual designs in art, iconography and architecture, in the cult of relics. Some scholars emphasize the monastic, scholarly tradition which made abstractions of these things, graphic reminders to the faithful of facts or qualities upon which they should meditate.[47] The scholarly monks, however, had to contend

[45] A. Rawlinson, 'Nāgas and the magical cosmology of Buddhism', *Religion*, 16 (1986), p. 144.

[46] Bailey, 'Problems'.

[47] J. Masson, *La religion populaire dans le canon Bouddhique Pāli* (Muséon, Louvain, 1942), distinguishes at many points between a popular type of religion which made its way into Buddhism to be accepted, rejected or transformed, and a scholarly type which made of mythical or divine beings allegories or philosophical categories. See for example pp. 109–13.

with the concrete realities of early Buddhism, which inevitably imported the unquestioned cosmological assumptions of its original cultural context and was perceived as bringing powerful forces out of the wilderness; what followed was a movement towards order and separation that came with domestication, sanitizing all the more strange or dangerous supernatural forces by turning them into laws of nature, eventually making of them intellectual abstractions.

One thing that Buddhism brought out of the wilderness was never wholly domesticated, although it came eventually to be ignored in practice by the overwhelming majority of all Buddhists – the doctrine of non-self, *anātman* or *anatta*. Of course, other *śramaṇa* movements with claims at least as strong to have found their truth in lonely places came up with different doctrines about the ontology of the self, but it is interesting that most of these doctrines shared a concern to dissolve the soul of man into thinghood. Among the new schools of holy men, Buddhism carried out perhaps the most systematic campaign to invert the teachings of brahmanism, and the Upaniṣadic glorification of the One, *ātman*, found its photo-negative in the Buddhist denial of any substantial immortal soul.

Such a claim, along with the 'materialistic' teachings of the Ājīvikas and others, should not be read as a simple reduction of the animate to the inanimate, a rejection of the ghost in favour of the machine (though in its most abstract and intellectual forms it came close). After all, the categories of Cartesian dualism do not precisely correspond to the categories of the ancient Indian thought world. The amorphous energies that haunt the wilderness belong to a primal chaos prior to categories; will and consciousness are not integrated within unique self-contained personalities but are stirred into a mixture of elements and impulses, physical and immaterial; and this mixture cannot adequately be described as animate or inanimate. Here divine energies move restlessly, without attachment to any abode; they are the wind that howls in desert places, *vāyu*, which was equated with the breath that quite literally constitutes the self, *ātman*.[48] Something of this ambiguity clings to the vision offered by the holy men. When the Buddha declined to say whether the soul is identical with the body or not, his chief purpose was probably to reinforce his constant emphasis upon practice, not metaphysics; but if the question were one that could be answered straightforwardly, without any complexity to detain the intellect and prompt a metaphysical enquiry, the demands of practice would not have been compromised by an answer. The fact is that, clearly enough,

[48] Malamoud, 'Village et forêt', pp. 3–20.

the Buddha and his disciples sensed an ambiguity that hung over the status of an individual's existence, an ambiguity that plagued the subsequent course of Buddhist teaching, and an ambiguity which had its origin in the otherness, the in-betweenness, of the empty spaces in which the *dhamma* found its birth. In its subsequent evolution, the doctrine of *anatta* turned into a preoccupation of philosophers concerned with learning rather than spiritual cultivation (*pariyatti*, rather than *patipatti*), but in its origins it was an instinctive response to the in-betweenness of the wild places where chaos rules, where everything is potential and nothing is complete. To say that personal beings exist there would be wrong; to say that they do not would be wrong too.

None of this, however, must be read as an attempt to interpret Buddhist doctrine as implied by the earliest scriptures; the Buddha was not a prophet of disorder. It is, rather, a description of the structure of the cosmos inhabited mentally by the Buddha's contemporaries, and it suggests the image presented to layfolk by the holy men who came out of the empty places to preach to townsmen.

Within the Indian thought world, then, the relationship between the animate and the inanimate was highly charged; the two terms were positive and negative poles capable of generating a powerful electricity. We need these principles for the understanding of the more abstract cosmology that was formulated within the Great Tradition and became part of the generally accepted Indian cultural heritage, including the popular or 'folk' environment within the totality of Indian religious culture.

Buddhism absorbed and digested the pre-existing Indian beliefs about the structure of the cosmos. It was a structure that postulated a cosmic order won from the primal absence of order that confounded personal and impersonal principles; in this cosmic order the gods presided over the continuing stability of the system. Cosmography pictured the world as an arrangement of four continents, or of seven ring-shaped continents separated by oceans, around a central point where Meru (Pāli *Sineru*), mountain of the gods, rose up towards the heavens.[49] Upon this cosmographic structure, Buddhism superimposed a scale of horizontal layers, *dhātus*, which are states of being reached in meditation and rising above Mount Meru as superior levels.[50] As Rawlinson said, '[I]t may well be that this magical

[49] W. Kirfel, *Die Kosmographie der Inder* (George Olms, Hildesheim, 1967 (Bonn and Leipzig, 1920); I. W. Mabbett, 'The symbolism of Mount Meru', *HR*, 23 (1983), pp. 64–83.

[50] E. Lamotte, 'Introduction à l'étude du bouddhisme de Śakyamuni d'après les textes anciens', *Nachrichten der Akademie der Wissenschaften in Göttingen I: Philologisch-Historische Klasse*, 1983, pp. 83–120.

cosmology is pre-Buddhist. But it would be wrong to think that Buddhism rejected it; the *rūpadhātu* and *kāmadhātu* of Buddhist cosmology are totally magical.'[51]

This superimposition has been seen as a conceptually awkward conflation likely to show the combination of traditions from different sources.[52] But, however it originated, Buddhist cosmology integrated the cosmic and psychological scales within a single vision. According to this vision, for example, the fourth *dhyāna* is a psychological state reached in meditation, from which enlightenment can be reached, but it is also a place, a realm within which rebirth is possible. The scheme is one which fuses what seems to the modern mind to be incommensurables, but as Peter Masefield has argued, perhaps the cosmography of tiered realms and the hierarchy of mental states should be seen not as more or less metaphorical designations of different things but as a single reality, apprehended from different points of view.[53] In similar vein, Rupert Gethin has argued that the Buddhist conception of states of existence does not distinguish them from states of mind.[54] The difference is one of time scale: different states of mind are reached within one lifetime; the cosmos evolves over aeons.

It would be wrong to identify the Buddhist cosmology with magic and folk culture, and divorce this from spirituality and meditation. Buddhism did not add a new mentality; it absorbed Indian cosmological traditions and reinterpreted them. It had no reason to reject the belief that power can be gained by insight into the fixed laws described by cosmology, which was a constant tributary to Indian tradition.

It is therefore important to recognize that magic – the manipulation of impersonal forces by one expert in the technology – was not something that Buddhist belief automatically rejected. The distinction between belief in impersonal principles and belief in sentient beings did not correspond to any difference between 'superstition' and 'religion'. Rhys Davids, who recognized very much the same two principles and called them normalism and animism, pointed out that the former persisted through the Vedas and was represented by the magic of names, numbers, propinquity and association.[55] The *Atharva Veda* clearly represents the belief in power based on

[51] Rawlinson, 'Nāgas', p. 144.

[52] On the hybrid origins of Buddhist hierarchies of meditation states, see Bronkhorst, *The Two Traditions*, pp. 75–80.

[53] P. Masefield, 'Mind/Cosmos maps in the Pāli Nikāyas,' in N. Katz (ed.), *Buddhist and Western Psychology* (Prajñā Press, Boulder, 1983), pp. 69–93.

[54] Rupert Gethin, 'Cosmology and meditation: from the *Aggañña Sutta* to the Mahāyāna,' *HR*, 36 (1997), pp. 183–217.

[55] Rhys Davids, *Dialogues of the Buddha*, vol. III, pp. 53–8.

knowledge of a system.[56] In the Pāli Canon, this Veda does not commonly figure alongside the earlier three, but the stream of magical belief which it represents was part of the cultural furniture of India.

The ascetic tradition, to which Buddhism belonged, lay squarely within the same cultural world. The literature of other ascetic schools is full of references to magic powers; Mahāvīra and Gosāla are represented as exercising precognition and duelling with the powers born of their austerities. One episode in the *Bhagavatī Sūtra*, for example, has Gosāla reducing enemies to ashes by magic, and attempting unsuccessfully to do the same to Mahāvīra.[57] Within the wider community, ascetics came to be seen as workers of magic. Ascetics, classed with learned brahmins, magicians and priests of miscellaneous cults, could be engaged for such purposes as protecting against the evil effects of rats, demons, pestilences of any sort, or famine. 'Persons acquainted with rituals of the Atharva Veda (*atharvavedavido*) and experts in sacred magic and mysticism shall perform such ceremonials as ward off the danger from demons.'[58] This is the world in which the monks stood forth to proclaim the *dhamma*. What they taught, and the roles they were able to play in society, had to fit within the same world. In the next chapter we shall explore a little further the Buddhist involvement in this world.

[56] For example, the creation of the human body is attributed to the magic action of the indwelling sacred brahman (conceived of as an impersonal force): *Atharva Veda* 10.2, discussed by L. Renou, *Etudes Védiques et Pāṇinéennes* (Boccard, Paris, 1956), vol. II, pp. 69–79. Renou emphasizes the theme of magically efficacious knowledge in the *Atharva Veda.*

[57] *Bhagavatī Sūtra*, cited by Basham, *Ājīvikas*, p. 60. [58] *AŚ* 4.3.37.

Mediation

7
The holy man

On the working hypothesis adopted here, the Buddha taught that truth is best to be found by leading the life of a wanderer who rids himself of all attachments and cultivates an austerely simple way of life, cut off from all social ties and possessions and following the path by which the causes of suffering and rebirth can be destroyed. This original idea is not to be regarded as determining a particular defined stage of Buddhism as a whole; it is, rather, one of a number of factors that co-operated in the shaping of the movement when the Buddha began to communicate his ideas to others. Nevertheless, the idea was original and basic, and it persisted, clearly and unambiguously, in the scriptures. It must therefore have been an element in the success of Buddhism in a particular sort of social environment. The purpose of this chapter is to advance a substantially new view of the way in which Buddhism (and similar ascetic movements) could first come to secure an important social role. This interpretation requires us to acknowledge that the life of the wandering ascetic was the original ideal of the Buddhist Order, and the one by which (despite its austerity and other-worldliness) it was first able to attract substantial support in some areas. First, therefore, it is necessary to survey briefly the reasons for accepting that the original impulse driving the order was indeed an ascetic one.

THE BUDDHISTS AS *ŚRAMAṆAS*

Seeking to explain Buddhism's social role, scholars often ignore the Buddhist scriptures' message of ascetic withdrawal and private pursuit of salvation. One objection to doing this – an objection rarely if ever recognized – is the simple fact that this message was perfectly familiar in society at the time as an important stream in religious life, the *śramaṇa* movement. We cannot ignore this stream. It therefore becomes difficult indeed to treat the Buddha's ideal of the homeless life of a wandering mendicant as an exotic theoretical notion on the margins of life, irrelevant to the processes of social evolution.

There were many groupings of ascetics who sought spiritual enlightenment by wandering from place to place and living on alms. Many of them engaged in more or less severe forms of self-mortification, hoping to detach themselves from the profane world and facilitate spiritual enlightenment. The Jains and the Ājīvikas were two major groups which practised severe asceticism. The Buddha's followers similarly lived as wandering mendicants but eschewed the severer practices because they did not regard these as conducive to enlightenment; they preferred a middle way, cutting ties with society and preferring simplicity and poverty to active self-mortification.[1]

So far as the Canon allows us to tell, the Buddha's path to salvation did not require the manipulation of *karma* as such by ascetic purification. The direct method which lay at the heart of the Buddha's message involved cutting the roots of ignorance and attachment by a special form of meditation cultivated as a method of insight.[2] Meditation may have been considered to produce good *karma*, but this was not essential to the quest for salvation; it has been argued by some that, though canonical teachings include doctrines about the Buddha's memory of past lives, this was an unsystematic borrowing from the cultural context, not an essential prop to Buddhist belief.[3]

This fact, if accepted, has important implications for our view of the social role of early Buddhism, for the early *bhikkhus* were, to the extent that they were imbued with the original ideals, simply not concerned with karmic interaction, the earning of merit as it has become institutionalized in subsequent Buddhist societies. They sought enlightenment by the short path. As Gombrich has argued, the Buddha was not a gradualist, and his message, despite its much gentler physical demands than those of the Jain teaching, called for uncompromising separation from society. 'The first Buddhists were asocial, even anti-social.'[4]

In general, the Buddhist rule was rather less strict than Ājīvika and substantially less strict than Jain practice. All were normally vegetarians by

[1] Bronkhorst's distinction between an older type of asceticism emphasizing physical austerities and the more psychological system represented by Buddhism is relevant here. Bronkhorst, *The Two Traditions*, pp. 76ff.

[2] J. W. de Jong, 'The Background of Early Buddhism', pp. 42ff. distinguishes between asceticism, yoga and shamanism, and points to the problems involved in tracing the historical origin of *śramaṇa* practices, which may have been influenced by the culture of non-Vedic peoples. See more recently the important insights of G. Samuel, *Civilized Shamans*, ch. 2.

[3] R. Gombrich, '*Karma* and social control', *Comparative Studies in Society and History*, 17 (1975), pp. 212–20.

[4] Ibid., p.216.

preference, though both the Buddha and the Ājīvikas were ready to eat meat.[5]

Sanction is also given in the Buddhist canon for austerities of some rigour. The Buddha is said to have washed rags to make himself a robe;[6] the *Vinaya* offered to monks the practices of living only on food scraps, wearing clothes taken from a dust-heap, sleeping at the foot of a tree, and using only decomposed urine as medicine; these are the four *nissayas*, things on which to depend.[7] The subsequent history of Buddhism demonstrates a persistent tendency to incorporate austere practices (stopping short of fanatical self-mortification), sometimes no doubt as a self-imposed challenge to the earnestness of the ascetic, sometimes possibly as a response to the perception that rigorously ascetic holy men attracted more prestige than others. One concept that brings out clearly the tension between the two approaches is that of the *dhutāṅga*, a set of thirteen ascetic practices which in later Theravāda Buddhism came to be esteemed for the dedication to the soteriological quest which it represented.[8] By the time of the *Milinda Pañha*, though not in canonical Buddhism, the *dhutāṅgas* could be recommended without qualification.[9] Despite the Buddha's rejection of severe austerities, in places he is represented as accepting some of the *dhutāṅgas* if they are practised without selfish intent. In the *Majjhima Nikāya*, nine of the *dhutāṅgas* are mentioned positively.[10] In one place the Buddha is said to have adopted a pragmatic attitude to the practice of austerities – it all depended whether profitable states arose in the practitioner.[11] Modern scholars are divided on the importance of these practices to the Buddha. In fact, what probably counted was motivation.[12]

5 See M. Wijayaratna, *Le moine bouddhiste selon les textes du Theravada* (Cerf, Paris, 1983), pp. 87ff.; Basham, *Ājīvikas*, pp. 122ff.

6 *Vin* I 28f., where Indra helps the Buddha make his rag robe ready.

7 *Vin* I 58, where each of the four primitive *nissayas* is supplemented by 'extra' allowable forms of food, clothing, dwelling and medicine which in all cases are much less austere. Cf. E. J. Thomas, *The History of Buddhist Thought* (Routledge & Kegan Paul, London, 1933), p. 23.

8 P. V. Bapat, 'Dhutangas (or the ascetic practices of purification in Buddhism', *Indian Historical Quarterly*, 13 (1937), p. 46 points to parallels with the Jain *Ayaraṅga*.

9 *MP* pp. 351–3 where the *dhutāṅgas* are praised and described as necessary for an understanding of the *dhamma*. See N. Tatia, 'The interaction of Jainism and Buddhism', in A. K. Narain (ed.), *Studies in History* (B. R. Publishing, Delhi, 1980), pp. 329ff.

10 See *M* III 40–2, where effectively the nine are identified among practices which do not tend to salvation if they are accompanied by a selfish attitude (implying they can be practised with an unselfish attitude).

11 *D* I 11.

12 See R. Ray, *Buddhist Saints in India*, passim. C. Prebish, 'Ideal types in Indian Buddhism: a new paradigm', *JAOS*, 115 (1995), pp. 651–66, reviews different scholarly attitudes. On the ambiguity of the status of these practices see Friedrich-Silber, *Virtuosity, Charisma, and Social Order*, p. 110.

The oscillation between the heroically austere (as reflected in parts of the *Theragāthā* and the *Sn*) and the moderate within the Buddhist tradition demands that we should be clear what we mean by asceticism. There is an important difference between the rigorous self-mortification represented especially by Jain practice and the gentler lifestyle taught by the Buddhist *dhamma*. Here, the term 'ascetic' will be applied to both, for the Buddhist self-discipline is in principle just as strict, and demands total dedication to a life without possessions or attachments.

One aspect of a monk's asceticism (Buddhist or other) which is so basic that it is easily forgotten about, but is in practice usually the most difficult for the ordinand to accept, is rigorous celibacy. The asceticism of Buddhists, however moderate, still involved total celibacy. That this was a problem in ancient times is evident from the need for the large number of rules in the *Vinaya* about sexuality, particularly those banning all abnormal forms. Sometimes, no doubt, recruits to the order were already married. An interesting episode from the *Udāna* offers a glimpse of the problems that could be faced by a would-be *pravrajita*. A monk is visited by his former wife, who seeks to persuade him that he must abandon his membership of the Order and return home to take up his family responsibilities; she shows him his baby son, seeking to appeal to his natural humanity.

> Then, putting the child down in front of the venerable Sangāmaji, she went off, saying, 'There's your child, *samaṇa*. Support him!' Then the venerable Sangāmaji neither looked at that child nor said anything to him. Then Sangāmaji's former wife, before she had gone far, looked back and saw the venerable Sangāmaji neither looking at the child nor saying anything to him. On seeing that, she thought to herself: 'This *samaṇa* is not desirous even of his child.' Then, turning back, she took up the child and went off.
>
> Now the Blessed One, with the divine eye, purified and transcending human vision, saw such impropriety on the part of Sangāmaji's former wife. At that time, seeing the meaning of it, he gave utterance to this *udāna* [solemn verse]: He does not rejoice at her coming, he is not sad when she goes. Sangāmaji is released (from all ties); him I call (a real) *brāhmaṇa*.[13]

A sutta story is not a historical record, but the purpose with which it is told may be historical evidence. The story of Sangāmaji was told as an example of steadfastness in the face of a strong inducement to lapse. It is a clue to the likelihood, prima facie strong, that followers of the Buddha might have to confront powerful opposition from their families.

We are entitled to wonder how often the radical rejection of any social role represented by 'going forth' provoked serious antagonism from the families

[13] *Udāna*, ed. P. Steinthal (Routledge & Kegan Paul (for the PTS), London, 1982 (1885)), pp. 5–6.

of ordinands. The Pāli texts vouchsafe few hints of this. One passage refers explicitly to such complaints:

People grumbled, took offence and became irritated, saying: 'The recluse Gotama has followed the path (*paṭipanno*) by causing childlessness, the recluse Gotama has followed the path by causing widowhood, the recluse Gotama has followed the path by splitting up families.'[14]

Bareau made a study of the reactions to having a family member become a Buddhist monk. Many of the cases recorded, unsurprisingly, tell of families enthusiastically supporting the Buddhist Order, but sometimes families are represented as expressing their indignation at the conversion of relatives. Bareau suggests two sources of this indignation: the social pride of high-caste families, and resentment at losing a son before he had time to produce an heir (thereby rendering family property liable to escheatment to the crown).[15]

WANDERING AND SOLITUDE

In Buddhist sources appear frequent statements of good reasons for preferring a peripatetic existence, operating alone or with only one or two companions. Teachers should seek seclusion; when their lay supporters crowd around them they may be corrupted.[16] Life in a house is treated as a symbol for indulgence in the sensual pleasures, which seriously obstruct spiritual progress.[17] The authority of other legendary Buddhas is called upon to justify the life of solitude. The Buddha Vipassin is said to have thought to himself: 'It is definitely not suitable for me that I should stay in the midst of a crowd. Better I should stay alone, distanced from the crowd.'[18] The praise of solitude is a constant refrain. The Buddha's disciples were known to frequent the wilderness.[19] The Buddha preferred wandering alone to the sort of gathering for the purpose of vain talk practised by other ascetics:

The Blessed One favours lodging in the remote wilderness among woods and forests, where there is scarcely a sound, scarcely a noise, pervaded by loneliness, utterly secluded and suitable for solitary meditation.[20]

14 *Vin* I 43. This is the only place it occurs in the Canon.

15 A. Bareau, 'Les réactions des familles dont un membre devient moine selon le canon bouddhique pali', in O. H. de A. Wijesekara (ed.), *Malalasekara Commemoration Volume* (The Malalasekara Commemoration Volume Editorial Committee, Colombo, 1976), pp. 15–22.

16 *M* III 115ff. 17 Collins, *Selfless Persons*, pp. 167ff. 18 *D* II 30.

19 *D* III 195. 20 *D* III 38.

We are told that the monk is likely to be found in the vicinity of a forest, trees, hillsides, glens, caves, charnel places or open fields.[21] This is indeed a stock formula, found in many descriptions of the monk's favoured haunts: 'A monk favours lodging in some isolated spot – the wilderness, the root of a tree, a mountain cleft, a hill cave, a cemetery, a wild wood, an (unsheltered) place out in the open, a pile of straw.'[22]

The Buddha's disciples were expected to make for remote haunts and stay in wild or forest areas.[23] The Buddha warned that monks who had not purified themselves or overcome their emotional fetters would only make things worse by dwelling in lonely dangerous places, but such a practice was right for those who had advanced in spirituality: 'I am one of those ariyas, purified in respect of behaviour, whose practice it is to lodge in the remote wilderness among woods and forests.'[24] When the Buddha discusses the factors of the prosperity of the Vajjians and lists the characteristics of the *saṅgha*, solitude occurs in this list.[25] The career of the Paccekabuddha involves ascetic renunciation and solitary wandering, conditions favouring prolonged meditation.[26] Mahāyāna later disparaged the image of the pratyekabuddha, but in the canonical Pāli texts the references appear in some of the oldest passages (for example in the *Udāna* and *Sutta Nipāta*, the *Majjhima Nikāya*, and the *Niddesa*) and unambiguously celebrate the values which the Paccekabuddha embodies. The whole character of Buddhist traditions about the careers of these enlightened beings displays the early values of the wandering forest ascetic. This has been argued in detail by Reginald Ray, whose study of the traditions about a whole series of such figures supports the ascetic paradigm for central Buddhist aspirations.[27] The peripatetic ideal is specially celebrated in the *Sutta Nipāta*, a text which has been seen as a probable *locus* for an early stage of Buddhist thought about a monk's life.[28] N. A. Jayawickrame has argued that the older parts of this text reflect a time before coenobitism flourished; the

[21] *D* III 49. [22] E.g., *M* I 274.

[23] *M* I 360: a monk is expected to abandon property and live with a minimum of food and clothing, but the point of this sutta is to emphasize that what matters is his psychological attitude, not his outward circumstances. Cf. *M* II 8.

[24] *M* I 4 generally. The quotation is at *M* I 17.

[25] *D* II 77: 'so long as the brethren delight in forest dwellings (*āraññakesu*)'.

[26] M. Kloppenborg, *The Paccekabuddha: a Buddhist Ascetic* (E.J. Brill, Leiden, 1974), pp. 31–73. Cf. J. W. de Jong's review in *IIJ*, 18 (1976), pp. 322–4.

[27] R. Ray, *Buddhist Saints in India.*

[28] Bronkhorst, *The Two Traditions*, p. 121. Vetter argues that the *Aṭṭhakavagga* contains the mystic teaching of a different monastic group that eventually came to merge with the Buddhist Order. T. Vetter, *The Ideas and Meditative Practices of Early Buddhism* (E.J. Brill, Leiden, 1988), appendix, pp. 101–5.

verse portions celebrating the peripatetic life of the *muni*, the *bhikkhu* or the *samaṇa* embody some of the oldest teachings, and the *Khaggavisāṇa* verses (praising the lonely wandering life of the rhinoceros) may survive from an original foundation upon which the collection of *suttas* was built.[29] Here we read that the Buddha takes the houseless state; housebound life causes defilement.[30] Solitude was the right condition for a monk.[31] The monk was to cut himself off from all the constraints of life in society and wander forth untrammelled by family or property:

'He who has sons takes pleasure in sons, and in the same way he who owns cows takes pleasure in his cows; for what supports a man gives him pleasure, and he who lacks support lacks pleasure.' [These are the words of Māra. The Blessed One however says:] 'He who has sons is made unhappy by sons, and in the same way he who owns cows is made unhappy by cows; for what supports a man makes him unhappy, and he who lacks support lacks unhappiness.'[32]

Having torn one's fetters asunder, like a fish breaking a net in the water, not returning, like a fire (not going back) to what is (already) burned, one should wander solitary as a rhinoceros horn.[33]

The implication was clear: the monk was to find release in solitude:

Happy is isolation for one who is content, who has heard the dhamma, who has vision. Happy is the avoidance of harm, restraining oneself from (injury to) living creatures in the world. Happy is freedom from passion, passing beyond the world of desire.[34]

Further, the many references to the Buddhist Order as the '*Saṅgha* of the Four Quarters' clearly designates the ideal character of the *saṅgha* as an order of homeless peripatetics all belonging equally to all places. Such references occur in the *Vinaya*, in some post-canonical Pāli literature, and in various early inscriptions (generally later than the period considered here).[35] The term was examined by S. Dutt in his classic study of early Buddhist residence patterns; he emphasized the peripatetic ideal.[36] Sometimes the Saṅgha of the Four Quarters is the entire Buddhist Order, sometimes (as the tendency

[29] N. A. Jayawickrame, Analysis of the Sutta Nipāta. A critical analysis of the Pāli Sutta Nipāta illustrating its gradual growth (London, unpublished PhD thesis, 1947), pp. 9, 304ff.

[30] *Sn* 273, 1003, 207; cf. 805, 963.

[31] *Sn* 45ff. One may wander in company with a wise and righteous companion, but in the absence of such a person, one must wander alone. Cf. *Sn* 208.

[32] *Sn* 32f.

[33] *Sn* 61 Trans. in K. R. Norman, *The Group of Discourses (Sutta-Nipāta) Volume II. Revised Translation* (PTS, Oxford, 1992), p. 7.

[34] *Udāna*, ed. Steinthal, p. 10.

[35] On the Saṅgha of the Four Quarters, see Wijaratna, *Le moine bouddhiste*, p. 18.

[36] S. Dutt, *Early Buddhist Monachism* (Munshiram Manoharlal, Delhi, 1984 (London, 1924)), pp. 90–5.

to form permanent monastic settlements set in) the expression designates particular local communities.

THE MONK AS GO-BETWEEN

But we must not go to extremes: to insist upon regarding the Buddha and his truest spiritual heirs as lonely hermits and nothing else would be to miss half the significance of the *dhamma*. The monks needed psychological detachment, just as a battery needs to be regularly recharged, and the best conditions for this lay in periods of solitude. But, in between, the whole point of the Buddha's way was to go from place to place, receiving offerings and imparting *dhamma*. Homelessness meant wandering (*pra-vraj*); wandering means going from place to place, not disappearing from human ken. We are not looking for hermits. In interpreting the earliest social form taken by Buddhism, the choice is not just between solitary hermits and community-involved coenobites. We should not describe the Buddha and his disciples purely as lonely mystics frequenting the wilds, and equally we should not describe them purely as cosmopolitans who attracted throngs and influenced the great and famous in the big cities. The point is that they were both, and indeed that they were commonly to be seen in the myriad villages where most people lived. This is fundamental to the sociology of Buddhism and the other *śramaṇa* movements; their leaders moved freely between two worlds, constantly moving from place to place.

The social role of the monk made him familiar with all conditions of men. He was to be found in the streets of a royal city, just as much as in a group of merchants hurrying along a forest track or among goatherds on upland pastures. Urbanization, in any society, pulls local elite groups into towns and cities; landlords gravitate to the city, at least seasonally,[37] and the best potential converts for the *dhamma* were likely to be found in the biggest settlements. In the fullest sense, then, the monk was a go-between.

All this goes some way to show that the role of the earliest transmitters of the *dhamma* was unlike that of the monk as a part of the settled rural order in modern Buddhist countries. It is not the case that, knowing what modern agrarian Buddhist societies are like, we can therefore recognize the dynamics of the society inhabited by the Buddha. The special conditions of early northeastern India during the urbanization process must have been different

[37] G. Sjoberg, 'The rise and fall of cities,' *International Journal of Comparative Sociology*, 4 (1963), pp. 110ff.

from those of later periods. In these conditions, Buddhism and the other non-brāhmaṇical teachings are likely to have found their niches in ways which cannot readily be inferred from the study of other places and times. In a modern setting, the community of monks participates in a stable social system. It facilitates the earning of merit by the lay population, with which it lives in symbiosis. Further, the order takes part in ceremonies, provides an avenue of advancement for the ambitious, keeps alive a tradition of higher values, and provides village education. Monks and nuns even participate in legal, social and economic exchanges in ways hardly countenanced by the letter of the monastic law. Indeed, inscriptions yield ample evidence of monastic involvement in various forms of social interaction in early times,[38] though they cannot tell us about the Buddha's own lifetime or the careers of the earliest converts.

It would be wrong to suppose that the essential character of this social involvement of the *saṅgha* provides a premise from which we can reason backwards to the mechanisms by which Buddhism as such first acquired any sort of social role. Such a proceeding may tempt us to dismiss as marginal or incidental the whole tradition of solitary asceticism and meditation which the canonical texts clearly identify as the predominant concern of the *dhamma*. We should seek to understand the *dhamma*'s origin by working from an understanding of the best evidence available. That evidence is furnished, for better or worse, by the texts. These represent the Buddhist monk as a wandering holy man, and it is this image to which we must give priority in the context of Buddhism's rise. In the next section we shall see that the image fits in its context very well.

COMMUNITY SELF-PERCEPTION IN AN AGE OF EXPANSION

On a map, or in a paragraph, the human settlements that made up an ancient Indian kingdom's population are anonymous and featureless, undifferentiated dots or notional quantities; we have little idea what it was like to live in them. But it was, ultimately, the feelings of their inhabitants that wrote the script – their loves and hates, their loyalties and distrusts – which determined how contests should end, what institutions should be

[38] In a series of articles G. Schopen has demonstrated this social involvement from inscriptions, dating primarily from the early centuries of the Christian era. See for example 'Doing business for the Lord: lending on interest and written loan contracts in the Mūlasarvāstivādavinaya', *JAOS*, 114 (1994), pp. 527–54; 'Monastic law meets the real world: a monk's continuing right to inherit family property in classical India,' *HR*, 35 (1996), pp. 101–23; 'Two problems in the history of Indian Buddhism: the layman/monk distinction and the doctrines of the transferences of merit', *Studien zur Indologie und Iranistik*, 10 (1985), pp. 9–47.

supported or abandoned. What motives drove them? It is all too easy to manufacture interpretative categories out of ignorance, imagining for example that 'the masses' were one significant class of people, and 'the elite' another, or that the four ritual *varṇas* were such classes, each following its perceived interest in dealing with the others. But we cannot know how often, or whether, these categories really shaped history. There must have been many categories of interest and affinity, often cross-cutting, that defined significant classes; and we have to deduce, if we can, what they might have been.

In modern society, significant groups of people which act on recognized shared interest tend to be horizontal – social classes or occupational groups. In ancient India the obvious working hypothesis must be different; it is much more likely that the significant groups were vertical – communities occupying particular areas. Features of the environment encouraging geographical separation, or facilitating one chieftain's control over an area, are more likely to have defined units of population with a natural coherence and cultural homogeneity.

Historical or social analysis favours simplicity of conceptualization and tends to interpret phenomena (such as religious movements) as products of continuing social or cultural patterns. But what if a phenomenon actually depends on social change, on transition? The period of the rise of Buddhism was one of expansion, as the rising urban-based kingdoms reached out to encroach upon hinterland communities. Paths first made by pioneers or refugees were increasingly trodden by traders, tax gatherers and war-bands or royal armies. With growing population, settlements grew and the patches of land they cleared grew and coalesced.

We have to recognize the major cultural adjustments that had to be made as the inhabitants of outlying settlements found their lives encroached upon by outsiders representing urban culture. Sometimes they could be recognized as fellow members of a cultural group, linked by lifestyle, language, religion, myth, ancestry, or any combination of these or other factors. Sometimes they could not. Either way, they might be seen as sources either of advantage or of danger.

When a state expanded into new territory, the people living there were under threat, but they might find opportunities too. They could suffer from armies, tax gatherers, press-gangs, and providers of goods and services in disastrous competition with local people. They could benefit from new trade opportunities, new resources, new employment possibilities, new wealth. All the time, they had to deal with an assertive and challenging set of cultural values and symbols coming from outside.

If these values and symbols belonged substantially to the set of shared culture and remembered history they already possessed, then brahmins, who were the custodians of acknowledged sacred truth, could mediate the fusion of separate groups, providing a language for the articulation of a common sense of community that integrated the locality within the larger unit. But what when shared cultural frameworks were absent or highly diffuse and there were no common cultural symbols? What when political dominance reached out quickly into the further hinterland where culturally unassimilated communities lived, strangers to brāhmaṇical rituals?

Not only would the extension of political hegemony have to be justified in other terms than a mere show of power, but different cultural positions would also have to be assimilated. Here, a different sort of cultural cement was required, neutral towards dominant culture and subordinated community alike. It is here that the figure of the holy man, a peripatetic symbol of power and wisdom, explicitly rejecting any stake in the institutions of power and authority, at home alike in the courts of kings and in the settlements of herdsmen or upland agriculturalists, had an important part to play.

This view of the social role of the Buddhist monk has the merit of relating the rise of Buddhism to the urbanization process in a more systematic way than do other accounts. The relationship lies in the role of the holy man, who, whatever his original personal motivation (and even in despite of it), could become an agent of acculturation, a middleman between the urban state and the remoter local cultures. But such a role was not part of the original ascetic and esoteric programme, as embodied in the earliest teachings; nor was it, in its evolution into a variety of social functions, envisaged by the villagers who first adopted a holy man as a repository of merit and protective energy. No doubt many monks, and very likely the Buddha himself, resisted the temptation to be drawn in, though at least the potentiality for this kind of role is implicit in some of the Buddha's activities.

At court, the monk could act as intercessor between a ruler and his potential targets or victims; but the traditional image of the Buddha as an adviser to kings makes clear the sensitivity of this role. It could so easily violate the other-worldly ideals of the ascetic path. Bareau has recognized this, emphasizing that the Buddha offered advice and teachings rather than attempting active mediation between two different cultures or world views.[39] In such situations, the Buddha encouraged kings to place their

[39] Bareau, 'Le Bouddha et les rois', p. 38.

actions in a much broader spiritual context than that provided merely by the language of Realpolitik.

However, as a matter of social history, the passage between ascetic and public forms of Buddhism has always been too easy to make. Just as may be observed in modern Buddhist states, when we examine the process of domestication studied by anthropologists, even those monks who were wedded to the ideals of the ascetic wanderer must have found themselves drawn into the web of social interaction by a thousand subtle strands.

They depended for subsistence upon lay supporters; these perceived themselves to be benefiting from the monks in ways that need not have corresponded to the world view or values of the ascetic wanderers; in the course of daily contact the dissonant perceptions adjusted to each other and the monks were brought to play an integral part in the society which they had originally forsaken. The more truly ascetic and detached they were, the more attractive they might be to villagers as sources of spiritual benefit.

This process of domestication in the interaction between monks and laity was not a straightforward development whereby an earlier situation (villagers regard ascetic holy men as sources of spiritual energy and give them alms) came to be superseded by a later (monks reside close to villages and act as mentors, priests and teachers). It was, if modern parallels are any guide, a complex form of evolution, both rapid and gradual, with cycles contained within cycles. Overall, in the long run, the *saṅgha* settled in monasteries and became a social institution. In detail, in innumerable micro-historical narratives, holy men gained reputations, formed links with villagers, and became quasi-icons at the centre of church-like institutions, which after their death sometimes inspired other ascetic holy men. Different facets of Buddhism, seen differently by different people, co-existed at any given stage. Here, we wish to abstract, artificially, the earlier and later stages and see how monks could be holy men, or village priests, or both.

HOLY MEN AS MIDDLEMEN. THE ANALOGY OF THE CHRISTIAN HOLY MAN

An interpretation of the monk as holy man mediating between diverse social groups finds support from the analogy of better documented historical episodes, where holy men have acquired a political role in the interaction between a cosmopolitan state and a culturally diverse local society. Conspicuous is the case of the Christian peripatetics of the Levant in late antiquity, as studied by Peter Brown.[40] Brown points to the need of hermits to separate themselves from society and frequent the wilderness. However, they also often visited public places wherever there were congregations of merchants, soldiers or migrant groups. The society that honoured them was not poverty-stricken, for there were big prosperous villages in Syria: 'The holy man did not arise from any misère of the country-folk, as is too often stated.'[41] Here as in India, we find no evidence for the assumption that social distress was a precondition of success for a message of salvation. Rather, with few exceptions, both economy and society appear on the evidence to have been expanding, and societies came into possession of more sophisticated technologies and broader cultural horizons.

The Syrian parallel is instructive. Holy men, once they had gained respect, could function as village patrons (replacing landlords, who were migrating to the towns); they could offer advice, use their influence as men of birth and education in matters of law and taxation; they could heal and exorcise; they could arbitrate in local disputes.

In 1995, Brown modified his earlier emphasis upon the political role of the holy man as a mentor of rulers, preferring to stress his mediating activity in the hinterland, in 'marginal' areas. The holy man 'in many regions, acted as a facilitator in the transition from paganism to Christianity';[42] examples show how the holy man could adapt to local perceptions of the sacred, and often directly confronted the local sorcerer, acting as healer or intercessor with divine power.[43]

These men had to separate themselves rigorously from society if they were to be trusted as neutral, disinterested helpers, spiritual or social. By his asceticism, even his eccentricity, a holy man marked himself off as a quintessential outsider wherever he went, standing 'outside the ties of family, and of economic interest . . . he was thought of as the man who owed nothing to society . . . whose attitude to food itself rejected all the ties of solidarity to kin and village that . . . had always been expressed by the gesture of eating'.[44] The more rigorous the asceticism, the greater the assurance of a holy power that transcended local horizons; Saint Simeon Stylites, perched atop his pole, was the holy man par excellence. He, like the Buddha, was credited with a 'lion's roar'.[45]

[40] P. Brown, 'The rise and function of the holy man in late antiquity', in *Society and the Holy in Late Antiquity* (Faber and Faber, London, 1982), pp. 103–52; P. Brown, *Authority and the Sacred. Aspects of the Christianisation of the Roman World* (Cambridge University Press, Cambridge, 1995).

[41] Brown, 'Rise and Function', p. 115.

[42] Brown, *Authority and the Sacred*, p. 64.

[43] Ibid., pp. 57–8, passim.

[44] Brown, 'Rise and Function', p. 131.

[45] 'Delegations from neighbouring villages, headed by their priests and elders . . . trooped up the side of the mountain to hear "the lion roar" as to how they should order their affairs,' ibid., p. 128.

Brown sees the holy man as a mediator between cosmopolitan and parochial cultures where society is fluid and social mobility is accelerating, where ancient institutional centres of religious certainty are losing relevance, where education is spreading, where the authority of the powerful individual is replacing that of the patriarch and where sanctity is coming to reside in people rather than places. He could have been describing northeastern India in the period of urbanization.[46]

THE HOLY MAN IN INDIA

India was already, in the fourth century BCE, highly diverse socially and linguistically; all the more timely, then, was the emergence of a group of figures who could aptly play the part of middlemen or facilitators. Their position did not depend in the least upon social distress, disease or increasing inequality among the ordinary folk; it arose from the stresses generated as the cultures of expanding states failed to fit within the world view of ordinary folk. A universal redefinition was needed in order to provide justification for the many changes that had taken place, producing a degree of culture shock not experienced before. Buddhism represented one such redefinition.

Another can be found in both Sanskrit epics, though the visions they offer are somewhat different, the *Mahābhārata* offering a much more fractured view of the changes, and the possible response to them. The brahmins had an ideology based on *varṇa* and ritual status that probably already existed by the time the *Brāhmaṇas* were composed, beginning in approximately 800 BCE, but this was tied into a particular language that was rapidly becoming archaic and increasingly different from any vernacular, and was quite socially exclusivist to begin with.

Buddhism (like some other ascetic schools) did not appear exclusive or particularistic, and could appeal where brahmins were seen as alien. This was where the wandering ascetic, intent upon salvation, could meet a need. His appeal was not to the gods of specific communities, but to impersonal principles that could be understood anywhere. Instead of taxes, he asked for left-overs. Instead of war-bands, he controlled untamed spiritual forces that lived in the wilderness. He could be regarded with favour, however cautiously, by kings as well as peasants. In an expanding state, it was natural for

[46] Ibid., p. 148. Friedrich-Silber, *Virtuosity, Charisma, and Social Order*, pp. 45ff. discusses Brown's analysis, emphasizing its social-functional approach. Such an approach, though, can be usefully married to a concern with the transcendent and ideological dimension of the monk's role, as the present study will show.

a ruler to seek association with such figures, even at the cost of disapproval from the priestly custodians of his own ancestral religious culture. This is because, if the state is to cohere, it must acquire a set of legitimizing principles in which all its constituent communities can recognize themselves. So long as the majority of the population under the lordship of a ruler consisted of people who recognized a single culture or ethnicity,[47] it was natural for the ruler to ground his legitimacy in this shared culture; when the majority of the population consisted of groups with quite different traditions, it was natural for the ruler to seek legitimacy in a new and universal ideology. It is therefore not surprising that a ruler such as Aśoka should have expressed disapproval of trivial ceremonies and patronized lavishly the communities of *śramaṇas*.[48]

The point is fundamental; *śramaṇa* teachers were not just rustic medicine men from the wilderness. They were active everywhere. They could therefore be co-opted to stand for the solidarity of the kingdom, a solidarity that was cemented by a new message that insisted upon the universality of values, and subverted the privileged authority of Vedic rituals and myths which were controlled by a special group. This sort of message was just what rulers needed when they were trying to bring beneath their dominion communities too diverse in culture and origins to be accommodated within a ready-made Sanskrit-brāhmaṇical image.

This whole situation was essentially transitional, but could last quite a long time. Generations of cultural interaction had to intervene before the brahmins could do their work, and cultural integration could occur. One could also add that the separation of monks from the king not only allowed an element of perceived independence to the monk, but released the king from dependence upon the brahmins, on whom he would have had to rely for major public ritual and legal interpretation. The Hindu king was circumscribed by the brahmins' role as the custodians of tradition, but this would never apply to a king's dealings with a Buddhist monk, who made no claim to superiority in a hierarchy.

[47] Ethnicity is a slippery concept which has changed its meaning in scholarly usage. Culture or even subjective world view has been replacing anything like biological ancestry as a main criterion. See for example Sian Jones, 'Discourses of identity in the interpretation of the past', in P. Graves-Brown, S. Jones and C. Gamble (eds), *Cultural Identity and Archeology: the Construction of European Communities* (Routledge, London and New York, 1996), pp. 62–80; Sian Jones, *The Archeology of Ethnicity: Constructing Identities in the Past and Present* (Routledge, London and New York, 1997), esp. p. 128.

[48] 'Women especially perform a variety of ceremonies, which are trivial and useless': Major Rock Edict IX; see R. Thapar, *Aśoka and the Decline of the Mauryas* (Oxford University Press, Oxford, 1961), pp. 253ff.

THE FIT BETWEEN BUDDHISM AND INDIAN HISTORY

The critical factors in the rise of holy men to importance operate in specific temporary conditions – rapid encroachment by a state upon diverse outlying communities. If the encroachment continues the conditions will change, and eventually, as cultures mingle through patronage and intermarriage, a single core tradition will emerge, and the brahmins – or monks who have come to behave like brahmins – will win. On this hypothesis, Buddhism and the other *śramaṇa* traditions were likely to prosper wherever and whenever a metropolitan culture expanded among alien populations speaking different languages and recognizing no shared ancestry; brahmanism was likely to prosper where expansion was among communities already sharing a cultural past. The difference between the two situations is one of degree, and in practice priestly and *śramaṇa* religious figures could compete for influence.

This interpretation is supported by the subsequent course of Buddhist history. The hypothesis would predict that, so long as it retained its original *śramaṇa* character, Buddhism would be particularly influential in the outer zones of expanding Sanskrit civilization, where the discontinuity between the old Aryan-Vedic culture and indigenous populations remained stark, and at the courts of imperial rulers. The success of Buddhism in the frontier zones of the northeast, the northwest and the south takes its place in this interpretation.

The hypothesis would also predict that, as Sanskrit civilization spread and consolidated, and different populations were gradually brought together by intermarriage and cultural osmosis, the role of mediator between metropolitan expansion and Little Tradition would fall increasingly to ritual priestly figures (in a word, brahmins) rather than ascetics, and Buddhism would retreat to the furthest social frontiers and beyond.

All religions change a great deal in the course of history; most of them turn into their opposites in some environments. Buddhism could lose much of its *śramaṇa* character in a new environment (though the scriptures were always available to inspire local revivals of it) and take on the particularistic features of a regional orthodoxy, its monks functioning like priests within local social structures; indeed, this tendency to institutionalization would have been present from the first, as an element in the interaction between different perceptions of the monks. This way of interpreting the history of Buddhism in India as a response to socio-cultural conditions is essentially new, although a few of its elements appear severally in the observations of some scholars – for example S. Dutt,[49] D. D. Kosambi,[50] M. M. Marasinghe,[51] Romila Thapar,[52] and Michael Carrithers.[53] Substantial empirical support for it may be found in the fit between what it predicts and the course of Indian Buddhist history, as sketched above. Spelling out this fit in detail would require another monograph, but familiar facts about the historical geography of Buddhism represent prima facie a persuasive case.

MODERN PARALLELS

It is dangerous to rely uncritically upon parallels from vastly different historical contexts; but, if there is any value at all in the proposal that holy men could prosper because there was a need for them as intermediaries between incommensurable cultural orders, the proposal abstracts something basic that is likely to be common to different societies. The much more accessible evidence of holy men linking polis with little tradition in modern times is worth noticing here, not as proof of anything, but because it can usefully illustrate the sorts of things that holy men in ancient India might have done.

The forest tradition in Thailand offers examples of monks whose fame as ascetics has involved them in the processes of politicization whereby isolated localities have been subjected to the influences of expanding national culture. Some have resisted the pressures to be drawn in – notably Acharn Man in the northeast, who early in the twentieth century inspired a strong and continuing movement.[54]

Such a movement genuinely offers a parallel to the religion of the frontier regions of expanding Sanskritic civilization in ancient India. The northeast of Thailand was relatively isolated until the nineteenth century; according to Sunait Chutintaranond, only in the late nineteenth century did anything like a centralized state begin to appear under the energetic policies of King Chulalongkorn.[55] The north-easterners were still adjusting to the crisis of cultural redefinition in Acharn Man's time.

[49] Dutt, *Early Buddhist Monachism*, pp. 153–6. [50] Kosambi, 'Early stages', pp. 45ff.

[51] M. M. Marasinghe, *Gods in Early Buddhism: a study in their social and mythological milieu as depicted in the Nikāyas of the Pali Canon* (University of Sri Lanka Press, Vidyalankara, 1974), p. 28, and citing G. P. Malalasekara, *Dictionary of Pāli Proper Names* (published for the PTS by Luzac, London, 1960), vol. I, p. 295 (Ālavī), vol. II, p. 1210, *M* III 268, *S* IV 61 (Sunāparanta), and *D* 2 166f. (Moriyas).

[52] Thapar, *From Lineage to State*, pp. 149ff. [53] Carrithers, *Buddha*, pp. 86, 90ff.

[54] See J. L. Taylor, *Forest Monks and the Nation-State* (Institute of Southeast Asian Studies, Singapore, 1993), for a study of this movement.

[55] Sunait Chutintaranond, '"Mandala", "Segmentary State" and the politics of centralization in medieval Ayudhya', *Journal of the Siam Society*, 78 (1990), pp. 89–100.

The pressures upon well-known monks to become part of the state apparatus have been real enough, with famous teachers sometimes attracting attention from the Thai monarchy and being made national icons.[56] One forest monk, Thui, was an effective mediator: 'Thui's linkage with influential élite helped to facilitate dialogue with local bureaucrats, and resultant attention on matters such as road repairs, bridge maintenance, or general village concerns.'[57] Important national figures liked to visit such famous monks, and wealthy supporters provided resources which could be used for the benefit of villages living in symbiosis with monasteries belonging to Man's tradition. Another monk, Baen, promoted the building of a road to a local village, using contacts in the government organization for rural development; he helped to establish a rice bank and a credit union, and 'arranged the distribution of used clothing and medicines to the isolated hived communities further into the Phuuphaan heartland'. Another monk, Wan Uttamo, promoted small-scale irrigation projects, with the King's benevolent interest. Such people combined their roles as meditation masters with the status of 'development monk' (*Phra Nakpathanaa*).[58]

Such monks acquire charisma which offers to lay supporters the means of making merit; they offer their donations to a famed monk, whether for public works or for the support of his monastic organization. As Acharn Tate recorded: 'Funds for [community projects] never seem to have dried up, and there remains a strong interest in aiding my projects . . . I have never gone out looking for even a penny, but funds have rolled in from all directions.'[59]

J. L. Taylor's important work on the forest monks of northeastern Thailand, cited above, shows how the tension between ascetic, public and popular images of the Buddhist monk is worked out. What has been happening repeatedly in the career of Acharn Man and the more renowned of his disciples is likely to have happened countless times since the lifetime of the Buddha. As Taylor summarizes it, the cycle typically begins with

56 Taylor, *Forest Monks*, pp. 214ff. Extensive government regulation of the training and organization of monks has even extended to the issue of identification cards for monks: ibid., p. 98.

57 Ibid., p. 242.

58 The Thai experience shows how readily Buddhist monks can slide into social roles as facilitators, mediators, counsellors and so forth. As Friedrich-Silber details, the modern Thai government is actively concerned to use monks as 'local agents in the implementation of its modernization policies', and the Thai Buddhist monastery has multiple social roles as 'a community center, counselling agency, hospital, school, community chest, free hotel, news agency, charity employer, bank (at low or no interest), clock, sports center, morgue, poorhouse, landlord . . .' See Friedrich-Silber, *Virtuosity, Charisma and Social Order*, p. 91, n. 38.

59 Ajahn Tate, *The Autobiography of a Forest Monk* (Wat Hin Mark Peng, Chiang Mai, Thailand, 1993), pp. 264ff.

a wandering monk, following an ascetic lifestyle,[60] favouring a particular spot for his rainy-season retreat and gaining a reputation for sanctity among local villagers; subsequently, other ascetic monks come, and buildings are put up; the site, with its shifting population, attracts patronage from further afield; the administrative apparatus of the state-sponsored *saṅgha* begins to absorb the monastery, and scholarly (not ascetic) monks are installed in it (that is, *pariyat* replaces *patibat*);[61] the monastery becomes a node in the national religious network. After the death of the original ascetic teacher who inspired the process, the settlement becomes a monument; devotees make pilgrimages to it in order to benefit from its concentrated spiritual energy, and great men endow it so that *pariyat* monks can study there, but the real ascetics forsake it and seek solitude elsewhere.[62]

This shows how forest monks continue an ancient tradition of asceticism. It also shows the tension between the image of the ascetic monk as a repository of talismanic spiritual power, and that of the institutionalized monk engaging in study and education; the tension produces various forms of Buddhism within a generation or so. But the superimposition of these images upon our map of ancient India, where so much space is blank, can only provide broad-brush strokes on the canvas. It depends in large part upon our acceptance of an interpretation that views the monk as a mediator between ill-assorted cultural groups being brought together willy-nilly.

THE DOMESTICATED MONK AS MIDDLEMAN

It must at least be clear, though, that the wandering holy man and the domesticated monk do not belong to two different institutions, stages of history, or cultural worlds. They interpenetrate; they can be one and the same man, seen from different points of view. This being understood, we may attempt some insight into the ways in which Buddhist monks, as their careers came to be shaped by the concerns of their lay supporters, became domesticated.

Buddhism grew to be a world religion because it succeeded so well in attracting lay supporters, especially those who were prepared to be munificent.

60 A monk following the forest tradition in its austere form; *thudong kammathaan*. These monks often observe the *dhutāṅgas* (see above, p. 163). Cf. Taylor, *Forest Monks*, pp. 326–8.

61 In Pāli scriptures occur the terms *pariyatti*, 'learning (the doctrine)', and *patipatti*, 'practising (the doctrine)' as two of the three stages of progress of the disciple (the third being realization of the goal of the doctrine); Nyanatiloka (ed.), *Buddhist Dictionary: manual of Buddhist terms and doctrines* (3rd edn, Frewin, Colombo, 1972), s.v. *pariyatti*.

62 This conflates summaries of the process by Taylor, *Forest Monks*, pp. 96ff., 202.

Without this success it could not have undergone the massive expansion it experienced after the reign of Aśoka, or left monumental evidence of its presence right across Asia.[63]

However, the study of the relationship between the laity and the Buddhist *saṅgha*, depicted in the earliest texts of Buddhism, is fraught with difficulty. True, there is much material, especially in the *Vinaya* and the *Nikāyas*, detailing interaction between laity and monks and nuns. Much of the description, though, is highly formulaic, and though this very fact is important in its own right, it does not allow us to tease out the details of daily interaction between monks and laity.

There are descriptions of a wide range of meals and alms-gathering activities; beyond this, the specific mechanisms of interaction are reduced to stereotypes and formulae. Material dealing with lay–monk interaction that is not structured round the meal relates mostly to the laity censuring monkish behaviour, so that the Buddha is required to declare a rule of conduct. Ostensibly the justification for many of the rules stemmed from the pressure of a censorious laity that required from the monks a strict adherence to a particular modest lifestyle. Whether this reflects the reality of lay pressure is very difficult to tell; we have no other evidence of such involvement beyond the texts, unless, on the basis of inscriptions which attest their active material support, we infer the lay supporters to have functioned somewhat like a modern-day pressure group. Rather, in the *Vinaya* passages the laity seems to represent an absolutely predictable body of opinion that could be drawn upon always by the Buddha or other senior monks as unwavering justification for the imposition on monks of particular standards.

At all events, the very fact that *Vinaya* rules were handed down in a framework of narratives explaining why such rules had to be proclaimed helps us understand the range of options within which early Buddhism could develop its images of monks and nuns, or, on the other hand, of the laity. It is especially important if we are to understand fully the role of the monk as social mediator. If the monk truly did derive status from mediating between different social classes, between different political and administrative groups and, above all, between outlying community and principal city, then it should be conceded, theoretically at least, that this mediatory function would have related the order of monks to lay non-Buddhists as well as committed Buddhists.

[63] See Jeffrey Samuels, 'Views of householders and lay disciples in the *Sutta Piṭaka*: a reconsideration of the lay/monastic opposition', *Religion*, 29 (1999), pp. 231–41.

One approach, which will be developed in further detail in the next chapter, is to speculate on the basis of the immense amount of material about the laity and the monk or nun in the *Vinaya*. This deliberate attention to the *Vinaya* is appropriate, since this corpus appears to have been shaped in a period later than that of the wandering mendicants. By then, monastic life was normal and the monks had a regular part to play, well understood on both sides, in interaction with villagers. Sensitivity about lay–monk relations is one of the fundamental parameters of the *Vinaya*.

In part this is because the Order was dependent on material support (financial support, once money came into use) for its survival. But it is also because the monk and the layperson were contrasted with each other as role models. The image of the monk is carefully circumscribed in the 318 rules of the *Vinaya* and tested continually in the many narratives accompanying the proclamation of the individual rules where monks and nuns are declared as coming into too close contact with laymen,[64] either in mimicking their activity, or mixing too often with them. As a symbol of immersion in a world dominated by the senses[65] the layman is portrayed as the opposite of what the monk should be. Of course, the image of the layman is much more nuanced than this in the texts and various degrees of attachment to sense objects are recognized. In short, the layman is both the opposite of what the monk should be and a control over the monk's behaviour.

The social role of the monk can be glimpsed by examining more closely contrasting paradigms – the monk enshrines what the layman could be, and the layman what the monk should not be – and different forms of authority (held by the laity by virtue of its possession of the wealth needed to support the Order, and the monk in having access to the conditions needed for *nibbāṇa*). Moreover, we must show that the role of monk as mediator was widespread, that it was not enshrined in the Buddha alone, even if he is always the ideal role model for the monk. We must recognize that as the originally unattached wandering monks became domesticated, settling in monasteries and serving the community, the tension between the original mission and the current social role became greater and greater.

64 See *Vin* II 7: 'At that time the venerable Seyyasaka was foolish and ignorant, had committed many offences against the Vinaya, did not take advice, lived in too close association with householders in ways that were inappropriate. So much so that the monks were fed up with granting him probation, sending him back to the beginning, imposing *mānatta*, rehabilitating him.'

65 As in the formulaic expression *Vin* II 105–6: 'People grumbled, took offence and became irritated, saying: "(the six monks) are just like householders, enjoying sensual pleasure,"' referring to the group of six monks using a bathing board; *Vin* II 106ff. refers to the six monks wearing bracelets, chains, etc., using a mirror, smearing their faces with ointment, wearing woollen clothes. The same expression occurs many times elsewhere in the *Cullavagga*.

The monk was a renouncer practising a mild asceticism, who could not ostensibly belong to any of the social networks[66] he might have served. He was an outsider, even in the midst of society. Thus the monk, because of his training in a doctrine having universal ramifications, could be seen as living at the edge of – yet necessarily beyond – two or more worlds. In assuming the role of social mediator, however it might be defined, was the monk denying the basic spirit, if not letter, of the eight-limbed path? Any theory of the monk as mediator must explain how this role would fit with the view of the monk constructed within the framework of *Vinaya* rules; we can see how such rules served to maintain something of the original spirit. They were specifically designed to prevent any kinds of attachments forming, and to uphold – by the power of enforceable discipline if necessary – the ulterior spiritual goal of the monk.

A closer examination of the monks' mediatory role after domestication had set in follows in chapter 10. Before we turn to this, one more important question deserves to be identified, although the present study does not answer it; but it needs to be recognized as an important area of enquiry linking the study of the monk's role to the study of the wider social environment. The question is how exactly, once settlement in monasteries has become normal for the Order, the monk who acts as mediator fits into his environment. If there were only a few monks in a district, they might well have no monastery. Would they live in the communities on which they depended for alms? How long, and in what places, did the monks maintain the genuinely homeless condition? And what were the necessary conditions in which monasteries were likely to be provided on the outskirts of particular settlements?

Particularly important here is the evidence of archaeology, which shows the association between Buddhist settlements and the network of economic and political activities that developed with the growth of kingdoms and empires. J. Heitzman notes that at the time of Aśoka Buddhist sites were 'closely linked to the major forms of political and economic organization that were developing at the same time', arguing that Buddhist communities played a part in the imperial state, 'serving as symbolic structures mediating social hierarchy within a new urban complex', and points to the continuing close association between Buddhist sites and trade routes or centres in later centuries.[67] We have already noticed that the geography of

66 See Greg Bailey, *Materials for the Study of Ancient Indian Ideologies: Pravṛtti and Nivṛtti* (Pubblicazioni di Indologica Taurinensia, Turin, 1985), pp. 88–94, drawing on the *Sutta Nipāta*.

67 J. Heitzman, 'Early Buddhism', pp. 121–37. Similar is H. P. Ray, *The Winds of Change: Buddhism and the maritime links of early South Asia* (Oxford University Press, Delhi, 1994), pp. 136–43.

Buddhism's subsequent history can provide indirect confirmation of the interpretation advanced here – it throve where changing political and economic conditions brought together discrepant cultural groups. We now see also how important to Buddhist history is its micro-geography, so to speak – the study of residence patterns in relation to the monks' go-between status.

8

Preparation of the monk for the mediatory role. Evidence from the Sutta Nipāta

Whilst the mediatory role of the monk is implied in many texts throughout the Canon and, in some very specific ways, is treated explicitly in the *Vinaya*, certain texts like the *Dhammapada* and the *Sutta Nipāta* allow us to construct a normative picture of the implications of this role better than the great majority of other texts in the Canon. Not that either text is built around this theme. They are not, but they do have special relevance for an understanding of the role. A case can be made that, like the *Dhammapada*, the *Sutta Nipāta*[1] offers a normative image of the monk and ties into this image the preliminary conditions – detachment and impartiality – essential for the monk who would be a mediator. This is not to say the normative monk described in this text would have performed this role, but it definitely creates the possibility that it could be so. If there is a problem here it is that the image given of the monk is surely of a hypothetical figure and stands in sharp contrast with the much more realistic image given in the *Vinaya* and the *Dīgha* and *Majjhima Nikāyas*.

The *Sn* is a text full of didactic verses replete with verbs in the optative, giving the text the strong impression of being injunctive in its intent, an impression strengthened by the constant use of privative nouns and particles of negation in many verses. Add to this the frequently appearing conversion frame which gives the Buddha a chance to preach some of his basic teachings, and a text is produced having direct relevance as a statement of both doctrine and ethical behaviour, which cannot be separated from each other. In the conversion stories the Buddha does not appear to play the mediatory role in the manner we describe it in this section of the book, but these narratives can be read as implying it. They depict the Buddha interacting with, and impressing, individuals of different classes, both human and

[1] We have used the *Sutta-nipāta*, ed. D. Andersen and H. Smith (Routledge & Kegan Paul, London, 1984 (1913)) and follow the translation of K. R. Norman, *The Group of Discourses*. Because of the excessive literalism of this translation we have modified some of his renderings.

non-human.[2] By extension the monk should have presented himself in a similar manner. Here the words 'presented himself' are pivotal, because it is how the monk appears to others – and meets the expectations of laypeople and those who were wary of holy men – that must have been the crucial factor for his success in mediating between the different cultural forces becoming ever more visible in the society of the time. The *Sn* is valuable in giving us, in a number of highly concentrated and repetitive passages, a sketch of what the expected behaviour of the monk should be, behaviour deriving from a stringently cultivated psychological attitude.

The *Sn* has been recognized[3] as an early text in the Canon, though its different parts have been stratified in accord with differing times of composition. A recent book by R. Ray argues, in deference to this temporal stratification, that the image of the Buddha depicted here is centred on the 'forest-dwelling' monk, that it conveys the possibility of a Buddhism whose spatial location is the forest, not the urban areas so prominently featured elsewhere in the Canon. Ray argues:

> The depiction of the Buddha in the *Suttanipāta* thus closely parallels, indeed exceeds, that of the *Buddhacarita* in its emphasis on the forest life and its values. This parallelism between the *Suttanipāta* and the *Buddhacarita* is important because it suggests that the understanding of the Buddha as an essentially forest personage goes back to an early time in Buddhism and that the 'urban Buddha' is not necessarily the earliest one.[4]

This assumes a very early date for the *Sn*, but it seems unnecessarily restrictive to distinguish between an 'urban' and a 'forest' Buddha. A shift in spatial emphasis may have occurred in the first few centuries of Buddhism, but our point here is that the whole ambit of the psychological approach of Buddhist teaching was that the monk would be at home in either the isolation of the forest or the bustle of the city. If this was not the case the monk could not have been a mediator in the sense we are arguing for this role here. Indeed, the whole thrust of the *Sn* is that the monk/sage should have cut ties with sufficient facility and absoluteness not to be affected by

[2] There is always an asymmetrical relationship operating here. The Buddha is consistently superior spiritually, though not socially, as several brahmins are amongst those converted.

[3] K. R. Norman, *Pāli Literature, Including the Canonical Literature in Prakrit and Sanskrit of All the Hīnayāna Schools of Buddhism* (Harrassowitz, Wiesbaden, 1983), pp. 63–70 and for relative dating of the particular parts see *The Group of Discourses*, pp. xxvii–xxix. See also R. Ray, *Buddhist Saints in India*, p. 74, n. 40; O von Hinüber, *A Handbook of Pāli Literature* (Walter de Gruyter, Berlin and New York, 1996), pp. 48–9; T. Vetter, 'Some remarks on older parts of the Suttanipāta,' in D. Seyfort-Ruegg and L. Schmithausen (eds), pp. 36–56.

[4] R. Ray, *Buddhist Saints in India*, p. 64.

any influences from human contact that would plunge him back into the *saṃsāra* from which he was seeking release.

Our response to this is that the *Sn* knows of the spatial opposition between the *gāma*, and the *nigāma* (995) and the *arañña* and also political concepts like the *raṭṭha* (287) and *janapada* (287, 683, 995, 1102). Although Ray is right to focus on its forest-like ambience, we argue that the main image presented in this text is that of the monk as wanderer.[5] The need for the monk to inhabit, if temporarily, the village in order to receive alms is certainly present (180, 710–11) throughout the text, and if the forest might be a place where the monk can perfect his psychological and social detachment, he is never constrained to remain there. From another perspective the injunction to wander is consistent with the mediatory role because the mobility it implies would be essential if the monk is to be able to communicate the views of the city and the expanding political bodies to those who had only ever lived in a village environment. The monk had to have knowledge of both areas.

CULTIVATION OF DETACHMENT

The disinterested attitude of the monk is the essential precondition of his role as mediator, an attitude constantly portrayed in the texts as detachment, a condition achieved only by the complete severing of all ties. Overwhelmingly in the *Sn*, statements about the holy man (the words *bhikkhu*, *muni* and *brāhmaṇa* seem to be used indiscriminately in the *Sn*) are given which exemplify the attitude of detachment and the required behaviour going with it. Verse 220 is instructive in its contrast of the householder with the sage, the two being treated as natural opposites.

> The two of them, having quite different dwelling place and way of life, are not the same. The householder supports a wife and the sage is unselfish and of good vows. The householder is not fully restrained in respect of the killing of other living creatures; the sage, being restrained, constantly protects living creatures.

Whilst the intent of the *Sn* is to prescribe ethical behaviour for both the householder and the monk from a Buddhist point of view, its unequivocal view is that there can be no accommodation between the two lifestyles (*vuttino*). The differences between the two are not just differences of degree.

[5] Even leaving aside those instances where derivatives of *car* can be translated as 'action, behaviour', there are multitudes of examples (25, 32–75, prose p. 21, 180, 208, 213, 218, 250, 328, 342, 344, etc.) of the monk being enjoined to wander, usually alone, and always the verb *car* is used, normally in the optative.

They are meant to be virtually absolute (see especially 214), though not inseparable. In spite of the sense of isolation in which the *Sn* seems to place the monk, it is always accepted the monk will approach the householder for material support. The layperson, irrespective of his class, will approach the monk for spiritual learning, as the *Sn* elaborates in its conversion narratives.

Yet an important sub-text of the *Sn*, and one crucial for defining the image of the monk, is the possibility of the monk's becoming entangled in the views of other sects, on the one hand, and in the disputes between factions in villages, on the other. That is why the wandering monk should be 'independent (*anissito*), not to be led by others . . .' (364),[6] a view given some context in 371: 'The learned believer, seeing the way (to salvation), not following any faction among the factious (*vaggagatesu na vaggasārī*).'[7] All the verses in this, the *Sammāparibbājanīyasutta*, describe the wandering monk as utterly impartial, one in whom all attachments to the world are completely broken. The refrain of sixteen of the seventeen verses reads *sammā so loke paribbajeyya*, 'he should wander properly in the world', where the resonance of renunciation is present in the verb *pari/baj*. Here the text joins the wandering theme with those of independence and detachment, which we are arguing constitute the minimum conditions for the mediatory role to be effective for those amongst whom it is exercised. A monk should be seen to be independent and detached as well as truly embodying both these characteristics in every aspect of his private and public life.

A fuller statement of the required attitude of a sage is given in verses 702–23, verses which repeat much of what occur in earlier verses in the *Sn*, but place the ascetic's behaviour in a more social context. Asita has asked the Buddha to explain the state of sagehood (*moneyyan*, 702). The resulting explanation turns on the sage's neutrality and implies how this might be utilized in the village context.

> One should practise equanimity (*samānabhāvaṃ*), for praise and abuse occur in a village. One should ward off faults in the mind. One should wander calmed, without pride. (702)

The point here is that the monk represents a constant amongst the changeable features of everyday life, summarized in this verse as the duality of praise and abuse. The duality implied here could be a result of the factionalizing suggested in other verses, yet is, no doubt, a normal part of village life. It is more speculative whether this is a reference to the way individual ascetics may have been treated. Praise and/or abuse were no doubt

[6] The same word occurs in a similar context in 66, 363, 756, 815, 853, 860, 951 and 1073.

[7] See also 800 and 912 for the compound *vaggasārī*.

expressed in respect of many monks by the large non-ascetic population with whom they come into contact. This could also correlate with calmness and absence of pride, the latter suggesting deliberately displayed satisfaction in the accomplishment of the ascetic role. Neither praise nor abuse is desirable, but both could be consequences of arrogant behaviour. Alone, equanimity (*sāmānabhāva*) – lit. 'even or unchanging nature' – is to be cultivated. Both calmness and absence of pride would seem go with *samāna* in a behavioural sense.

One of the reasons for this is given in the next verse:

> Various sorts of things emerge, like the flames of a fire in a forest. Women will seduce a sage, do not let them seduce you. (703)

Surely this verse must be understood as recommending an attitude of constant vigilance against provocation of any kind, sex and heat being brought together because of their common characteristic of provoking inflammatory reactions. The sage may have been regarded as a sexual object, since he was supposedly untouchable, and the *Vinaya* rules are much taken up with the lapse of monks back into sexual misdemeanours. It is likely this recommendation referred to actual possibilities, as much as to a general statement that equanimity could not exist within the presence of sexual desire. Verse 704 reiterates the use of sexual intercourse as a symbol of all other desires which must be renounced if the monk is to be neither opposed (*aviruddho*) to nor attached (*asāratto*) to living things. It is not enough to be detached, he must also harbour no negative emotions towards living things.

The next verse takes a different tack and recommends strongly against the performance of violent acts.

> 'As I am, so are these; as are these, so am I.' With this idea and comparing himself with others, he should not kill or cause to kill. (705)

If this suggests a similarity with all other humans, the following verse adds a further qualification which immediately belies this.

> Having abandoned desire and lust, to which the ordinary individual is attached, one with vision should set out (on the path). He should cross over this hell. (706)

Here hell (*naraka*) is surely a synonym of *saṃsāra* and 'cross over' the technical term so often used to indicate the passing over *saṃsāra*. It is as though the previous verse has laid down the conditions of the monk's humanity as being identical with the normal person and the present verse indicates the initial attitudes to be cultivated if the monk's path is to be followed in any realistic way. The monk could not be a mediator if the conditions of the first two *pādas* of verse 705 applied to his habitual thoughts and activities. Of course, there must be some recognition of similarity if he is to have awareness of human problems experienced by those still trapped within *saṃsāra*, yet verse 706 makes it clear that rejection of desire must begin the process of differentiation of the monk. Moreover, the preconditions for the success of the mediatory role would be absent if he was still in thrall to desire and lust.

The next seven verses are concerned with the appropriate way in which a monk should beg for food. However, they offer guidance in all aspects of a monk's life and highlight his uniqueness by virtue of his removal from the concerns of everyday life. His need to demonstrate a deliberate distance is especially stressed in the two following verses.

When he has been on his alms-round, he should take himself to a grove. Standing at the foot of a tree, (or) come to a seat, he is a sage. (708)

Intent on meditation, he should remain, in a state of delight (*ramito*), in the grove. He should meditate at the foot of a tree, satisfying himself. (709)

We assume the injunction to meditate is designed not just for religious purposes but to function as a visible instance of the monk's uniqueness measured by his capacity to cut himself off by use of meditative practices. In addition, it is likely that it was a deliberate decision that the injunction requiring the monk to return to the village in order to engage in begging should follow these two verses. It is a means of recording the causal relation between the contemplative lifestyle and the capacity it gives to remain separate from all his surroundings even when surrounded by the forces of socialization and acculturation which the monk originally renounced in order to become a monk.

But the monk does have to eat, and this means an element of socialization with villagers as verse 710 enjoins, a socialization which is severely limited.

Then at the end of the night, he should take himself to a village. He should not rejoice at an invitation or a present from the village.

A clear statement of neutrality and complete detachment from any external influence, this attitude makes full sense in terms of the Buddhist emphasis on psychological and social detachment. Equally, it could also establish the monk as somebody who could be approached for advice without any fear of partiality or desire for reward. The next verse confirms this:

Having come to a village, a sage should not pursue his search for food inconsiderately (*sahasā*) among the families. Cutting off all conversation, he should not utter a word with an ulterior motive. (711)

The two verses following this reiterate what has just been said, implicitly stressing the uniqueness of the holy man and his need to live within and without the village, a perfect position from which to be able to give advice that is not actuated by any other motive than to present a situation as it should be seen within the context of Buddhist ethical teaching. The subsequent verses are more difficult to comprehend in an unambiguous sense, enjoining acuity (716) in the same breath as restraint in food, the need neither to have an inactive mind, nor to think too much (717), almost a statement of the middle way.

The mediatory role requires the capacity to communicate effectively between different cultural groups and so communications skills and knowledge of conditions – metropolitan and local – will be essential qualifications. Yet any communication skills the monk may possess are severely qualified. Restraint of speech is stressed in 723 and often elsewhere, as in 850:

> Without anger, without trembling, not boasting, without remorse, speaking in moderation, not arrogant, he indeed is a sage who is restrained in speech.

Note the negatives here, all redolent of cutting away from the kind of emotive discourse associated with everyday life that the sage/monk is required to eschew. Restrained use of language could also be seen as a reflection of the monk's refusal to be captured by a particular view, a position put often in the *Sn* and yet another requirement for the development of impartiality required of the mediator.

Much of what we find in later sections (especially Book IV) of the *Sn* stresses how crucial it is for a *bhikkhu* not to cling to a particular view, the consequence of which is to take positions in a dualistic sense. VI 5 is especially pointed on this subject, as 798 teaches:

> That very (view) the experts call a tie, dependent upon which he sees the rest as inferior. Therefore a bhikkhu should not depend upon (anything) seen, heard or thought, or virtuous conduct and vows.

Further

> Abandoning what has been taken up, and not taking it up (again), he should not depend even upon knowledge. He indeed does not follow any faction amongst those who hold different views (*sā ve viyuttesu na vaggasārī*). He does not fall back on any view at all. (800, cf. 371, 912, cf. 845–6)

And the effect:

> By him not even a minute notion has been formed here in respect of what is seen, heard or thought. How could anyone here in the world have doubts (*kenīdha lokasmiṃ vikappayeyya*) about that brahmin, who does not adopt a view? (801)

Despite the play on words between the *pādas*, it may be too free an interpretation to take this as a judgement about the *bhikkhu* and the acceptance of his status by the general public. Nonetheless the stressing of the distinction between those who still cling to views and the *bhikkhu* who has renounced all such is utterly clear.

But what other clues do we have about the public attitude towards this idealized vision of the *bhikkhu/muni* depicted here? Two verses are quite specific about the monk's acceptance of commonplace opinions:

> That on account of which the common people (*puthujjanā*), and ascetics and brahmins, might accuse him, is not preferred by him. Therefore he is not agitated in (the midst of) their accusations. (859)

> A man with knowledge does not get involved at all with whatever opinions are commonplace (*sammutiyo puthujjā*). Why should a man who is without involvement (*anūpayo*) become involved (*upayaṃ . . . eyya*), when he shows no preference for what is seen and heard. (897)

Surely this is the point. The *Vinaya* texts, which are not straightforwardly normative in the way of the *Sn*, show us that the monks do become constantly involved in the life of the laity, even if this involvement does not correspond to the kind of mediation we are writing about in this book. That so many verses in the *Sn* repeat the injunction of 897 is a recognition on the part of the compilers of the text that monks, because of their eremitic lifestyle and their need to visit villages, often daily, had to cultivate the sense of detachment necessary for preventing the 'attachment, clinging, involvement' associated with the acquisition of new *karma*. In this it is consistent with everything Buddhism teaches, especially in its more contemplative aspects, yet it establishes the conditions for the monk to give unprejudiced advice, whether or not the authors of the text were aware that this was what they may have been teaching. Involvement is unavoidable, but it should not lead to attachment.

Sections IV.13–IV.15 of the Chapter of Eights repeat substantially the injunctions given in the previous verse and several of the other verses cited above. Section IV.14 does not differ appreciably in its teachings from this, but is slightly more expansive in depicting the *bhikkhu* as a totally autonomous island in the midst of a sea of turmoil. This theme is expressed already in 915 where the Buddha is asked about detachment (*viveka*) – psychological as much as social – and peace, and its direct opposite, avoidance of grasping in the world (*anupādiyāno lokasmiṃ*). The world is, of course, *saṃsāra*, and given the emphasis early Buddhist doctrine places on the individual's creation of *saṃsāra* through the mind, the teachings which will follow have a dual ambience; they define the mind's grasping what it perceives in the world and the monk's relations with the world after he has learnt to detach himself from false perceptions. That is, the monk is still in the world, though not of it: paradoxically, it is this quality which gives him his facility for mediation.

So often in these verses the world is described in psychological terms of ties, motivated by grasping. Because it was probably so difficult to attain to a level of complete psychological detachment, the *Sn* and other Buddhist texts take great pains to describe attachment and its content. Sometimes though, normative texts like the *Sn* do present the monk in the more empirical conditions he must have encountered in his wanderings.

He would not pay much attention to sleep. Being energetic he would apply himself to wakefulness. He would abandon sloth, deception, laughter, sport, (and) sexual intercourse, together with their appurtenances. (926)

He would not practise Atharva charms, or (interpretation of) dreams, or signs, or even astrology. My follower would not devote himself to (the interpretation of animal) cries, or (the art of) impregnation, or healing. (cf. 927, 360)

A bhikkhu would not tremble at blame; he would not be puffed up when praised. He would thrust aside greed together with avarice, anger and slander. (928)

A bhikkhu would not engage in buying or selling; he would not incur blame in any respect. He would not linger (*nābhisajjeya*) in a village; he would not talk boastfully to people with a desire for gain. (929)

We suggest these are included here as injunctions because Buddhist monks may on occasion have gone beyond the required detachment from mundane life and, like other holy men, have acted as advisers on the basis of status acquired from their perceived spiritual power, a quality that would have made them attractive to some laypeople. Verse 927 is reminiscent of some of the occupations listed in the *Brahmajālasutta* and almost certainly represents the manner in which some monks would have acted and in which many brahmins did, in fact, act. Similar is 929 which recommends against basic mercantile activities of a kind that could not help but plunge the monk into the mundane life of the village, a danger surely implied in the use of *abhi/sajj* 'linger' (Norman) which semantically corresponds with clinging and attachment.

The śāstric style marked by the continued use of the optative makes these verses reminiscent more of dharmaśāstric literature than they do of

Vinaya rules. The effect of the injunctions they encode is to distinguish sharply the Buddhist monk from the other varieties of holy men who would have had no hesitation in using their powers, gained from *tapas* performed in the forest, to enhance their status, especially in village society where they would have had fewer competitors than in the urban environment of the large towns. But leaving aside the restraining effect of the injunctions, we must note that on the positive side they maintain the image (and the actuality) of the monk as an aloof figure, involved in none of the mundane activities of the village and *known by the village population to be such*. He could be approached for advice in the full knowledge that he would not take sides in any of the disputes known to have occurred in the village, that pecuniary reward would have no influence on him, that he was not tied into the society in the manner of the brahmin.

Finally, the *Sn* contains a few verses which can be taken as indicating the high status of the ascetic at the Buddha's time, a status surely essential for underscoring the validity of the mediatory role. An instance is the opinion of Sabhiya who believes, 'An ascetic (*samaṇo*) is not be despised nor to be treated with contempt because he is young. Even if an ascetic is young he has great power and influence (*so ca hoti mahiddhiko mahānubhāvo*)' (prose p. 93). This is not repeated elsewhere in this text, but the whole thrust of the many other verses (see the whole of III 6 on Sabhiya) is to reaffirm the image of the *bhikkhu/brāhmaṇa/samaṇa* as utterly detached and gone beyond any ties to the world. This virtually superhuman detachment must have been a powerful factor in allowing the judgement suggested in the sentence just cited to be made. It is well known from Hindu literature of various ages that ascetics could be rogues, but this roguishness must have been measured against this stringent standard of detachment rehearsed so often in the *Sn*.

SOCIAL CONDITIONS

Given the emphasis on detachment and isolation the *Sn* teaches, it is a little surprising that a few passages contain highly concentrated statements about social life in the world of the *putthujjana*. The *Sn* demonstrates very clearly the contrast between social engagement and spiritual isolation, but to understand the need for isolation, an equivalent understanding of the conditions of society, beyond the more abstract psychological conditions associated with mental attachment to worldly things, was needed. Every indication in the Canon is that the Buddha had an excellent knowledge of social mores and different cultures. In the *Sn* passages containing such information are significant for our argument in suggesting the monk's acceptance of the reality of social networks and aspirations and his own need to be able to deal with these from the perspective of Buddhist ethics. Section 1.6 of the *Uragavagga* details the defining features of the 'unsuccessful man'[8] (*parābhavantaṃ purisaṃ*), which means a man who will ultimately be unsuccessful within business or in terms of social values centred on family cohesion across generations. Here is a list of the causes given in summary:

He does not like (Buddhist) doctrine. 92
Bad men (*asanta*) associate with him. 94
He sleeps too much, likes company, is lazy and subject to anger. 96
He does not support his parents when they are old. 97
He lies to anybody. 99
A wealthy man enjoys his wealth alone (*eko bhuñjati sādūni*). 102
Arrogance leads him to disregard his own kinsman. 104
He squanders wealth because of women, gambling and alcohol. 106
He betrays his own wife, he is seen with prostitutes and other women. 108
As an old man he brings home a young girl and lusts for her. 110
He puts wrong people into positions of authority. 112
He can be a man of little wealth but huge desire, like a *khattiya* who wants to be a king. 114

The conclusion (115) is brief, stating that a wise man who possesses insight will enjoy the auspicious world (*lokaṃ bhajate svam*). Arguably section I.7 is an extension of this teaching, offering a range of reasons as to why a person can be called an 'outcaste' (*vasala*), a category that seems also to be confused with those of *samaṇa* and *muṇḍaka*.[9]

The parallel of the content of these verses with the passage from the *Vinaya* cited in chapter 3 and also with the *Sigālovādasutta* is striking, and reaffirms how strong was the Buddha's knowledge of the new economic elite and how acute were his observations as to how wealth, when gained, could be kept. But these admonitions are not simply about maintenance of wealth; they are also about maintenance of status that must have accrued to the man who has acquired wealth either from land or mercantile activity.

Their opposite is given in II.4 (258) when a *deva* comes and asks the Buddha to adjudicate about 'auspicious things' (*maṅgalāni* 'good

[8] See Norman's discussion of this word in *The Group of Discourses*, p. 168.

[9] See prose preceding vs. 116. Because of the correlation of these three terms it is possible this entire section could be read as a description of the conditions under which a monk or an ascetic becomes regarded as a rogue.

fortunes' N). Of the verses which follow, 259–64 virtually give the opposite of the twelve reasons for becoming an unsuccessful man. Verses 265–9, however, are more applicable to the monk, rehearsing the qualities of detachment, mental calmness and the practice of austerities.

These passages can be taken as a guide to the kind of knowledge a monk should possess and, more pointedly, give advice upon, and so demonstrate with clarity the degree to which a monk's knowledge should cover an extensive range of affairs, and not just be restricted narrowly to the understanding of the dhamma. In truth, the dhamma was extended to the social world of ethics and honesty, meaning that the monk had to be able to give advice on matters pertaining to business and social interaction. This knowledge would have been regarded as valuable by a layperson only if a monk was recognized as transcending the conditions in which such knowledge would be valuable to him in a material sense. His advice would be sought because, as an outsider, he had no personal interest in the result to be gained from the application of his advice. Verses 268 exemplifies this when saying of the person enjoying 'supreme good fortune' – a virtual analogy of the monk – that he is one 'whose mind is not shaken when he is touched by the phenomena of the world (*phuṭṭhassa lokadhammehi cittaṃ yassa na kampati*), being without grief, unpolluted, secure . . . '. In other words, worldly affairs have no effect on him in terms of emotional or physical entanglement within them. The next verse enunciates the consequences of this in saying, 'Having done such things, (being) unconquered everywhere, they go everywhere in safety (*sabbatthā sotthiṃ gacchanti*) . . . ' Thus, in many ways, our text sets out the ideal condition for one who would play a mediatory role between different groups.

9

The Dhammapada *and the images of the* bhikkhu

294 Destroying mother and father and two *khattiya* kings, destroying [likewise] the country and the attendant (*sānucāra*),[1] the brahmin comports himself (*carati*) without trembling.

295 Destroying mother and father and two learned (*sotthiya*) kings, destroying also those (hindrances) of which the fifth is like a tiger (*veyyagha*), the brahmin comports himself without trembling.

At first glance, these two verses from the *Dhammapada* may look like a volley of polemic against the Buddhists' rivals for popular influence, the brahmin priests. The impression will not last long, however. Buddhist complaints against brahmins do not normally allege savage and degenerate criminality; they lament rather the corruption of present-day brahmins who have fallen from the high standards set by the wise and diligent priests of old. The Buddha is very commonly represented as praising the true brahmin, the one who seeks enlightenment, cultivating restraint and virtue.

The later Pāli commentarial tradition automatically interprets these verses as a celebration of the achievements of the truth-seeker who follows in the footsteps of the Buddha and finds enlightenment through spiritual cultivation. The brahmin is this seeker, and his victims are metaphors: mother and father are craving and egoism or self-conceit, the two kings are the false beliefs in eternalism and annihilationism, the country is the senses and their spheres, the attendant (or revenue officer) is the pursuit of sensory pleasure, and the tiger's domain is the group of five hindrances of which sceptical doubt, seen as a source of fear like the tiger, is the fifth member.[2]

[1] Literally, 'with the follower(s)' (Rhys Davids and Stede (eds), *Pali-English Dictionary*, *s.v. sānucāra*). The metaphor likens the government apparatus of a kingdom (in the Pāli commentary, 'revenue officer') to the bases and objects of the senses.

[2] The annotated edition and translation of the *Dhammapada* by J. R. Carter and M. Palihawadana, *Dhammapada* (Oxford University Press, New York, 1987), is the authority in this chapter for references to the Pāli commentary, which is extensively used by the editors in their notes.

Certainly the Ceylonese tradition is correct in taking the term *brāhmaṇo* here as equivalent to *arahant*. These are not the only verses in this text where normally pejorative expressions are used in a new and special sense to denote the world-denying values of the seeker after enlightenment.[3] But the identification is put beyond doubt by the text's twenty-sixth and last division, the *brāhmaṇa-vaggo*, in which verses commemorating the wisdom and serenity of the enlightened monk all end with the words *ahaṃ brūmi brāhmaṇam* – '[that one] I call a brahmin'. This sustained identification of the ideal Buddhist monk with the socially eminent class of priests, in many other contexts represented as scornful or condescending detractors of the Buddhist *saṅgha*, must have meant something to the monks and laity through whose interest this text acquired its place in the Canon, and it is clearly of value to examine what resonances the semantics of such a text could acquire. The *Dhammapada*, which belongs within the *Khuddaka Nikāya*, is generally considered to be among the earlier of the collections of canonical material, or at least to contain parts which are early, and, for reasons which matter here, it came to be very popular. Other schools than the Theravāda had their versions of it, and some of these survive.[4] It consists, as normally edited, of 423 verses grouped under headings according to their main topics. To some extent, the collection is arbitrary, bringing together a wide variety of sayings, some of which occur elsewhere in the Canon. There is no uniting structure of argument, and the themes are various. For the most part, the teachings imparted seem to be exhortations and memoranda for monks living a wandering life, and some of them contain technical points of psychological or ethical doctrine. Yet, for whatever reasons, this anthology came to be treasured in many places.

The text therefore embodies features of the process by which canonical texts acquired meaning and importance in Buddhist culture. The concern of this chapter is with the way in which teachings are likely to have acquired a significance for different audiences, not only monks. The *Dhammapada*, however it originated, acquired sets of meanings from the cultural contexts

[3] Particularly verse 97 which commemorates faithlessness and other seeming defects. It has sometimes been misunderstood.

[4] The Sanskrit *Udānavarga*, the Prakrit *Gāndhārī Dharmapada* and the *Patna Dharmapada*. On all of these see Norman, *Pāli Literature*, pp. 59ff. See also G. Roth, 'Text of the Patna Dharmapada', in H. Bechert (ed.), *Die Sprache der ältesten buddhistischen Überlieferung: the Language of the Earliest Buddhist Tradition* (Vandenhoek and Ruprecht, Göttingen, 1980), pp. 97–135; K. Mizuno, 'A comparative study of Dharmapadas', in G. Dhammapala, R. Gombrich and K. R. Norman (eds), *Buddhist Studies in Honour of Hammalava Saddhātissa* (Buddhist Research Library Trust, Nugegoda, 1984), pp. 168–75.

in which it figured, and these contexts affect the way in which we read it as a document for the *dhamma*'s historical role.

There is not just one meaning which uniquely and absolutely belongs to such a text. There is indeed an original intention in the mind of whoever first uttered each verse; and it is certainly of value to seek plausible inferences about the character of these intentions. For what it is worth, the great majority of the verses can be read as statements about the values of the wandering monk, lacking possessions and deliberately cutting himself loose from the entanglements of social relationships and worldly status. That is, the *Dhammapada* could well be used to support the claim that, so far as an original Buddhism can be recovered (however quickly augmented by other Buddhisms), it was the solitary pursuit of enlightenment through meditation and a moderately ascetic lifestyle. The present chapter, though, is concerned with the further claim that, by being spoken and listened to in different contexts, these verses acquired other meanings as well.

The Ceylonese scholar-monks of later centuries read it in a particular way. Like the original anonymous authors of the several verses, they wished to forge a tool of monkish discipline conducive to the pursuit of spiritual goals and to a mode of life that would uphold the highest standards of the *saṅgha*. Unlike the original authors, they were interested in the text as an object of intellectual analysis, they used an elaborate technical vocabulary of Buddhist psychology, and they cultivated erudition in the traditional lore that had been transmitted alongside the Canon, containing numerous stories that could be used in explanation of the meaning of obscure passages. But, between the original authors and the Ceylonese monks, there was a series of other participants in the tradition, shadowy but indispensable to its evolution. The teachings passed on by older monks to novices in edifying verses were not, after all, secrets. They embodied the *dhamma* that the Buddha offered to all with an open hand. Whatever features made them easy for novices to learn would, up to a point, have made them easy for lay followers. It stands to reason that they would often have been used in the course of *dhamma* talks by monks to lay groups and individuals, recited with emphasis as wise and ancient sayings invested with the authority of the earliest *saṅgha*. Much in the *Dhammapada* is apt for such purposes, as indeed are other texts that came to be grouped in the *Khuddaka Nikāya*. The *Dhammapada* has the character of an anthology, its units consisting of single verses or of pairs or generally short sequences of verses, and such a selection from available stock, eventually compiled by selection according to value, is particularly likely to have responded to its effectiveness in providing material for *dhamma* talks as well as its perceived importance for the wandering monk's own spiritual cultivation. Over the generations, the reciting of verses could give them meanings on different levels, all congruent with a set of core ideas and values but meeting the needs of different audiences.

To be quite specific, we can read here not only messages for wandering monks but also messages for ordinary people in the settlements where the monks came with their teachings, and for the representatives of expanding states in their dealings with subject communities. That is, to over-simplify somewhat, there were folk and there were public or political messages. That is, the text served both the 'asocial' version of Buddhism and the 'social', the latter in both its Great Tradition and its Little Tradition forms as described above in the Introduction. The monks who delivered these messages were able to face in two directions – towards the subject communities, where people needed ways of accommodating the forces of an intrusive and threatening outside world to their indigenous traditions, and towards the expanding state, which needed a new ideology of universal values capable of reinterpreting the rulers' ancestral culture and bringing together a multiplicity of disparate communities lacking shared traditions. The *dhamma* fitted the monks to function as intermediaries, each party able to read its own needs in their teachings.

Let us take first the public or political messages. They represent an important aspect of religion familiar in other traditions.

Doctrines important in the evolution of a religion, whether as orthodoxy or heresy, can often be read as encoded political statements. To say this is not to say anything about their real spiritual meaning, and it is not to offer any simplistic reduction of religious statements to political ones; it is only to recognize that, in its historical interaction with the profane world, a religion inevitably comes to be involved in political issues, and rival doctrines (however indifferent to worldly values originally) become tokens in the debate between political interests. To identify the political content of a doctrine is not to exhaust its meaning, but it may help us to see how the doctrine played a part in society.

However complex the assessment of such propositions may be, they indicate ways in which doctrine may come to function as a badge of political interest. The lines of political interest in ancient India are mere speculative reconstructions from the mist of history for us now, but they surely acted to give meaning to often-repeated doctrinal formulae.

393 Not by matted locks, not by clan, not by birth is one a brahmin. He is the brahmin, he the pure, in whom there is truth and dhamma.

395 One who wears a garment made of rags, who is emaciated, marked by spreading veins (*dhamanisanthataṃ*), a solitary meditator in the forest – him do I call a brahmin.
405 The one who, abandoning the rod [of punishment] in dealing with all beings, the movable and the immovable (those who lack and those who possess calmness and restraint, *tasesu thāvaresu ca*), who does not kill and does not have killed – him do I call a brahmin.

Here the values of the meditating monk, who cultivates asceticism and pacifism, are squarely equated to the status of brahmin. Yet those who received this message knew that brahmins were people qualified by birth to study the Vedas and officiate at sacrifices. Rulers employed brahmins to perform rituals, and bestowed offerings upon brahmins as demonstrations of power. The radical reinterpretation of such an institution inevitably challenged orthodox ideas.

Buddhism had to be adapted substantially to function as an alternative to the brāhmaṇical ideology. Buddhism as it first took shape rejected the ritual and kin-based claims of the tight-knit group, and with its prescriptions for the wandering, independent life of the solitary ascetic, it likewise rejected the claims of political organization, secular or otherwise. If it was to serve the purposes of the expanding state, it had to be reinterpreted. It already had the universal values, but it lacked an appropriate term by which authority could be mediated.

On a strict interpretation, it was indeed antagonistic to any involvement in authorities and networks. The *Dhammapada* itself is a good text for the ascetic detachment of original Buddhism: the eradication of all craving, of all attachment to the bonds of sensual gratification. The emphasis is upon inner freedom, won by mastery of the recalcitrant elements within one's own mind; but it is a freedom that works outwards to the calming of attachment even to the closest of one's possessions:

62 A fool is vexed (*vihaññati*) thinking: 'I have sons, I have wealth'; but there exists no self belonging to oneself, so how much less can there be sons, how much less wealth?

Any sort of attachment, any vestige of craving, is to be patiently eradicated. One whole division of the text, the *taṇhā-vaggo*, is devoted to verses teaching the elimination of craving. For example:

353 I am the conqueror of all, the knower of all, undefiled (*anūpalitto*) amid all *dhammas*, abandoning all, released at the destruction of craving; what teacher can I have, when I myself comprehend all?

Such a doctrine, unadapted, could not serve the purposes of state organization. It rejected the claims of society upon the individual; it thus lacked principles apt for the validation of authority. Traditionally, this sort of validation was associated with brahmins. Everybody accepted that there were invisible forces and beings capable of affecting human fortunes; through the brahmins a particular community could as a unit make contact with this beyond through the sacrifice in order to ward off dangers or attract benefits; the patron capable of sponsoring this contact thereby had sacrally legitimized authority. Before urban-based kingdoms began to spread into new areas, while the culture of a state was still homogeneous, priestly sacrifice was the appropriate expression of a ruler's authority; the *Upaniṣads* tell stories of kings making lavish offerings to brahmins, who competed for patronage.[5] But in the new world of the rising northeastern states things had to be different; a new sort of contact with the beyond mediated by a holy man was needed. Sacrifice was denigrated, and the spiritual self-mastery of the holy man became the new vehicle of superhuman forces no longer conceived of in terms supplied by myths of familiar gods.

Seen from outside, ascetic values could be reinterpreted: the *arahant*, the holy man, precisely to the extent that he was uninvolved in social relationships and authority structures, became in his own person the vessel of offering, replacing the brāhmaṇical sacrifice:

106 One person might make a thousand offerings month after month in sacrifices a hundred times over, and another might offer worship for one moment to him whose self is spiritually refined (*bhāvitattānaṃ*); the (latter) worship is better than what is offered for a hundred years.

The redefinition of the brahmin as a holy man, and the devaluation of sacrifice in favour of worship offered to the spiritually pure, fit the *dhamma* as an ideology for the validation of state authority. The holy man's very indifference to social relationships and political hierarchy magnifies his value; the more spiritually pure he is, the greater the value of worship offered to him, and by the making of offerings to monks the state can attach itself to the moral power of cosmic forces.

Hence the domestication of Buddhism in the expanding state modelled it upon the structure of brahmanism. Certainly, in many contexts, holy men such as the wandering Buddhist mendicants were contrasted as a category with the worldly brahmins; but sometimes, equally, the two categories

[5] For example, see *BṛhU* 3.1.1.

could be twinned as sharers in the profession of sacred knowledge. This is the sense apparent in the Aśokan inscriptions, in which reverence towards *śramaṇas* and brahmins is enjoined as part of Aśoka's own *dhamma* or code of social morality. Aśoka's empire is the supreme example of an expanding state in which many cultures were brought together; we should expect to see in it Buddhist values superimposed upon brāhmaṇical religion.

This equation provided a lever for the redefinition of an ascetic teaching in terms suitable for the culture of an expanding state. The embodiment of this function was patronage, the making of offerings to holy men for the practical benefit of the community. Sometimes extravagant claims are made for the amount of merit earned by making offerings to spiritually advanced monks, and we should see in this the possibility of another audience, the political one for which the point of the monk's spiritual advancement was as a suitable vehicle for sacramental actions by the representatives of the community. Such actions were to be praised even if they did not issue in any food or comforts for monks, but simply consisted of honour and respect:

108 Whatever oblation or sacrificial offering a seeker after merit may make in the world for a year long, even the whole of it is not worth one quarter as much as what is better – to give honour to those whose going is straight [i.e., leads to enlightenment].

An ideology suitable for the expanding state in a culturally diverse environment needs to dispense with particularistic traditions such as sacrifice. What had to take their place was a concept of virtue which was neutral towards birth and community. Buddhist teachings were not the only ones to redefine the sacrificial act in moral terms; but they proved particularly appropriate to the changing environment.

The concept of *karma* as a moral law of cause and effect was not of course new with Buddhism, but the Buddhist interpretation of it had advantages from the point of view of the secular state. The Buddhist *karma* was preeminently psychological and moral – the effects of *karma* were determined by the moral quality of the agent's intentions. This gave a strongly ethical cast to Buddhist cosmology.[6]

Actions could have consequences for those who performed them from their moral (not ritual or mechanical) character, and a science of virtue was

[6] The imposition of a theory of good and bad actions upon a previously impersonal or amoral cosmology, a concept identified by Weber as ethicization, has been discussed in its application to Buddhism by G. Obeyesekere, 'Theodicy, sin and salvation in the sociology of religion', in E. R. Leach (ed.), *Dialectic in Practical Religion* (Cambridge University Press, Cambridge, 1968), p. 21.

integral to an ideology of universal values.[7] The *dhamma* teachings of the monks therefore emphasized the role of *kamma*, in its sense of moral cause and effect, and when we read in their texts of the importance of liberality or other virtues it is this process of ethicization that we must recognize; it was not just edification for the novice – it was intensely relevant to the concerns of the wider urban culture of the state.

Thus many of the maxims of the *Dhammapada* read like exhortations to upright conduct in society:

50 One should not bother about the anomalies or the commissions and omissions in the case of others; one should bother about one's own commissions and omissions.
55 There are the scents of sandalwood, rhododendron, lotus, and jasmine, but the scent of virtue (*sīla*) is incomparable.[8]
57 Māra [death personified] cannot find the path of those who are endowed with virtue, who are not lacking in mindfulness, liberated by right knowledge.
78 One should not consort with bad friends or inferior people; one should consort with worthy friends and with superior people.

Frequently enough the context clearly refers to the concerns of the ascetic monk, but the vocabulary is appropriate for the celebration of social virtue, as where praise is lavished on one who initiates resolute enterprise (*viriyam ārabhato daḷhaṃ*, *Dhp* 112). Similarly the section on *dhamma* (*Dhp* 256–72), concerned with righteousness in following the ascetic path, can be read as teaching righteousness as embodied in society. Any empire in the making had to deal with a multitude of communities with different customs, and fairness to all was important.

256 One is not an upholder of righteousness (*dhammāṭṭho*) by making a wild decision; a wise man will decide only after considering both what is and what is not the case.
257 A wise man, a protector of righteousness (*dhammassa*), governs others[9] with impartial righteousness, without wildness, and he is called an upholder of righteousness.

[7] There is an important parallel here in the way that Confucianism imposed a moral framework upon an old magico-auguristic cosmology. As Waley has written about the concept of *te*, often translated 'virtue', 'Only when the moralistic position was thoroughly established, that is to say, after the doctrines of Confucianism had become a State orthodoxy, did *te*, at any rate among the upper classes, come to mean what we usually mean by virtue.' A. Waley (ed. and trans.), *The Way and its Power: A Study of the Tao Te Ching and its Place in Chinese Thought* (Grove Press, New York, 1958), p. 32.

[8] The meanings of the botanical terms in Pāli are not at all certain. Here the translation of Daw Mya Tin is followed, *The Dhammapada* (Rangoon, 1993).

[9] Lit. 'lead others', *nayatī pare*. On variant readings, see the Carter and Palihawadana edn, p. 480, n. 3.

Here the word translated 'impartial' is *samena*, 'same', 'uniform', and it reflects the concern for uniform justice that is evinced also by Aśoka's inscriptions: sameness or fairness is to be desired, he says, in trials and punishments.[10]

In a kingdom where the ruler sought to impose a new universal code, as Aśoka did, the message of abstention from harm, a monkish virtue, was also apt as a principle of state, and a division of the *Dhammapada* (29–145) preaches the virtue of restraint towards all beings.

129 All are afraid of the rod (*daṇḍassa*); all are afraid of death; putting oneself in the place of another, one should not harm or kill others.

This is exactly what Aśoka claimed to have done after the appalling loss of life caused by his war with Kaliṅga; he sought to replace conquest by the sword with conquest by his own *dhamma*.

137 He who harms those who are harmless, without offence, will quickly go to one of the ten (harmful) states.

These are then listed; they are physical and material sufferings, including notably 'danger from the king'. If we imagine a king or a minister listening to the rhythmically insistent exhortations to virtue embodied in the text, it is easy to understand how it could speak to the ethics of government. Aśoka's own code of social morality is clearly at one with the message about reverence to seniors:

109 For one whose custom is constantly to respect and give honour to the aged, four benefits (*dhammā*) increase – longevity, complexion, contentment and strength.

This is remarkably like the teaching of Aśoka's edicts, which commonly exhort his subjects to honour parents along with brahmins and *śramaṇas*. The original intention may have concerned respect to senior monks, but the projection to society at large is readily made.[11]

The social ethic appropriate to the management of a large state containing heterogeneous cultures demands values of fairness and respect. It cannot easily be combined with local cults and culture-bound myths. Hence the appeal of the impersonal rule of moral law, *kamma*. One group of verses insistently links actions with moral consequences:

[10] Pillar Edict 4: *ichitaviye hi esā kimti viyohāla-samatā ca siya daṃda samatā.*

[11] Aśoka's concern with social harmony and bonds of respect is evident for example in Rock Edicts 3, 4, 7, 9–11 and all Pillar Edicts.

67 That deed is not well done which one regrets after performing it, experiencing the consequence of it with tears and weeping.
68 That deed is well done which one does not regret after performing it, experiencing the consequence of it with delight and happiness.
69 So long as a bad deed does not bear fruit, the foolish one thinks it sweet as honey; but, when the bad deed bears fruit, then the foolish one undergoes suffering.

There are many such aphorisms. To the modern ear, they may sound banal, rather like many of the platitudes attributed to Confucius – which is an apt analogy, since his teachings similarly imposed a framework of impersonal morality upon an older culture of ritual, supplying an ideology for the state. However, what gave them freshness to their first hearers, as well as authority for later generations, is their promise of contact with the forces that govern our lives, not through a priest with controversial cultural credentials, but through virtue. Such a programme could only commend itself to growing state power.

None of this is intended to suggest that the *Dhammapada* or any other text was consciously redacted in order to interest the rulers of kingdoms in the potential of the Buddhist *dhamma* to furnish a state orthodoxy. The verses generally reflect the ascetic values of original Buddhism, and were composed chiefly with a view to keeping in the monk's mind a clear understanding of the noble path. But audiences invisible to the modern reader had a hand in the history of a text that has attained such a rank as has the *Dhammapada*, influencing the selection of maxims and helping to give the collection its final shape. One such audience was the expanding state.

But the early *saṅgha*, with its ascetic values, faced in two directions, and by being able to do so was able to supply an essential joint in the articulation of a multi-cultural society. One direction, just considered, was towards the state. The other was towards the towns and villages, especially communities far removed in culture and power from the dominant urbanized groups. There are various ways in which popular Buddhist texts demonstrate the orientation of the *saṅgha* in this direction, towards popular culture. A particularly important one has to do with the attitude of ordinary people to ascetic holy men coming as outsiders among them. The *dhamma* held up high ideals of detachment and passionlessness running strongly counter to ordinary human nature. There were soteriological reasons for such teaching; but it is easy to overlook their implications for laymen who came to know about them, however little inclined they might be to adopt ascetic ideals themselves.

We must picture the wandering monks arriving as strangers, ready to impart an unfamiliar *dhamma* to any who would listen. If they were lucky, or had the appropriate talents or personality, the monks inspired trust, and if they stayed long enough or visited often enough they would become familiar and eventually become part of the local scene, valued perhaps as healers, counsellors or seers. Of course they had not been trained as counsellors in village politics, as umpires, as go-betweens, as interpreters of government demands, or as vehicles of healing power or sacred energy, but what matters is simply that their carefully studied calmness, detachment, dignity and lack of private agenda were likely to be excellent qualifications for just such roles; we see the same thing happening today in remote rural areas visited by forest monks.

The texts which teach the importance of these qualities therefore must be recognized as signals to laymen who knew something about the discipline and education of monks. The teaching that a monk should aim at a seemingly superhuman indifference to his surroundings could be recognized within the *saṅgha* as a discipline for focusing upon the path, but it was also an assurance to laymen that monks were expected to live by a much higher standard than ordinary mortals, perhaps thereby gaining a higher state that would give them special powers and insight.

35 The mind (*citta*) is hard to hold on to firmly, volatile (*lahuno*), alighting where it fancies, and it is good to have control of it; a controlled mind brings satisfaction.
37 The mind roams far afield, wandering on its own, bodiless, lying hid; those who can restrain the mind are released from the bonds of Māra.

That is, those who succeeded in meeting the demands of the *Vinaya* were able to reach a status inaccessible to ordinary people. This aspiration was not seen as mere rhetoric; it was a believable consequence of the strenuous self-purification ideally expected of monks. Those monks whose aloof detachment and apparent wisdom were truly impressive might inspire the belief that they actually possessed the awe-inspiring superhuman powers recognized among the fruits of arahantship.

They were supposed to have eradicated all craving, and to be uninvolved in worldly concerns, uninterested in receiving honour and veneration:

75 The way of gaining possessions (*lābhūpanisā*) is one thing, and the passage to nibbāṇa is another. A mendicant (*bhikkhu*) who recognizes this to be so should not rejoice in receiving veneration (*sakkāra*), but should cherish his detachment (*viveka*).

Even the gods loved one who had complete control over his mind (*Dhp* 94), and such a being was not subject to the round of *saṃsāra* (*Dhp* 95).

The description of the *arahant* is reminiscent of the shadowy forest spirits thought to haunt the wilds in modern times; he is elusive, unaffected by normal physical influences, and not dependent upon sustenance (*āhāre ca anissito*: *Dhp* 93). It is his calmness that will instantly mark him out: 'Calm is his mind, calm his speech and action' (*Dhp* 96). One who is steadfast, moderate and restrained, 'Māra in no degree can defeat, any more than the wind can defeat a mountain crag' (*Dhp* 8). One who conquered the defilements (*āsava*) with self-control and with truth was truly worthy of his robe (*Dhp* 9–10); here the laity could read a clear message that it should distinguish between the worthy and unworthy and respond accordingly. The true monks, the virtuosi, gained a higher consciousness that enabled them to overcome even death:

21 Awareness (*appamādo*) is the abode of deathlessness; lack of awareness is the abode of death. Those who have awareness do not die; those who lack it perish.

From the point of view of a monk, no doubt, lack of awareness was a familiar obstacle to successful meditation, a natural human propensity to relaxation and distraction. The term *appamādo* covers all the monk's needed qualities of mindful consciousness. From the point of view of the layman, awareness was something superhuman, setting its possessor upon a higher plane. Awareness is stressed in many verses, and the second division, *Appamādo-vagga*, is devoted to it.

The *Dhammapada*, therefore, could function as a guide for the lay population (from which, after all, every monk had to be recruited) to the qualities of an advanced monk, and an assurance of the value of the attainments of such a person. How could the villagers hope to benefit?

Here it is useful to consider the type of cosmology, implicit in folk ways of thought rather than specified in any particular system, that gave meaning to contact with holy men in disparate local cultures not necessarily versed in Vedic lore or its associated myths. The rudiments of such a cosmology can be detected in the texts of *dhamma*.

One verse, likening the passing mendicant to a bee taking off pollen, is eloquent:

49 Just as a bee takes nectar from a flower and flies away without harming its colour and fragrance, so would a sage pass through a village.

The bee disappears into its abode in the wilds to make honey, which is sweet and sustaining. Similarly, the mendicant takes away something from the villagers, and in some sense he transforms it, for their benefit.

What he takes away is the offering placed in his bowl. He takes it away and eats it, thereby enabling the donors to obtain the benefit of his own advanced spirituality. This transaction fits easily within the world of popular cosmological belief in almost any folk culture.

But there had to be stringent conditions. No mere ritual giving was likely to be efficacious. The recipient had to be purified, wholly unlike ordinary people. It was necessary to purge away his own human frailty, the clutter of selfishness and ignorance that had constituted his ego before he became a monk, for these could only smother the offering and prevent the action upon it of cosmic forces. In simple terms, the purification was effected by emptying himself, making himself a blank. The begging bowl was a good symbol of this emptiness: one places one's offering within the bowl, which is a pure vehicle of selflessness, empty space, without distinction or adornment, and the bowl is taken away to be used in a sacramental act of eating, subject to remarkably elaborate rules of discipline designed to ensure that involuntary manifestations of personal pleasure do not sully the enactment. Some forest monks today take a great deal of trouble to make their bowls duly anonymous, ensuring that they have a uniform dull matt finish. Monks also keep up rigorously the ancient routine of collecting offerings, going by the village doorways so that householders can make their individual offerings. This is done even where the begging round is not strictly necessary – lay supporters later come to the *vihāra* and prepare a proper meal.

So the holy man has to be, in an important sense, a blank space. The particular fleshly mortal being is transmuted, becomes an insubstantial image of a reality that lives on a higher plane, cannot be localized and is without individual personality. Something of this idea can be detected in the *Dhammapada*:

> 93 One in whom the defilements [*āsavā*] are thoroughly destroyed, who is not tied to [a source of] sustenance, whose territory is freedom, void and unmarked – the passage of such a one is hard to trace (*durannayam*) like that of birds in the sky.

Lay Buddhist understanding of nibbāṇa has proved a complication for the study of Buddhism in its social setting: though theoretically of supreme importance, for the ordinary Buddhist it is remote, obscure and uninteresting as a goal of aspiration.

Yet it instantly becomes central, and acquires a major role in the sociology of Buddhism, when we shift perspective and treat its occurrence in a text not as the specification of the most desirable goal worth aspiring after for oneself but as a description of something that happens to other people. If the monk obtains nibbāṇa, or if he even sets his feet firmly upon the road that leads in the right direction, then offerings given to him will surely earn the highest possible benefit.

There are several references to nibbāṇa in the *Dhammapada*, all celebrating it as the summit of a holy man's self-purification. He studies mindfulness, aiming at nibbāṇa, thereby eliminating the *āsavas* (*Dhp* 226). Nibbāṇa is the supreme contentment (*paramaṃ sukhaṃ*, *Dhp* 204), the seat of the deathless (*amataṃ padaṃ*, *Dhp* 114), the unshakeable abode (*Dhp* 225); it is the prize for cutting away all passion and hatred (*Dhp* 369), masters distraction, and achieves total mindful awareness:

32 The *bhikkhu* who takes pleasure in awareness (*appamāda*), seeing danger in lack of awareness, is not likely to lapse (*abhabho parihānāya*); he is in the vicinity of nibbāṇa.

Nibbāṇa thus figures as the seal or crown of the qualities repeatedly emphasized as necessary for the monk seeking salvation – mindfulness, self-control, total detachment, passionlessness. These are qualities which fit a holy man to act as advocate and adviser for the local community in its dealings with the outside world – and also, in a religious sense, qualities which fit him as a medium between the supplicant making offerings and the cosmic forces which can turn the offerings into karmic benefit. There are two levels of action: Buddhism operates both in the public arena, as an integrating social force, and in the context of folk belief, as a superior conduit of sacred energies, but the two converge in the language of spiritual discipline which belongs to neither but is directed to the needs of salvation for the ascetic.

Those who made offerings needed the ascetics to be bent upon nibbāṇa, but were not seeking it for themselves. What they sought was happiness in this world and the next. Even a 'secular' culture, one with a cosmology privileging impersonal forces, could believe in a next world, so long as access to it was conceived of in impersonal terms not involving divine choice; the doctrine of *kamma* supplied this. A pair of verses refers to the beyond in terms which made sense to ordinary people; both verses end in the refrain: 'One who observes *dhamma* sleeps in contentment in this world and the world beyond' (*Dhp* 168–9). These verses refer in generic terms to the good conduct which conforms to *dhamma*, but they could also be taken as maxims for upright life in society, not just for monks (though, as usual, the Pāli commentary resolutely interprets them as referring to a monk's spiritual discipline[12]).

Here we can recognize the notion of contentment in a fully imaginable human life, which is more likely to have made sense to most hearers of

[12] See the Carter and Palihawadana edn, p. 233. On the tendency of the Theravāda scholastic commentators to apply such textual prescriptions specifically to the discipline of the monks, see G. Bond's review of Carter and Palihawadana, *JAOS*, 111 (1991), p. 173.

the text, not as a bodiless abstraction. This is the cultural context in which Buddhism must have had most impact, and it is significant that in Aśoka's inscriptions *dhamma* is a this-worldly concept, in which nirvāṇa does not figure, but the concept of benefits in this life and the next is likewise present.[13] Some of the epithets for nibbāṇa, such as 'supreme contentment', suggest images of heavenly happiness, and one verse indeed refers to the heavenly noble land (*dibbaṃ ariyabhūmiṃ*, *Dhp* 236) – that is, the heavens in which are reborn those destined for enlightenment and nirvaṇa after one more rebirth.

To ordinary lay followers, the *dhamma* texts alluded to a hierarchy of increasingly happy states, with nibbāṇa as a theoretical abstraction at the top. It was not so much a desirable state to which one could aspire; it was an ideal condition which the better ascetic monks were thought to be approaching, and its significance was precisely that such monks were fitted thereby to act as conduits for the offerings given to them. The actual content of nibbāṇa, as something realized by the ascetic monks, was infinitely less interesting than its value for others.

So benefit for the givers of offerings is mechanically linked to the purity and spiritual advancement of their recipients. Several passages indicate that the merit of offerings to a monk is precisely congruent with that monk's advancement. The propensity to generate bad *kamma* can be neutralized by offerings to one who has eliminated that propensity.

356 In fields, it is grass [growing as weeds] that is the defect; in humans, it is passion that is the defect. Therefore there is great fruit from what is given to those in whom passion is eliminated.
357 In fields, it is grass [growing as weeds] that is the defect; in humans, it is hatred that is the defect. Therefore there is great fruit from what is given to those in whom hatred is eliminated.
358 In fields, it is grass [growing as weeds] that is the defect; in humans, it is delusion that is the defect. Therefore there is great fruit from what is given to those in whom delusion is eliminated.
359 In fields, it is grass [growing as weeds] that is the defect; in humans, it is desire that is the defect. Therefore there is great fruit from what is given to those in whom desire is eliminated.

[13] See Major Rock Edict IX (the performance of *dhamma* leads to merit in the next life: Kālsi version); X (all Aśoka's efforts were 'with a view to the after-life, that all men may escape evil inclinations'); XIII (victory by *dhamma* is pleasurable only to the extent that it has benefits in the next world); Dhauli and Jaugaḍa Separate Edict (good principles of administration conduce to the attainment of heaven); Second Separate Edict (the border peoples should follow *dhamma* and thus gain this world and the next); Minor Rock Edict (implying that if people are pious they come nearer to the gods and can reach heaven easily); 1st Pillar Edict (referring to happiness in this world and the next); 4th Pillar Edict (condemned criminals can use their three days' respite to fast for the sake of better rebirth).

Texts such as the *Dhammapada*, then, could speak in various ways. They could confirm with total authority that a good monk was reliable as a truly detached, unthreatening figure, totally unconnected with the agenda of powerholders in the state. They also described the discipline and training of a monk in ways that represented the holy man as a pre-eminently potent intermediary between the individual or his group and the forces that determine people's fate; these claims were couched in terms that presupposed no local or ancestral cult but appealed to universal values, and yet fitted in with folk beliefs.

These texts were therefore neutral towards different cultures with different repertoires of lore and myth. They contained very little that presupposed a hearer's familiarity with any specific particularistic tradition, such as the brāhmaṇical one. The contrast with brāhmaṇical texts is striking; Vedic and post-Vedic literature is replete with allusions that presuppose knowledge of a rich tradition. The brāhmaṇical texts could draw confidently upon a stock of motifs that had meaning for a whole people – the 'Aryan' communities and their descendants who recognized their brotherhood in the Vedic Sanskrit traditions. The Buddhist texts were different: they did not seek to give expression to an ancestral culture of a particular people, and they expected to deal frequently with communities to which their ideas were unfamiliar.

The difference is measurable in the number of references to mythical beings, in general or as individuals, and, in simple terms, in the frequency of proper names. The *Dhammapada*, for example, has very few. Gods are mentioned generically at a number of points (*Dhp* 94, 105, 420), not as specific beings to be invoked but just as part of the background scene. (*Dhp* 94: 'Even the gods' love one who is passionless and self-controlled; the point is to magnify the achievement of the ascetic, not to say anything about gods.) Gandhabbas, celestial beings, appear alongside humans and gods simply to map the total of beings who are unable to follow the path of an *arahant* (*Dhp* 420).

Maghavan (a name of the Vedic Indra) makes an appearance (*Dhp* 30), but the allusion, as the commentary asserts, is to the story of a young brahmin Magha, who became known as Maghavan.[14] There are very few proper nouns generally. Points are illustrated by reference to the horses from Sindh

[14] Implicitly, perhaps this cuts the Vedic god down to size as a manifestation of karmic rebirth like the rest of us. The *Dhammapadaṭṭhakathā* tells the story that Sakka, king of the gods, was in a former life Magha, called Maghavā, who came to be reborn as Sakka through good deeds. See E. W. Burlingame (trans.), *Buddhist Legends. Translated from the original Pāli Text of the Dhammapada Commentary* (Luzac, London, 1969 (Cambridge, Mass., 1921)), part 1, pp. 314–19.

(*sindhavā*) (*Dhp* 322), and to the elephant Dhanapālaka, which figured in a story (*Dhp* 324). A group of verses about fault-finding is represented as being spoken to Atula, described in the story as a notorious fault-finder (*Dhp* 227).[15] There is not much else. The vein of allusion to legendary lore is thin indeed. In the long run, certainly, a rich store of Buddhist legends accumulated, and later sources such as the *Jātakas* tapped in to a treasury of folk memory; but the canonical texts are simply not concerned with the traditions of particular communities.

There is one exception, which needs to be particularly noticed: Māra, or Yama, Death. This figure is mentioned a number of times, as the enemy who is bested by the holy man.

274 This is the path, there is no other for purification of vision. Take this path; it will confound Māra.

It is not entirely clear just how far this Māra is really personalized in Buddhist thought, but on the whole, in the *Dhammapada* at least, every mention of him is little more than a metaphor, like references to the Devil in colloquial English. He normally stands for ignorance and attachment that may be overcome by restraint and mindfulness, or for the delusive power of life in *saṃsāra* which traps ordinary mortals. Sometimes Māra is mentioned not by name but as the king of death (*Dhp* 170). As a representative of forces to be overcome, he is only weakly personalized (*Dhp* 7, 8, 40, 175, 276, 350). There are references to 'Māra's flowers', which designated the flux of life in *saṃsāra*, or the defilements. There can be no certainty how vivid was the concept of Māra as a personal force to be trembled at in the minds of early Buddhists, but it is clear at least that canonical texts such as the *Dhammapada* did little to encourage the notion of him as a real person active in human affairs.[16]

And that is what we should expect in a period when the appeal of the *dhamma* was to a multi-cultural audience subject to the stresses of encroachment by rising states with their urban culture. Texts have a secular character that is in some ways curiously modern in flavour. Man is in control of his own fate, at least to the extent that present actions can determine future consequences, not dependent upon the favour of personal divine beings. This accords with Mary Douglas' proposition: 'The essential difference between a cosmos dominated by persons and one dominated by objects is the impossibility of bringing moral pressures to bear upon the

[15] Again the story is told by the *Dhammapadaṭṭhakathā*. See ibid., part III, pp. 113–15.

[16] *Dhp*, ed. Carter and Palihawadana, p. 442.

controllers: there is no person-to-person communication with them.'[17] The small community managed by rituals addressed to gods was being displaced by the large impersonal state.

It was in this situation that monks could play an important part in the articulation of society. To kings and officials, their teachings appeared to offer ideals of peace and harmony within the body politic, where all should respect the wise and cultivate civic virtue. To the subordinate or marginal tribes and clans, their teachings appeared to offer a buffer between the local community and the state, and a culture-neutral mechanism for the accumulation of merit by making offerings.

In this context, the *Dhammapada* can be read on several levels, according to the several audiences likely to have had a hand in its shaping. For the anonymous individuals originally responsible for the composition of its individual verses, its message was ascetic, directed to those who had wandered forth as mendicants. For the state, its message was political or public; for the little man, it was spoken to folk belief.

This at least is a plausible interpretation, supported by an analysis of the text. Most verses, it should be emphasized, can be adequately understood in the way they were probably first intended, as props to the self-discipline of the mendicant practising meditation and detachment; but the public and folk messages can be read as alternatives in the language of the anthology in its final form. An analysis of the whole text identifies three main categories: verses which can be read only in the ascetic sense; verses which can be taken in this sense or equally in the public sense (directed to the state); and verses which can be taken in either the ascetic or the folk sense.

Which verse goes in which category is a matter of judgement, and there would be little point in a detailed tabulation of all verses. For what it is worth, though, the examination undertaken for this chapter counted only a minority of unambiguously ascetic verses that come in the first category – fifty-four, out of the 423. The public message can be read alongside the ascetic in many more – 115. What is most impressive, though, is the large number – 233 – which can be read on either the ascetic or the folk levels. (There are other permutations, which account for only a few verses.) The abundance of verses into which can be read a message for folk culture arises in large part because the many verses enjoining such qualities as detachment and calmness are also important as assurances to the local community that the wandering monk is totally neutral, and can be expected to exhibit wisdom and spiritual purity.

[17] M. Douglas, *Natural Symbols: explorations in cosmology* (Penguin, Harmondsworth, 1973), p. 61.

The interplay of different ways of understanding a single verse can be illustrated by a single example drawn from the (very small) class of verses capable of being read on all three levels:

391 That one who does no ill in deed or word or thought, who is restrained in respect of these three – him do I call a brahmin.

The cultivation of restraint by cleaving to proper thought, proper speech and proper action is of course integral to the path followed by the wandering monk bent upon enlightenment. The ascetic message is plain enough. But so is the public: this verse asserts that the holy man, marked not by his birth or his training in officiating at rituals but by his supreme mental self-control, is the proper mediator between the community and the forces that bring about its weal or woe, and he is a paradigm of social virtue, fostering no dissidence or division. Meanwhile, the villager living on the fringes of Sanskrit civilization is reassured by the verse's popular message: unlike the official brahmins, with their pretensions and their exclusive customs, the monk is a truly benign figure, easy to approach yet powerful as an intercessor on account of his spiritual purity.

Certainly, Buddhist monks were of all sorts. But the ideals of detachment and spiritual purity were always prominent in the *dhamma*, and the training in calmness and dignity was integral to the discipline. Those monks who came at all close to embodying the recognized values of the Order were necessarily well placed to stand forth, not only as good role models for novices, but also as potential mediators between the culturally isolated locality and the cosmopolitan state. This point is easy enough to document in respect of the careers of forest monks in modern times. It is not so easy in respect of ancient times, with sources contaminated by centuries of historical evolution; but it is still possible to see how readily the protagonists of the middle path could slip into the role of middleman at a time of cultural dislocation.

10

The mediating role as shown in the Canon

This chapter examines the role of the monk as middleman in a domesticated, monastic environment, as reflected mostly in the *Vinaya*. Evidence is scanty, but a few passages identify specific kinds of mediation forbidden to monks. The tone of admonition indicates that what is forbidden must have been practised. A role as middleman is not the same as the mediatory role, but the negative aspects of it as laid down in the texts are deserving of attention because of the restrictions they would implicitly place on the mediatory role.

One significant example concerns the ubiquitous monk Udāyin, who is portrayed attempting to make a match linking two families, and is sitting down in a secluded place with the girl in question, a man, and a woman. A prominent woman in the area, Visākhā, found out about this. She came and spoke to Udāyin, saying: 'Sir, this is not pleasing, it is not right, it is inappropriate for the master to sit with a woman – one man with one woman – on a secluded, comfortable seat. Although, sir, the master rightly has absolutely no ulterior motive, it is hard to convince people who are unconvinced.'[1] This uncompromisingly asserts that in certain respects monks were *not* to act as middlemen in local affairs and the example given is certainly of behaviour alien to the original ascetic ideal. Nevertheless, it must acknowledge a reality; a teaching transmitted down the centuries would not hold up such behaviour as a bad example unless it actually characterized some monks. The proscription is evidence of what it proscribes.

CONDITIONS LIMITING AND PROMOTING THE ROLE OF MONK AS MEDIATOR

In general, the monk was required to be modest in behaviour. One instance alleging the laity's insistence on this is in a passage portraying monkish

[1] *Vin* III 187–8.

greed. King Bimbisāra offers the monks access to his mango grove, and they abuse his hospitality by taking far too many. Then:

These people told the matter to King Seniya Bimbisāra of Magadha. He said: 'Look! The masters have really enjoyed eating the mangoes, but the Lord has stressed moderation.' People . . . spread it about, saying: 'How is it that these recluses, sons of the Sakyans, will enjoy eating the king's mangoes because they do not know moderation?'

And so the Buddha initially prohibited them, but allowed their limited use in curries.[2] The discipline of moderation is imposed not only upon a monk's apprehension of all sense objects, but also in the garments he wears, the implements he carries and his behaviour inside or outside the monastery.

A difficult area here for the Order was the temptation to demonstrate psychic capacities, believed to be a by-product of advanced meditational accomplishments; it was considered threatening to the spirit of moderation. For example, a story tells of an expensive sandal-wood bowl made to the order of a wealthy merchant of Rājagaha. He had it placed at the top of a pole and offered it to anyone who could bring it down by psychic means. The so-called six heretical teachers tried and failed, then Piṇḍola the Bhāradvāja, a 'perfected one as well as of psychic power', rose up in the air and brought it down. The merchant gave it to the monk, filled with expensive food. Then:

People heard it said, 'The master Piṇḍola made the bowl of the merchant of Rājagaha come down.' Then these people, making a loud noise, followed very close behind the venerable Piṇḍola the Bhāradvāja. Then the Lord heard the great noise, and, after hearing it, said to the venerable Ānanda, 'What on earth, Ānanda, is this loud noise? . . . ' [The Buddha rebuked the monk:] 'It is not suitable, Bhāradvāja, it goes against the grain, it does not look right, it is not worthy of a recluse, it is inappropriate . . . Bhāradvāja, how could you reveal this extraordinary condition, this amazing psychic power, to householders, because of a miserable wooden bowl? . . .

Then he went on to prohibit such exhibitions in general and ordered that the bowl be broken up and made into ointment.[3]

No doubt men who appeared to demonstrate psychic powers provoked various reactions. Hindu narrative literature is full of the awe and fear evoked by ascetics who use their ascetic heat destructively, or for sexual adventures, and in contemporary Indian villages people believed to be

[2] *Vin* II 109. Cf. *Vin* IV 258–9. [3] *Vin* II 110–12.

possessed by a deity are often credited with much power.[4] The same applies here: the monk who has psychic powers inspires fear, but also attraction. For the Order this was unacceptable for several reasons – because it violated the principle of moderation in all things, because the monk should not make a public show of himself, and because it was potentially expressive of sensuality. If the laity was impressed, it was for all the wrong reasons.

Nonetheless, the display of psychic powers must have been very tempting; if nothing else, it would have attracted an audience of monks or potential supporters. Thus there was conflict between the Order's interest in attracting contributions and its fundamental principle of utter detachment, to which the public demonstration of psychic powers was repugnant.

Nor are the texts utterly consistent, for elsewhere the Buddha endorses householders' requests for the monks 'to look out for lucky signs. I allow you monks when being asked by householders for good luck's sake, to tread on a cloth carpeting.'[5] Perhaps this could have been justified by the need for a monk to communicate his merit in whatever way he could, and need not be considered a demonstration of psychic power.

People who are seen as impartial and honest brokers are likely to be appealed to as mediators of any sort, and indeed monks are portrayed as honest brokers throughout the canon. It is one of the reasons why the *Vinaya* rules are so extensive and why there is so much emphasis placed on the monks' own and the laymen's disparagement of other monks who do not appear to act with the utmost probity. Honesty is not the most apposite word, for the monk is supposed to surpass all other men in his detachment from all material things. This perceived impartiality must have helped qualify him as a 'go-between', a kind of messenger between different groups, whose persuasive power was underpinned by his reputation as a monk. An additional factor in a monk's utility as a mediator must have been his knowledge of a relatively extensive region; this knowledge, enhanced by current news he picked up from other wandering monks, would have been much richer than that possessed by a typical villager.

Here is a negative example of this honesty taken from the *Vinaya*:

A certain caravan was desirous of going from Rājagaha to the south. A certain monk said this to the people belonging to the caravan: 'I will go with you venerable people.'

'But we, sir, will evade the customs tax.'

[4] See K. Erndl, *Victory to the Mother: the Hindu Goddess of Northwest India in Myth, Ritual and Symbol* (Oxford University Press, New York, 1993), ch. 5.

[5] *Vin* II 128.

The overseers heard about this, ransacked the caravan and asked the monk why he had travelled with a caravan which he knew was engaged in theft. Nonetheless, they set him free. Other monks found out and the Buddha rebuked him with the stock phrase, 'It is not, foolish man, to please those who are not pleased.'[6]

Another similar story tells of an honest monk to whom a woman attaches herself. Her husband assaults the monk, but later apologizes. The Buddha rebukes the monk, using the same terms as in the previous case.[7]

A final example: the nun Thullanandā takes into the Order a Licchavi adulteress whose husband wishes to kill her. The adulteress takes valuables belonging to him; he then complains to King Pasenadi. The Buddha thereupon prohibits the ordination of anyone in trouble with the law.[8]

If the monks' perceived honesty is a source of attraction for the laity, a danger for their mediatory role is the monks' constant vulnerability to accusations of being tainted with worldly attitudes and concerns. Caesar's wife must be above suspicion. One instance among many concerns the (probably apocryphal) 'group of six monks' who 'entered a village at the wrong time, sat down in a hall and talked a variety of worldly talk' on topics such as politics, clothes, household goods, town gossip, women and useless metaphysical speculation. Householders criticized them for this; the Buddha heard about it, and declared a general prohibition of entering villages at the wrong time. This criticism may have been made because the spiritual aspirations of monks require them to stand above worldly life, which they renounced at ordination. (But nuns such as Thullanandā do go to a village on business (*karaṇīyena*), though it is not clear what this business was.)[9] On the other hand, it would have been difficult to function as mediators between different groups if they did not possess a good knowledge of affairs and if they could not move freely between different levels of society. Delicate balancing was required. The monk, to be of use to competing parties, needed to be familiar with rural problems; yet, by direct personal involvement in worldly affairs, he risked impairing his status as an impartial wise man. The monk placed himself firmly within a transcendent universal framework of values, much broader than the villagers' more narrowly directed aspirations and values.

Yet the frequent references to monks being supported by a particular family or householder in a given village indicate that they must have been provided with a good working knowledge of family problems and of the

[6] *Vin* IV 131. [7] *Vin* IV 132ff. [8] *Vin* IV 225–6. [9] *Vin* IV 230–1.

difficulties of subsistence at both family[10] and village level. The Buddha's admonitions may have been directed simply at preventing them from airing their knowledge casually or frivolously, without judiciousness or restraint. Consider a conflict of interest, where Sāriputta is potentially torn between breaking a *Vinaya* rule and offending the family which supports him:

The Lord stayed in Sāvatthī . . . at that time the family who supported the venerable Sāriputta sent a youth to the venerable Sāriputta, saying: 'May the elder let this youth go forth.' Then the venerable Sāriputta thought: 'A rule of training the Lord has designated says that one monk should not attend upon two novices and this Rāhula is my novice. Now what path of action should I follow? . . .' [The Buddha then promulgated a rule allowing an experienced monk to have two novices.][11]

TYPES OF MEDIATION

The texts, virtually our only evidence for the early history of the *saṅgha*, were compiled by selection and rearrangement over a long period to meet the purposes of edification and pedagogy in the interests of monastic and lay education in much later times. These purposes are remote from those of the modern social historian, and it is not surprising that, in presenting all their narrative material as generic object lessons or as ideals, the texts do not tell us the ways in which monks actually dealt with the public. We have to read between the lines. Generally, we can infer monks' actual behaviour only from what they are told not to do. The *Vinaya* does provide some instances suggestive of the monk's middleman role. In each case, an example of monkish activity is subsequently used by the Buddha to promulgate a particular rule of conduct. Many of the examples we have found are trivial enough in themselves, but their value is in drawing attention to the variety of ways in which, despite the detachment from worldly involvement professionally required of the wandering monk, the Buddha's followers were involved in lay affairs.

To count as mediation, a monk's action must involve two different parties who wish to communicate in order to achieve a particular goal unrelated to the monk himself; both regard him as an honest broker. Mediation is more than mere interaction, for monks inevitably had to interact with laity and non-Buddhists simply by undertaking an alms round. Nor can it be

10 Eg. *Vin* IV 178: '. . . in Sāvatthī there was a certain family which became favourable towards the middle way and as it grew in faith, it decreased in wealth. Any solid food or soft food the family obtained they gave to monks before it was eaten and sometimes they went without food.'

11 *Vin* I 83.

simply offering advice to interested parties. Into such categories would fall the sermons monks give to donors and, the most spectacular, advice that the Buddha is depicted giving to kings.

There are many cases of monks giving advice to laymen about dealings with the Order. One such is the monk Sudhamma,[12] who 'was a builder and resided in the Maccikāsaṇḍa of the householder Citta where he ate permanently (*dhuvabhattiko*).[13] When Citta wished to invite an Order, a group or an individual person, he would not . . . [do so] before he had asked the venerable Sudhamma.' A problem emerges when Sudhamma thinks he alone can decide with which monks Citta will have relations. When several very prominent monks, including Sāriputta and Moggallāna, are invited by Citta for a meal, without first consulting Sudhamma, the latter becomes unhappy and begins criticizing the quality of the meal. The Buddha finds out what has happened and rebukes Sudhamma, saying,

> It is not suitable, foolish man, it goes against the grain, it does not look right, it is not worthy of a recluse, it is inappropriate, it should not be done. How could you, foolish man, scold and jeer so contemptuously at the householder Citta, who has faith, who believes, who is a donor and supporter of the Order?[14]

Only in an oblique sense can this be taken as an example of mediation: Sudhamma is the conduit by which Citta, a prominent layman, is enabled to interact with other monks. Sudhamma assumes something approaching dominance over Citta. No doubt there was always a danger of this happening, given the awe in which certain monks were held – especially those credited with psychic powers. It may also signal the tensions arising when monks entered the territory of others and encroached on the families on whom the latter depended.

One type of mediation was that of matchmaker, a curious job for a monk given his supposed distance from matters of the heart. It may not represent mediation between different ethnic or political groups, but it is a sort of mediation between kin groups. Several such examples can be found in the *Vinaya*, usually involving the monk Udāyin:

> . . . At Sāvatthī in the Jeta grove in Anāthapiṇḍika's park . . . the venerable Udāyin was dependent (*kulupago hoti*) on families at Sāvatthī, and he went up to many families. Whenever he saw a young boy without a wife and a young girl without a

[12] *Vin* II 15ff.

[13] There are some oddities with this passage. Why would a monk – the word here is not *bhikkhu* but *āyasmā* – work for a householder? In addition, *dhuvabhattiko* could also translate as 'permanent servant'.

[14] *Vin* II 18.

husband, he spoke of her beauty in the presence of the young boy's parents, saying: 'The young girl from that family is beautiful, good looking, pleasant, learned, wise, intelligent, capable and energetic. That young girl is right for that young boy.'

They said: 'They don't know us, sir, neither who we are, nor to whom we belong. If, sir, the noble monk were to make them give, we would bring that young girl to this young boy.'

He spoke of the boy's handsomeness in the presence of the girl's parents, saying: 'The young boy of that family is handsome, good looking, pleasant, wise, intelligent, capable and energetic. That young boy is right for that young girl.'

They said: 'They don't know us, sir, neither who we are, nor to whom we belong, nor what is this young girl's property. If, sir, the noble monk were to make them ask, we might give this young girl to that young boy.'

In this way he caused bridegrooms to be led out, brides to be brought out, and so caused marriages to happen.[15]

What is significant here is that Udāyin is dealing – in a very sensitive area – with families with whom he has a relationship circumscribed by alms-giving. No doubt this has allowed them to build up confidence in him and his competence to negotiate. In addition, since neither family knows the other, yet he knows both, it appears that his circle of acquaintances was much wider than that of the laymen with whom he had dealings. Nor is he simply an informant. He has to make a case as well. Why would a monk want to do this? Was it because he felt an obligation for alms given to him by the families on whom he was dependent? Was the transfer of merit an insufficient inducement always to give food? That this form of mediation was not a single case is demonstrated by the tales directly following it which show similar efforts at matchmaking.

A more down-market version of this was the use of the monk in the act of communicating between potential marriage partners of substantially different status. Another anecdote dealing with Udāyin tells of disciples of the Ājīvikas, arriving from afar, who asked a former prostitute to give her daughter to their son.

She refused, saying, 'Sir, I don't know you, nor who these are, nor to whom he belongs; and I will not give my only daughter to go to a distant village.' [The disciples were then advised to approach Udāyin as he 'will make her give her daughter'. Udāyin did as requested, telling her to give her daughter as he knew them. To this she responded positively,]

'If, sir, the master knows them, I will give (her.)'

[She gave her daughter to the disciples of the Ājīvikas; however, they began treating her like a slave, and she sent a message of complaint to her mother, asking

[15] *Vin* III 135.

to be taken away. In response her mother went to see them and asked them not to mistreat her daughter, but they told her they would not deal with her, only with the monk (*samaṇena saddhiṃ amhākaṃ āhārūpahāro . . .*). After a second letter of complaint the courtesan approached Udāyin, who subsequently asked the disciples not to mistreat the young girl. But now they said, shiftily,]

'We do not want anything to do with you; we only want to deal with the courtesan. A recluse should have no occupation. A recluse should be a genuine recluse. You go away, we don't know you.'

[A third message was sent, then the courtesan went directly to Udāyin who told her what had happened to him, and suggested she go herself. In response she cursed Udāyin to be miserable and unhappy and her young daughter put the same curse on him. After that, many other women who were unhappy with their in-laws denounced him, whilst others who were happy praised him, wishing prosperity for him.

Other monks saw what happened and the so-called modest monks asked,] 'How can the venerable Udāyin act as a go-between?' (*kathaṃ hi nāma āyasmā udāyī saṃcarittaṃ samāpajjissasi*) [He became upset and complained to the Buddha. The Buddha condemned Udāyin with the words,] 'Whatever monk should act as a go-between for a woman who wants a man or for a man who wants a woman, whether as a wife or as a mistress, that is an offence entailing a formal meeting of the Order.[16]

This kind of activity does count as mediation. The monk is well acquainted with both parties involved in the exchange. Knowledge of the other party is essential here as the reason given for the courtesan's reluctance to marry her daughter to the son of the Ājīvika is her lack of knowledge of them. The monk's acquaintance with both parties indicates not just his wide local knowledge but also his acquaintance with people who live beyond the locality. Further, he is dealing with a rival sect, the Ājīvikas, thereby showing that the monk could operate between different status groups within society. This inference gains weight from the status difference of the two implicated categories of people: prostitutes, and lay Ājīvikas, a religious group conspicuous by its extreme behaviour in the Buddha's time.

However, this mediatory function can go wrong. Ultimately the monk cannot compel the two parties to behave ethically. His own behaviour is carefully circumscribed by *Vinaya* rules, and that of Buddhist laypeople is ultimately defined by the Buddha's five basic rules for lay followers. Yet lay moral observance is voluntary, nor should the Buddhist monk intervene to apply pressure in any way. This would compromise his status as a monk, an impartial figure, in the eyes of those with whom he is dealing. Hence the critique of him made by the Ājīvikas. This is more than opportunism;

[16] Summary of *Vin* III 135–8.

it is a genuine indictment that Udāyin has stepped beyond his legitimate sphere.

The cursing and blessing by the women of the town constitute a more broad-based and potentially devastating indictment. Not only does it present the monk as having a divisive influence on the layfolk of the village, but it also epitomizes the sort of unprofitable states that are so condemned in early Buddhist literature. Life in the world is all *dukkha*, and any activity within society, even activity directed towards satisfaction of legitimate wants, whilst it may have provisional value, is ultimately a valueless tinkering with concerns that should have been abandoned by one on the path of the *dhamma*. Such activity was therefore a potential trap for a monk.

This narrative is followed by another of a similar kind where the persons requiring the 'go-between' are a prostitute and a group of men seeking to have sexual intercourse with her. Some of the dialogue is illuminating for the light it throws on Udāyin's role. The men sent a messenger to bring her but she refused to go with him:

> She said, 'Masters, I don't know you, nor who you are, nor to whom you belong; and I have many possessions and resources, but I will not go outside the city.' . . .
>
> [A man said,] 'Sir, why are you soliciting this prostitute? Surely master Udāyin should be told. Master Udāyin will bring (*uyyojessati*) her here.'
>
> When he had said this, a certain layman said to that man: 'Do not say that, master; it is not right for recluses, sons of the Sakyans, to act like that. Master Udāyin will not do it.'
>
> When he had said this, they said, 'Will he do it, or won't he do it?' and they made a bet.
>
> Then these dissolutes approached the venerable Udāyin . . .
>
> Udāyin went and asked the prostitute to go to the men. She agreed, saying, 'If, sir, the master knows them, I will go.'
>
> [A layman complained about a monk acting as a 'go-between' for a 'temporary wife' (*taṃ khaṇikaṃ sañcarittaṃ sampajjisatīti*) and the Buddha declared the activity to be a *saṅghādiseso* offence.][17]

The same themes are present as in the previous example, and this is presumably why they were all grouped together as *saṅghādisesa* rules. In both examples the crucial words are *sañcarittaṃ sampajjissati*, where the latter word can occur in several variant forms. Deriving from *sam/car*, the noun *saṃcarittar* conveys the idea of wandering about, though in the few examples where it occurs (almost all restricted to this section of the *Vinaya*) the prefix *sam* could have a sociative sense as well as indicating the act of

[17] *Vin* III 138–9.

moving between different parties. The repetition of the prefix *sam* in both words gives emphasis to the concept of intermediation.

Does this episode describe anything more than an act of procurement? Certainly a lay follower has considerable doubts about the integrity of a monk persuading a prostitute to go with men of whom she has no knowledge at all. Yet she trusts him. All these examples share this theme. The monk is approachable because of his knowledge and honesty. But is the monk truly neutral? If the lay follower could doubt his neutrality, perhaps the Buddha himself would have doubted it.

Often the Buddha is depicted dealing with prostitutes, so it is arguable that the monk Udāyin was simply helping her in her specific occupation, that truly he was acting as a 'go-between' without making any moral judgement on those for whom he was acting. However, as always in dealing with the laity, the Buddhist Order needed to heed its perceptions, and lay opinion had always to be accommodated. So if the monk was to act as mediator in the specific examples just cited he would do so only within defined boundaries.

Perhaps, therefore, the *Vinaya*'s attribution to the Buddha of acute sensitivity towards monks demonstrating bad conduct is, in a way, good evidence that in principle monks were qualified to play the mediatory role.

An extreme example concerns the followers of the monks Assaji and Punabbasu, located at Kiṭāgiri, who have to be reprimanded because of the many forms of outrageous behaviour they engage in.[18] According to the text, what concerns the Buddha is that 'their evil conduct is seen and also heard, and respectable families corrupted by them are seen and also heard'. In the course of this the Buddha lays down the right conduct for monks living in a state of material dependency on particular families:

> If a monk who lives in dependence on some village or small town corrupts families and does evil, and if his evil activities are seen and heard about and families he had corrupted are seen and heard about, the monks [as advised by the Buddha] should speak to him in this way, 'The venerable monk must depart from this residence where he has lived long enough.'[19]

It is not just the conduct itself which is condemned. Rather, the cumulative effect leads to an evil reputation being spread abroad, one capable of detriment to the Order in every area of its operation.

[18] *Vin* III 179ff.; *Vin* II 13–17.

[19] *Vin* III 184. Note the commentary upon this: '"Families corrupted by him" means that formerly having acquired faith, they no longer have faith because of him. Having been convinced, they are no longer convinced.'

MONK AS RECONCILER

None of the examples just cited could be described as fulfilling a mediatory role in the sense in which a wandering ascetic might do. Cumulatively, however, they do show the monk as capable of acting as a neutral channel for communication between groups who are engaged effectively in some form of exchange, not necessarily involving money. What is being exchanged is women, and it may simply be a logical extension of the monk's professed chastity that (perhaps like eunuchs in Chinese imperial harems) he is chosen for this task. A different kind of mediatory task, though, involves the monk in reconciliation. For example:

Once, a certain woman, having quarrelled with her husband, went to her mother's house.

A monk dependent on her family effected a reconciliation. He was 'remorseful . . . so this was not considered an offence'.[20] Yet, when on the next page of the same text a monk acts as a go-between for a eunuch, that is branded an offence. Both instances refer to situations involving family and possibly sexuality. Yet again it is the monk's chastity and his capacity to draw upon local knowledge of people that are brought into play, giving him a special status as reconciler.

The story of Pilinda, as told in the *Mahāvagga*, depicts the monk as reconciler, but also presents the potential dangers of conflict of interest that can beset a monk as mediator. Here is a summary of the passage:

Pilinda was a monk who wished to make a cave, so had a mountain slope cleared in Rājagaha. King Bimbisāra went up to him and offered an attendant for a monastery, but this was refused because the Buddha would not allow it. Pilinda agreed to ask the Buddha if it was acceptable and then gave the king a talk on *dhamma*. On being asked the Buddha agreed to a request for an attendant, and Bimbisāra came up and made the offer again. This time it was accepted, but he forgot to give the order and did not do so until after five hundred days. In consequence of the passing of five hundred days his chief minister gave five hundred attendants to the monk.

They established a village and Pilinda used it for his alms collection. One day the villagers held a festival where the young girls were decked out with ornaments. One young girl did not have any and cried. The monk Pilinda asked the girl's mother why the girl was crying. When told the reason, he had the girl's mother put a roll of grass on her head, and through his psychic power had this changed into gold. Bimbisāra heard about it, believed the family had stolen the gold, and so had them jailed.

[20] *Vin* III 144.

Pilinda found out what had happened, went to see Bimbisāra, and, exercising 'volitional force', had the king's palace turned into gold. In response Bimbisāra released the family. Pilinda became famous and was given ghee, fresh butter, oil, honey and molasses by the laity. He acquired so much it began to overflow and the people complained that he was storing up things, like the king. Other monks accused the monks associated with Pilinda of storing up abundance and the Buddha laid down a rule allowing only seven days' storage.[21]

Pilinda already has high status as a monk in the eyes of the king, a status seemingly enhanced by his knowledge of *dhamma*. From the village he receives all kinds of offerings of food. His close relation with the king allows him to intercede when the king inadvertently causes injustice. His entitlement stems specifically from his status as a monk, not his individual qualities such as chastity and honesty. But presumably also his outsider status is important. Finally, this passage shows the monk bringing some kind of arrangement between two parties which exist in a relation of asymmetrical power.

Whether we can generalize from this example to the entire *saṅgha* is a moot point. The evidence does not show conclusively whether village elites respected monks simply because they were monks, or whether monks first had to display psychic powers or knowledge of the *dhamma*.

Another example of possible mediation concerns a monk being used by a layman to determine who is worthy of an inheritance:

At one time in Vesalī, the householder who was the supporter of the venerable Ajjuka had two children, a son and a nephew. Then the householder said this to the venerable Ajjuka: 'Sir, will you grant an audience to whichever of these two children has faith and conviction?' At that time the householder's nephew had faith and conviction. So the venerable Ajjuka granted an audience to that child. With his wealth, he set up an estate and made a gift. Then the householder's son said to the venerable Ānanda:

'Ānanda, sir, which is the father's heir, the son or the nephew?'

'The son, friend, is the father's heir.'

'Sir, this master Ajjuka has shown that our wealth belongs to our associate. Your reverence, the venerable Ajjuka is not a (true) recluse.'[22]

Here it seems a monk is credited with influencing somebody as to who should receive an inheritance. Upāli declared no offence was accrued. This is surely not just an instance of a monk being appealed to on the score of his honesty. It must reflect the layman's belief that just as a monk has

[21] Summary of *Vin* I 207–9. [22] *Vin* III 66.

abandoned sexuality, so too has he abandoned material or any other wealth. Therefore his attitude in matters regarding wealth should be wholly detached and impartial. Here we see a figure committed to transcendent values being able to offer impartial adjudication between interested parties. In theory, this is the minimum condition for one who would play a mediatory role.

A related example concerns a monk being used by a trader:

> Once, a certain man took a valuable jewel and went along the main road in the company of a certain monk. Then the man saw the customs house, put the jewel into the monk's wallet without him knowing it, and so took it past the customs house.[23]

The Buddha declares this was not an offence since the monk had no awareness of it. Precisely because the monk is regarded as belonging to a special category to which the rules appropriate for normal laypeople do not apply, he can be used for fraudulent purposes. No wonder the *Vinaya* rules are at such great pains to preserve the public impression of the monk's indifference to material possessions and sensuality.

Further on in the same book of the *Vinaya*, there is a whole series of brief passages where women beseech monks to provide preparations either to prevent barrenness or to produce an abortion.

> Once, a certain woman whose husband was living away from home became pregnant by a lover. She said to a monk, who was dependent for alms on her family, 'Look here, master, you must know of an abortive preparation.'
>
> 'All right, sister,' he said, and he gave her an abortive preparation. The child died. He was remorseful . . . 'You, monk, have fallen into an offence involving defeat,' he said.[24]

In all of these examples the monk is said to be 'dependent for alms on her family'. He is credited with local knowledge, as well as either medical skill or sufficient knowledge to be able to find somebody else with it.

Another case relates once more to the monk's medical role:

> Once, a certain man whose hands and feet had been cut off was in the paternal home surrounded by relations. A certain monk said to these people, 'People, do you want him to die?'
>
> 'Certainly, sir, we want that,' they said.
>
> 'Then you should make him drink buttermilk,' he said. They made him drink buttermilk, and he died. He was remorseful . . .[25]
>
> Nonetheless, this was regarded as a *pārājika* offence.

[23] *Vin* III 62. [24] *Vin* III 83; cf. *Vin* III 139. [25] *Vin* III 86.

Here is a final example which, strictly, does not count as showing a monk as a mediator, but it is interestingly suggestive. The monks go to spend the rains at Vaggumudā. Then

> Vajjī was short of alms-food and it could be obtained only with difficulty. It was white with bones and people were living by digging out little pieces of grain from holes in the ground using sticks. Nor was it easy to nourish oneself by gleaning or from kindness. . . . [The monks then proposed they would superintend the householders' business and execute householders' commissions.] Those who rejected superintending the work of householders said, 'We've had enough, your reverences, of overseeing the business of householders. Look, your reverences, we will take the householders' messages (. . . *mayaṃ āvuso gihīnaṃ kammantaṃ adhiṭṭhitena . . . handa maya āvuso gihīnaṃ dūteyyaṃ harāma . . .*) . . . thus they will think of giving to us; thus being entirely on friendly terms and not disputing, we will spend a comfortable rainy season and will not go short of alms-food.'
>
> [Others suggested they praise the supernatural powers of certain monks. In this they succeeded. The monks were well fed, the people went hungry. The Buddha subsequently criticized them.][26]

If there is a problem here it is that monks definitely seem to be acting like householders. Rather than mediation, their job of running messages is something anybody employed by the householder would be able to do. In addition, they are working for the sake of shelter and alms-food, commodities they would normally receive from begging. By undertaking a householder's task and doing it for a specific goal they forsake their positions as monks. The misdemeanour may be minor, but it shows how monks may compromise themselves by acting as mediators or involving themselves in the affairs of different social and occupational groupings.

In describing the monk as a mediator between various elements of society and levels of power, as an unappointed functionary made attractive because of his detachment and his rich knowledge of local (and perhaps regional) affairs, we need to be very careful not just to focus on the figure of the Buddha himself. The need for this caveat has already been signalled here. If the application of Brown's theory is to be valid in the Indian case, then we should expect that some of the monks initially dedicated to meditation and solitude should be gradually sucked into a degree of social involvement by the expectations of the laity, and that many of the less dedicated ordinary monks should readily and willingly take on socially active roles. Because of this, we have cited as many examples as practicable of instances where monks are dealing with people of demonstrably different social groups, occupations and political status. However banal, these examples do reveal the qualities

[26] *Vin* III 87–91.

laypeople expected of monks as middlemen between conflicting groups – local knowledge, chastity and indifference to the material world. The latter two qualities contributed to the high trust in which laypeople must have held the *saṅgha* as a special body of men and women standing always in an ambiguous position: in the world whilst outside of it.

THE CONTRASTING MEDIATORY ROLE OF THE BRAHMINS

If one set of role model contrasts in Buddhist literature turns on the distinction between monks and laymen, another is between brahmin and monk. It was suggested in chapter 7 that monks had a role to play as middlemen between the urban culture of state capitals and the folk culture of outlying communities where the cultural gap between the two was great, while brahmins did the same where the cultural gap was small – at least, the outlying communities could recognize themselves in the world view offered by the brahmins. The contexts did not differ radically – there was necessarily a substantial overlap. This situation, we might naturally infer, provoked tension between brahmins and monks. In a sense they were competitors.

The difference between the role of the holy man or *śramaṇa* and that of the brahmin lies in the different settings in which they could operate successfully. Both moved between the seat of political and economic power and the communities upon which this power was encroaching, interpreting each to the other and *representing* (without necessarily possessing) education and high culture in the village.

It is therefore useful to notice how the process can be illustrated from the better-attested later history – derived mainly from epigraphic sources – when brahmins were acting as go-betweens mediating high culture, professing universal values, to the Little Tradition in communities already possessing, or valuing, some elements of the core traditions represented by brāhmaṇical culture. Here the brahmin could find the materials to co-opt local cults and myths, identifying regional deities as forms of great gods known to the Great Tradition. Note though that we are not arguing for a sharp distinction between a Great and a Little Tradition. The cultural ambassadors for the Great Tradition could operate successfully within the localized traditions only because they were immersed in both.

Such processes of acculturalization are known to history, offering valuable examples of the middleman process by which brahmins assisted in the acculturation of people who derived their identity from a localized culture. Two scholars in particular have chronicled the role of the brahmin as a cultural mediator in different areas. Hermann Kulke, in his important book on the political role of the Jagannātha Cult in the history of Orissa, has given a significant lead, successfully demonstrating the role played by brahmins as agents in the spread of brāhmaṇical (and *kṣatriya*) culture to areas where it had not previously been authoritative. Kulke gives much attention to the need for Hindu kings and *rājas*, who colonized the coastal areas of Orissa, to domesticate the tribal people of the mountainous areas, where they were a potential threat to the agricultural expansion of the new growing Hindu kingdoms. Kulke shows that a community's pre-existing beliefs could be integrated into the brāhmaṇical tradition so as to allow the community to become integrated into a larger political unity with shared trans-local beliefs.[27]

Even when the empire supposedly extended over a large area there was always doubt whether many of the subordinate tribes were, in fact, subordinate at all. In Samudragupta's time, '[t]he lords quite frequently proclaimed hugely successful expeditionary conquests in their inscriptions; however, rarely did they succeed in permanently connecting the subjugated princedoms with their own area of rule'.[28] Accompanying these conquests was a process of ideological conversion alluded to in the previous paragraph. This functioned like a process of domestication where the so-called 'barbarian tribes' came to pay obeisance to the larger state rulers and integrated themselves, to varying degrees, into the trans-local world view. In this process the brahmins played a vital part, and we are convinced this role was not a new one for them, that it had been played out well before the time of the explicit evidence provided in Orissan inscriptions. Kulke sets out the main lines of this process:

> The consolidation of the princes' power in the new core regions was a protracted process . . . Even if the relations between Hindu society and the tribes were certainly never without tensions, it can however be confirmed that they were characterized in Orissa by a continual process of indoctrination and partial integration rather than by a constant suppression or complete destruction of tribes. In this context the brahmins played an exceedingly important normative role in Orissa. They defined and codified the obligations of tribes, which (as in the *Mahābhārata*) 'resided in the area of (Aryan) kings' . . . This was one of the most important duties of those brahmins who lived in the outer parts of the core region: to propagate this ideal of a domesticated tribe for their own welfare and that of their king.[29]

[27] H. Kulke, *Jagannātha-Kult*, p. 8. See also Burton Stein, 'Formation of the medieval agrarian order: brahman and peasant in early South Indian history,' in *Peasant, State and Society in Medieval South India* (Oxford University Press, Delhi, 1980/1994), pp. 63–89, writing about the Coromandel Plain from the sixth to tenth centuries ACE.

[28] Kulke, *Jagannātha-Kult*, p. 11. [29] Ibid., p. 17.

This occurred by integrating tribes into the lower levels of the caste system and by pressing many of their menfolk into the army. But note: 'Both routes for the assimilation of tribesmen into the Hindu society led to a powerful mutual influence, a development which is generally known as "Hinduization".'[30] 'Hinduization', or, perhaps better, 'Indianization', is a process which extended to South East Asia, where the interactions which furthered it are a field open to speculation.[31] In the further extension of Indian religions over later centuries, no doubt, brahmins could play ascetic roles, and Buddhist monks could play priestly roles (as they do in many places today). But in India, as in South-East Asia, the textual sources do not offer us historical records of the very earliest forms taken by the spread and encroachment of the culture of urban states among alien populations, except to the extent that stories of the Buddha may offer us distorted echoes. In the nature of his role as an outsider, a social blank, the wandering ascetic seeks to leave no footprints. The priestly figures who came later, acting as mediators among populations already to some extent culturally assimilated, are much easier to recognize.

[30] Ibid., p. 18.

[31] See H. Kulke, 'Indian colonies, Indianization or cultural convergence?', in H. Schulte Nordholt, (ed), *Onderzoek in Zuidoost Asië* (Rijkuniversiteit de Leiden, Leiden, 1990), pp. 8–32. Alternatively, we could call the process 'Sanskritization'. M. N. Srinivas' concept has been much debated and the debate cannot be explored here, but the use of cultural themes from the religion of the Great Tradition to integrate a community into an embracing metropolitan culture must have important parallels in the more ancient, undocumented, processes of political expansion.

11

Exchange

As soon as he had made the decision to convert followers to the homeless life, the Buddha, as the first leader of the *saṅgha*, had to establish means of raising material support to sustain the *saṅgha*, none of whose members engaged in any productive work. This effort required at least three sustaining factors:

(1) The presence of sufficient material support – whether from an economic surplus or elsewhere.
(2) The intellectual motivation for people to give this support, a motivation fully acceptable to the laity, as to why they should give freely to the Order or to individual holy men.
(3) A marketing or communicative technique designed to spread news of the *saṅgha*'s need for support without giving the impression this need was motivated by avarice or grasping.

His success in harnessing material support can be judged by the minimal evidence in the texts pertaining to the development of these ideas. Even in the Buddha's time there must have been a widespread belief that *śramaṇas* were entitled to receive offerings and that benefits would flow directly from the giving of such offerings. How long it took to make the transition from individual to institution as receiver of gifts cannot be determined from the evidence at hand. From a quantitative perspective the difference is a fundamental one.

The offering of alms to monks looking for food in the early morning was the most habitual and conspicuous form of giving a layperson could make, at least when the *saṅgha* was first established. For the more wealthy the option was to offer land for a monastery, money or large quantities of food. Several centuries after the establishment of Buddhism, when it was successful in attracting many converts, it is clear from a study of inscriptions that even the less wealthy in society were offering financial donations for the construction of monuments. However, what becomes very apparent from studying the Pāli texts is that even in the earliest period of Buddhism the exchange of food *during a meal* had acquired other symbolic resonances simply than functioning as a glorified form of alms-giving. But the meals in question are not normal meals. They are characterized by their large size and strong ritualistic ambience. One could be forgiven for assuming they are almost entirely demonstrative, as if they are serving a kind of sumptuary consumption role. In studying these meals, therefore, we are studying a specific system of exchange, sumptuary consumption, systems of hierarchy within a clear Buddhist context and the Buddha's public dealings with elite members of society.

Most of the texts taken to illustrate the themes in this chapter are from the *Vinaya* and the *Majjhima Nikāya*. We have treated them from the perspective that they encode a set of values and are not just a careful description of specific historical events. At the same time we do not doubt that something like the meals described here did occur.

MERIT-MAKING

Given that the doctrine of the transfer of merit functions as one of the principal frames for gift exchange throughout Buddhist history and is a central frame in defining lay–monk relations we must say something about it before going on to the more specific case of what we call the ritual meal. So much has already been written on this subject that it is hardly necessary to enter into any detail. Ivan Strenski has summarized as well as anybody the interrelationships implied by the transference of merit:

> . . . a domesticated *saṅgha* will, second, maintain a range of ritual relations with the lay communities outside it. Above all, the *saṅgha* is a ritual receiver of gifts. Weber even argued that the only real rule laid upon the Buddhist laity was the obligation to maintain the *saṅgha* by giving it gifts. This in turn leads to the first of the *saṅgha*'s two chief symbolic relations with the lay world: the *saṅgha* is the chief occasion for merit-making (only superficially 'given' by the *saṅgha* for gifts received), thus making the *saṅgha* the chief exemplar of non-reciprocity. It is a passive symbol of independence even as it depends upon active lay donors (*dāyakas*). In this passive symbolic role, the *saṅgha* also exemplifies (and, of course, actively pursues) the *dhamma* and beyond this, Nibbāna itself. In an active role, the *saṅgha* provides preachers, teachers, scholars and, in certain cases, healers. Note well however, that none of these services is, strictly speaking, reciprocated cleanly to the laity for gifts given, but is an obligation, to some extent, freely assumed as appropriate to the new domesticated role of the *saṅgha* and its members. I shall argue that these relations constitute the basis of what is properly called a Buddhist culture or civilisation, and that they are in some sense the critical features of a domesticated *saṅgha*.[1]

[1] Ivan Strenski, 'On generalized exchange and the domestication of the sangha', *MAN*, ns.18 (1983), p. 465.

And further:

> In each case, we have a circle of giving beginning with the lay *dāyaka*, passing to the *saṅgha*, then from the *saṅgha* to other recipients, and ultimately, it can be argued, either in this or the next life to the initial giver. Thus the *saṅgha* does not necessarily reciprocate to the *dāyaka* for gifts given (least of all merit!) but instead acts to benefit a third party, which in turn eventually brings benefit back to the original donor. In some cases, where a 'trickle down' effect might occur, people would enjoy the same economic benefits and profitable estate would provide to the community at large . . . Rather than considering merit-making and the so-called transfer of merit a matter of spiritual accounting, we have something quite different: a *dāyaka* gives *dāna* to the *saṅgha* and thereby (automatically) earns merit (remembering all the while that this is not given the *dāyaka* by the *saṅgha*, only 'occasioned' by it); in turn the *saṅgha* then invites the *dāyaka* to invite others (the dead, the gods) to rejoice in the merit earned. The *saṅgha* gives an occasion for others to rejoice in the merit made by the first gift, and thus gain merit thereby.[2]

Whilst the idea of merit-making might presuppose a surplus, it is not dependent on a natural surplus of production over subsistence level of living, whatever that might have been. It would have occurred whether this kind of surplus prevailed or not. Merit was the reward for the deposition of goods and services with monks and was one way a surplus could both be used and justified. But the use of a surplus, individual or institutional, may have been popular because like the *śrauta* sacrifice it too had benefits over and above what might have accrued to the individual taking or giving the alms. In this we can agree with the judgement of the Ernfors: 'This contribution [derived from a surplus] is utilized for public works, which need not be physical and are typically ceremonial in nature, or concern the building of holy palaces, stupas or whatever of that kind. These things serve auspiciousness and maintenance of good life and order, enjoyed by all.'[3]

The centrality of the theory of the transference of merit guaranteed that aspects of it would be carefully defined in the texts. We cite two instances of such definitions to indicate the presentation of ideal types of monks as alms-receivers and of those who have fallen away from this ideal.

> [At Sāvatthī:]
>
> What do you think of this monks! What kind of monk is worthy to approach a family and what kind of monk is unworthy to approach a family?
>
> Indeed, monks, a monk may approach families thinking, 'They must give to me. They should not refuse to give. They must give a lot, not a little. They must

[2] Ibid., pp. 473–4.

[3] E. B. Ernfors and R. F. Ernfors, *Archaic Economy and Modern Society* (Studia Sociologica Upsaliensia 31, Acta Universitatis Upsaliensis, Uppsala, 1990), p. 148.

give me excellent things only, not poor things. They must give to me quickly, not slowly. They must give to me respectfully, not disrespectfully.' When they do not give anything to that monk who thinks like this, he feels annoyed because of that and consequently experiences pain and sorrow. And he feels like this if they give a little and not a lot, and if they give what is poor and not excellent, and if they give slowly and not quickly. The monk is annoyed by that and consequently experiences pain and sorrow. They give without respect, not respectfully. The monk is annoyed by that and consequently experiences pain and sorrow.

Monks, this kind of monk is not worthy to approach a family.

But indeed, monks, a monk may approach families thinking, 'How could I possibly think in regard to other families that "they must give to me. They should not refuse to give. They must give a lot to me, not a little. They must give me excellent things only, not poor things. They must give to me quickly, not slowly. They must give to me respectfully, not disrespectfully."' The monk is not annoyed by that and consequently he does not experience pain and sorrow.

Monks, this kind of monk is worthy to approach a family.[4]

The second passage seems to propose a historical change in the status of the monk, the Buddha lamenting the passing from the forest dwelling monk to the dweller in a monastery.

'Lord it is difficult to speak right now to the monks since they are full of qualities arising from wrong advice, they are impatient and do not respond quickly when taught.'

'In the past, Kassapa, the elder monks were forest dwellers and praised the forest life; they ate only alms-food and praised living off alms-food; they wore rags from a dust heap; they wore three robes and praised the wearing of three robes; they desired little and praised the attitude of desiring little; they were wholly satisfied and praised the attitude of being wholly satisfied; they were secluded and praised seclusion; they did not mix and praised lack of contact; they were energetic and praised the application of energy . . .

. . . Then the senior monks invited the monk – who was a forest dweller and praised the forest life – to a seat, saying, "Come monk! What is your name, monk! This monk is certainly of high repute. This monk definitely wants to learn. Come monk, sit on this seat!" . . .

But now the senior monks are not forest dwellers and do not praise the forest life; they do not simply eat alms-food and do not praise living off alms-food; they do not wear rags from a dust heap and do not praise the wearing of rags from a dust heap; they do not simply wear three robes and do not praise the wearing of only three robes; they do not desire just a little and do not praise the attitude of desiring just a little; they were not wholly satisfied; they were not secluded and did not praise seclusion; they mixed and did not praise lack of contact; they were not energetic and did not praise the application of energy.

[4] *S* II 199–200.

There is a monk who is well-known, renowned, who receives gifts of clothes, alms, lodgings and all the requisites and medicines for illness; it is he the senior monks invite to a seat, saying, "Come monk! What is your name, monk? This monk is certainly of high repute! This monk certainly wants to be with other ascetics. Come monk, sit on this seat!" '[5]

It would be possible to see the last paragraph of this passage as an admission of the elite nature of the early *saṅgha*; what had originally hoped to produce a community dedicated to an ideal succeeded only, under the influence of patronage for the wrong reasons, in providing a career path for the sort of politically adept monk who, in modern society, would be good at getting his face on television and making friends with the rich and famous. Perhaps the real burden of both these passages is the obvious one: that there will always be a temptation for a monk to spruik for alms, or if not, to use with more subtlety his reputation as a monk as a specific means of acquiring alms. This would represent a misunderstanding of the merit-making relationship, for, as Strenski says, it is as much about an opportunity for the laity to obtain merit as it is for the *saṅgha* to receive material support.

We must assume the simplest form of alms-giving and alms-seeking was a highly ritualized demonstration of one form of exchange between laity and monk. Yet this form of exchange, scarcely a 'gift exchange', was not one taking in the idea of contract and reciprocity. On the surface the gift of food in return for a sermon might conjure up the idea of a relation of reciprocity, which is what we find underlying the Hindu notion of sacrifice. The problem with the Hindu model is that it would have tied the monk into a form of obligation to the donor – almost a form of attachment in the Buddhist reading of it. Nevertheless the Hindu model of obligation to provide hospitality to guests must have been one of the dominant ones known within the cultures inhabited by the Buddha and his followers, even if the model was not formalized until several centuries later in the Dharmaśāstras. As Jamison[6] has stressed in a recent book, the situation described in Hindu texts from the *Brāhmaṇas* to the *Dharmaśāstras* is one where a guest must be received and hospitality given, irrespective of the giver's inclination or his material circumstances. From the Buddhist point of view the *bhikkhu* is not an *atithi* (guest) and, whilst the lay Buddhist does

[5] *S* II 208.

[6] S. W. Jamison, *Sacrificed Wife. Sacrificer's Wife* (Oxford University Press, New York, 1996), pp. 153–69. Cf. also F. Wilhelm, 'Hospitality and the caste system', *Studien zur Indologie und Iranistik*, 20 (1996), pp. 523–9; T. Brekke, 'Contradiction and the merit of giving in Indian religions', *Numen*, 45 (1998), pp. 303–8 for the view of giving as sacrifice.

have an implicit obligation[7] to feed the monk, for the Hinduized layperson no such obligation need exist in theory. In practice, of course, the situation might have been considerably different and the success of monks' begging for food might have been a consequence of the dominance in northeastern India of the Hindu model of hospitality.

But what does this tell us about non-monastic economics and the role of the *saṅgha* in the early Indian economy? We should at this stage note that this was not just a barter arrangement where food and materials would be provided to a monk who was held to be a field of merit. No bargaining would ever take place. In the Buddha's time, and certainly in contemporary Buddhist countries, the exchange becomes impersonalized when money intervenes, though the merit component is certainly still present. However, it is our conviction that the meal functioned as a form of gift exchange, where reciprocity was certainly implied. In this sense it brings with it all the qualities associated with the gift in what the Ernfors describe as archaic societies:

> The gift is a sign of the norm, the obligation or duty and right, and as such a carrier of a normative order of various widths and scopes. Being presented, it demands a return, whether this be in the form of a material thing, behaviour, gesture of the body or mind or whatever. And this return is a gift as well, whether it be called '*service*', '*favour*', '*duty*' or a '*gift*'. The gift in its archaic context is *the beginning and the end of essential social activity, the realization of the norm and its initiation.* It commands a cycle of duties and right . . .[8]

The subsequent part of this chapter attempts to unpack this statement as it applies to the meal understood as gift.

THE IMPORTANCE OF MEALS AS A MEASURE OF SOCIAL INTERACTION

The image of the monk as an almsman (and the doctrine of the transfer of merit used to circumscribe the mode of exchange) is such a familiar one in Buddhist literature as to be taken for granted as the privileged image of exchange between monk and laity in early Buddhism. It is not the only such image, however. Another one, also occurring frequently in the texts, is structured around a meal between the Buddha or another monk and a layman. It is normal in such cases for the meal to be enframed within

[7] Though the obligation to accept may not have been equally stringent. See Brekke, 'Contradiction', p. 298.

[8] Enfors and Enfors, *Archaic Economy*, pp. 59–60; emphasis in the original.

the larger context of conversion, a common frame in Buddhist literature and not always including the kind of meal with which we are concerned here. All the meals presented in such cases are large, highly demonstrative and deliberately ritualized, offering possibilities for sumptuary display on the part of the patron who pays for the meal and an exalted status for the Buddha who receives it. It may be problematic that the great majority of cases of meal narratives portray the Buddha as the recipient of the meal and so, to be fully conclusive, evidence of other monks receiving the kind of adulation implied by the meal should be found, so that it is not exclusively a marker of the Buddha's own charisma.[9]

A passage taken from the *Jīvakasutta* of the *M* lays down some of the conditions under which a monk is approached by a layperson for a meal and the required attitudes that should prevail in the monk. It also demonstrates, we think, that the prior invitation to a meal distinguishes it from the typical alms-gathering round the monk is ideally supposed to take each morning.

> . . . Jīvaka, a monk lives in reliance on a village or market town. He lives having suffused the first quarter with a mind of friendliness, likewise the second, likewise the third, likewise the fourth; just so above, below, across; he lives having suffused the whole world everywhere, in every way, with a mind of friendliness that is far-reaching, wide-spread, immeasurable, without enmity, without any ill-will. A householder, or a householder's son who has gone to him, invites him for a meal on the next day. If he wants to, the monk accepts, Jīvaka. When the night has passed, he dresses in the early morning, takes his bowl and robe, and approaches the dwelling of that householder or householder's son. Once he has gone there he sits down on the appointed seat, and the householder or householder's son waits on him with sumptuous alms-food. The thought does not occur to him: 'It's really good that a householder or a householder's son waits on me with similar kinds of sumptuous alms-food. A householder or a householder's son should wait on me in the future with sumptuous alms-food of the same kind'. This does not occur to him. He enjoys that alms-food without being ensnared, infatuated or enthralled by it, but seeing the danger in it, aware of the outcome . . .[10]

Even in defining normative attitudes, this text itself notes the particular specificity of this kind of meal: it is sumptuous. Hence our suggestion that this meal is in considerable measure an opportunity for sumptuous display on the part of the wealthy. But if the attitude of the monk is to be one of absolute indifference, identical with what is required in the more habitual kind of alms round, the text tells us nothing of the attitude of the donor. As we will see this is often characterized by competitive zeal.

[9] See *S* IV 288ff., where Citta offers a meal to the 'elder monks'. This is elaborated in ch. 10 above.
[10] *M* I 368ff.

A question that arises here, of course, is how the Buddha and the Order's acceptance of these fabulous sumptuary meals fitted with their commitment to poverty and absence of ostentation.

Whatever the answer, the evident tension between the ideal of spartan simplicity and the practice of lavish honour is a reminder that, in the process of the growth of Buddhism, there had to be different Buddhisms. Add to this the likelihood that the practice of devotees surrounding renouncers with great wealth was becoming increasingly common in India during the Buddha's time, then to the extent that Buddhism became part of society, it was inevitably going to adapt, acquiring a multiple personality as it did so.

A classic instance of the meal as ritual of exchange, with all the signification of hierarchy and transformation this implies, is recorded in the *Abhayarājakumārasutta*:

[The Buddha was staying near Rājagaha. Prince Abhaya went up to Nātaputta, a Jain monk. Nātaputta tried to persuade Prince Abhaya (son of King Bimbisāra) to defeat the Buddha – who, he said, was 'of such great psychic power' – in argument as this would give him much fame (*te kalyāṇo kittisaddo*). Abhaya agreed and Nātaputta presented him with a dilemma to put to the Buddha, one designed to make the Buddha say something disagreeable to someone.] . . . and (p. 61) Abhaya 'answered Nātaputta the Jain in assent, rose from his seat, greeted Nātaputta the Jain keeping his right side towards him, went up to the Lord; and when he had arrived there he greeted the Lord and sat down at a respectful distance'.

He thought, 'It is not the right time today to refute the Lord, but tomorrow I will refute the Lord in my own house,' and he spoke thus to the Lord: 'Revered sir, may the Lord agree to take a meal with me tomorrow with three others?' (*adhivāsetu me bhante bhagavā svātanāya attacatuttho bhattan – ti*) The Lord agreed by becoming silent. Then Prince Abhaya, having understood the Lord's agreement, rising from his seat, having acknowledged the Lord, departed keeping his right side toward him. Then the Lord, at the end of that night, having dressed in the early morning, taking his bowl and robe, went up to Prince Abhaya's dwelling; and when he had reached there he sat down on the appointed seat. Then Prince Abhaya with his own hand served and satisfied the Lord with sumptuous solid and soft foods (p. 62) (*atha kho abhayo rājakumāro bhagavantaṃ paṇītena khādaniyena bhojaniyena sahatthā santappesi sampavāresi*). Then when the Lord had eaten and had withdrawn his hand from the bowl, Prince Abhaya, taking a low seat, sat down at a respectful distance. Prince Abhaya, sitting down at a respectful distance, spoke thus to the Lord.

[After this the conversation proceeded, with the Buddha offering a lengthy disquisition on the types of subjects about which he talked and the conditions under which he said them. Abhaya had the last word, saying,]

'It is excellent, revered sir, it is excellent, revered sir. It is as if one might set upright what had been upset, or might disclose what had been covered, or show the way to one who had gone astray, or bring an oil-lamp into the darkness so that those with vision might see material shapes, even so is *dhamma* made clear in many a figure by the Lord. Revered sir, I am going to the Lord for refuge and to *dhamma* and to the order of monks. May the Lord accept me as a lay-disciple going for refuge from this day forth for as long as life lasts.'[11]

The ritual prescriptions of the meal are here followed to the letter. We can isolate the following sets of acts which occur in the same sequence in most, though not all, of the meal narratives:

(1) An introduction detailing time, place and social context of the donor;
(2) an implied or actual dispute between the donor and the Buddha (this does not occur in all cases);
(3) the spoken invitation to attend the meal made in speech;
(4) the Buddha's acquiescence by remaining silent;
(5) the ritual departure of the figure who makes the request;
(6) the Buddha coming to eat in the guise of a monk on a begging round;
(7) the Buddha sitting down on the appointed seat;
(8) the donor serving food to the Buddha with his own hand;
(9) the donor taking a seat lower than the Buddha;
(10) the donor sitting down at a respectful distance;
(11) the donor speaking to the Buddha;
(12) the Buddha giving a teaching;
(13) the donor becoming a convert.

Any other name could be substituted for that of Prince Abhaya, although, even if the sequence of the events does not change, the *vaṇṇa* reference is significant in altering the status implications of the interaction between the two figures. Apart from the frame, virtually standard in all the 'meal narratives', formed by the set of events structuring the meal, there is a conversion frame operative here; it offers us different possibilities for the interpretation of these 'meal narratives'. It is possible, of course, to assert the interrelation of both frames, the meal functioning as the consummation and the demonstration of the conversion experience conceived of as a public event. However, the conversion frame is found frequently in situations where the meal is not given any kind of consummatory role.[12]

The initiatory structure of the offering of a seat to the Buddha may well have brāhmaṇical precursors, as B. Oguibenine has shown.[13] Perhaps we are entitled to go even further and interpret the ritual significance of the meal as a deliberate reworking of the Vedic sacrifice, where initiation into the

[11] *M* I 392–6. [12] For many examples drawn from the *Sn* see Bailey, 'Problems'.

[13] Oguibenine, 'Vedic Ritual', pp. 107–23. More generally see P. Masefield, 'The pursuit of merit: sacrificial devotion in the Pāli Nikāyas', in G. M. Bailey and I. Kesarcodi-Watson (eds), *Bhakti Studies* (Sterling, New Delhi, 1992), pp. 292–308.

saṅgha, even as a lay supporter, is sanctified by the ritual structure present in the invitation and the meal. We assume this is because the Buddha was fully aware of the brāhmaṇical cultural bedrock on which so many of his potential converts operated and knew that to extend his influence he would be required to present his teachings and normative forms of conduct within the traditionally patterned forms of behaviour. The new was once again drawing on the traditional for social confirmation.

The meal narrative just summarized is highly structured and quite repetitive in narrative sequence and language, a feature it shares with the other examples of the genre. But whilst it is important to be aware of the structural aspects of the narrative, our task must be to penetrate beneath these virtually formalized features to discover the high emotion and excitement that must have accompanied the actual event of the meal. In *Mahāvagga* VI there are twelve meal narratives and at least one more in *Mahāvagga* VII. Taken in conjunction with many others found in the *M* and other parts of the Canon, we have a set of rich resources available from which this subject can be studied. Each of the narratives found in the *Mahāvagga* contains the conversion frame and the meal frame, but is further anchored in the *Vinaya* as such by the proclamation of a *vinaya* rule at the end of the narrative. Within these three frames different kinds of content can be inserted and the individual narratives become superficially quite different in spite of a similarity induced by the frames, the motifs and the sequences in which these are arranged. These differences are invaluable for forcing us to consider what the historical conditions producing such narratives might have been.

Whilst each of the meal narratives contains a sequence of events illustrated by the Abhaya episode, we do not find absolute identity in all the sequences,[14] but the same motifs, within a tight range of possible variants,[15] seem to recur in virtually every narrative. The content of the individual narratives differs considerably, as does the *vinaya* rule the Buddha proclaims at the end of the tale. The other principal differences relate to the characters involved and the locations where the meals are given. These locations occur over most of the territory where the Buddha wandered. They confirm the text's desire to have us believe he was widely known and esteemed over this area and that the large-scale feeding of the Buddha and the monks was well

[14] For example, in the case of the wealthy householder Meṇḍaka (*Vin* I 242) the progressive talk is given before the meal.

[15] In *Vin* I 224–6 and 238–40 there is no formal invitation followed by a meal, only cooking of particular foods which people, following the path of the Buddha and the Order, consider them not to have had yet.

accepted as a means whereby a lay follower or a prominent person could publicly express his adherence to the Buddha's *dhamma*.

Many of the meal narratives[16] do not begin with a particular person hearing of the arrival of the Buddha with the *saṅgha*. They simply begin with a particular person approaching the Buddha and then the interaction leading to the meal takes place. But of those in the *Mahāvagga* there are five instances where the person concerned hears of the Buddha's imminent arrival (*Vin* I 231–3; 242; 243–5; 247) or hears him being praised when he is already there (*Vin* I 236ff.); and expressing a wish to see (*dassanāya*) him, mounts a chariot and goes to visit him attended by an entourage. It is not just out of respect for him that people strove to see him when he was on tour, nor can we be at all certain that, when a noun or verb derived from *das* 'to see' is used of the person who wants to see the Buddha, that usage corresponds to the devotional sense so common in later Hinduism. At least two of the meal narratives in the *Mahāvagga* depict camp followers, whose purpose[17] for following is to feed a member of the Order. In the first of these examples (*Vin* I 220–1) the desperation of one of the followers is illustrated very vividly. The Buddha was walking on tour from Benares to Andhakavinda, followed in carts by many camp followers each of whom was hoping to have a turn to feed the Buddha or one of the monks.

> Then it occurred to a certain brahmin who did not receive his turn, 'For the last two months I have been following the Order of monks with the Awakened One at its head, thinking, "When I get my turn, I will make a meal for them", but I have not got my turn. I am alone, and my household affairs are in great decline. What if I were to look into the kitchen and prepare what I can not see there?'[18]

This points to a strong competitive attitude amongst those wishing either to see the Buddha or to gain the merit achieved by the offering of food. We will notice more of this in other meal narratives.

All of the meal narratives are given within the context of the Buddha being on tour at a particular time. No doubt touring occupied the majority of his time except during the rainy season. Though we would not want to suggest these tours were carefully stage-managed, they were centred on the figure of the Buddha himself and the evidence from the texts, especially given the elite background of those who host the meals, is that his fame has preceded him. Most people are very eager to see him, an eagerness

[16] *Vin* I 212–13; 216–18; 220–1; 222–4; 224–6; 228–30.

[17] If that is what we read in the sentence '*yadā paṭipātiṃ labhissāma, tadā bhattaṃ karissāmeti*', *Vin* I 221; 238.

[18] *Vin* I 220.

played down dramatically by the inevitably formulaic wording used in the narratives,[19] and this bespeaks a fame, possibly cultivated, as we explored in chapter 5, apparently enabling him to remain aloof from the hustle and bustle of the tour and daily life in the places where he stops and definitely giving him all the more esteem because of this. In no sense does he need to pursue converts, they come to him. Their eagerness to approach him directly and the forewarning many of those who give meals have of his coming must have worked to build up the anticipation of the people who lived in the areas through which he travelled, and would ultimately contribute to the creation of the public spectacle the meal must often have been.

As far as it is possible to ascertain, all the people offering the meals fall into the category of elites. Most are named with their occupational status. Here is the list:

(1) *Vin* I 212–13 A certain brahmin.
(2) I 216–18 The wealthy lay followers Suppiya and Suppiyā.
(3) I 220–1 A brahmin.
(4) I 222–4 The young minister of little faith.
(5) I 224–6 Belaṭṭha Kaccāna who gives sugar to each of the 1,250 monks. We presume he is a merchant.
(6) I 229 Sunidha and Vassakāra, chief ministers in Magadha (cf. *D* II 87ff.).
(7) I 231–3 Ambapālī. A wealthy courtesan (cf. *D* II 96–8).
(8) I 233–238 Sīha, the general who was formerly a Jain.
(9) I 238–40 Country people who hitch their wagons outside a monastery as it is their turn to make a meal.
(10) I 240–5 Meṇḍaka, a wealthy householder (i.e., farmer) and possessor of psychic powers.
(11) I 245–6 Keniya the matted-hair ascetic.
(12) I 247–9 Roja, a well-known Malla who wants to provide a succession of meals. He wants his turn like the people in No.6.
(13) I 290 Visākhā, Migāra's mother, who gives food to the Order and then makes an offer of total material support.

[19] For example, the following form of words is typical: 'Then Belaṭṭha Kaccāna went up to the Lord. After he had gone up and greeted the Lord, he stood at a respectful distance. As he was standing at a respectful distance, Belaṭṭha Kaccāna said this to the Lord.' (*atha kho belaṭṭtho kaccāno yena bhagavā tenupasaṃkami. Upasaṃkamitvā bhagavantaṃ abhivādetvā ekamantaṃ atthāsi. Ekamantaṃ thito kho belaṭṭho kaccāno bhagavantaṃ etadavoca.*) *Vin* I 224. A striking exception here would be the instance of Roja the Malla who went to meet the Buddha only because his tribe had made an agreement that anyone who did not would be fined five hundred (?) if they did not go to meet him (*Vin* I 247).

A schematic list of the individuals and their class status produces the following:

brahmins (2) [*Vin* I 212; 217];
political elites (2) [I 222; 229];
wealthy householders (5) [I 216: 238; 242; 247; 290];
a general (1) [I 233];
a Jain ascetic (1) [I 245];
a merchant (1) [I 224];
a courtesan (1) [I 231].

This cannot be taken as a complete cross-section of ancient Indian society roughly covering the period from about 600–200 BCE, but it fits very closely the image of elite figures who populate Buddhist literature (see chapter 2 above). Noting that these meals are specified always for the *saṅgha* as well as for the Buddha, and that in the *Mahāvagga* narratives, the Buddha is usually accompanied by 1,250 monks, the logistics of the meal production requires the person who provides them to have been somebody of considerable means. Imagine how much space and food would have been needed to feed the Buddha and five hundred monks, let alone twelve hundred and fifty monks, the number usually given.

Not all supporters of the Buddha came from the elite classes, though it is they who figure most in the literature. It is therefore instructive to examine one meal narrative, not taken from the *Mahāvagga*, but from the *M* (II p. 45ff.), where status difference between potential donors is strongly emphasized. The Buddha tells a story about a past Buddha named Kassapa. He lived in a town called Vebhaliṅga where he had a monastery. His chief supporter (*upaṭṭhāko ahosi aggupaṭṭhāko* . . . p. 46) there was Ghaṭīkāra the potter, whose best friend was a brahmin named Jotipāla.

Ghaṭīkāra said to the brahmin:

> Let us go, dear Jotipāla, we will go up to the Lord Kassapa . . . in order to see him. I think a sight of the Lord, perfected one, fully Self-Awakened One, is really worthwhile.[20]

However, Jotipāla was unconvinced and said,

> Yes, dear Ghaṭīkāra, but of what use is it to see this little shaveling recluse (*muṇḍakena samaṇakena*)?

Ghaṭīkāra then tried various means of persuasion to bring Jotipāla round to his way, finally pulling his hair. Jotipāla was so amazed, he thought,

[20] *Āyāma, samma Jotipāla, Kassapaṃ bhagavantaṃ arahantaṃ sammāsaṃbuddhaṃ dassanāya upasaṅkissāma; sādhusammataṃ hi me tassa bhagato dassanaṃ arahato sammāsaṃbuddhassāti.*

It's really wonderful, it's really marvellous, that this potter Ghaṭīkāra, a recluse of lowly birth, should touch my hair, when my head has been bathed, and should think, 'Indeed this is definitely not insignificant.'[21]

Both finally approached Kassapa and sat at a respectful distance.

Then, Ānanda, the potter Ghaṭīkāra and the brahmin youth Jotipāla went up to the Lord Kassapa . . . When they had reached him, Ghaṭīkāra the potter greeted the Lord Kassapa . . . and sat down at a respectful distance. But the brahmin youth Jotipāla exchanged greetings with the Lord Kassapa . . . conversed pleasantly and politely, and sat down at a respectful distance.[22]

Ghaṭīkāra then asked Kassapa to teach the *dhamma* to Jotipāla and he did this. Then Jotipāla asked Ghaṭīkāra why he had not renounced after having heard the *dhamma*. In response he said that he was required to look after his blind parents.

Jotipāla said he understood and declared his intention to renounce. He and Ghaṭīkāra went back to Kassapa and this time both sat at a respectful distance from him, but only after gaining his permission.

[Kassapa then went to Benares. Kikī, King of Benares, heard of his arrival and] '. . . had many splendid vehicles harnessed, mounted a splendid vehicle and set off for Benares with the many splendid vehicles and with great royal pomp in order to see (*dassanāya*) the Lord Kassapa . . .'

On finding Kassapa he approached him and sat at a respectful distance. Kassapa gave him a talk on *dhamma*. Then the king said,

'Revered sir, will the Lord agree to have a meal with me tomorrow, together with the Order of monks?' Ānanda, the Lord gave his agreement by becoming silent. Then, Ānanda, Kikī the king of Kāsi understood the Lord Kassapa's consent, rose from his seat, saluted the Lord Kassapa, and departed, keeping his right side towards him.

Then, Ānanda, the Lord Kassapa dressed in the morning, took his bowl and robe, and went to the dwelling of Kikī, king of Kāsi. After he gone there, he sat down on the designated seat (*paññatte āsane nisīdi*) accompanied by the Order of monks. Then, Ānanda, Kikī the king of Kāsi with his own hand served the Order of monks, headed by the enlightened Kassapa, with sumptuous foods, solid and soft, and satiated them. Then, Ānanda, when the Lord Kassapa had eaten and had withdrawn his hand from the bowl, Kikī, the king of Kāsi, taking a low seat (*nīcaṃ āsanam*), sat down at a respectful distance.

[21] *Acchariaṃ vata bho, abbhutaṃ vata bho. Yatra hi nāmāyaṃ Ghaṭīkāro kumbhakāro ittarajacco samāno amhākaṃ sīsanahātānaṃ kesesu parāmasitabbaṃ maññissati; na vat' idam orakaṃ maññe bhavissatīti.* p. 47.

[22] . . . *saddhiṃ sammodi, sammodaniyīyaṃ kathaṃ sārāṇīyaṃ vītisāretvā ekamantaṃ nisīdi.*

After this Kassapa did not, as one would expect, give a talk on *dhamma*, in response to the meal given by the king. Before he was given the chance, the king asked him to accept a 'rains-residence' (*vassāvāso*) with him. Kassapa refused, saying he had already accepted such an invitation. Twice more he is asked and both times refuses. After the final refusal, the king became unhappy.

He then asked Kassapa if he had another supporter. Kassapa said the potter Ghaṭīkāra was his chief supporter. Recognizing the king's depression he explained why Ghaṭīkāra did not and would not grieve. He enumerated a list of qualities he possessed (pp. 51–2):

> He has taken the triple refuge.
> He refrains from killing creatures, from theft, from incorrect enjoyment of sense pleasures, from lying and from sloth.
> He has unwavering confidence in the three jewels.
> He has the correct morality.

And so on, until finally, recounting that he looked after his blind parents, he predicted he would attain final *nibbāṇa* and not be reborn.

Kassapa then tells another anecdote about the potter. One day whilst in Ghaṭīkāra's village he went up to the potter's parents and asked where the potter had gone. They confirmed his departure, but added that he had left behind instructions for the Buddha to be provided with food to eat. The Buddha ate the food, rose up from his seat (*uṭṭhāy' āsanā*) and departed. Later, when Ghaṭīkāra returned and discovered Kassapa had had a meal at the house, he believed himself to have gained (*lābhā vata me suladdhaṃ vata me*) through Kassapa's having been there.

He then recounted a second anecdote about Ghaṭīkāra. Kassapa was staying in the potter's village and discovered his own hut was leaking. Kassapa told the monks to go and take grass from Ghaṭīkāra's hut. His parents asked who was taking the grass and why. When told it was for Kassapa they encouraged its being taken away. Ghaṭīkāra took the act of taking the grass as a vote of Kassapa's confidence in him and then, as the narrative tells us, no rain fell into the open roof for three months. King Kikī then sent five hundred cartloads of food to Ghaṭīkāra. The potter expressed his satisfaction to the king's messenger, saying he knew the king had much to do. Finally the Buddha declared himself to have been the brahmin Jotipāla.[23]

A folk-tale theme may lie at the basis of this narrative. The poor potter Ghaṭīkāra outdoes the wealthy king by his piety and (measured by his

[23] *M* II 45ff.

commitment to his blind parents as much as by anything else) gains a material fortune from the very same king, a fortune matched by the religious fortune he has received from the Buddha's recognition of the potter's devotion towards him, thus confirming the persistent Buddhist view that a person's measure is determined by conduct, not by source of birth. But above all this narrative is about the means of measuring the status of people who interact with the Buddha. The three highest classes are in evidence here, represented by Jotipāla, Kikī and Ghaṭīkāra respectively. Each represents a different degree of devotion. The king and the potter both wish to experience a *dassana* of the Buddha Kassapa, with all the devotional implications that act entails. Jotipāla alone is almost hostile to this and is prevailed upon to attend the *dassana* only by mild violence. Yet, of the three, he is the only one who becomes a member of the Order and renounces, the other two retaining the status of lay follower. Even then Kikī's status remains unclear, suggesting his sumptuous feeding of the Order and Kassapa may have been a demonstration of conspicuous generosity. He does not even receive the habitual progressive talk, although Kassapa's justification as to why he will spend the rain retreat with Ghaṭīkāra rather than with the king contains much in it that is clearly of a doctrinal nature. It is as though the brahmin was the prize convert into the Order, an observation supported by the statistics of conversion we have at our disposal. Anybody else could be converted as a lay follower, but a brahmin brought status with him. He was of the highest class and was more associated with the high-status world view associated with the world of Sanskrit learning than was a representative of any other class. His was a religious vocation, even if by the time of the Buddha, this was probably observed in the breach. Conversion of a brahmin meant that the Buddha's teaching was becoming considered a viable alternative to the prevailing dominant cultural position, or at least this was what it was intended to mean.

Both Kikī and Ghaṭīkāra play the traditional roles expected of members of their groups. In the magnitude and the opulence of the meal Kikī supplies to Kassapa and then subsequently to Ghaṭīkāra, presumably as a mediating figure in respect of Kassapa, the role of the political elites as providers of large-scale support to the Order is expressed. As for Ghaṭīkāra, he is the archetypal image of the village lay Buddhist who supports the individual monk in whatever manner he can. The symbolism of the blind parents, found often elsewhere in Indian literature (e.g., the ascetic killed by Pāṇḍu in the *Ādiparvan* of the *MBh*), lends more dramatic emphasis to his domestic responsibility than would the simple declaration that he has a family to support. He must perform his household responsibilities whilst continuing to function as a Buddhist and modifying his behaviour accordingly. Note that both figures offer the Buddha a meal.

The size and nature of the meals is perfectly consonant with the social and economic standings of the respective donors and as such there is no message of status disjunction being expressed here. Where the latter assumes its full force is in Kassapa's refusal of Kikī's invitation to spend the rains retreat with him. The contrasting emotions experienced by the favoured donor and the one who is refused are quite symmetrical, but do not explicitly turn on status disjunction so much as failure and joy in the wake of Kassapa's refusal. Perhaps this is how the Buddha would have wanted the situation to be given his firmness on evaluating a person by his expressed moral action rather than by his hereditary status.

The meal the Buddha takes with King Kikī is typical of those formal meals that require a public invitation: an acceptance by silence, a gap of time between invitation and meal, the setting up of a designated seat, the clear manifestation of status distinction – a kind of obeisance before the Buddha – and the Buddha's acceptance of the meal by offering a teaching on *dhamma*. As for the meal associated with Ghaṭīkāra, this is nothing other than the normal begging round, given more significance here because of what it is being contrasted with.

THE MEAL AS PUBLIC EVENT

For a large town of twenty thousand the visit of the Buddha whilst on tour would have been a major event, no doubt attracting widespread interest, even considering the short notice given for the meal. But for a small village, whose population would have probably been at least doubled at the time of the visit, the coming of the Buddha or a prominent monk must have been a huge event. The magnificence of all the events surrounding the visit and the possibilities for sumptuary display would therefore have been enormous. This magnificence is communicated as much by the positions and the wealth of those who give the meals as it is by the occasional formulaic descriptions of the ornate chariots[24] used by certain of the meal givers (Ambapālī, the Licchavi princes, Meṇḍaka, General Sīha), in contrast to the Buddha who would have been on foot, dressed in a totally unostentatious manner. Nor was the display just for the sake of display, if it is ever. It

[24] Ambapālī hears of the Buddha's arrival in Koṭigāma, then 'the courtesan Ambapālī had some magnificent vehicles harnessed, mounted a magnificent vehicle, and, accompanied by the magnificent vehicles, left Vesālī in order to see the Lord.' *Vin* I 231; 242. These words are not used of General Sīha, but he did go and meet the Buddha with an entourage of 500 chariots.

must have been a recognition of the financial power of the person who paid for the meal, a conviction strongly supported by the jealousy aroused in the minds of those parties unsuccessful in receiving the Buddha's attentions, signalled by his acceptance of their invitation for a meal. The most famous example of this is given in the narrative where the Licchavi princes offer money to Ambapālī to entice her to give up the meal with the Buddha (*Vin* I 232; *D* II 196). Even after her refusal they still invite the Buddha but he declares he is unable to accept their invitation because of his prior engagement with Ambapālī. At this they angrily declare, amazingly in front of the Buddha, 'We have been defeated by this mango-girl' (*Vin* I 232). Clearly, there is an element of obligation here on the Buddha's part.

The tinge of jealousy, undergirded by competition, is even more pronounced in one of the prominent passages in the *Vinaya* dealing with Anāthapiṇḍika. Described as (*Vin* II 154) 'the husband of a sister of a (great) merchant of Rājagaha', Anāthapiṇḍika goes to Rājagaha at the same time as the Buddha and members of the Order have been invited to a meal at the merchant's place. So lavish are the preparations Anāthapiṇḍika sees that he wonders, 'Now is this householder holding the ritual journey to the bride's house or the ritual departure from the bride's house, or has a great sacrifice been organized or has King Seniya Bimbisāra of Magadha been invited tomorrow together with his troops?' (155) The merchant denies any of these as the explanation for the gathering and says, 'I have organized a huge sacrifice. I have invited the Order led by the Buddha for tomorrow.'[25] Although such events seem commonplace in the world of the Pāli Canon, we are still entitled to ask if a more nuanced reading of the passage is to be expected. Would the feeding of a religious person normally attract such approbation and munificence as this? The appearance of the Buddha is being explicitly compared to an event of great secular importance. Or are such events reflections of the magnitude of the large *śrauta* sacrifices – coming into desuetude even in the Buddha's time – where large crowds must have been present and the idea of the special status of the sacrifice as a ritual meal was always in the minds of those attending the performance?

By way of illustration of similarity between the *śrauta* sacrifice and the 'total' event of the Buddha visiting a village we cite the *Kūṭadantasutta* where both events are obliquely juxtaposed. The plot of this *sutta* concerns the transformation of Kūṭadanta from a traditional brahmin into a figure who becomes devoted to the Buddha, though he does not appear to become

[25] *Vin* II 155. The sentence 'I have organized a huge sacrifice' seems anomalous here. The Buddha was a well-known critic of animal sacrifice. It is possible that *yañño* could refer to any type of celebratory occasion or that the sentence '*Api ca me mahāyañño paccupaṭṭito*' really implies a negative.

a convert. When the Buddha arrives at the brahmin village of Khāṇumata with 500 monks and locates himself at the Ambalatthikā park, Kūṭadanta is about to sponsor a huge sacrifice:

> At that time a huge sacrifice was being prepared for Kūṭadanta the brahmin. A hundred bulls, a hundred steers, a hundred heifers, a hundred goats, and a hundred rams had been brought to the post for sacrifice.[26]

But his plans are upstaged by the Buddha's arrival. All those – brahmins and householders – attending the sacrifice hear that the Buddha has arrived in the Ambalatthikā park and leave the sacrifice in order to visit the Buddha.[27] The text is much more florid than is the description of their departure. They are portrayed hearing a set of standard epithets of the Buddha's achievements, including his enlightenment. As such he is placed in competition with the brahmin.

Kūṭadanta asks his doorkeeper why all the people are leaving. Informed that the Buddha is staying outside of the village he goes to meet him, though only after some other brahmins question the respective status of the Buddha and Khāṇumata. Kūṭadanta meets the Buddha and asks him about a success in performing a sacrifice in its three modes and its sixteen accessories. The Buddha provides a long explanation in which he describes a sacrifice performed by a mythical king which uses ghee, oil, butter, milk, honey and sugar, but no animals. The Buddha then explains how any sacrifice should be transformed into a procedure for becoming a lay Buddhist and practising the five abstinences and the other requirements for the laity. At the end Khāṇumata is so impressed he invites the Buddha to a meal, and

> The Blessed One dressed early in the morning, put on his outer robe, and taking his bowl with him, went with the collection of monks to Kūṭadanta's sacrificial site, and sat down there on the seat designated for him. And Kūṭadanta the Brahmin satisfied the collection of monks led by the Buddha, with his own hand, with sweet food, both hard and soft . . .[28]

Pointedly the text tells us the meal was held on the site for Kūṭadanta's *śrauta* sacrifice and, therefore, that it replaced it. The significance of this is emphasized by virtue of the amount of space given in the narrative to the mythical king Mahāvijita's preparation[29] of a *śrauta* sacrifice and especially of the recommendation given him by his purohita:

> Then let his majesty the king send invitations to whosoever there may be in his realm who are kṣatriyas, vassals of his, either in the country or the towns; or who are ministers and officials of his, either in the country or the towns; or who are

[26] *D* I 128–29. [27] Ibid. [28] *D* I 149–50. [29] *D* I 135–42.

wealthy householders, either in the country or the towns, saying: 'I intend to offer a large sacrifice. Let the venerable people acknowledge what will be conducive to my happiness and welfare for many days and nights.'[30]

Both the *śrauta* sacrifice and the public meal for the Buddha were opportunities for public display, status validation and delimitation of social hierarchy.

Returning to the narrative dealing with Anāthapiṇḍika and the merchant of Rājagaha, we note competition also emerges as a theme later in it. Anāthapiṇḍika is said to have become a lay devotee and invited the Buddha for a meal. On discovering this a merchant of Rājagaha says to him, 'It is said that you invited the Order with the Buddha at its head, householder, for tomorrow. But you are a newcomer. Householder, I will give you the money (*veyyāyikam*) so that you will be able to feed the Order with the Buddha at its head.' To this Anāthapiṇḍika responds, 'Thank you, householder, but I have the money to make a meal for the Order with the Awakened One at its head.'[31] The urban council of Rājagaha makes the same offer and receives the same response. Both the great merchant of Rājagaha and the urban council of Rājagaha must be reckoned important symbols of wealth here and elsewhere in the Nikāyas.

We should never underestimate the display component in the meal as an expression of competition. Here is a case where it is known the Buddha is on tour and will be visiting a town or a city at a particular time. A large number of monks are moving across the countryside, presumably on the trade routes connecting the large cities, their itinerary probably being known by the direction in which they are moving. Always the event, when it happens, concentrates on the public display of the aloof figure of the Buddha being personally fed by the wealthy person who has paid for the meal. Even when they have slaves, as in the case of Suppiya and Suppiyā, it is not the slaves who feed the Buddha but the two donors. Whilst this must be taken as a personal display of homage (and respect, if the devotional aspect of the whole event is downplayed), especially since it is witnessed by the *saṅgha* as well as those in the household of the donor and any other onlookers, its effects for the on-going acceptance of Buddhism must have been considerable. One of the most prominent people in the village or town, where prominence is determined by wealth, occupation or social position, is demonstrating obeisance to the famous new teacher, whose reputation spreads like wildfire. Given the importance of the role model provided by the elites who organize the meals, the Buddha's public gaining

[30] *D* I 137. [31] *Vin* II 157.

of a convert must have raised or simply confirmed the status of the new belief system with its rigorous social practices. Moreover, it establishes a direct connection between the teachings, the practice and the creation of wealth, in a way quite astonishing in view of the Buddha's own level of renunciation. As such, in a kind of perverse way it gives dramatic emphasis to the entire new discourse the Buddha attempts to inculcate through his teachings.

But there is much more to it than this. We suggested earlier that the meals, in spite of the conversion frame in which they are partially structured, offered the possibility for sumptuary display. Huge expense would be incurred in feeding twelve hundred and fifty people and the extent of this expense would surely have been recognized by all who participated in the event. The time frame also becomes important as in most instances where the meal occurs in a fixed location, and not intermittently whilst the monks and the Buddha are moving along the road, it is only held one day after the Buddha has arrived. Surely this would have been enough time for the news that the Buddha was to be fêted at a particular meal to have spread around the entire village or town. In an environment where conspicuous patronage to brahmins and other sects had been long established, the offering of huge meals would not have been undertaken just as a means of acquiring merit, but also as a failsafe means of displaying wealth as such to those who lived in the districts surrounding them. It could be regarded as confirming the socio-economic status the meal-giver had acquired through the material wealth he/she had accumulated.

Beyond the coding of status differences tied up in the ritual meal, and the strongly initiatory structure of the meal as a process of social interaction, we are entitled to suggest there may have been different pragmatic motivations for the Buddha's accepting meals with wealthy brahmins (for which see chapter 5 above) who were renowned for their knowledge and learning and whatever spiritual accomplishments they might have achieved, as well as with elites whose position was owed to material possessions more than to religious virtuosity. That is, from one he receives material support, from the other he receives direct cultural legitimacy, if we consider how important the brahmins were as purveyors of a cultural position they themselves, at least, would have liked to be hegemonic. Both were essential if the fledgling Buddhist *saṅgha* was to survive beyond the Buddha's own death. We have to bear in mind continually that, like the brahmins, the Buddha himself was offering a total position about culture and society. He could not be reduced to the level of another sectary deriving his principal inspiration from some offshoot of brāhmaṇical thought.

The subject of competition between religious sectaries, whether implied or otherwise, is constantly in play in the meal narratives. In an overt sense the passage where Abhaya provides the meal involves the abandonment of his allegiance to the Jains, at least in his acceptance of their beliefs, and the same applies in the case of General Sīha. For these situations the Buddha's grasp of metaphysical argument is sufficient to guarantee his victory. Yet there are other instances where his wish to demonstrate his own unique status comes to the fore. Of these instances the most spectacular, and no doubt productive of social esteem, are those where he displays his supernormal powers. Several of the meal narratives in the *Mahāvagga* instance this use of his powers. One concerns[32] interaction between the Buddha and the two wealthy laypeople, Suppiya and Suppiyā.

The Buddha and the monks were staying at the Deer Park. Suppiyā wandered from cell to cell asking, 'Who, honoured sirs, is ill? Can something be brought for someone?'

One monk, having drunk a purgative, asked for meat-broth (*paṭicchādiya*) and was told by Suppiyā it would be supplied. She asked a servant to find the meat, but none was to be found because it was a meatless day. On being informed of this, and not wanting to lie to the monk, she cut a piece from her own thigh. She instructed her servant to say that if anybody came around looking for her they should be told she was ill.

Then her husband Suppiya returned and asked the servant about the whereabouts of his wife. He went in to see her and she told him the whole story of what had happened.

> 'Why are you lying down?'
> 'I am ill,' she said.
> 'What is causing you pain?' Then the laywoman Suppiyā raised the matter with the layman Suppiya, thinking, 'It is really marvellous, it is wonderful, that Suppiyā is so faithful and believing that she even gives up her own flesh. Is there anything else she would not give?'[33] . . .

Then in a state of joy he went to see the Buddha and respectfully invited him to a meal, an invitation the Buddha accepted. A magnificent meal was organized and the Buddha arrived on the following morning. The Buddha then enquired as to the health of Suppiyā and was told she was ill. In spite of this the Buddha asked for her to be brought before him:

[32] *Vin* I 216–18.
[33] *Vin* I 217, *atha kho Suppiyo upāsako acchariyaṃ vata bho abbhutaṃ vata bho yāva saddhāyaṃ Suppiyā pasannā, yatra hi nāma attano pi maṃsāni pariccattāni.*

Then the layman Suppiya took hold of the laywoman Suppiyā and brought her along. With the Lord's sight on her, that huge wound was healed, the skin became good and small hairs appeared on it.[34]

On witnessing this both Suppiya and Suppiyā remarked upon the great psychic powers of the Buddha. Then they served the meal to the Buddha and the *saṅgha* and received a progressive talk from the Buddha who then departed.

The Buddha then asked which monk requested food from Suppiyā and asked if he had enquired about it. When he said he had not the Buddha rebuked him and forbade monks to eat human flesh.

Although perhaps an extreme example to cite because of its reference to cannibalism – whose historical veracity we might question – it is a typical instance of the kinds of obligations bearing on both parties participating in the meal where the Buddha is the honoured guest. As soon as the husband and wife find out about the presence of the Buddha they undertake to make contact with him. We can be certain of their wealth by their possession of slaves and their capacity to feed all the monks.

Their generosity towards the monks is twofold. In the first place Suppiyā attempts to provide succour to any monk who is ill and in doing so engages in an amazing form of self-sacrifice by offering a piece from her own leg.[35] This is subsequently rewarded by the Buddha in a scene which is a clear structural reversal of her own action – woman heals monk, Buddha heals woman. His action is an implicit reward for her own self-sacrifice and, considered in a broader frame, is both an expression of the reward for her faith and a demonstration of the Buddha's super-normal powers, his vision in this case. It is almost a sanction of her action, though this kind of action is disallowed when the relevant *vinaya* rule is promulgated. The second expression of generosity is the standard offering of the meal as a reward for which the two laypersons receive a teaching in the *dhamma*. In itself the very visit of the Buddha must have functioned as a confirmation of the lay status of the layman, but it may have also indicated a kind of status marker amongst Buddhists even at that very early time in the development of the Order.

The devotional quality of the narrative is manifest and it focuses on both the Buddha and Suppiyā. Her devotional credentials are considered impeccable by her husband, for when she cuts the flesh from her own leg,

[34] *Vin* I 219, *tassā saha dassanena bhagavato tāvamahā vaṇo rūḷho ahosi succhavi lomajāto.*

[35] This section of the narrative – reward for devotion – seems strongly folkloric with the addition of a Buddhist tinge in demonstrating the direct workings of merit.

he says, 'It is really marvellous (*acchariyaṃ*), it is wonderful (*abbhutaṃ*), that this Suppiyā is so faithful and believing that she gives up even her own flesh.' The words *acchariyaṃ* and *abbhūtaṃ* both convey the idea that the event to which they refer is in some measure absolutely extraordinary. In the West we might say supernaturally so. Both words, and especially the latter, are used in the myriads of devotional narratives found in the later Hindu *Purāṇas*.[36] But to bring the message fully home Suppiya and Suppiyā virtually give the same expression verbatim as a reaction to the Buddha's healing of Suppiyā's leg by his divine vision. The whole exchange can perhaps be explained in terms of the transfer of merit doctrine. Equally, the devotional ambience of some of the terminology and the emphasis placed on building up a picture of Suppiyā's own devotional attitude (*passanā*) and the Buddha's great psychic powers, to be used beneficially for his devotees, must have had the effect of depicting an enormously enhanced figure in contrast to many other *śramaṇas* claiming similar powers.

The second example of this is found in the fairly lengthy narrative dealing with the wealthy householder Meṇḍaka.[37] Because Meṇḍaka was already famed for his great psychic powers in producing huge quantities of grain and food, King Bimbisāra ordered one of his ministers to observe such powers in person. Meṇḍaka gave a demonstration of his power by feeding the minister's army and the minister returned to Rājagaha in order to inform Bimbisāra. The narrative could easily end there and be self-contained, yet it is really just the preface to a meal narrative.

> [The Buddha set out on tour for Bhaddiya [where Meṇḍaka lived] and Meṇḍaka heard of his imminent arrival, given almost in the form of a Hindu *stotra*. After describing all the Buddha's achievements it ends with the words] It would be good to see perfected ones like this (*Sādhu kho pana tatharūpānaṃ arahataṃ dassanaṃ hotu ti*).
>
> [Immediately he decided to see the Buddha, only to be hampered by members of other sects who declared that as a Jain, it was inappropriate for him to court the Buddha. When he saw the Buddha he was given the progressive talk and assumed lay status. It was then that he invited the Buddha for a meal on the next day. As soon as the Buddha arrived he preached a progressive talk, ate the meal, then left.
>
> After he had gone Meṇḍaka ordered his workmen to load food on to carts so they could follow the Buddha and feed him on his travels.]

Here the Buddha performs no miraculous deeds expected of a holy man. Instead that honour goes to Meṇḍaka, already a special person when the

[36] For examples, see Greg Bailey, 'The semantics of bhakti in the Vāmana Purāṇa', *Rivista degli Studi Orientali*, 62, 1988, pp. 25–57.

[37] *Vin* I 240–5.

Buddha meets him, and publicly known as such. His open acts of obeisance to the Buddha, first deliberately rejecting the protestations of the Jains and then receiving the Buddha's teachings and holding a meal, are explicit and deliberately communicated signs that the Buddha is of a higher status than himself. In addition, already knowing of his special status, he betrays the devotional ambience of the whole narrative in his wish 'to see the Buddha'.

The emphasis laid on figures such as Meṇḍaka and others mentioned in the meal narratives successfully conveys their own importance in the communities where they lived. Equally, as a reflection of them, each narrative measures the great significance of the Buddha as a new, perhaps unique, figure who has temporarily entered the same community. When the meal is introduced it offers the possibility of sumptuary display, a procedure absolutely applicable to both principal participants in the meal event. For the donor it is an offering of merit and an expression of his status in the local area. As applied to the Buddha, it underscores for non-Buddhists, who witness or hear of the meal, his capacity to enter an area and to be immediately fêted as a regional religious figure of proven fame and achievement. When we note the frequent addition of the conversion frame to the meal narrative, it is clear that the meal event forms a valuable 'marketing' function for the Buddha.

Conclusion

Buddhist Studies have been prosecuted in the West for the last one hundred and eighty years, if not longer. During that time the basic sources, at least in Indic languages, have begun to be excavated, some extensively. The contours of the teachings of the various schools have been outlined and their overlaps recognized. Increasingly the full context of the emergence of Buddhism on Indian soil has been clarified and its complexity determined. In turn this has allowed scholars to work in the understanding that the Buddhist evidence is just one component of the complete body of primary sources defining the total environment of North Indian history in the last five centuries of the first millennium BCE. An important implication of this is that the development of Buddhism can be ascertained in a more comprehensive way on the basis of evidence coming from other than Buddhist sources, such that we will not have to rely simply on inference from literary texts not necessarily designed to mirror the day-to-day realities of the empirical world. Thus the emergence and growth of Buddhism can now be understood as just one of several developments in ancient North Indian culture registering on the historical record from the sixth to the second centuries BCE. Its use as a governing interpretative tool for this history will be correspondingly modified so that it will no longer be allowed to assume the broad hermeneutical priority it has had even for areas far beyond itself.

To bring the time frame closer to the contemporary period, we note that during the last two decades any perception of a monolithic Buddhism has been severely dissipated as a result of the input from the anthropology of lived Buddhism and the re-evaluation of the early *Vinaya* texts from a perspective emphasizing social history, especially through the gaze supplied by the interaction between monk, nun and laity, whether Buddhist or not. Buddhism has come to be looked upon as a rich religio-cultural tradition operating successfully at different levels of society and as flourishing because it succeeded in adjusting itself to all these levels, being simultaneously influenced by, and influencing, them.

Throughout this book we have stressed the seeming paradox between the intense ascetic and renunciatory imperative associated uncompromisingly with the founding of early Buddhism, on the one hand, and on the other its capacity to adapt itself to the very real changes occurring in all the non-religious areas of life during the early centuries of its emergence. In itself this is a theme running consistently across every chapter, though sometimes, especially in section one 'Context', it is present beneath the surface rather than standing in the front line. Conceived in a totalistic sense, as a cultural system Buddhism was always able to operate with these two, potentially antagonistic, components, the first of which was essential for the distinctiveness of the early Buddhist Order, the second for its on-going survival. The latter it has done with great success in many cultures because it could maintain an integrity of doctrine and practice in the midst of variant forms consistent with this integrity. In short, Buddhism makes sense only if it is conceded that there are several different Buddhisms operative even within the one culture.

This book rests firmly on the assumption that it could not be otherwise. Despite the possibility of identifying a distinct doctrinal and practical integrity within Buddhism, it is always necessary to remember that even in the Buddha's time it is likely to have developed in a society consisting of many distinct communities, communities which contextualized a growing religion and fragmented it in the mirror of this society. In the third section of the book we have laid focus on this fragmentation of culture – not fragmented to the individuals within it, but to an outsider looking in from without twenty-five centuries later – and have argued that the Buddhist monks operated in terms of it in two ways. On the one hand, as representatives of a relatively uniform transcendent view – mirroring the wish for uniformity of the newly emergent political elite running large-scale states – standing outside of pluralistic cultures, they acted as an ideological glue. On the other hand, they identified rival elite groups in society – groups such as the brahmins, the Jains and other *śramaṇa* groups – each of which claimed the superiority of its own transcendental and totalistic vision of human existence. Towards such groups their attitude was defined by competition, the intensity of which varied according to the Buddhists' perception of the potential success of these competitors in winning souls. Hostility was directed by the Buddhists as much towards those figures – exemplified by the six heretical teachers – whose views were not too far from those of the early Buddhists, as it was towards the brahmins. The latter not only had a distinctive vision of the transcendent, into which was anchored a totalistic view of society and culture, but also basked in the complacency of an elite knowing its success in defining patterns of influence and control.

Whilst likely an elite movement in its beginnings, the early Buddhist Order had to struggle to influence the non-religious elites to support it financially, materially and, more subtly, with the general imprimatur of the elites acknowledging Buddhism both as distinct from other rival groups and as a public group with as much legitimacy as the brahmins. Success in its struggle was clearly achieved by the time of Aśoka (269–242 BCE) – where religious patronage is so strongly reflected in his inscriptions – and this perhaps compels us to read this success back into the Pāli sources where the evidence of strivings towards such a result is to be sought in the Buddha's own interaction with political and economic elites. Even without the kind of relative certainty available from the Aśokan material, we still need to have some precision as to why the Buddha's message would have been attractive to the elites whose status rested on political and economic foundations. We have suggested that the Buddha taught a universal philosophy, cutting aside the more partial views of the brahmins and the other *śramaṇa* groups, both more tied to particular power bases than was Buddhism, which, at least in theory, sought independence from any power base. To identify with such an outlook may have provided psychological justification to the kings of the expanding new polities who fought their enemies with ideological tools as well as with armies and tried to promote a commonality of culture over its plurality, ultimately an impossible task. Similarly, for the newly emerging groups who lived off trade and the use of 'capital', being tied down to a specific pressure group or social hierarchy could act as an obstacle to the execution of their vocation. Wealth at least was always regarded as of universal substance and the merchant's quest for wealth was analogous in its lack of boundaries to the Buddhist quest, even if it was totally different in content.

Focusing on the relationship between emergent Buddhism and the non-religious elites in northeast India of the sixth to second centuries BCE raises a conundrum encountered constantly in our work. Was the emergence of Buddhism a response to the substantive changes that appear to have occurred by the time the Buddha became active as a holy man or was it in some way complicit in the historical forces and the subsequent justification, primarily by the elite groups of society, of the direction of historical change? Or was it both? Responses to radical and sustained change are many, ranging along the entire gamut from outright refusal to adapt, to an attitude – practised in a wholly opportunistic way – of on-going adjustment to the perceived changes. In stressing the practical application of a rigorous path, requiring the adoption of an uncompromising form of asceticism, Buddhist teaching sought to place its adepts in a constancy operating outside of change as this was perceived in the 'secular' world.

To respond to the conundrum by adopting either of these positions as providing the privileged hermeneutical guide is of course far too simplistic when dealing with a highly complex cultural phenomenon like Buddhism. On the basis of all the evidence at our disposal we still cannot say with certainty why the Buddha felt inspired to develop a highly original message about the nature of existence, one emphasizing the centrality of *dukkha*, always a deceptively difficult word to comprehend. It is true that the early texts allow inferences to be made about the social environment in which the Buddha and the first members of the Order made their mark; yet we are constrained only to know of the reaction of these figures to their immediate historical context. And, as part of this, we are provided with no firm evidence as to what specific (whether particular events or memories of rapid and comprehensive change) material, social or political conditions impelled the Buddha to develop such a rigorously consistent doctrine of *dukkha*. Had he had direct experience of large-scale displacement brought about by the political and economic factors that impressed themselves upon his sensitive mind? And did this experience, in conjunction with the perception of the apparent arbitrariness associated with death and disease, lead to this exposition of metaphysical doctrine asserting the omnipresence and interrelation of *dukkha* and change?

Or was it more likely that – as we have consistently argued – the economy was in a stage of steady growth during the Buddha's lifetime, pressure on land use was minimal and cultural plurality, though not political independence, still tolerated? In such an environment the elite speculate on the impossibility of material wealth and psychological security precluding the certainty of death and focus instead on the juxtaposition between all forms of distress, personal and social, in the midst of flourishing material conditions. To state the obvious, the texts do not enable us convincingly to confirm or deny this assertion, nor does the archaeological evidence.

What we must be fully confident in asserting is that the early Buddhist Order of monks and nuns had emerged and developed in the new urbanism, with all the other changes accompanying this, without showing much awareness of an immediately prior historical situation – unless we exclude the idealized reflections on the condition of the 'brahmins of old', asserted as a role model for right behaviour in the Buddha's time. That is, early Buddhism developed as a consequence of *a changed situation*, rather than of a rapidly changing one. Arguments about repressed memories of earlier situations lack substance because there exists neither implicit nor explicit textual evidence to support them. This aside, the development of the renunciatory life was just one response to a heightened recognition of substantially changed living conditions. If Buddhism had not developed as an institution, as opposed to a loosely grouped set of individuals, it would have had to foster the development of its own opposite – a lay body which identified itself as Buddhist by following particular ethical precepts, venerating the Buddha and materially supporting monks. At the same time this lay body must have continued to worship Hindu gods and immersed itself in the economic order of the day with all that that life entailed.

The need to accommodate a lay following meant there would always be several Buddhisms. If this promotes a picture of plurality, how much more the different emphases within monastic Buddhism where we can most easily distinguish the fund-raising parish priest from the meditator in the monastery and the forest-dwelling ascetic. Plurality becomes more and more reified the longer the institution of Buddhism flourishes and survives.

An inevitable consequence of the successful growth of Buddhism by Aśoka's time was the noticing of this growth in all of its manifestations by others who would have considered the Buddhists as potential rivals. Of these rivals the brahmins were the most significant. Certainly, the Buddhist texts, with their extensive portrayal of the often humorous interaction between Buddhist monks and brahmins, have a vested interest in creating an impression of concern by the brahmins. Always the latter are depicted in various postures of defeat, and potential humiliation, at the hands of their Buddhist antagonists. Yet we might well see such a picture as being entirely subjective, painted as it is from the Buddhist perspective.

Hindu evidence of brāhmaṇical sensitivity to on-going rivalry from Buddhist and other śramaṇic sects comes primarily from the *Mahābhārata*.[1] An integral part of its plot is taken up with the destructive and bloody revenge warrior brahmins take against the entire class of *kṣatriyas*, from whom the kings were recruited. On one reading this theme enshrines a brahmin reaction against the development of a polity where brāhmaṇical values are no longer being regarded by the rulers as hegemonic. From the brahmin point of view, their class needed to do more than just survive as one body of opinion jostling with several others; it had always to be *primus inter pares*. Its attack then was directed not so much against the Buddhists as against those supposedly Hindu kings who did not utterly privilege the brahmins,

[1] Our thinking on this subject has been substantially influenced by the continuing work of Professor Jim Fitzgerald of the University of Tennessee.

but offered largesse more widely. Thus the very extensive satirization of the brahmin, as both a class and a cultural position, in the Pāli Canon, has its direct reflex in the *Mahābhārata* where a class believing themselves dispossessed use a literary instrument – the epic itself – to fight back. The emerging Hinduism, dominated by a brāhmaṇical codification of society and religion within the frame of brahmin self-interest, saw the brahmins thriving on the cultural integration of a politically fractured society (which ultimately became the norm in India where political fracturing has been the norm). Buddhism, on the other hand, throve on the ideological integration of a culturally diverse fragmented society subject to political and economic expansion.

Bibliography

BOOKS IN INDIC LANGUAGES

Aṅguttara Nikāya, ed. Morris, R. and Hardy, E. (6 vols, PTS, London, 1958–76 (1885–1910)).

Atharva Veda, ed. Roth, R. and Whitney, W. D. (Berlin, 1855).

Corpus Inscriptionum Indicarum, Vol. 1 Inscriptions of Asoka, new edn ed. Hultzsch, E. (Indological Book House, Delhi and Varanasi, 1969). Original edn: *Inscriptions of Asoka* (Clarendon Press, Oxford, 1925).

Dhammapada, eds and trans. Carter, J. R. and Palihawadana, M. (Oxford University Press, New York, 1987).

Dhammapada, ed. von Hinüber, O. and Norman, K. R. (PTS, Oxford, 1995).

Dharmasūtras: the law codes of Āpastamba, Gautama, Baudhāyana, and Vasiṣṭha. Annotated text and translation, Olivelle, P. (Motilal Banarsidass, New Delhi, 2000).

Dīgha Nikāya, ed. Rhys Davids, T. W. and Carpenter, J. E. (3 vols, PTS, London, 1960–7 (1890–1911)).

Divyāvadana, ed. Cowell, E. B. and Neil, A. (Oriental Press, Amsterdam, 1970 (Cambridge, 1886)).

The Early Upanishads: annotated text and translation, trans. and ed. Olivelle, P. (Oxford University Press, New York, 1998).

Eighteen Principal Upaniṣads, ed. Limaye, V. P. and Vadekar, R. D. (Vaidika Samsodhana Mandala, Poona, 1958).

Jātaka, ed. Fausböll, V. (6 vols, PTS, London, 1962–4 (1887–97)).

Kātyāyanasmṛti or Vyavahāra, law and procedure, ed. [reconstructed] and trans. Kane, P. V. (Bombay, 1933; reprinted from *Hindu Law Journal*).

The Kauṭilīya Arthaśāstra: A critical edition with a glossary, ed. and trans. Kangle, R. P. (3 vols, University of Bombay, Bombay, 1969–72).

Mahābhārata, ed. Sukthankar, V. S. et al. (19 vols, BORI, Poona, 1933–66).

Majjhima Nikāya, ed. Trenckner, V., Chalmers, R. and Rhys Davids, C. A. F. (4 vols. PTS, London, 1960–74 (1888–1925)).

Digital version produced by the International Buddhist Research and Information Center.

The Milindapañho, ed. Trenckner, V. (Luzac, London, 1962 (1880)).

Patañjali, Mahābhāṣya. Vyākaraṇamahābhāṣyam Kilhornnamna, ed. Kielhorn, F., rev. Abhyankar, K. V. (Bhandarkar Oriental Research Institute, Poona, 1962–5).
Saṃyutta Nikāya, ed. Feer, L. (6 vols, PTS, London, 1960–75 (1884–1904)).
Śatapatha Brāhmaṇa, ed. Weber, A. (Benares, 1964 (Berlin, 1855)).
Sutta-nipāta, ed. Andersen, D. and Smith, H. (Routledge & Kegan Paul, London, 1984 (1913)).
Udāna, ed. Steinthal, P. (Routledge & Kegan Paul (for the PTS), London, 1982 (1885)).
Vinaya Piṭaka, ed. Oldenberg, H. and Pischel, R. (5 vols, PTS, London, 1929 (1879–83)).
The Vyākaraṇa-Mahābhāṣya of Patañjali, ed. Kielhorn, F. (3 vols. Osnabrück, 1970 (1880)).

BOOKS AND ARTICLES IN EUROPEAN LANGUAGES

Acharya, P. K. *Architecture of Mānasāra* (Oxford University Press, London, 1934; reprint: Oriental Books Reprint Corp., Delhi, 1980).
Agrawal, D. P. and Kusumgar, S. *Prehistoric Chronology and Radiocarbon Dating in India* (Munshiram Manoharlal, Delhi, 1972).
Ali, D. 'Technologies of the self: courtly artifice and monastic discipline in early India', *JESHO*, 41 (1998), pp. 159–84.
Allchin, B. and Allchin, F. R. *The Rise of Civilization in India and Pakistan* (Cambridge University Press, Cambridge, 1982).
Allchin, F. R. 'City and state formation in early historic South Asia, I', *South Asian Studies*, 5 (1989), pp. 1–16.
Allchin, F. R. (ed.). *The Archaeology of Early Historic South Asia* (Cambridge University Press, Cambridge, 1995).
Amore, R. C. *The Concept and Practice of Doing Merit in Early Theravāda Buddhism* (University Microfilms, Ann Arbor, Xerox, 1971).
Auboyer, J. *Le trône et son symbolisme dans l'Inde ancienne* (Presses Universitaires de France, Paris, 1949).
Bailey, G. *Materials for the Study of Ancient Indian Ideologies: Pravṛtti and Nivṛtti* (Pubblicazioni di Indologica Taurinensia, Turin, 1985).
'The semantics of bhakti in the Vāmana Purāṇa', *Rivista degli Studi Orientali*, 62 (1988), pp. 25–57.
'Problems of the interpretation of the data pertaining to religious interaction in ancient India: the conversion stories in the *Sutta Nipāta*', *Indo-British Review*, 19 (1991), pp. 1–20.
'Max Weber's *Hinduismus und Buddhismus*: a new interpretation', paper contributed to *Max Weber, Religion and Social Action*, conference in Canberra, September 1999.
Bajpai, R. *Society in the 7th Century* (Chand, Delhi, 1992).
Bapat, P. V. 'Dhutangas (or the ascetic practices of purification in Buddhism)', *Indian Historical Quarterly*, 13 (1937), pp. 44–51.

Bareau, A. 'Les réactions des familles dont un membre devient moine selon le canon bouddhique pali', in Wijesekara, O. H. de A. (ed.), *Malalasekara Commemoration Volume* (The Malalasekara Commemoration Volume Editorial Committee, Colombo, 1976), pp. 15–22.

'Le Buddha et les rois', *Bulletin De L'École Française D'Extrême-Orient*, 80/1 (1993), pp. 15–39.

Barth, F. 'Ecological relationships of ethnic groups in Swat, North Pakistan', *American Anthropologist*, 58 (1956), pp. 1079–89.

Barth, F. (ed.). *Ethnic Groups and Boundaries* (Little, Brown, Boston, 1969).

Basham, A. L. *History and Doctrine of the Ājīvikas: A Vanished Indian Religion* (Luzac, London, 1951).

'The background to the rise of Buddhism', in Narain, A. K. (ed.), *Studies in History* (B.R. Publishing, Delhi, 1980), pp. 13–32.

Beaujeu-Garnier, J. *Geography of Population*, trans. Beaver, S. H. (Longman, London, 1966).

Béteille, A. 'On the concept of tribe', *International Social Science Journal*, 32 (1980), pp. 825–8.

Biardeau, M. and Malamoud, C. *La Sacrifice dans L'Inde Ancienne* (Presses Universitaires de France, Paris, 1976).

Blackburn, A. 'Looking for the Vinaya: monastic discipline in the practical canons of the Theravada', *JIABS*, 22 (1999), pp. 281–309.

Bloch, J. *Les Inscriptions d'Aśoka, traduites et commentées* (Société d'édition 'Les Belles Lettres', Paris, 1950).

Bodhi, Bhikkhu. *The Connected Discourses of the Buddha: A New Translation of the Saṃyutta Nikāya* (2 vols, Wisdom Publications, Boston, 2000).

Bond, G. Review of J. R. Carter and M. Palihawadana, *Dhammapada*, *JAOS*, 111 (1991), p. 173.

Bongard-Levin, G. M. *Mauryan India* (Sterling, New Delhi, 1985).

Brekke, T. 'The early saṅgha and the laity', *JIABS*, 20/2 (1997), pp. 28–9.

'Contradiction and the merit of giving in Indian religions', *Numen*, 45 (1998), pp. 287–320.

Bronkhorst, J. *The Two Traditions of Meditation in Ancient India* (Steiner, Stuttgart, 1986).

Brown, P. 'The rise and function of the holy man in late antiquity', in *Society and the Holy in Late Antiquity* (Faber and Faber, London, 1982), pp. 103–52.

Authority and the Sacred. Aspects of the Christianisation of the Roman World (Cambridge University Press, Cambridge, 1995).

Brucker, E. *Die Spätvedische Kulturepoche nach den Quellen der Śrauta-, Gṛhya und Dharmasūtras. Der Siedlungsraum* (Steiner, Wiesbaden, 1980).

Bühler, G. 'The Bhattiprolu inscriptions', *Epigraphica Indica*, II (1894), pp. 323–9.

Burlingame, E. W. (trans.), *Buddhist Legends. Translated from the original Pāli Text of the Dhammapada Commentary* (Luzac, London, 1969 (Cambridge, Mass., 1921)).

Caillat, C. 'Aśoka et les gens de la brousse (XIII M-N)', *Bulletin des Etudes Indiennes*, 9 (1991), pp. 9–13.

Caritthers, M. Review of S. J. Tambiah, *World Conqueror, World Renouncer*, *Journal of the Anthropological Society of Oxford*, 8 (1977), pp. 95–105.
The Buddha (Oxford University Press, Oxford, 1983).
Carter, J. R. and Palihawadana, M. (eds and trans.). *Dhammapada* (Oxford University Press, New York, 1987).
Chakrabarti, D. K. 'The beginning of iron in India', *Antiquity*, 50 (1976), pp. 114–24.
'Iron and urbanization: an examination of the Indian context', *Purātattva* 15 (1984–5), pp. 68–74.
Chakravarti, U. *The Social Dimensions of Early Buddhism* (Oxford University Press, Delhi, 1987).
Chattopadhyaya, B. D. 'The city in early India: perspectives from texts', *Studies in History*, 13/2 NS (1997), pp. 181–208.
Chattopadhyaya, D. P. *Lokāyata. A study in ancient Indian materialism* (People's Publishing House, Delhi, 1959/1973).
Chutintaranond, S. ' "Mandala", "Segmentary State" and the politics of centralization in medieval Ayudhya', *Journal of the Siam Society*, 78 (1990), pp. 89–100.
Collins, S. *Selfless Persons: Imagery and Thought in Theravāda Buddhism* (Cambridge University Press, Cambridge, 1982).
'The Discourse on What is Primary (Aggañña-Sutta). An annotated translation', *Journal of Indian Philosophy*, 21 (1993), pp. 301–95.
Coningham, R. A. E. 'Dark Age or Continuum', in F. R. Allchin (ed.), *The Archaeology of Early Historic South Asia* (Cambridge University Press, Cambridge, 1995), pp. 54–72.
Coomaraswamy, A. K. *Yakṣas* (2 parts, Munshiram Manoharlal, Delhi, 1971).
Cribb, J. 'Dating India's earliest coins', in Schotsmans, J. and Taddei, M. (eds.), *South Asian Archaeology 1983* (2 vols, Istituto Universitario Orientale, Naples, 1985), pp. 535–54.
Dehejia, V. 'The collective and popular basis of early Buddhist patronage: sacred monuments, 100BC–AD250', in Stoler Miller, B. (ed.), *The Powers of Art. Patronage in Indian Culture* (Oxford University Press, Delhi, 1992).
de Jong, J. W. 'The background of early Buddhism', *Journal of Indian and Buddhist Studies*, 12 (1964), pp. 34–47.
Review of M. Kloppenborg, *The Paccekabuddha: a Buddhist Ascetic*, *IIJ*, 18 (1976), pp. 322–4.
Review of R. Gombrich, *Theravāda Buddhism*, *IIJ*, 32 (1989), p. 241.
Deloche, J. *La Circulation en Inde, avant la Révolution des Transports* (2 vols, École Française D'Extrême-Orient, Paris, 1980).
Despres, L. A. (ed.). *Ethnicity and Resource Competition in Plural Societies* (Mouton, The Hague/Paris, 1975).
Douglas, M. *Purity and Danger: an analysis of concepts of pollution and taboo* (Routledge and Kegan Paul, London, 1966).
Natural Symbols: explorations in cosmology (Penguin, Harmondsworth, 1973).
Drekmeier, C. *Kingship and Community in Early India* (Stanford University Press, Stanford, 1962).

Dumont, L. *Homo Hierarchicus* (Paladin, London, 1966).
Durkheim, E. *The Elementary Forms of the Religious Life*, trans. Swain, J. W. (Free Press, New York, 1965).
Dutt, S. *Early Buddhist Monachism* (Munshiram Manoharlal, Delhi, 1984 (London, 1924)).
Erdosy, G. 'Origins of cities in the Ganges valley', *JESHO*, 28 (1985), pp. 81–109.
'Early historic cities of northern India', *South Asian Studies*, 3 (1987), pp. 1–23.
'City states of North India and Pakistan at the time of the Buddha', in Allchin, F. R. (ed.), *The Archaeology of Early Historic South Asia* (Cambridge University Press, Cambridge, 1995), pp. 99–122.
Erndl, K. *Victory to the Mother: the Hindu Goddess of Northwest India in Myth, Ritual and Symbol* (Oxford University Press, New York, 1993).
Ernfors, E. B. and Ernfors, R. F. *Archaic Economy and Modern Society* (Studia Sociologica Upsaliensia 31, Acta Universitatis Upsaliensis, Uppsala, 1990).
Falk, N. 'Wilderness and kingship in ancient South Asia', *HR*, 13 (1974), pp. 1–15.
Fausbøll, V. *Sutta Nipāta* (Sacred Books of the East, vol. x, Oxford, 1881).
Fick, R. *Die Soziale Gliederung in Nordöstlichen Indien zu Buddhas Zeit* (Kiel, 1897).
Friedrich-Silber, I. *Virtuosity, Charisma, and Social Order: a comparative sociological study of monasticism in Theravada Buddhism and medieval Catholicism*, (Cambridge University Press, Cambridge, 1995).
Geertz, C. 'Religion as a cultural system', in *The Interpretation of Cultures* (Basic Books, New York, 1973), pp. 87–125.
Gethin, R. 'Cosmology and meditation: from the *Aggañña Sutta* to the Mahāyāna', *HR*, 36 (1997), pp. 183–217.
Ghosh, A. *The City in Early Historical India* (Institute of Advanced Study, Simla, 1973).
Glover, I. *Early Trade between India and Southeast Asia* (Centre for Southeast Asian Studies, University of Hull, Hull, 1990).
Gokhale, B. G. 'The Buddhist social ideals', *Indian Historical Quarterly*, 32 (1957), pp. 141–7.
'The early Buddhist elite', *Journal of Indian History*, 42 (1965), pp. 391–402.
'Early Buddhist kingship', *Journal of Asian Studies*, 26 (1966), pp. 15–22.
'The merchant in ancient India', *Journal of the American Oriental Society*, 97 (1977), pp. 125–30.
'Early Buddhism and the urban revolution', *JIABS*, 5/2 (1982), pp. 7–22.
Gombrich, R. *Precept and Practice. Traditional Buddhism in the Rural Highlands of Ceylon* (Oxford University Press, London, 1971).
'Karma and social control', *Comparative Studies in Society and History*, 17 (1975), pp. 212–20.
Theravāda Buddhism. A Social History from Ancient Benares to Modern Colombo (Routledge & Kegan Paul, London, 1988).
'How the Mahāyāna began', *Journal of Pali and Buddhist Studies*, 1 (1988), pp. 29–46; reprinted in Skorupski, T. (ed.), *The Buddhist Forum: Seminar Papers 1987–88, Volume 1* (School of Oriental and African Studies, London, 1990), pp. 5–20.

Granoff, P. 'The ambiguity of miracles. Buddhist understandings of supernatural power', *East and West*, 46 (1996), pp. 79–96.

Gupta, S. P. 'Two urbanizations in India: a side study in their social structure', *Purātattva*, 7 (1974), pp. 53–60.

Harris, M. *Cultural Materialism: the struggle for a science of culture* (Random House, New York, 1979).

Heesterman, J. C. 'Was there an Indian reaction? Western expansion in Indian perspective', in H. Wesseling (ed.), *Expansion and Reaction: Essays on European Expansion and Reaction in Asia and Africa* (Leiden University Press, Leiden, 1978), pp. 31–58.

Heitzman, J. 'Early Buddhism, trade and empire', in Kennedy, K. A. R. and Possehl, Gregory L. (eds), *Studies in the Archeology and Paleoanthropology of South Asia* (Oxford and IBH Publishing Co., New Delhi, 1984), pp. 121–37.

Hodder, I. 'Economic and social stress and material cultural patterning', *American Antiquity*, 44 (1979), p. 446–54.

Horner, I. B. *The Book of the Discipline* (6 vols, Luzac & Co. (PTS), London, 1938).

Indian Archaeology – A Review (Archaeological Survey of India, Delhi, 1957–8, 1982–3, 1984–5, 1986–7, 1989–90).

Jamison, S. W. *Sacrificed Wife. Sacrificer's Wife* (Oxford University Press, New York, 1996).

Jayawickrame, N. A. Analysis of the Sutta Nipāta. A critical analysis of the Pāli Sutta Nipāta illustrating its gradual growth (London, unpublished PhD thesis, 1947).

Jones, S. 'Discourses of identity in the interpretation of the past', in Graves-Brown, P., Jones S. and Gamble C. (eds), *Cultural Identity and Archeology: the Construction of European Communities* (Routledge, London and New York, 1996), pp. 62–80.

The Archeology of Ethnicity: Constructing Identities in the Past and Present (Routledge, London and New York, 1997).

Kaelber, W. O. '*Tapas*, birth and spiritual rebirth in the Veda', *HR*, 15 (1976), pp. 343–86.

Kahane, R. 'Priesthood and social change: the case of the brahmins', *Religion*, 11 (1981), pp. 353–66.

King, A. 'Some archaeological problems regarding Gangetic culture', in Kennedy, K. A. R. and Possehl, Gregory L. (eds), *Studies in the Archeology and Paleoanthropology of South Asia* (Oxford and IBH Publishing Co., New Delhi, 1984), p. 109–19.

Kirfel, W. *Die Kosmographie der Inder* (Georg Olms, Hildesheim, 1967 (Bonn and Leipzig, 1920)).

Kloppenborg, M. *The Paccekabuddha: a Buddhist Ascetic* (E. J. Brill, Leiden, 1974).

Knox, R. *Amaravati: Buddhist Sculpture from the Great Stupa* (British Museum, London, 1992).

Kölver, B. 'Kauṭalyas Stadt als Handelzentrum: der Terminus *puṭabhedana*', *ZDMG*, 135 (1985), pp. 299–311.

Kosambi, D. D. 'Early stages of the caste system in northern India', *Journal of the Bombay Branch of the Royal Asiatic Society*, 22 (1946), pp. 33–48.

'Ancient Kosala and Magadha', *Journal of the Bombay Branch of the Royal Asiatic Society*, 27, 1952, p. 183.

An Introduction to the Study of Ancient Indian History (Popular Book Depot, Bombay, 1956).

'The beginnings of the iron age in India', *Journal of the Economic and Social History of the Orient*, 7 (1963), pp. 309–18.

Kuiper, F. B. J. *Varuṇa and Vidūṣaka. On the Origin of the Sanskrit Drama* (North Holland, Amsterdam, 1979).

Kulke, H. *Jagannātha-Kult und Gajapati-Königtum* (Steiner, Wiesbaden, 1979).

'Indian colonies, Indianization or cultural convergence?', in H. Schulte Nordholt, H. (ed.), *Onderzoek in Zuidoost Asië* (Rijksuniversiteit de Leiden, Leiden, 1990), pp. 8–32.

'Grāmakāma – "das verlangen nach einem Dorf". Überlegungen zum Beginn frühstaatlicher Entwicklung im vedischen Indien', *Saeculum*, 42 (1991), pp. 111–28.

'THE RĀJASŪYA. A paradigm of early state formation', in Van Den Hoek, A. W., Kolff, D. H. A. and Oort, M. S. (eds), *Ritual, State and History in South Asia. Essays in Honour of J. C. Heesterman* (E. J. Brill, Leiden, 1992), pp. 188–98.

Lal, B. B. 'The two Indian epics vis-à-vis archaeology', *Antiquity*, 50 (1981), pp. 27–34.

Lal, M. *Archaeology of Population: A Study of Population Change in the Ganga-Yamuna Doab from 2nd Millennium B.C. to the Present* (Dept of Ancient Indian History, Culture and Archaeology, Banaras Hindu University, Varanasi, 1984).

Settlement History and Rise of Civilization in Ganga-Yamuna Doab, from 1500 B.C. to 300 A.D. (B.R. Publishing, Delhi, 1984).

'The stages of human colonization of the Ganga-Yamuna doab: archaeological evidence', *South Asian Studies*, 3 (1987), pp. 25–32.

'Population distribution and its movement during the second–first millennium B.C. in the Indo-Gangetic divide and Upper Ganga plain', *Purātattva*, 18 (1987–8), pp. 35–53.

Lamotte, E. 'La légende du Buddha', *Revue de l'Histoire des Religions*, 134 (1946), pp. 37–71.

'Introduction à l'étude du bouddhisme de Śakyamuni d'après les textes anciens', *Nachrichten der Akademie der Wissenschaften in Göttingen I: Philologisch-Historische Klasse*, 1983, pp. 83–120.

Law, B. C. *Geography of Early Buddhism* (Bharatiya Publishing, Varanasi, 1973 (K. Paul, Trench, Trubner, London, 1932)).

Lewis, I. T. 'Newar-Tibetan trade and the domestication of the *Simhalasārtha-bāhu Avadāna*', *HR*, 33 (1993), pp. 1–35.

Mabbett, I. W. *Truth, Myth and Politics in Ancient India* (Thomson Press, Delhi, 1971).

'The symbolism of Mount Meru', *HR*, 23 (1983), pp. 64–83.

'Weber, Protestantism and Buddhism', paper contributed to *Max Weber, Religion and Social Action*, conference in Canberra, September 1999.
'The rise of Buddhism in a period of urbanization and state formation', *Aichi Bunkyo Review*, 4 (2001), pp. 35–59.
'The early Buddhist *Saṃgha* in its social context', *Nagoya Studies in Indian Culture and Buddhism: Saṃbhāṣā*, 21 (2001), 101–29.
'Buddhism and freedom', in Kelly, D. and Reid, A. J. S. (eds.), *Asian Freedoms. The Idea of Freedom in East and Southeast Asia* (Cambridge University Press, Cambridge, 1998), pp. 19–36.
McCrindle, J. W. *Ancient India as Described in Classical Literature* (Philo, Amsterdam, 1971).
McNeill, W. *Plagues and Peoples* (Anchor, New York, 1976).
Majumdar, R. C. *Classical Accounts of India, Being a Compilation of the English Translations of the Accounts Left by Herodotus, Megasthenes . . .* (Mukhopadhyay, Calcutta, 1960).
Malalasekara, G. P. *Dictionary of Pāli Proper Names* (2 vols, published for the PTS by Luzac, London, 1960).
Malamoud, C. 'Village et forêt dans l'idéologie de l'Inde brāhmaṇique', *Archives Européennes de Sociologie*, 17 (1976), pp. 3–20.
Marasinghe, M. M. *Gods in Early Buddhism: a study in their social and mythological milieu as depicted in the Nikāyas of the Pali Canon* (University of Sri Lanka Press, Vidyalankara, 1974).
Masefield, P. *Divine Revelation in Pali Buddhism* (Allen & Unwin, London, 1986).
'Mind/Cosmos maps in the Pāli Nikāyas', in Katz, N. (ed.), *Buddhist and Western Psychology* (Prajñā Press, Boulder, 1983), pp. 69–93.
'The pursuit of merit: sacrificial devotion in the Pāli Nikāyas', in Bailey, G. M. and Kesarcodi-Watson, I. (eds), *Bhakti Studies* (Sterling, New Delhi, 1992), pp. 292–308.
Masson, J. *La religion populaire dans le canon Bouddhique Pāli* (Muséon, Louvain, 1942).
Mayrhofer, M. *Kurzgefasstes etymologisches Wörterbuch des Altindischen* (4 vols, Winter, Heidelberg, 1953–75).
Milner, M. *Status and Sacredness. A General Theory of Status Relations and an Analysis of Indian Culture* (Oxford University Press, New York, 1994).
Misra, G. S. P. *The Age of Vinaya* (Munshiram Manoharlal, Delhi, 1972).
Mizuno, K. 'A comparative study of Dharmapadas', in Dhammapala, G., Gombrich, R. and Norman, K. R. (eds), *Buddhist Studies in Honour of Hammalava Saddhātissa* (Buddhist Research Library Trust, Nugegoda, 1984), pp. 168–75.
Moore, E. *Moated Sites in Early North East Thailand* (British Archaeological Reports, Oxford, 1988).
Morrison, K. 'Trade, urbanism and agricultural expansion: Buddhist monastic institutions and the state in early historic western Deccan', *World Archeology*, 27 (1995), pp. 203–21.
Mourer, R. 'Préhistoire du Cambodge', *Archéologia*, 23 (1988), pp. 40–52.

Mus, P. *India Seen from the East* (Centre for South East Asian Studies, Clayton, Victoria, 1975).

Narain, A. K. and Roy, T. N. *Excavations at Rājghāt* (Benares Hindu University Press, Varanasi, 1976).

Norman, K. R. 'A note on Attā in the Alagaddupama Sutta', in *Studies in Indian Philosophy. A Memorial Volume in Honour of Pt Sukhlalji Sanghvi* (LD Institute of Indology, Ahmedabad, 1981), pp. 19–29.

Pāli Literature, Including the Canonical Literature in Prakrit and Sanskrit of All the Hīnayāna Schools of Buddhism (Harrassowitz, Wiesbaden, 1983).

The Group of Discourses (Sutta-Nipāta) Volume II. Revised Translation (PTS, Oxford, 1992).

Nyanatiloka Bhikkhu (ed.). *Buddhist Dictionary: manual of Buddhist terms and doctrines* (3rd edn, Frewin, Colombo, 1972).

Obeyesekere, G. 'Theodicy, sin and salvation in the sociology of religion', in Leach, E. R. (ed.), *Dialectic in Practical Religion* (Cambridge University Press, Cambridge, 1968).

O'Connor, R. 'Agricultural change and ethnic succession in Southeast Asian states: a case for regional anthropology', *Journal of Asian Studies*, 54 (1995), pp. 968–96.

Oguibenine, B. 'From a Vedic ritual to the Buddhist practice of initiation into the doctrine', in Denwood, P. and Piatigorsky, A. (eds), *Buddhist Studies Ancient and Modern* (Curzon Press, London, 1983), pp. 107–23.

Olivelle, P. *Saṃnyāsa Upaniṣads: Hindu Scriptures on Asceticism and Renunciation* (Oxford University Press, New York, 1992).

The Āśrama System (Oxford University Press, New York, 1993).

Pande, G. C. *Studies in the Origins of Buddhism* (Motilal Banarsidass, Delhi, 1974 (Department of Ancient History, Culture and Archeology, University of Allahabad, 1957)).

Parpola, A. 'The coming of the Aryans to Iran and India and the cultural and ethnic identity of the Dāsas', *Studia Orientalia*, 64 (1988), pp. 195–302.

Pearson, H. W. 'The economy has no surplus: critique of a theory of development', in Polanyi, K., Arensberg, C. M. and Pearson, H. W. (eds), *Trade and Market in the Early Empires* (Free Press, New York, 1957), pp. 320–41.

Pleiner, R. 'The problem of the beginning of the iron age in India', *Acta Praehistorica et Archaeologica*, 2 (1971), pp. 5–36.

Polanyi, K., Arensberg, C. M. and Pearson, H. W. (eds). *Trade and Market in the Early Empires* (Free Press, New York, 1957).

Prebish, C. 'Ideal types in Indian Buddhism: a new paradigm', *JAOS*, 115 (1995), pp. 651–66.

Quigley, D. 'Is a theory of caste still possible?', in Searle-Chatterjee, M. and Sharma, U. (eds), *Contextualising Caste: post-Dumontian approaches* (Blackwell, Oxford and *Sociological Review*, Cambridge, Mass., 1994), pp. 54–72.

Rahula, W. 'Humour in Pali literature', *Journal of the Pali Text Society*, 9 (1981), pp. 156–74.

Rau, W. *Staat und Gesellschaft Im Alten Indien Nach Den Brāhmaṇatexten Dargestellt* (Harrassowitz, Wiesbaden, 1957).

Zur vedischen Altertumskunde (Akademie der Wissenschaft und der Literatur, Mainz, 1983).

Rawlinson, A. 'Nāgas and the magical cosmology of Buddhism', *Religion*, 16 (1986), pp. 135–53.

Ray, A. *Villages, Towns and Secular Buildings in Ancient India* (Firma K. L. Mukhopadhyaya, Calcutta, 1964).

Ray, H. P. *Monastery and Guild. Commerce under the Sātavāhanas* (Oxford University Press, Delhi, 1986).

The Winds of Change: Buddhism and the maritime links of early South Asia (Oxford University Press, Delhi, 1994).

'Trade and contacts', in Thapar, R. (ed.), *Recent Perspectives of Early Indian History* (Popular Prakashan, Bombay, 1995), pp. 142–75.

Ray, N. 'Technology and social change', *Purātattva*, 8 (1975–6), pp. 132–8.

Ray, R. *Buddhist Saints in India* (Oxford University Press, New York, 1994).

Renou, L. *Etudes Védiques et Pāṇinéennes* (19 vols, Boccard, Paris, 1956).

Reynolds, F. 'The two wheels of Dharma: a study of early Buddhism,' in Obeyesekere, G., Reynolds, F. and Smith, B. L., *The Two Wheels of Dharma: Essays on the Theravāda Tradition in India and Ceylon* (The American Academy of Religion, Chambersburg, Pa. 1972), pp. 6–30.

Rhys Davids, T. W. *Buddhist India* (T. Fisher Unwin, London, 1903; 8th edn: Susil Gupta (India) Private, Calcutta, 1959).

Rhys Davids, T. W. and Oldenberg, H. 'Introduction to the Vinaya' (Sacred Books of the East, vol. XIII, Oxford, 1881).

Rhys Davids, T. W. and Stede, W. *The Pali Text Society's Pali-English Dictionary* (PTS, London, 1972 (1921–5)).

Ritschl, E. 'Brahmanische Bauern. Zur Theorie und Praxis der brahmanischen Ständeordnung im alten Indien', *Altorientalische Forschungen*, 7 (1980), pp. 177–87.

Roth, G. 'Text of the Patna Dharmapada', in Bechert, H. (ed.), *Die Sprache der ältesten buddhistischen Überlieferung: the Language of the Earliest Buddhist Tradition* (Vandenhoek and Ruprecht, Göttingen, 1980), pp. 97–135.

Dialogues of the Buddha (3 vols, Luzac, London, 1956–66 (Oxford University Press, London, 1899–1921)).

Russell, J. C. *Medieval Regions and their Cities* (Indiana University Press, Bloomington, 1972).

Ryan, J. D. 'The Civakacintamani in Historical Perspective' (unpublished thesis, University of California, Berkeley, 1985).

Sakurai, Y. 'Tank agriculture in South India: an essay on agricultural Indianization in Southeast Asia', in Jayawardena, S. D. G. (ed.), *Transformation of the Agricultural Landscape in Sri Lanka and South India* (Kyoto University Centre for Southeast Asian Studies, Kyoto, n.d.), pp. 117–58.

Samuel, G. *Civilized Shamans* (Smithsonian Institute Press, Washington and London, 1993).

Samuels, J. 'Views of householders and lay disciples in the Sutta Piṭaka: a reconsideration of the lay/monastic opposition', *Religion*, 29 (1999), pp. 231–41.

Sankalia, H. D., Ansari, Z. D. and Dhavalikar, M. K. 'Excavations at the early farming village of Inamgaon, 1968–82', in Lukacs, J. (ed.), *The Peoples of South Asia. The Biological Anthropology of India, Pakistan, and Nepal* (Plenum Press, New York and London, 1984), pp. 91–103.

Sarao, K. T. *The Origin and Nature of Ancient Indian Buddhism* (Eastern Book Linkers, Delhi, 1989).

Sarkisyanz, E. *Buddhist Backgrounds of the Burmese Revolution* (Nijhoff, The Hague, 1965).

Urban Centres and Urbanisation as Reflected in the Pāli Vinaya and Sutta Piṭakas (Vidyanidhi, Delhi, 1990).

Schopen, G. 'Two problems in the history of Indian Buddism: the layman/monk distinction and the doctrines of the transference of merit', *Studien zur Indologie und Iranistik*, 10 (1985), pp. 9–47.

'Burial *ad sanctos* and the physical presence of the Buddha in early Indian Buddhism: a study in the archeology of religions', *Religion*, 17 (1987), pp. 193–225.

'Doing business for the Lord: lending on interest and written loan contracts in the Mūlasarvāstivādavinaya', *JAOS*, 114 (1994), pp. 527–54.

'Monastic law meets the real world: a monk's continuing right to inherit family property in classical India', *HR*, 35 (1996), pp. 101–23.

Searle-Chatterjee, M. 'Caste, religion and other identities', in Searle-Chatterjee, M. and Sharma, U. (eds), *Contextualising Caste: Post-Dumontian Approaches* (Blackwell, Oxford, 1994), pp. 147–66.

Shaffer, J. 'Bronze age iron from Afghanistan', in Kennedy, K. A. R. and Possehl, Gregory L., *Studies in the Archeology and Paleoanthropology of South Asia* (Oxford and IBH Publishing Co., New Delhi, 1984), pp. 41–62.

Sharan, M. K. 'Origin of republics in India with special reference to the Yaudheya tribe', in Mukherjee, B. N. et al., (eds), *Sri Dinesacandrika – Studies in Indology. Shri D.C. Sircar Festschrift* (Sundeep Prakashan, 1983), pp. 241–52.

Sharma, J. P. *Republics in Ancient India 1500 B.C. to 500 B.C.* (Brill, Leiden, 1968).

Sharma, R. S. *Light on Early Indian Society and Economy* (Manaktalas, Bombay, 1966).

Material Culture and Social Formations in Ancient India (Macmillan India, Delhi, 1983).

'Trends in the economic history of Mathurā (c.300 B.C.–A.D. 300)', in Srinivasan, D. M. (ed.), *Mathurā. The Cultural Heritage* (Manohar, American Institute of Indian Studies, New Delhi, 1989), pp. 31–8.

Sinha, A. K. 'The historical urbanization – a suggestive date', *Purātattva*, 11 (1979–80), pp. 151–5.

Sjoberg, G. 'The rise and fall of cities', *International Journal of Comparative Sociology*, 4 (1963), pp. 107–20.

Smith, G. *Classifying the Universe. The Ancient Indian Varṇa System and the Origins of Caste* (Oxford University Press, New York, 1994).

Southwold, M. *Buddhism in Life: the anthropological study of religion and the Sinhalese practice of Buddhism* (Manchester University Press, Manchester, 1983).

Spiro, M. 'Buddhism and economic action in Burma', *American Anthropologist, 68* (1966), pp. 1163–73.

Buddhism and Society: a Great Tradition and its Burmese Vicissitudes (Harper and Row, New York, 1970).

Sprockhoff, J. F. 'Āraṇyaka und Vanaprastha in der vedische Literatur', *WZKSA*, 25 (1981), pp. 19–90.

Stein, B. 'Formation of the medieval agrarian order: brahman and peasant in early South Indian history', in *Peasant, State and Society in Medieval South India* (Oxford University Press, Delhi, 1980/1994), pp. 63–89.

Strenski, I. 'On generalized exchange and the domestication of the sangha', *MAN*, ns. 18 (1983), pp. 463–77.

Tambiah, S. J. *World Conqueror and World Renouncer: a study of Buddhism and polity in Thailand against a historical background* (Cambridge University Press, Cambridge, 1976).

Tate, A. *The Autobiography of a Forest Monk* (Wat Hin Mark Peng, Chiang Mai, Thailand, 1993).

Tatia, N. 'The interaction of Jainism and Buddhism', in Narain, A. K. (ed.), *Studies in History* (B.R. Publishing, Delhi, 1980), pp. 321–38.

Taylor, J. L. *Forest Monks and the Nation-State* (Institute of Southeast Asian Studies, Singapore, 1993).

Taylor, T. 'The Interaction of the Settled and Wild Lands According to the Jātakas' (unpublished thesis, Monash University, 1983).

Tenbruch, F. H. 'The problem of thematic unity in the works of Max Weber', *British Journal of Sociology*, 31/3 (1980), pp. 315–51.

Thapar, R. *Aśoka and the Decline of the Mauryas* (Oxford University Press, Oxford, 1961).

Ancient Indian Social History: Some Interpretations (Orient Longman, New Delhi, 1978).

'The Rāmāyaṇa: theme and variation', in Mukherjee, S. (ed.), *India: History and Thought* (Subarnarakha, Calcutta, 1982), pp. 221–53.

From Lineage to State (Oxford University Press, Delhi, 1984).

'Patronage and community', in Stoler Miller, B. (ed.), *The Powers of Art. Patronage in Indian Culture* (Oxford University Press, Delhi, 1992), pp. 19–34.

'The first millennium B.C. in northern India', in R. Thapar (ed.), *Recent Perspectives of Early Indian History* (Popular Prakashan, Bombay, 1995), pp. 80–141.

Thomas, E. J. *The History of Buddhist Thought* (Routledge & Kegan Paul, London, 1933).

Tin, D. M. *The Dhammapada* (Department for the Promotion and Propagation of the Sāsanā, Rangoon, 1993).

Tsuchida, R. 'Two categories of brahmins in the early Buddhist period', *The Memoirs of the Toyo Bunko*, 49 (1991), pp. 51–95.

Vetter, T. *The Ideas and Meditative Practices of Early Buddhism* (E.J. Brill, Leiden, 1988).

'Some remarks on older parts of the Suttanipāta', in Seyfort-Ruegg, D. and Schmithausen, L. (eds), *Earliest Buddhism and Madhyamaka* (E.J. Brill, Leiden and New York, 1990), pp. 36–56.

von Hinüber, O. *A Handbook of Pāli Literature* (Walter de Gruyter, Berlin and New York, 1996).

von Simson, G. 'Die zeitgeschichtliche Hintergrund der Entstehung des Buddhismus und seine Bedeutung für die Datierungsfrage', in Bechert, H. (ed.), *The Dating of the Historical Buddha* (4 parts, Vandenhoek & Ruprecht, Göttingen, 1991).

Wagle, N. K. *Society at the Time of the Buddha* (Popular Prakashan, Bombay, 1966).

Waley, A. (ed. and trans.). *The Way and Its Power: A Study of the Tao Te Ching and Its Place in Chinese Thought* (Grove Press, New York, 1958).

Walters, J. 'A voice from the silence. The Buddha's Mother's Story', *HR*, 33/34 (1994), pp. 358–79.

Warder, A. K. 'On the relationships between Buddhism and other contemporary systems', *Bulletin of the School of Oriental and African Studies*, 18 (1956), pp. 43–63.

Watters, T. (trans. and ed.) *Yuan Chwang's Travels in India* (Munshiram Manoharlal, Delhi, 1961 (Oxford, 1896)).

Weber, M. *Die Wirtschaftsethik der Weltreligionen. Hinduismus und Buddhismus*, ed. Schmidt-Glintzer, H. (J.C.B. Mohr, Tübingen, 1998 (Tübingen, 1921)).

The Religion of India: the sociology of Hinduism and Buddhism, trans. and ed. Hans H. Gerth and Don Martindale (Free Press, Glencoe, Ill., 1958/1962). Translation of *Die Wirtschaftsethik der Weltreligionen.*

Wheatley, P. 'Presidential address: India beyond the Ganges – desultory reflections on the origins of civilization in Southeast Asia', *Journal of Asian Studies*, 42/1 (1982), pp. 13–28.

Wijayaratna, M. *Le moine bouddhiste: selon les textes du Theravada* (Cerf, Paris, 1983).

Wilhelm, F. 'Hospitality and the caste system', *Studien zur Indologie und Iranistik*, 20 (1996), pp. 523–9.

Wilson, P. J. *The Domestication of the Human Species* (Yale University Press, New Haven and London, 1989).

Witzel, M. 'Tracing the Vedic dialects', in Caillat, C. (ed.), *Dialectes dans les littératures indo-aryennes* (Institut de Civilisation Indienne, Collège de France, Paris, 1991), pp. 97–264.

'The development of the Vedic Canon and its schools: the social and political milieu', in Witzel, M. (ed.), *Inside the Texts. Beyond the Texts* (Harvard Oriental Series, Opera Minora 2, Cambridge, Mass., 1997), pp. 257–345.

Index

9 780521 831161